American Literary Scholarship 1992

American Literary Scholarship
An Annual 1992

Edited by David J. Nordloh

Essays by David M. Robinson, Leland S. Person, Jr.,
Benjamin F. Fisher, John Wenke, Gary Lee Stonum,
Tom Quirk, Richard A. Hocks, George Kearns,
Cleo McNelly Kearns, Alexander J. Marshall, III,
Albert J. DeFazio III, William J. Scheick,
Gary Scharnhorst, Jo Ann Middleton, Catherine Calloway,
Jerome Klinkowitz, Michael Fischer, Algerina Neri,
Hiroko Sato, Jan Nordby Gretlund,
Elisabeth Herion-Sarafidis, and Hans Skei

Duke University Press   Durham and London 1994

© 1994 Duke University Press

All rights reserved

LC 65-19450   ISBN 0-8223-1480-0

Printed in the United States of America

on acid-free paper ∞

Contents

Foreword

With this volume *American Literary Scholarship,* originally conceived by James Woodress and first published in 1965, marks its 30th anniversary. Such longevity deserves at least modest recognition, so I will take the opportunity to recognize all those contributors, present and past, who have made this series a lasting, lively, and substantial resource.

Some users of the series may not have 30 years' experience with it, and may benefit from having a brief statement of its aim and its methods. *American Literary Scholarship* offers a selective survey of significant and substantial publications from the great quantity of current work on American literature. Each volume covers work published during the calendar year identified in its title, though occasionally items published in the year or two immediately preceding and missed in previous volumes are also mentioned. Though our contributors make every effort in preparing their essays to examine all relevant items, generally they report only those that in their judgment are worth the reader's serious attention. For the convenience of both the reader and the contributing reviewer, material published in English and in the predominantly English-speaking countries is subdivided for coverage by major authors (Part I of the table of contents) and by historical periods and genres (Part II). Also included in Part II are a "Themes, Topics, Criticism" chapter as well as surveys of foreign-language scholarship and an overview of recent reference works. The author index provides access to the names of all scholars whose work is discussed or mentioned, and the subject index to all authors written about. To conserve space, journals and publishers are cited in the text in abbreviated form (journals by their MLA abbreviations if such exist). Book titles which occur frequently are represented by short title only—that a title *is* a short title is further signaled in the text by the absence of publisher information. The three sections of the "Key to

Abbreviations" following this foreword provide full citations for these books, journals, and publishers.

The series continues unflinching, but participants inevitably come and go. New to the roster this year are Leland S. Person, Jr. ("Hawthorne"), Tom Quirk ("Mark Twain"), Albert J. DeFazio III ("Fitzgerald and Hemingway"), and Catherine Calloway ("Fiction: 1900 to the 1930s"). In addition, Richard A. Hocks returns to "Henry James" after a year's sabbatical, and Hiroko Sato alternates turns at "Japanese Contributions" with Keiko Beppu.

Next year will see further changes. Gary Scharnhorst steps in for his first turn at editing the volume. (Authors are invited to direct review copies of books and articles to him at the Department of English, University of New Mexico, Albuquerque, NM 87131.) Replacing him as author of the chapter on "19th-Century Literature" is Lawrence I. Berkove. In another bit of internal reorganization, Gary Lee Stonum moves from "Whitman and Dickinson" to "Themes, Topics, Criticism," replacing Michael Fischer. Replacing Stonum in the former chapter is Martha Nell Smith. Richard Hocks takes leave once again from "Henry James," but has engaged in his place Robert Gale, a long-time past contributor of that chapter. And thanks to Gary Scharnhorst's productive recruiting efforts, several chapters not present in the current volume will return next year: Timothy Materer will contribute "Poetry: 1900 to the 1940s"; Lorenzo Thomas, "Poetry: The 1940s to the Present"; James Martine, "Drama"; and Daniel Royot, "French Contributions."

Chapter authors labor in the foreground, and receive their modest rewards in bylines. Other people support the enterprise less publicly, and deserve recognition too. My thanks to Terence Ford, director, and his staff at the Center for Bibliographic Services, Modern Language Association, for supplying a preprint of relevant portions of the *International Bibliography* for our use; to Nancy May-Scott, my secretary in the Graduate Program in American Studies, Indiana University, for assistance and patience; and to Pam Morrison and Bob Mirandon of Duke University Press, who made the job as close to enjoyable as relentless deadlines permit.

David J. Nordloh
Indiana University

Key to Abbreviations

Festschriften, Essay Collections, and Books Discussed in More Than One Chapter

The Aching Hearth / Sara Munson Deats and Lagretta Tallent Lenker, eds., *The Aching Hearth: Family Violence in Life and Literature* (Insight Books)

African American Imagination / Carol Aisha Blackshire-Belay, ed., *Language and Literature in the African American Imagination* (Greenwood)

American Literature and Science / Robert J. Scholnick, ed., *American Literature and Science* (Kentucky)

American Modernism / Michael J. Hoffman and Patrick D. Murphy, eds., *Critical Essays on American Modernism* (Twayne)

American Women's Autobiography / Margo Culley, ed., *American Women's Autobiography: Fea(s)ts of Memory* (Wisconsin)

The Continuing Presence of Walt Whitman / Robert K. Martin., ed., *The Continuing Presence of Walt Whitman: The Life After the Life* (Iowa)

The Critics Bear It Away / Frederick C. Crews, *The Critics Bear It Away: American Fiction and the Academy* (Random House)

The Culture of Sentiment / Shirley Samuels, ed., *The Culture of Sentiment: Race, Gender, and Sentimentality in Nineteenth-Century America* (Oxford)

De/Colonizing the Subject / Sidonie Smith and Julia Watson. eds., *De/Colonizing the Subject: The Politics of Gender in Women's Autobiography* (Minnesota)

Desert, Garden, Margin, Range / Eric Heyne, ed., *Desert, Garden, Margin, Range: Literature on the American Frontier* (Twayne)

Destruction of Knowledge / Ronald E. Martin, *American Literature and the Destruction of Knowledge: Innovative Writing in the Age of Epistemology* (Duke, 1991)

Early American Literature and Culture / Kathryn Zabelle Derounian-Stodola, ed., *Early American Literature and Culture: Essays Honoring Harrison T. Meserole* (Delaware)

Ezra Pound and America / Jacqueline
  Kaye, ed., *Ezra Pound and America*
  (St. Martin's)
Faulkner and the Short Story / Evans
  Harrington and Ann J. Abadie,
  eds., *Faulkner and the Short Story:
  Faulkner and Yoknapatawpha, 1990*
  (Miss.)
Female Pastoral / Elizabeth Jane Har-
  rison, *Female Pastoral: Women
  Writers Re-visioning the American
  South* (Tennessee)
Fiction of the Home Place / Helen Fid-
  dyment Levy, *Fiction of the Home
  Place: Jewett, Cather, Glasgow, Por-
  ter, Welty, and Naylor* (Miss.)
Fictions of the Past / Alide
  Cagidemetrio, *Fictions of the Past:
  Hawthorne and Melville* (Mass.)
Gaiety Transfigured / David Bergman,
  *Gaiety Transfigured: Gay Self-
  Representation in American Litera-
  ture* (Wisconsin, 1991)
Image and Ideology / David B. Down-
  ing and Susan Bazargan, eds., *Im-
  age and Ideology in
  Modern/PostModern Discourse*
  (SUNY)
Images of the Self as Female /
  Kathryn N. Benzel and Lauren
  Pringle De La Vars, eds., *Images of
  the Self as Female: The Achievement
  of Women Artists in Re-envisioning
  Feminine Identity* (Mellen)
L'Imaginaire-Melville / Viola Sachs,
  ed., *L'Imaginaire-Melville: A French
  Point of View* (Vincennes)
Imagining Language in America /
  Michael P. Kramer, *Imagining Lan-
  guage in America: From the Revolu-
  tion to the Civil War* (Princeton)
Language Unbound / Nancy Gray,

*Language Unbound: On Experimen-
  tal Writing by Women* (Illinois)
Literary New Orleans / Richard S.
  Kennedy, ed., *Literary New Or-
  leans: Essays and Meditations* (LSU)
Louisiana Women Writers /
  Dorothy H. Brown and Barbara C.
  Ewell, eds., *Louisiana Women
  Writers: New Essays and a Com-
  prehensive Bibliography* (LSU)
Mapping American Culture / Wayne
  Franklin and Michael Steiner, eds.,
  Mapping American Culture (Iowa)
Multicultural Autobiography / James
  Robert Payne, ed., *Multicultural
  Autobiography: American Lives*
  (Tennessee)
*Neo-Realism in Contemporary Ameri-
  can Fiction* / Kristiaan Versluys,
  *Neo-Realism in Contemporary
  American Fiction* (Rodopi)
Playing in the Dark / Toni Morrison,
  *Playing in the Dark: Whiteness and
  the Literary Imagination* (Harvard)
Poetry and Pragmatism / Richard
  Poirier, *Poetry and Pragmatism*
  (Harvard)
The Politics of Voice / Malini Johar
  Schueller, *The Politics of Voice: Lib-
  eralism and Social Criticism from
  Franklin to Kingston* (SUNY)
Russian Eyes on American Literature /
  M. Thomas Inge and Sergei
  Chakovsky, eds., *Russian Eyes on
  American Literature* (Miss.)
Seeking Awareness / Scott Slovic, *Seek-
  ing Awareness in American Nature
  Writing: Henry Thoreau, Annie Dil-
  lard, Edward Abbey, Wendell Berry,
  Barry Lopez* (Utah)
Sitting at the Feet of the Past / Gary D.
  Schmidt and Donald R. Hettinga,

eds., *Sitting at the Feet of the Past:
Retelling the North American
Folktale for Children* (Greenwood)

Styles of Creation / George Slusser and
Eric S. Rabkin, eds., *Styles of Cre-
ation: Aesthetic Technique and the
Creation of Fictional Worlds*
(Georgia)

Subject to History / David Simpson,
ed., *Subject to History: Ideology,
Class, Gender* (Cornell, 1991)

To Blight with Plague / Barbara Fass
Leavy, *To Blight with Plague:
Studies in a Literary Theme*
(NYU)

Victorianism in the United States /
Steve Ickingrill [i.e., Ickringill] and
Stephen Mills, eds., *Victorianism in
the United States: Its Era and Its
Legacy* (VU)

The Wicked Sisters / Betsy Erkkila,
*The Wicked Sisters: Women Poets,
Literary History, and Discord* (Ox-
ford)

Women in Search of Literary Space /
Gudrun M. Grabher and Maureen
Devine, eds., *Women in Search of
Literary Space* (Gunter Narr)

The Word in Black and White /
Dana D. Nelson, *The Word in
Black and White: Reading "Race" in
American Literature, 1638–1867*
(Oxford)

Writing the Woman Artist /
Suzanne W. Jones, ed., *Writing the
Woman Artist: Essays on Poetics, Pol-
itics, and Portraiture* (Penn., 1991)

Periodicals, Annuals, and Series

AAR / *African American Review*
ABSt / *A/B: Auto/Biography Studies*

*A.C.D.: The Journal of the Arthur
Conan Doyle Society*
ADEB / *ADE Bulletin*
AI / *American Imago*
AJS / *American Journal of Semiotics*
AL / *American Literature*
ALR / *American Literary Realism,
1870–1910*
American Periodicals
American Review (Tokyo)
AmerS / *American Studies*
AmerSS / *American Studies in Scan-
dinavia*
AmLH / *American Literary History*
Amst / *Amerikastudien*
Annali-Anglistica
Annali di Ca' Foscari
Annals of Wyoming
*ANQ: A Quarterly Journal of Short Ar-
ticles, Notes, and Reviews*
AQ / *American Quarterly*
ArielE / *Ariel: A Review of Interna-
tional English Literature*
ARLR / *American Renaissance Literary
Report*
ArQ / *Arizona Quarterly*
ASch / *American Scholar*
ASInt / *American Studies International*
ATQ / *American Transcendental Quar-
terly*
BB / *Bulletin of Bibliography*
Biography / *Biography: An Inter-
disciplinary Quarterly*
Black Music Research Journal
BoundaryII / *Boundary 2: An Interna-
tional Journal of Literature and Cul-
ture*
BSWWS / Boise State University
Western Writers Series
The Californians
*Callaloo: A Black South Journal of Arts
and Letters*

CanL / *Canadian Literature*
CCTEP / *Conference of College Teachers of English Studies*
CCur / *Cross Currents*
CE / *College English*
CEA / *CEA Critic*
Chasqui: Revista de Literatura Latinoamericana
ChH / *Church History*
Cithara: Essays in the Judaeo-Christian Tradition
Città di Vita
Civil War History
CL / *Comparative Literature*
CLAJ / *College Language Association Journal*
CLAQ / *Children's Literature Association Quarterly*
ClioI / *CLIO: A Journal of Literature, History, and the Philosophy of History*
CLQ / *Colby Library Quarterly*
CLS / *Comparative Literature Studies*
Clues: A Journal of Detection
CML / *Classical and Modern Literature*
CollL / *College Literature*
ConL / *Contemporary Literature*
Connecticut Review
CRCL / *Canadian Review of Comparative Literature/Revue Canadienne de Littérature Comparée*
CRevAS / *Canadian Review of American Studies*
Crit / *Critique: Studies in Modern Fiction*
CritI / *Critical Inquiry*
Criticism: A Quarterly for Literature and the Arts
Critique of Anthropology
Culture

DicS / *Dickinson Studies: Emily Dickinson (1830–86), U.S. Poet*
Dionysos
DLB / Dictionary of Literary Biography
Doshisha Literature (Kyoto)
DrS / *Dreiser Studies*
DSA / *Dickens Studies Annual: Essays on Victorian Fiction*
EA / *Etudes Anglaises*
EAL / *Early American Literature*
ECS / *Eighteenth-Century Studies*
EdWR / *Edith Wharton Review* [formerly *Edith Wharton Newsletter*]
EigoS / *Eigo Seinen* (Tokyo)
EIHC / *Essex Institute Historical Collections*
ELH [formerly *Journal of English Literary History*]
ELN / *English Language Notes*
ELWIU / *Essays in Literature* (Western Ill. Univ.)
Emily Dickinson Journal
English: The Journal of the English Association
EONR / *Eugene O'Neill Review*
ES / *English Studies*
ESC / *English Studies in Canada*
ESP / *Emerson Society Papers*
ESQ: A Journal of the American Renaissance
Ethnic Forum
Expl / *Explicator*
Extrapolation: A Journal of Science Fiction and Fantasy
Faulkner Studies
Film & Television
Fitzgerald Newsletter
FJ / *Faulkner Journal*
FNS / *Frank Norris Studies*
GaR / *Georgia Review*
Genre

Gerontologist

GettR / *Gettysburg Review*

GPQ / *Great Plains Quarterly*

GQ / *The German Quarterly*

HJR / *Henry James Review*

HLB / *Harvard Library Bulletin*

HN / *Hemingway Review*

The Horn Book

HSL / *Hartford Studies in Literature*

HudR / *Hudson Review*

Humor: International Journal of Humor Research

HUSL / *Hebrew University Studies in Literature and the Arts*

IFR / *International Fiction Review*

Il Lettore di Provincia

Il Confronto Letterario

Il Ponte

Imprint

Indice

L'Indice

JACult / *Journal of American Culture*

JADT / *Journal of American Drama and Theatre*

JAmS / *Journal of American Studies*

JAH / *Journal of American History*

JASAT / *Journal of the American Studies Assn. of Texas*

JELL / *Journal of English Language and Literature*

JEP / *Journal of Evolutionary Psychology*

JER / *Journal of the Early Republic*

JH / *Journal of the Humanities* (Japan)

JJQ / *James Joyce Quarterly*

JMAS / *Journal of Modern African Studies*

JNT / *Journal of Narrative Technique*

Journal of Religion

JPC / *Journal of Popular Culture*

KPR / *Kentucky Philological Review*

Kritik (Copenhagen)

LAmer / *Letterature d'America: Rivista Trimestale*

L&LC / *Literary and Linguistic Computing*

L&P / *Literature and Psychology*

L&U / *The Lion and the Unicorn: A Critical Journal of Children's Literature*

Legacy: A Journal of Nineteenth-Century American Women Writers

Leggere

LHRev / *Langston Hughes Review*

Linea d'Ombra

LitR / *Literary Review: An International Journal Devoted to English Studies*

M&H / *Medievalia et Humanistica: Studies in Medieval and Renaissance Culture*

Medieval Perspectives

MELUS: The Journal of the Society for the Study of Multi-Ethnic Literature of the United States

Menckeniana: A Quarterly Review

MFS / *Modern Fiction Studies*

MichA / *Michigan Academician*

Midamerica: The Yearbook of the Society for the Study of Midwestern Literature

MissQ / *Mississippi Quarterly*

MLQ / *Modern Language Quarterly*

MLR / *Modern Language Review*

MLS / *Modern Language Studies*

MMisc / *Midwestern Miscellany*

MQR / *Michigan Quarterly Review*

MR / *Massachusetts Review*

MSEx / *Melville Society Extracts*

MTJ / *Mark Twain Journal*

Names: Journal of the American Name Society

N&Q / *Notes and Queries*

NCF / *Nineteenth-Century Literature*

SELit / *Studies in English Literature* (Tokyo)

SHR / *Southern Humanities Review*

Signs: A Journal of Women in Culture and Society

SLitI / *Studies in the Literary Imagination*

SLJ / *Southern Literary Journal*

SN / *Studia Neophilologica*

SNNTS / *Studies in the Novel* (North Texas State Univ.)

SoAR / *South Atlantic Review*

SoQ / *Southern Quarterly*

SoR / *Southern Review*

SoSt / *Southern Studies*

Southern Folklore

SPAS / *Studies in Puritan American Spirituality*

SR / *Sewanee Review*

SSF / *Studies in Short Fiction*

Stephen Crane Studies

StHum / *Studies in the Humanities* (Indiana, Pa.)

Strathclyde Modern Language Studies

StQ / *Steinbeck Quarterly*

Style

Sulphur

SWR / *Southwest Review*

TCL / *Twentieth-Century Literature*

Thought: A Review of Culture and Idea

TPB / *Tennessee Philological Bulletin*

TSB / *Thoreau Society Bulletin*

TSLL / *Texas Studies in Language and Literature*

TUSAS / Twayne's United States Authors Series

TWN / *Thomas Wolfe Review*

UDR / *University of Dayton Review*

UMSE / *University of Mississippi Studies in English*

VN / *Victorian Newsletter*

Voices in Italian Americana

VQR / *Virginia Quarterly Review*

VRev / *Victorian Review: The Journal of the Victorian Studies Association of Western Canada*

W&I / *Word and Image: A Journal of Verbal / Visual Enquiry* (London, England)

W&L / *Women & Literature*

WAL / *Western American Literature*

WCPMN / *Willa Cather Pioneer Memorial Newsletter*

Weber Studies

Western Journal of Black Studies

WF / *Western Folklore*

Wilson Library Bulletin

Wisconsin Academy Review

WLT / *World Literature Today*

WMQ / *William and Mary Quarterly*

Women's Art Journal

WS / *Women's Studies*

WWR / *Walt Whitman Quarterly Review*

YER / *Yeats Eliot Review*

YULG / *Yale University Library Gazette*

Publishers

Alabama / Tuscaloosa: Univ. of Alabama Press

Almqvist and Wiksell / Stockholm: Almqvist and Wiksell

Anchor / New York: Anchor Books

Arkansas / Fayetteville: Univ. of Arkansas Press

Atheneum / New York: Atheneum (imprint of Macmillan Publishing Co.)

Bantam / New York: Bantam Books

Beacon / Boston: Beacon Press, Inc.

Belknap / Cambridge, Mass.: Belknap Press of Harvard Univ. Press

Black Sparrow / Santa Rosa, Calif.:
Black Sparrow Press

Blackwell / Oxford: Basil Blackwell,
Ltd.

Borgen / Copenhagen: Borgen

Bowling Green / Bowling Green,
Ohio: Bowling Green State Univ.
Popular Press

Brandeis / Hanover, N.H.: Brandeis
Univ. Press (dist. by Univ. Press of
New England)

Brown / Providence, R.I.: Brown
Univ. Press (dist. by Univ. Press of
New England)

Bucknell / Lewisburg, Pa.: Bucknell
Univ. Press (dist. by Associated
Univ. Presses)

Bulzoni / Rome: Bulzoni Editore

Bunkashobo Hakubunsha (Toyko)

Calif. / Berkeley: Univ. of California
Press

Cambridge / New York: Cambridge
Univ. Press

Camden House / Columbia, S.C.:
Camden House

Cass / London: F. Cass

Chelsea / New York: Chelsea House
Publishers (div. of Main Line Book
Co.)

Chicago / Chicago: Univ. of Chicago
Press

Clarendon / Oxford: Clarendon
Press

Clarkson Potter / New York: Clarkson Potter

Columbia / New York: Columbia
Univ. Press

Confluence Press (Lewiston, Idaho)

Cornell / Ithaca, N.Y.: Cornell Univ.
Press

Da Capo / New York: Da Capo Press
(div. of Plenum Publishing Corp.)

Dalkey Archive / Elmwood Park, Ill.:
Dalkey Archive Press

Delaware / Newark: Univ. of Delaware Press (dist. by Associated
Univ. Presses)

Dent / London: J. M. Dent

Duke / Durham, N.C.: Duke Univ.
Press

Edward Arnold / London: Edward
Arnold

Epoch / Kenmore, N.Y.: Epoch
Books

Faber / Winchester, Mass.: Faber &
Faber, Inc. (affil. of Faber & Faber,
Ltd., London; dist. by American
International Distribution Corp.)

Facts on File / New York: Facts on
File, Inc.

Fairleigh Dickinson / Teaneck, N.J.:
Fairleigh Dickinson Univ. Press
(dist. by Associated Univ. Presses)

Feminist Press / Feminist Press of the
City University of New York

Florida / Gainesville: Univ. of Florida
Press

Fordham / New York: Fordham Univ.
Press

Four Walls / New York: Four Walls
Eight Windows

Francke / Tübingen: A. Francke Verlag GmbH

Gale / Detroit: Gale Research, Inc.
(subs. of International Thompson
Publishing, Inc.)

Garland / New York: Garland Publishing, Inc.

Georgia / Athens: Univ. of Georgia
Press

Gordon and Breach / Philadelphia:
Gordon and Breach

Greenwood / Westport, Conn.:
Greenwood Press, Inc.

Gunter Narr / Tübingen: Gunter Narr Verlag

Hall / New York: G. K. Hall & Co. (div. of Maxwell Macmillan International)

Harvard / Cambridge: Harvard Univ. Press

Heritage / Bowie, Md.: Heritage Books

Hopkins / Baltimore: Johns Hopkins Univ. Press

Houghton Mifflin / Boston: Houghton Mifflin Co.

Howard / Washington, D.C.: Howard Univ. Press

Illinois / Champaign: Univ. of Illinois Press

Indiana / Bloomington: Indiana Univ. Press

Insight Books (New York)

Iowa / Iowa City: Univ. of Iowa Press

Kaibun-sha / Tokyo: Kaibun-sha Shuppan

Kenhyu-sha (Tokyo)

Kent State / Kent, Ohio: Kent State Univ. Press

Kentucky / Lexington: Univ. Press of Kentucky

Kirihara-shoten (Tokyo)

Knopf / New York: Alfred A. Knopf, Inc. (subs. of Random House, Inc.)

Library of America / New York: Library of America (dist. by Viking Penguin, Inc.)

Locust Hill / West Cornwall, Conn.: Locust Hill Press

Longman / White Plains, N.Y.: Longman, Inc.

LSU / Baton Rouge: Louisiana State Univ. Press

McFarland / Jefferson, N.C.: McFarland & Co., Inc.

Macmillan / London: Macmillan Publishers, Ltd.

Madison Books / Lanham, Md.: Madison Books (dist. by National Book Network)

Manly/Omnigraphics (Detroit)

Mass. / Amherst: Univ. of Massachusetts Press

Maxwell Macmillan / New York: Maxwell Macmillan International

Meckler / Westport, Conn.: Meckler Publishing Corp.

Mellen / Lewiston, N.Y.: Edwin Mellen Press

Mentor / New York: Mentor Books (imprint of New American Library)

Michigan / Ann Arbor: Univ. of Michigan Press

Midwestern / East Lansing, Mich.: Midwestern Press, The Society for the Study of Midwestern Literature, Michigan State Univ.

Minnesota / Minneapolis: Univ. of Minnesota Press

Miss. / Jackson: Univ. Press of Mississippi

Missouri / Columbia: Univ. of Missouri Press

MIT / Cambridge, Mass.: MIT Press

MLA / New York: Modern Language Assn. of America

Morrow / New York: William Morrow & Co., Inc. (subs. of Hearst Corp.)

NAL / New York: NAL/Dutton (division of Penguin)

NCTE / Urbana, Ill.: National Council of Teachers of English

Nebraska / Lincoln: Univ. of Nebraska Press

New Directions / New York: New Directions Publishing Corp. (dist. by W. W. Norton & Co., Inc.)

New England / Hanover, N.H.: Univ. Press of New England

New Mexico / Albuquerque: Univ. of New Mexico Press

No. Car. / Chapel Hill: Univ. of North Carolina Press

No. Ill. / DeKalb: Northern Illinois Univ. Press

Northeastern / Boston: Northeastern Univ. Press

Norton / New York: W. W. Norton & Co., Inc.

NYU / New York: New York Univ. Press

Odense / Odense Univ. Press

Ohio / Athens: Ohio Univ. Press

Okla. / Norman: Univ. of Oklahoma Press

Oxford / New York: Oxford Univ. Press, Inc.

Pace / New York: Pace University

Partington / Whittier, Calif.: Partington

Penguin / New York: Penguin Books

Penn. / Philadelphia: Univ. of Pennsylvania Press

Persea / New York: Persea Books

Peter Lang / New York: Peter Lang Publishing, Inc. (subs. of Verlag Peter Lang AG [Switzerland])

Pittsburgh / Pittsburgh: Univ. of Pittsburgh Press

Praeger / New York: Praeger Publishers

Princeton / Princeton, N.J.: Princeton Univ. Press

Purdue / West Lafayette, Ind.: Purdue Univ. Press

Random House / New York: Random House, Inc.

Rodopi / Amsterdam: Editions Rodopi BV

Routledge / New York: Routledge, Chapman & Hall, Inc.

Rubena / Bloomington, Ind.: Rubena Press

Rutgers / New Brunswick, N.J.: Rutgers Univ. Press

St. James / Chicago: St. James Press

St. Martin's / New York: St. Martin's Press, Inc. (subs. of Maxwell Macmillan International)

Salem Press (Pasadena, Calif.)

Scandinavian / Oslo: Scandinavian Univ. Press

Scribner's / New York: Charles Scribner's Sons

Seymour Lawrence / Boston: Houghton Mifflin/Seymour Lawrence

Shoe String / Hamden, Conn.: Shoe String Press

Signet / New York: Signet Books

Simon & Schuster / New York: Simon & Schuster, Inc. (div. of Paramount Communications, Inc.)

Smithsonian / Washington, D.C.: Smithsonian Institution Press

So. Car. / Columbia: Univ. of South Carolina Press

So. Ill. / Carbondale: Southern Illinois Univ. Press

South End / Boston: South End Press

Spinifex / North Melbourne, Australia: Spinifex Press

SR Books / Wilmington, Del.: SR Books

Stanford / Stanford, Calif.: Stanford Univ. Press

Starmont / Mercer Island, Wash.: Starmont House, Inc.

Sun & Moon / Los Angeles: Sun & Moon Press

SUNY / Albany: State Univ. of New York Press

Susquehanna / Selinsgrove, Pa.: Susquehanna Univ. Press (dist. by Associated Univ. Presses)

Syracuse / Syracuse, N.Y.: Syracuse Univ. Press

Temple / Philadelphia: Temple Univ. Press

Tennessee / Knoxville: Univ. of Tennessee Press

Texas / Austin: Univ. of Texas Press

Thunder's Mouth: New York: Thunder's Mouth Press

Ticknor and Fields / Boston: Ticknor and Fields

Toronto / Toronto: Univ. of Toronto Press

Twayne / Boston: Twayne Publishers

(imprint of G. K. Hall & Co., div. of Maxwell Macmillan International)

Union / Schenectady, N.Y.: Union College Press

Utah / Salt Lake City: Univ. of Utah Press

Viking / New York: Viking Penguin, Inc.

Vincennes / Saint-Denis, France: Presses Universitaires de Vincennes

Virginia / Charlottesville: Univ. Press of Virginia

VU / Amsterdam: VU Univ. Press

Wayne State / Detroit: Wayne State Univ. Press

Whitston / Troy, N.Y.: Whitston Publishing Co.

Wisconsin / Madison: Univ. of Wisconsin Press

Yale / New Haven, Conn.: Yale Univ. Press

Yamaguchi-shoten (Kyoto)

Part I

1 Emerson, Thoreau, Fuller, and Transcendentalism

David M. Robinson

Heading the year's list of important work on Transcendentalism were new volumes of Thoreau's *Journal* and Emerson's sermons, important compilations of the early reviews of Emerson and Thoreau, and several significant critical studies, including the first installment of a major scholarly biography of Fuller.

i Source Materials

Two valuable bibliographical references offer extremely useful grounding for scholars interested in questions of reception, canon formation, and cultural transformation. Joel Myerson's *Emerson and Thoreau: The Contemporary Reviews* (Cambridge) reprints the most significant contemporary reviews of Emerson and Thoreau and includes a checklist of other reviews. In assessing the patterns of reception in these reviews, Myerson notes the persistent comments on Emerson's lapses in style, and he finds that early reviewers' engagement with Emerson's ideas, whether critical or supportive, was "religiously and nationalistically based." Myerson identifies Theodore Parker's 1850 review of Emerson's works (reprinted pp. 224–47) as "arguably the most incisive" review of Emerson's work during his life. Gary Scharnhorst's *Henry David Thoreau: An Annotated Bibliography of Comment and Criticism Before 1900* (Garland) is an impressively thorough listing with helpful descriptive annotation of 19th-century comment. Scharnhorst's bibliography "contains more than twice the number of relevant items previously known to exist," and it includes references to other collections of Thoreau criticism. The volume will be crucial to the ongoing assessments of Thoreau's 19th-century reputation and cultural impact. Scharnhorst also reprints Maria S. Porter's "A Day at Concord" (*TSB* 198:1–2), an account of Edward Waldo Emerson's 1890 lecture on Thoreau. Walter Harding's "A Bibliography of Thoreau in Music" (*SAR,* pp. 291–315) lists more than 160 musical tributes to Thoreau, "most of them published and many of them recorded," with information on publication, recording, location, and in many cases descriptive comments by the composers.

Wesley T. Mott's edition of the fourth volume of *The Complete Sermons of Ralph Waldo Emerson* (Missouri) includes sermons from 1 December 1831 through 17 July 1836, a period of crucial transition which encompassed Emerson's resignation from his pastorate at the Second Church, his first European journey, and the beginning of his career as a lecturer and essayist. The volume includes a section of occasional discourses and sermon fragments as well as appendices which include Second Church records on Emerson's ministry and his letter to the church of 22 December 1832, before his departure to Europe. Emerson's sermon of 9 September 1832 on the Lord's Supper (Sermon CLXII), which outlined his public reasons for resigning his pulpit, here edited from the delivery manuscript, is of particular interest. Also notable are Sermons CXLIV and CLX, which indicate Emerson's growing commitment to a vision of the religious life as progressive or dynamic. The volume contains extensive informational and textual annotations and a detailed chronology of Emerson's preaching from late 1831 through 1839. Albert J. von Frank, the chief editor of *The Complete Sermons of Ralph Waldo Emerson,* deserves particular commendation for guiding this edition to timely completion and for crucial contributions to each of the four volumes. Emerson scholars also will be interested in Delores Bird Carpenter's new edition of Ellen Tucker Emerson's *The Life of Lidian Jackson Emerson* (Mich. State), which includes Carpenter's revised introduction and annotations.

The publication of Thoreau's *Journal, Volume 4: 1851–1852,* ed. Leonard N. Neufeldt and Nancy Craig Simmons (Princeton), is of particular importance, given the growing stature of Thoreau's *Journal* in contemporary criticism and the pivotal period, 21 August 1851 through 27 April 1852, covered in this volume. These were intensely creative months for Thoreau, when he was writing crucial parts of *Walden*—descriptions of the sand foliage, the battle of the ants, his meditation on leaving the pond—and using the *Journal* increasingly as a literary form of its own. As Neufeldt and Simmons point out in their "Historical Introduction," Thoreau's "method of creating his 'daily' entries is more complicated than the record would indicate," since he sometimes composed entries from penciled field notes on the evening or morning after an excursion, using "the present tense to create the impression of immediacy of perception and composition." This installment of the *Journal,* which includes helpful annotations, Thoreau's indexes, and extensive notes on the text, will make a valuable contribution to the ongoing consideration of his creative process. In "Textual Instability in the Riverside Edition of Thoreau" (*PBSA* 85 [1991]:347–419), Joseph J. Moldenhauer describes the Riverside Edition as "a startling modern case example of textual instability," details the "frequent modifications in wording, arrangement of matter, spelling, and punctuation between the reprintings" of the edition from 1894 to 1914, and includes a comprehensive table of those changes.

ii Emerson

Two important books on Emerson led the year's critical studies; while very different in scope and procedure, each finds Emerson's struggle for intellectual self-conception as crucial to his stature as a thinker. In *Emerson on the Scholar* (Missouri) Merton M. Sealts, Jr., has produced a comprehensive intellectual biography centered on Emerson's evolving concept of the "scholar" as a term of both self-definition and social purpose. Sealts's study has two major sections. In the first, he traces Emerson's early development of the concept of the "scholar" as a projected ethical and vocational ideal, a process that culminates in "The American Scholar." In the second, Sealts describes Emerson's resulting effort to measure and modify this ideal under the pressures of ethical commitment and social engagement. Of particular importance, therefore, is Sealts's recognition that the term "scholar" is a key to understanding Emerson's complex, lifelong meditation about the place of "action" in the intellectual life, an important element in our current attempt to gauge Emerson's political consciousness and relevance. *Emerson on the Scholar* makes two signal contributions to our understanding of Emerson's development: it completes the line of inquiry about Emerson's "problem of vocation" raised in Henry Nash Smith's landmark 1939 essay, and in so doing it restores to us a sense of the importance of Emerson's "later" work, those essays and addresses from the mid-1840s to the mid-1860s that, compared to other periods, have received so little attention from Emerson scholars. The Emerson that Sealts presents here is no static Transcendental sage, but a constantly engaged and evolving intellectual whose responses to the political and social pressures of America in the 1840s and 1850s were crucial to our comprehension of him. In a sense, we have been working with half an Emerson for a number of years. *Emerson on the Scholar*, in conjunction with Len Gougeon's *Virtue's Hero: Emerson, Antislavery, and Reform* (see *ALS 1990*, pp. 4–5), will help us rediscover the entire man, especially as newly edited volumes of Emerson's later work approach publication in Harvard's *Collected Works* edition. Sealts's study, which began in his editorial work for the *Journals and Miscellaneous Notebooks*, is deeply cognizant of the importance of the journals to any assessment of Emerson's development, and the book reminds us of the continuing legacy provided to Emerson's readers by the *JMN* edition.

In *Poetry and Pragmatism* Richard Poirier convincingly traces a line of "Emersonian pragmatism" from Emerson through Whitman and William James to Frost, Eliot, Stein, and Stevens, all of whom were moved less by Emerson's vision than by his example. Poirier's elegantly written volume is an important contribution to the developing discourse on Emerson and pragmatism, and it offers a new and persuasive articulation of Emerson's influence on American modernist writers. For Poirier, the key to Emerson's achievement and influence was the way "his writing enacts the struggles by which he tries to keep his own language from becoming 'faked.'" Emerson's enactment of this struggle authenticates his work in a way that mere description of such a struggle could not. While Emerson was constantly aware of the "metaphorical proliferation, slippage and excess" of language, he treated that indeterminate or "superfluous" quality as "a surplus of meaning in the face of always incipient impoverishment," and he insisted that "words may be kept in motion by human agency." Poirier argues cogently for Emerson's stature in American intellectual life—his emphasis on Emerson's philosophical importance complements the recent work of Stanley Cavell—and grounds his pragmatist genealogy in discerning textual analysis of "Experience" and "History."

Interest in the theological context of Emerson's thinking, nurtured by publication of the Emerson sermons and the reevaluation of early Unitarian theology, continues to be high. Emerson's relationship with his step-grandfather, Concord minister Ezra Ripley, is explored in Ronald A. Bosco's "'[M]ercy to Pardon & Grace to Help': Ezra Ripley's Ordination Diary, 1778–1836" (*SPAS* 2:153–92), which reprints Ripley's lifelong diary of meditations marking the anniversary of his ordination. Elizabeth Addison's "Compensation and the Price of Purity: An Old Quaker Impresses the Young Emerson" (*SAR*, pp. 107–20) describes Emerson's meeting Edward Stabler in 1827, and it notes the impact of Stabler's theology, especially his version of the doctrine of compensation, on Emerson's early preaching. Elisabeth Hurth offers an informative and solidly researched consideration of the impact of German biblical scholarship on early New England Unitarianism in "Sowing the Seeds of 'Subversion': Harvard's Early Göttingen Students" (*SAR*, pp. 91–106). Hurth describes the exposure of Edward Everett, George Bancroft, William Emerson, and other Harvard ministerial students to the curriculum of biblical studies under J. G. Eichorn at Göttingen, noting that Eichorn's approach to "the Bible as the product of a particular historical and cultural conditioning" was fundamentally at odds with the Unitarian emphasis on evidentialism. Hurth explains their resistance to Eichorn, but she also describes how the exposure unalterably distanced them from the conservative Unitarian theological program, leaving them instead with an openness to the religion of experience promulgated by Schleiermacher, the basis of Transcendentalism. Hurth notes that Ralph Waldo Emerson was profoundly affected by these experiences, chiefly through his correspondence with William, and struggled with skepticism as he pursued his own ministerial studies. I found Robert D. Habich's "Emerson's Reluctant Foe: Andrews Norton and the Transcendental Controversy" (*NEQ* 65:208–37) an illuminating addition to the material on the Divinity School Controversy. Habich convincingly connects Norton's opposition to Transcendentalism to his frustration with his own role at Harvard—a surprise, I suspect, to many scholars who may have taken him as a Harvard spokesman. Norton objected to a pattern of governance that had resulted in a "steady erosion of faculty control" and weakened academic discipline. The building disorder seemed to come to a point of crisis in the "fractious summer" of 1838 when many Unitarian ministers "had already been rubbed raw by tests of their authority, criticism of their commitment, and a sense of their own vulnerability." Norton's "New School of Literature and Religion," Habich argues, was less an attack on Emerson specifically than on a series of events that signaled disorder and confirmed a long-standing complaint about "the Unitarian hierarchy's lack of responsibility." Habich augments Lilian Handlin's revisionist essay on Norton (see *ALS 1989*, p. 15); and while to know Norton, even in revisionist terms, is not necessarily to love him, both essays remind us that he is a complex figure whose connections with mainstream Unitarianism, which he is usually supposed to be defending, have not been adequately explored.

Two essays approached Emerson's religious and cultural context by undertaking to revise Perry Miller's classic "From Edwards to Emerson." Alan D. Hodder's incisive " 'After a High Negative Way': Emerson's 'Self-Reliance' and the Rhetoric of Conversion" (*HTR* 84 [1991]:423–46) describes how "Emerson's rhetoric of self-reliance recapitulates the constructional schemes and strategies of Puritan conversion rhetoric," most notably the pattern of "contrition and humiliation followed by rapture and assurance." Hodder emphasizes Emerson's expression of a "theology of negation . . . made necessary by a blinding recognition of the absolute transcendence of God," a theological disposition influenced in part by Coleridge, but rooted ultimately in "the traditional patterns of New England orthodoxy." Hodder's important essay should be compared with Robert Milder's "Emerson's Two Conversions" (see *ALS 1988,* p. 7), both of which make a strong case for the Puritan roots of Emerson's spirituality. In "The Road Not Taken: From Edwards, Through Chauncy, to Emerson" (*ArQ* 48, i:45–61), I argue that Miller's definition of Emerson as an Edwardsean mystic distorts our sense of Transcendentalism by deemphasizing the movement's concern with questions of work, ethics, politics, and human relationships. Although Miller defined both Edwards and Emerson against the Arminian rationalism represented by Charles Chauncy or Andrews Norton, his own portrayal of what he felt was Emerson's irresponsible mysticism bears an ironic resemblance to Norton's earlier attacks on Emerson.

Emerson's involvement with science was the subject of two essays. In "The Emerson Museum" (*Representations* 40:57–80) Lee Rust Brown offers an illuminating reading of the impact of Emerson's 1833 visit to the Muséum d'histoire naturelle, with its Jardin des plantes, in Paris. Brown explains that in the Muséum's organization of the specimens, intended to exhibit the methods and conclusions of botanical and zoological classification, "the representative aspect of the thing superseded the thing itself." Emerson thus came to see the act of classification as an intellectual paradigm, and the effect on his conception of his project as a scholar, and on his compositional practice, was profound. "Natural history taught Emerson to treat the 'facts' of his own writing as natural objects," Brown maintains, "and to see them as constituted by the same sort of 'history' as that exposed in natural subject matter." More secure about the emergence of larger patterns of unity in his writing, Emerson could give himself over more completely to the discrete moment of observation or insight: "One notices, after October 1833, a decided turn to the aphorism, a less limited range of subjects, a far greater willingness to experiment with radical statements and thoughts that could not be completed." My survey of Emerson's evolving attitudes toward science, "Fields of Investigation: Emerson and Natural History" (*American Literature and Science*, pp. 94–109), begins with the assumptions of "natural theology" prevalent in early Unitarianism and traces Emerson's deepening immersion in science in the early 1830s, emphasizing the 1837 lecture "Humanity of Science" as a summation of his early views. Emerson's enthusiasm for science waned, however, in the 1840s, coinciding with a certain estrangement from nature that one can detect in "Nature" (1844) and an increasing absorption in questions of social reform. His later *Natural History of Intellect*, however, aspired to a systematization of mental processes similar to the great classifications of scientific knowledge of the 18th and 19th centuries.

Several essays extend the current exploration of what we might broadly term Emerson's political identity. In "Emerson's *Nature:* A Materialistic Reading" (*Subject to History*, pp. 119–42), R. Jackson Wilson places the composition of *Nature* in the framework of Emerson's literary ambition, arguing that in "the figure of the poet" Emerson "masks the motives of a professional writer who is trying to get a start in the literary marketplace after quitting a most respectable ministry." Christopher Newfield focuses on *Nature* in "Controlling the Voice: Emerson's Early Theory of Language" (*ESQ* 38:1–29) to argue that Emerson "anchors free expression in preexisting authority," a linguistic and perceptual dynamic in which "the moment of freedom is constituted by the moment of submission to superior, active power." Newfield's larger subject is the connection of linguistic practice to American politics, and he implies that this "authoritarian" theory of language is revelatory of contradictions within American liberal individualism. To my mind, Linck C. Johnson's "Reforming the Reformers: Emerson, Thoreau, and the Sunday Lectures at Amory Hall, Boston" (*ESQ* 37:235–89) is the most important new assessment of Emerson's politics. Johnson reconstructs the contributions of Emerson and Thoreau to an 1844 series of reform lectures which reveal important differences within the reform movement of the period over the political relevance of religion and the theory of "non-resistance." Johnson argues that Emerson's contribution to the series, "New England Reformers," was a "reply to the communitarians, who had steadily sought to enlist him in their cause," a critique sharpened by the 1844 adoption of a Fourierist constitution at Brook Farm. Following Emerson in the series, Thoreau expressed a similar skepticism of communitarian ideas, accusing the reformers of wanting to "replace [existing institutions] with new ones." Johnson's analysis of Thoreau's unpublished lecture, parts of which were later incorporated into *Walden,* is an important analysis of his development within the context of reform thinking. In "The Gender of Transparency: Masculinity and the Conduct of Life" (*AmLH* 4:584– 606), Julie Ellison argues that "the essays in Emerson's *Conduct of Life* participate in the aspirations of the contemporary conduct-of-life literature," work marked by its "belief in the split between socioeconomic position and personal authority." Ellison interrogates Emerson's depiction of male relationships as "epiphanies in which closeness depends on mutually revealed authority," and she argues that in "Behavior," the focal text of her essay, "gaze, manners, and American nationality are linked in passages that rewrite the 'transparent eye-ball' and 'axis of vision' passages of *Nature* as encounters between men." In such encounters, "the hierarchy of social position is replaced by a hierarchy of personal force." The record of Emerson's stand on racial issues is explored in two pieces. Wesley T. Mott's "Emerson and the New Bedford Affair in Boston Newspapers" (*ESP* 3, i:3–4) reprints two articles critical of Emerson's refusal to lecture at the New Bedford Lyceum in 1846 because of its exclusion of blacks. In "Did Emerson Blackball Frederick Douglass from Membership in the Town and Country Club?" (*NEQ* 65:295–98), Thomas Wortham establishes that Emerson did not block Douglass's membership, as James Russell Lowell suspected he might have, and as William S. McFeely, in a recent biography of Douglass, reported that he did. Wortham returned to the manuscript minutes of the club for 2 May 1849, which show that Emerson opposed any exclusion from the club on the basis of race. In "Emerson and the Worcester Lyceum, 1855–1857: Two New Letters" (*NEQ* 65:290–95), Kent P. Ljungquist and Wesley T. Mott print letters to Thomas Earle that add information on Emerson's lecture schedule in the mid-1850s.

In "From Merlin to Faust: Emerson's Democratization of the 'Heroic Mind,'" pp. 113–35 in *Merlin versus Faust: Contending Archetypes in Western Culture,* ed. Charlotte Spivack (Mellen), Monika Elbert argues that "when Emerson conceived of the ideal poet, he envisioned Merlin, and when he thought of the representative man of his era, he thought of Faust." Neither aspect of this argument is compelling, but Elbert makes

the stronger case for Merlin and offers commentary on the rarely discussed poems "Merlin I" and "Merlin II." In "Scanning 'Hamatreya':
Emerson as Miltonic Prosodist" (*ESP* 3, ii:1–2), Richard R. O'Keefe
proposes lines in *Paradise Lost* as the metrical precedent for lines 1 and
3 of "Hamatreya." Richard Tuerk provides a useful interpretation of
"Emerson's 'Woodnotes' Poems" (*ATQ* 6:295–305), explaining the relationship of the two poems and stressing the theme of metamorphosis or
"flux" that emerges in "Woodnotes II." As Tuerk rightly argues, the
poems complicate the received opinion of Emerson's abstracted or distanced stance toward nature (see also Boudreau and Zimmerman, below), and they deserve further critical attention. Linda K. Urschel's
explication of "Emerson's 'The Snow Storm' " (*Expl* 50 [1991]:15) places
the poem in the context of other images of snow in Emerson's prose to
emphasize not only the snow's beauty but its potential destructiveness
and illusion-making power.

In addition to Poirier's very important *Poetry and Pragmatism* (see
above), there were several other discussions of Emerson's influence, but
no consensus on whether to regard it as salutary. Merton M. Sealts, Jr.'s
"Emerson Then and Now" (*Wisconsin Academy Review* 38:29–32) describes the Emerson revival now in progress and charts the changes in
Emerson's reputation during his career and after. Sealts points to the
journals as a key to the revival, arguing that "the current interest in
Emerson is directly traceable to the rediscovery of the man behind the
formal writings." In *Nietzsche and Emerson: An Elective Affinity* (Ohio),
George J. Stack explores the "profound and intimate philosophical and
valuational relationship of thought" between Nietzsche and Emerson,
presenting Nietzsche as an "ultraradical Emersonian who transcended
this standpoint in scope and depth and by dint of philosophical acuity."
Stack argues that Emerson's work entered Nietzsche's through "an unconscious process of cognitive-linguistic assimilation," and much of his
book is devoted to cataloguing and comparing Emerson's articulation of
nascent forms of Nietzsche's characteristic doctrines. "At the center of all
reality, for both Emerson and Nietzsche," Stack finds, "is dynamic
energy or, to employ the word they ordinarily use, *power.*" This emphasis
on power accounts for their common rejection of "the torpidity, the
mediocrity, timorousness, conformity, and untruth of conventional social morality" and their rhetorical embrace of immoralism. In "Emersonian Self-Reliance and Self-Deception Theory" (*P&L* 15 [1991]:286–94),
Kenneth Marc Harris compares Emerson's discussion of will and motiva-

tion in "Self-Reliance" with those of Pascal and of the contemporary philosopher Alfred R. Mele. In " 'The Woman's Flesh of Me': Rebecca Harding Davis's Response to Self-Reliance" (*ATQ* 6:131–40), Kristin Boudreau describes Davis's "The Wife's Story" (1864) as a fictional critique of Emersonianism, challenging both "the cultural fantasy of bodily transcendence" and "the Emersonian notion of self-reliance." In a similar vein, Lee Zimmerman's "An Eye for an I: Emerson and Some 'True' Poems of Robinson Jeffers, William Everson, Robert Penn Warren, and Adrienne Rich" (*ConL* 33:645–64) argues that the "bodiless, autonomous self" of the transparent eyeball passage, with its "fantasy of limitlessness," poses ideological difficulties for several modern poets. Jeffers, for instance, exhibits this problem when he achieves his "closest contact with nature" only "at the expense of his connections to a humanity which he mostly disdains." Zimmerman finds in Rich's "Transcendental Etude" a "very different understanding of selfhood" that is "rooted in the body" and "constituted, not diminished, by social relation." In "Life in the Transitions: Emerson, William James, Wallace Stevens" (*ArQ* 48, iii:75–97), Jonathan Levin proposes a model of Emersonian influence similar to Poirier's (see above), in which James and Stevens are linked with Emerson because "each cultivates a peculiar style of attention, directed not toward intellectual or verbal mastery but toward the dynamic processes that suffuse and inflect intellectual, and linguistic, activity." For Levin, Emerson's central theme is the "valorization of the dynamic dimension," and he argues that Emerson's dynamism is directed less at imposing a commanding will than it is "fueled by incessant and thoroughly unpredictable transformations." Angela Elliott's "The Eidolon Self: Emerson, Whitman and Pound" (*Ezra Pound and America,* pp. 43–54) traces Pound's use in the *Cantos* of the neoplatonic concept of the *eidolon,* or image of the soul, a concept transmitted to him in the work of Emerson and Whitman.

iii Thoreau

Raymond R. Borst has provided Thoreauvians with an important reference work in *The Thoreau Log: A Documentary Life of Henry David Thoreau, 1817–1862* (Hall), a compilation of information on Thoreau's daily life in the tradition of Jay Leyda's *The Melville Log.* Borst records Thoreau's activities year by year, and where possible, day by day, using the *Journal* as the principal reference, and supplementing it with Thoreau's "letters and other writings" and "the journals, diaries, and letters of his contemporaries; church, school, legal, and other records; newspaper reports; mentions and reviews in contemporary periodicals; and reminiscences." The resulting pool of information will aid in close-grained examinations of particular periods and seasons in Thoreau's life and help us see more clearly the relationship between his published literary work and his daily activities. Every scholar of Transcendentalism will want to read two fascinating essays by Walter Harding, "The Adventures of a Literary Detective in Search of Thoreau" (*VQR* 68:277–97) and "Adventures in the Thoreau Trade" (*ASch* 61:277–89), both of which offer accounts of the pleasures and frustrations of Harding's lifetime of distinguished biographical research. Harding includes anecdotes of his discoveries of previously unrecorded information on Thoreau's life, including the proposal of marriage to Ellen Sewall. Princeton also has reprinted Harding's important biography, *The Days of Henry Thoreau,* with an afterword that surveys important scholarship since 1965 and discusses what Harding feels was "a major *lacuna*" in his biography, a more detailed discussion of Thoreau's sexuality. Harding summarizes the case he recently made for Thoreau's homoerotic sexual identity (see *ALS 1991,* p. 15, and also Michael Warner, below), and he describes the marriage proposal to Sewall as motivated primarily by a desire to satisfy social expectation. Sewall is brought to our attention in more detail in George E. Ryan's "Love of Thoreau's Life a Remarkable Woman" (*Quincy* [Mass.] *Patriot-Ledger,* 7 Dec., pp. 11–12). Ryan describes Sewall's life after she rejected Thoreau in 1840 and later married Unitarian minister Joseph Osgood, and he notes that scholars have not yet sufficiently acquainted us with "the real, intelligent, and fascinating woman who was able to inspire in Henry Thoreau the closest thing to romantic love he ever acknowledged." Philip F. Gura's helpful "Travelling Much in Concord: A Sampling of Recent Thoreau Scholarship" (*ESQ* 38:71–86) is an overview of eight recent volumes on Thoreau, in which Gura notes "the particular strengths of scholarship [on Thoreau] based solidly in contextual and biographical study."

It is perhaps a measure of Thoreau's rhetorical achievement in *Walden* that we do not ordinarily think of him as an aspiring writer ambitious to succeed on the literary scene. I was impressed with Steven Fink's *Prophet in the Marketplace: Thoreau's Development as a Professional Writer* (Princeton) because of the new perspective it gave me on Thoreau's professional ambitions. As Fink demonstrates in persuasive detail, Thoreau was motivated by a desire for a broad readership, but his interaction with the literary market, dominated by frustration and missed opportunity, eventually forced him to reconceive his role as a writer. Fink underlines the modest success that Thoreau achieved with "picturesque travel narratives," a mode that Horace Greeley encouraged him to pursue, but Fink notes Thoreau's unwillingness to devote himself to shorter works as his commitment to *A Week on the Concord and Merrimack Rivers* grew. Fink finds that the "resounding and absolute [commercial] failure" of *A Week* was due in large part to the utter delinquency of his publisher James Munroe and Co., "who made the book virtually inaccessible to the public unless they applied for it directly." This defeat forced Thoreau to reconsider his hopes for a wide audience, and it affected the final shape of *Walden* and other works such as "Wild Apples," which Fink reads allegorically as Thoreau's attempt to characterize his own life. Robert Sattelmeyer's "A Walk to More than Wachusett" (*TSB* 202:1–4) explains the importance of "A Walk to Wachusett" in allowing Thoreau to cultivate the "excursion" as a usable literary form.

Walden received much new interpretive attention this year, keyed by Robert F. Sayre's useful volume of *New Essays on* Walden (Cambridge), which includes his introductory essay on the writing and reception of the book (pp. 1–22) and four substantial essays. Lawrence Buell's "Henry Thoreau Enters the American Canon" (pp. 23–52) explains how the efforts of 19th-century editors and publishers intersected with a rising cultural valuation of "the literary nature essay" to establish Thoreau as a major author. Buell calls particular attention to Bliss Perry's advocacy of Thoreau within Houghton Mifflin at the turn of the century, which resulted in the firm's decision to publish a complete edition of his works (including the *Journal*) in 1906 and to include Thoreau in their promotions as a major American author. Thoreau gradually acquired stature as "father of a genre of 'out-of-door' literature," a reputation that gave him a measure of bourgeois respectability, even as he was also being hailed for "his opposition to genteel norms." But in the 1990s, Buell argues, "Thoreau's naturism looks more like a mode of dissent than it would have in 1910 to a radical critic gagging on repeated tributes to Thoreau the poet-naturalist." Anne Labastille's " 'Fishing in the Sky' " (pp. 53–72) contains a personal account of the gradual process by which she came to appreciate *Walden* and her reactions to the book as a cabin-dweller, a woman, and an ecologist. In "The Crosscurrents of *Walden*'s Pastoral" (pp. 73–94) H. Daniel Peck defines the pastoral quality of *Walden*,

noting that by Thoreau's time pastoral had become "not so much a literary form as a state of mind, or mode of thought." Peck argues that the
pastoral necessarily exists through its establishment of a "boundary"
against the world, but that the forces bounded out are always a "felt
presence" in the work. The pastoral is in this sense always a work of tension and one of reconciliation, aspects that he illustrates by comparing
the pastoral techniques of *Walden* with those of two paintings by George
Inness, *The Lackawanna Valley* and *On the Delaware River.* Michael R.
Fischer's consideration of "*Walden* and the Politics of Contemporary
Literary Theory" (pp. 95–113) emphasizes the way that Thoreau's insistent demand that his readers engage themselves in self-examination
helps him to overcome the dilemma of contemporary literary theory:
"how to overcome authority without claiming it—without, in other
words, reappropriating the vocabulary we have discredited." Fischer
finds Stanley Cavell's interpretation of Thoreau in the light of ordinary-
language philosophy helpful in understanding that "Thoreau is asking
[his reader] for something other than belief in his many opinions," an
experimental attitude that emphasizes a critical "self-knowledge."

Martin Bickman's Walden: *Volatile Truths* (Twayne) is an effective
overview of *Walden* which emphasizes the book's concern "with transitions, with passage." Bickman argues convincingly that its structure
must be seen in terms of transitions—the passage from winter to spring,
or fall to winter, is more meaningful to Thoreau than the quality of the
season itself. Bickman traces Thoreau's strategies to revitalize language in
his diction and phrasing, and he argues that Thoreau uses his inventive
skill to transform his "pining for the loss of his own childhood . . . into a
more general mythography of the culture." Malini Johar Schueller applies Bakhtin's concept of "carnivalistic" language to *Walden* to describe
Thoreau's "parodic appropriation and dialogic questioning of liberal
capitalism" (*The Politics of Voice*, pp. 31–46). Schueller notes Thoreau's
creation of reader-characters whose conformity to conventional notions
of success is mocked, and she contends that Thoreau "tries to destroy
commonplace expressions . . . in which ideology is masked and mysti-
fied." Thomas D. Birch and Fred Metting argue that "The Economic
Design of *Walden*" (*NEQ* 65:587–602) can be understood in the context
of the economic theories of Adam Smith and Jean-Baptiste Say. By
measuring activities by the standard of " 'life' rather than labor," Thoreau
established an "alternative theory of value" in which the principle of
"minimizing cost" was recast as "the most productive use of time." In

"Thoreau's Bottom" (*Raritan* ii, iii:53–79) Michael Warner argues that Thoreau articulated "an extreme version of liberal individualism" but "repeatedly expressed a longing for self-transcendence through the love of another man." Warner explores this contradiction in the context of the modern construction of sexual identity, and he calls attention to Thoreau's pond imagery as evidence of a "displaced sexual imagination": "For every passage about the attraction of seeing himself reflected in the water's surface, there is another passage about the lure of penetrating that surface to the bottom beneath it." Gordon Boudreau's "Transcendental Sport: Hunting, Fishing, and Trapping in *Walden*" (*Thought* 67:74–87) is a witty appreciation of "the paradoxical levity in Thoreau's master-piece," tracing Thoreau's humorous uses of the various outdoor sports described in *Walden*. In "Nineteenth-Century American Attitudes To-ward the Classics" (*CML* 12 [1991]:7–14), L. R. Lind labels "Reading" as "the most eloquent and spirited defense of the Classics ever written in America." In addition to these critical studies of *Walden,* I am very pleased to welcome a second edition of Walden *and* Resistance to Civil Government (Norton), ably assembled by William Rossi. Both *Walden* and "Resistance to Civil Government" are edited from the first editions, and the volume includes a generous section of "Selections from the Journal, 1845–54" (pp. 255–307) and Rossi's essay "The Journal and *Walden*" (pp. 249–54). The critical material includes a particularly dis-cerning selection of criticism from the past two decades.

As the interest in ecological criticism grows, Thoreau is being read less as a "Transcendentalist" than as a nature writer, and the extent of his immersion in natural history is a concomitantly important question. Robert D. Richardson, Jr., has contributed a valuable assessment of "Thoreau and Science" (*American Literature and Science,* pp. 110–27), premised on the observation that "the more serious Thoreau's involve-ment in science becomes, the more intense his questionings become." Richardson notes that Thoreau's "bright and uncomplicated" early atti-tude toward science gave way to a more divided one as his actual scientific expertise grew. The depth of his immersion in scientific reading and observation by 1852 resulted in a conflict with his underlying intel-lectual adherence to idealism, eventually leaving him in a state of intel-lectual division that he never entirely resolved. Richardson also reminds us that there remains "a mass of unarranged, undigested manuscript" relevant to this subject "that has never been taken adequately into account." Scott Slovic's consideration of Thoreau's "habit of attention" in his journal (*Seeking Awareness,* pp. 21–59) stresses Thoreau's use of the *Journal* for "exploration of his own mental processes" as they "coincide intermittently with those of the natural world." Slovic emphasizes the *Journal*'s "experimental" nature, and he argues that Thoreau came to recognize its aesthetic potential, quite apart from any connection to potentially publishable works. In "Marginality, Midnight Optimism, and the Natural Cipher: An Approach to Thoreau and Eiseley" (*Weber Studies* 9:25–43), Slovic observes that both Thoreau and Loren Eiseley cultivated a sense of "marginality" that was essential to their work as acute observers of nature. For Thoreau, marginality meant both a stance of "voluntary exile from society" and a "glimpsing" or indirect method of observing nature, both of which contributed to his capacity "to experience the immediacy, the multiplicity, and the beauty of the natural world." In an essay of considerable significance for the appraisal of Thoreau's *Journal* ("Thoreau's *Journal:* The Creation of a Sacred Place," pp. 139–51 in *Mapping American Culture*), Don Scheese uses Joseph Campbell's definition of the "archetypal pattern" of "Separation, Transformation, and Return" to analyze the structure of Thoreau's daily excursions, finding each of them "a kind of vision quest" and a "mode of self-culture." Scheese demonstrates this pattern convincingly in a discussion of Thoreau's 30 August 1856 walk to Beck Stow's swamp, in which Thoreau comes "to associate wildness with a particular place" and discovers "that wildness can be found almost anywhere." Herman Nibbelink's "Thoreau and Wendell Berry: Bachelor and Husband of Nature" (pp. 135–51 in *Wendell Berry,* ed. Paul Merchant [Confluence, 1991]) notes that Berry as a 20th-century nature writer must face ecological "malady as heritage." While noting their deep affinities, Nibbelink reminds us of the fundamental "difference between bachelor [Thoreau] and husband [Berry], between naturalist and farmer."

In "Thoreau's *Cape Cod:* The Unsettling Art of the Wrecker" (*AL* 64:239–54), John Lowney observes "the dramatic tension between Thoreau's desire for initiation into the Cape Cod world and his desire to differentiate his narrative from previous accounts of initiation." Lowney finds Thoreau's act of marking found objects on the beach, a mimicry of the work of the community's wreckers, a sign of his ambivalent affirmation and criticism of Cape Cod life and American culture in general. In "The Moose and the Whale: Thoreau's 'Chesuncook' as a Terrestrial *Moby-Dick*" (*ATQ* 6:77–94), Gregory M. Pfitzer notes "the striking resemblance" between "Chesuncook" and *Moby-Dick,* finding that both works attempt "to bring narrative life to ancient hunter mythologies." While I can accept these parallels as products of a shared cultural milieu, I am not persuaded by Pfitzer's suggestion of "the possibility of a direct appropriation of Melville's epic themes."

iv Fuller and the Transcendentalist Movement

Charles Capper's *Margaret Fuller: An American Romantic Life, The Private Years* (Oxford), the first volume of a projected two-volume biography, traces Fuller's life in detail through the beginning of her editorship of the *Dial* in 1840. Capper combines sound evaluative judgment with scrupulous research in primary documents, drawing in particular on a wide range of contemporary correspondence, to offer an illuminating portrait of Fuller's early development and intellectual emergence. The book is notable for its sensitive and balanced depiction of Fuller's intense relationship with her father, Timothy Fuller, whose exacting generosity was crucially formative for Fuller but also left her with a significant psychological burden. Capper vividly describes Fuller's pursuit of self-culture through a series of deep and demanding relationships with a number of men and women, notably James Freeman Clarke, Anna Barker, and Emerson in these years. This analysis reminds us of the importance of friendship and social orientation in molding the presumably individualist movement of Transcendentalism. Capper also reconstructs the importance of Fuller's early work as a teacher, first in Bronson Alcott's Temple School, and later in the Greene Street School in Providence, and of her "Conversations" for women that grew out of this teaching. This is certainly the definitive account of Fuller's early career, and I look forward to Capper's treatment of her experience in New York and Italy. In "The Call of Eurydice: Mourning and Intertextuality in Margaret Fuller's Writing," pp. 271–97 in *Influence and Intertextuality in Literary History*, ed. Jay Clayton and Eric Rothstein (Wisconsin, 1991), Jeffrey Steele offers a discerning discussion of Fuller's creation of "a series of self-representations shaped by nineteenth-century discourses of mourning" which chart her articulation of a socially defined self. Steele focuses on the year 1840, when Fuller's mourning for her father was exacerbated by her sense of loss over the marriage of Samuel Gray Ward and Anna Barker. In a resulting psychological breakthrough, Fuller realized that her dependent grief for her father "recapitulated the dependence of women in general upon patriarchal narratives." Fuller consequently reconstructed her female and maternal identity by "defining the self through extended reference to the lives of numerous women, both real and imaginary," a process that is reflected in the dense "medley of voices" in *Woman in the Nineteenth Century*. In a related essay, "Freeing the 'Prisoned Queen': The Development of Margaret Fuller's Poetry" (*SAR*, pp. 137–75), Steele offers a comprehensive overview of Fuller's poetry, arguing that it offers previously unexplored information about her emotional and psychological development. Steele finds that the poetry falls into three chronological periods—an early grouping of poems (1835–38) written primarily to Anna Barker, a middle period (1839–43) centering on her "spiritual crisis of 1840–41," and a later outburst of 37 poems written in 1844. These essays by Steele constitute an important psychological portrait of Fuller in the crucial decade after her father's death in 1835. Teachers of Fuller's work also will welcome Steele's anthology, *The Essential Margaret Fuller* (Rutgers), which includes a wide range of selections from her writings and a solid introductory essay and annotations. Marcia Noe's "The Heathen Priestess on the Prairie: Margaret Fuller Constructs the Midwest" (*ON* 16:3–12) discusses Fuller's description of the Midwest in *Summer on the Lakes* as both "an abundant natural garden" and a "cultural desert" and argues that Fuller's midwestern tour was crucial to her intellectual development. Paula Kopacz discusses Fuller's friendship with James Freeman Clarke and her consideration of a move to Kentucky in " 'As to your School-Keeping Project': Margaret Fuller's Kentucky Connection" (*KPR* 6 [1991]:21–26).

The continuing interest in the political nature of Transcendentalism has focused attention on Brook Farm, as evidenced by Sterling F. Delano's *Brook Farm: A Retrospective and Celebration* (Falvey Memorial Library, Villanova University, 1991), a catalogue of a 1991 exhibition commemorating the founding of the commune. The descriptions and photographs of the exhibits constitute a valuable resource for research on the social dimension of Transcendentalism. Joel Myerson's "Rebecca Codman Butterfield's Reminiscences of Brook Farm" (*NEQ* 65:603–30) is an account of life there by one of its members and includes valuable descriptions of the farm's setting and daily life. Butterfield stresses the commune's commitment to the "Equality of the Sexes," noting that "no distinction was made between the sexes in the ordinary conduct of affairs." In "Emerson and Brook Farm" (*ESP* 3, i:1–2) Len Gougeon proposes that Emerson's consideration of joining Brook Farm "was serious and extensive," and he cites an unpublished letter from William

Emerson urging him not to join such a community. Scholars interested in the connections of Transcendentalism and political reform may also be interested in Deborah Pickman Clifford's *Crusader for Freedom: A Life of Lydia Maria Child* (Beacon).

In "Channing's Influence on Peabody: Self-Culture and the Danger of Egoism" (*SAR*, pp. 121–35), Susan H. Irons explains how the elder Channing's "recognition of self-culture's danger of 'egotheism'" had a strong impact on Peabody's development, leading her to emphasize the importance of Christ more heavily than other Transcendentalists. Irons describes Peabody's attempt to defend Emerson's Divinity School Address to Channing, an attempt to reconcile the position of two important mentors. Diane Brown Jones characterizes "A Vision" (1843) as "Elizabeth Palmer Peabody's Transcendental Manifesto" (*SAR*, pp. 195–207), noting that this account of a visionary experience rests finally in Christ as "the fountain of life." Jones finds that Peabody resorts to history as a complementary element of the visionary, helping to prevent mysticism from degenerating into "Egotheism."

Francis B. Dedmond's "The Selected Letters of William Ellery Channing The Younger (Part Four)" (*SAR*, pp. 1–74) concludes this excellent edition, continuing the richly detailed annotations that have characterized each installment. Of particular interest in this installment are Channing's references to his work on Thoreau's manuscripts and information on his declining health and estrangement from his children in his later years. In "Christopher Pearse Cranch's Struggle with the Muses" (*SAR*, pp. 209–27), Julie M. Norko has provided a much-needed study of Cranch's early career, emphasizing the growing rift between his aesthetic sensibility and his commitment to the ministry in the late 1830s.

Oregon State University

2 Hawthorne

Leland S. Person, Jr.

According to "Highlights of the MLA's 1990 Survey of Upper-Division Literature Courses" (*ADEB* 101:34–60), Hawthorne ranks first among writers judged "particularly important" for 19th-century American literature courses, while *The Scarlet Letter* ranks second to *Walden* as an important work. Even though this year is nowhere near the banner year that 1991 proved to be, with sixty-plus entries the year's output reinforces claims of Hawthorne's "particular" importance. Richard Millington's is the only general book-length study, but Evan Carton's extended analysis of *The Marble Faun*, Gary Scharnhorst's compilation of *Scarlet Letter* criticism, James Schiff's account of that novel's influence on John Updike, and a welcome study of the children's books by Laura Laffrado certainly deepen the reach of Hawthorne criticism. Add to those books a major Lacanian reading of *The Scarlet Letter* by James Mellard and significant essays or chapters by Emily Miller Budick, Laurie Sterling, Michael P. Kramer, and Robert C. Grayson, and the year's work appears very respectable.

i Bibliography, Biography, and Reference Guides

In *The Critical Response to Nathaniel Hawthorne's* The Scarlet Letter (Greenwood), Gary Scharnhorst has edited a useful research tool for those interested in the 19th- and early 20th-century reception of the novel. (The section on "Modern Criticism" absurdly spans the past 50 years with only six reprinted essays—by Neal Frank Doubleday, Chester E. Eisinger, Darrel Abel, Nina Baym, Robert E. Todd, and Elizabeth Aycock Hoffman—and a new one by Marilyn Mueller Wilton [see below].) Scharnhorst includes 25 early reviews to illustrate the novel's "Contemporary American Reception," including lengthy notices from the *Salem Register, Literary World, Christian Register,* and *Christian Inquirer* (Hawthorne is a "pearl-diver" into the "morbid . . . exceptional regions of our nature"), and important essays by Charles C. Hazewell, Orestes Brownson (who calls Hawthorne a "moderate transcendentalist"), Arthur C. Coxe, Henry T. Tuckerman, and Amory Dwight Mayo. Seven notices represent the "Early British Reception" and reinforce American tendencies to test the novel's morality—one reviewer noting Hawthorne's "moral restraint," another citing the "unwholesome fascination" of the romance.

"The Growth of Hawthorne's Posthumous Reputation" features several well-known pieces from the period 1869–1939 (by Howells, Trollope, James, George Woodberry, William C. Brownell, Carl Van Doren, and others). My favorite is Trollope's imagining himself "so loving the image of Hester Prynne as to find himself on the verge of treachery to the real Hester of flesh and blood who may have a claim upon him"—priceless testimony to Hawthorne's sexiness. Reviews of "*The Scarlet Letter* on Stage and Screen" through 1934 are interesting, but the "Selected Bibliography" will be dangerous for anyone to rely on. Nevertheless, *Critical Response* is a welcome addition to Hawthorne studies.

ii Critical Books

In *Practicing Romance: Narrative Form and Cultural Engagement in Hawthorne's Fiction* (Princeton), Richard Millington reconstructs Hawthorne as a New Anthropologist. Synthesizing Freudian psychoanalysis, New Historicism, reader-response theory, and other critical methodologies, Millington provides a twist on an old idea: the interplay of individual and community in Hawthorne's fiction. Millington argues that Hawthorne's "neutral territory" of romance provides a contested space in which revisionary cultural work can be accomplished, and he emphasizes the "disciplinary" power of Hawthorne's fiction to bridge the personal and the cultural. Such emphases enable him to generate informative readings of "Roger Malvin's Burial" and several other tales, as well as of the four major romances. *The Scarlet Letter,* for example, becomes an attempt to locate the "meaning of living within a community"; whereas Dimmesdale is inscribed by the conscience-ridden narrative of his culture, Hester forges a new commonality in the romance-space at the margins of culture. *The House of the Seven Gables* becomes a "narrative of the cultural system" and explores a "range of cultural positions" available to readers and characters alike while moving toward a "new cultural alliance." A "counternovel" to *Gables* and a "striking act of cultural diagnosis," *The Blithedale Romance* represents a bitter attack on predation and self-aggrandizement. In the narrative "civil war" that marks the "double novel" of *The Marble Faun,* Millington traces the triumph of a "culture of conscience" represented by Kenyon and Hilda over a culture of pleasure embodied in Miriam and Donatello. Such readings would be even more useful if Millington had examined 19th-century New England culture rather than Culture as a universal abstraction, but *Practicing Romance* still makes a significant contribution to Hawthorne studies and will seem refreshing to those tired of seeing Hawthorne patronized as a victim of cultural ideology.

Where Millington sees Hawthorne as synthesizer, in *The Marble Faun: Hawthorne's Transformations* (Twayne) Evan Carton sees him as dialectician and considers *The Marble Faun* the best example of the polarities and instabilities in Hawthorne's writing. Carton successfully breathes fresh critical life into the novel by aligning himself with those (Robert S. Levine, Richard Brodhead, Luther Luedtke, T. Walter Herbert) who emphasize the work's social and political dimensions. After obligatory chapters on the historical and critical background, Carton performs his own "critical transformations," approaching the novel from several different perspectives, while remaining healthily committed to the idea that it resists critical closure. In a scintillating chapter he coordinates the religious and aesthetic debates in the novel, grounding that discussion in Levine's observations about American anti-Catholicism. Carton discusses *The Marble Faun*'s sexual politics in terms of a rather pat 19th-century "separate spheres" paradigm that, not surprisingly, shows the triumph of "domestic ideology" at the expense of female Otherness. Carton also turns a psychological and New Historical lens on Hawthorne himself, rehearsing Gloria Erlich's argument about Hawthorne's conflicted gender identity to show how sexual politics, psychology, and aesthetics all work together in the novel. In his final chapter Carton plays deconstructionist and, using Freud's "The Uncanny," uncovers numerous repressed contents from *The Marble Faun*'s "unconscious." Eschewing simplistic allegorization for deft New Historical analysis, Carton argues that Hawthorne was troubled by pre-Civil War events and inscribed those concerns into the novel through the races of Miriam and Donatello. As an exceptionally intelligent and always insightful—if necessarily introductory—reading of a complex work, this one is unsurpassed.

In *Hawthorne's Literature for Children* (Georgia) Laura Laffrado produces the first book-length treatment of the six collections of children's
stories Hawthorne published between 1841 and 1853. Laffrado makes an
effective case for the children's books as integral points in Hawthorne's
literary career, barometers of his literary and extraliterary confidence.
Hawthorne's narrators reflect his own felt "status and authority." Especially in her discussion of the four collections from the 1840s, Laffrado
emphasizes Hawthorne's experimentation with a "neutral territory" well
before he coined the term in "The Custom-House," and she helps us
realize Hawthorne's early fascination with the "fluid boundaries of time
and reality." Devoting separate chapters to each volume, Laffrado offers
close readings of each tale, and she interests most when she links the
stories with Hawthorne's writerly condition. With his writing still relatively unsuccessful, "reality takes a stranglehold in *Biographical Stories*,"
but when he felt flush from the success of *The Scarlet Letter* and *The
House of the Seven Gables*, he confidently created a younger narrator
(Eustace Bright) and a happier, prelapsarian world for his listening
children. In contrast, *Tanglewood Tales* with its pervasive images of
"death and loss, and sanitized and coded sexual relationships," is a "more
troubled and problematic text," largely because of the deaths (his sister
Louisa, Sophia's mother) and losses (a sense of pre-Civil War stability)
that Hawthorne had suffered. Laffrado has left plenty of room for other
scholars, but as a groundbreaking study of a neglected portion of Hawthorne's canon, this one provides good service.

In "Updike's *Scarlet Letter* Trilogy: Recasting an American Myth"
(*SAF* 20:17–31), "Updike's *Roger's Version*: Re-Visualizing *The Scarlet
Letter*" (*SoAR* 57, i:59–75), and finally in *Updike's Version: Rewriting* The
Scarlet Letter (Missouri), James A. Schiff naturally focuses more on
Updike than on his predecessor, but Hawthorne scholars may profit
from his analysis of the "dialogue between Updike's texts and Hawthorne's *Scarlet Letter*." In addition to its manifold allusions, Updike's
trilogy offers the Hawthorne scholar a set of new lenses through which to
view the novel. Thomas Marshfield's affair with Ms. Prynne in a *Month
of Sundays*, for example, forces us to recognize the roles of power and
sexuality in Dimmesdale's affair with Hester, while Updike's emphasis on
Marshfield as writer focuses our attention on Dimmesdale's conflicted
verbalizations. The creative voyeurism and triangularity in *Roger's Version*
make us "reconsider the dynamics of the *Scarlet Letter* triangle" and to
give more emphasis to the relationship between the two men. *S.* includes

more allusions to *The Scarlet Letter* than either of Updike's other novels. Sarah resembles Hester more closely than any previous heroine, Schiff says, and her solitary transcontinental journey fleshes out the untold prehistory of Hester's tale. Schiff, however, believes that Updike has designed his portrait to demystify recent views of Hester as feminist saint and to confirm D. H. Lawrence's emphasis on Hester's anger and vengeance. From a Hawthornean point of view, *Updike's Version* propounds a more scarlet *Scarlet Letter* that may intrigue contemporary readers and encourage renewed awareness of the degree to which sexual tensions drive Hawthorne's novel. The letter A, "gules," indeed.

iii General Essays

One of the year's best essays is Emily Miller Budick's "Sacvan Bercovitch, Stanley Cavell, and the Romance Theory of American Fiction" (*PMLA* 107:78–91), a wide-ranging engagement with recent American literary theory that, like many others, uses Hawthorne and *The Scarlet Letter* to test for the presence of ideology. Budick, however, has no particular ax to grind, and her essay represents a scintillating example of cogent theorizing. Taking aim at recent challenges to the romance theory of American fiction associated with Richard Chase, Budick puts Sacvan Bercovitch "into conversation" with Stanley Cavell on the question of textual dissent or consent. Cavell helps reopen "what Bercovitch sees as the closed ending of a text like *The Scarlet Letter,*" Budick claims, because his theory of "aversion" ("the ability of individuals equally to turn away from and toward one another" and ideological pressures) enables us to see how Hester's return expresses both consent and dissent, placing her and her creator in a "richly aversive relation with America."

In "Hawthorne and Two Types of Early American Romance" (*SoAR* 57, i:33–51), John Engell works some of this same ground in arguing that Hawthorne created a hybrid American romance that combined gothic (or "affective") and historical features. Not an original idea, but Engell supplements previous work by comparing Hawthorne's comments on romance-writing with commentary and fiction by other male writers (Charles Brockden Brown, John Neal, Poe) who took greater license with subject matter, point of view, and ties to historical reality, as well as by still others (Cooper, Simms, James Kirke Paulding) who grounded their writing more conservatively in historical reality.

In "Reading, Writing, and Recycling: Literary Archaeology and the

Shape of Hawthorne's Career" (*NEQ* 65:238–64), James C. Keil begins with a provocative idea about Hawthorne's career and methods, but his follow-through is weak. Claiming that the archaeological Hawthorne tended to "recycle" other men's texts in his early years as a writer and voracious reader, Keil sees a crisis point in 1836, after which Hawthorne increasingly wrote from his own experience. Unfortunately, Keil doesn't flesh out this structure effectively, sifting no early fiction for its recyclables, paying too little attention to dates of composition (for "The Old Manse" and "Ethan Brand," in particular), and begging the question of Chillingworth's embodiment of Hawthorne's archaeological tendency.

In *Fictions of the Past*, pp. 5–103, Alide Cagidemetrio expands on the old and New Historicist work of many recent critics to identify a modernist Hawthorne in the forefront of constructing the "modern historical consciousness" and interested more in "referentiality" than in "representation." Cagidemetrio ingeniously links Hawthorne with 19th-century theories of mind and technological advances (theories of visuality, phantasmagoria shows, the transatlantic telegraph cable) in examining the "symbolic logic" in which historical events become subject to constant reconstruction by the ordering power of contemporary consciousness. For cogent illustrations of this subjective, or affective, history, Cagidemetrio examines *Legends of the Province-House* and the unfinished Claimant manuscripts.

Nathaniel Philbrick's "Hawthorne, Maria Mitchell, and Melville's 'After the Pleasure Party'" (*ESQ* 37 [1991]:291–308) quotes several passages from Hawthorne's *French and Italian Notebooks* to demonstrate that Mitchell inspired the characterization of Zenobia in *The Blithedale Romance* as well as Melville's poem. In "Solving the Mysteries of Hawthorne's Fiction" (*DUJ* 83 [1991]:187–94), David Seed provides brief analyses of the four major novels in order to rehearse the very familiar idea of Hawthorne's interest in secrets, multiple significations, and interpretive relativity.

iv **Essays on the Novels**

a. *The Scarlet Letter* Few works of criticism truly astonish, but James M. Mellard's "Inscriptions of the Subject: *The Scarlet Letter*," pp. 69–106 in his *Using Lacan, Reading Fiction* (Illinois, 1991), is one of those few—a richly detailed reading of Hawthorne's novel that should engage even those not inclined toward literary psychoanalysis. Regardless of his

Lacanian paradigms, for example, Mellard's attention to all four major characters, whom he analyzes as "four inscribed subjectivities," enriches our understanding of the novel. At the same time, Mellard reveals uncanny parallels between Hawthorne's text and Lacan's theories. Pearl passes from the *infans* stage of the "child-without-speech" through the mirror stage to the assumption of gender, and to resolution of the Oedipus complex in her "introjection of the Name-of-the-Father." Hester's story suggests a subject "caught between the Imaginary and the Symbolic," but it also illustrates her "acceptance of her life under the burden of the Law, under the rule of the Symbolic Other." The pathological Dimmesdale, in Lacanian terms, has "foreclosed" the "authority of the father." Gestating the letter (phallus) on his own body (a "hysterical pregnancy") and ascending the scaffold mean reclaiming "the place of the Father." Hawthorne progressively unmasks Chillingworth as a "paranoid psychotic," in Mellard's view, who surrenders ego functions to the "domain of the Other," the "destiny" that directs his actions. Mellard's impressive work is destined in its own right, I think, to become a classic essay—as important to the current generation as Frederick Crews's work was to an earlier one.

In "Beyond Symbolism: Philosophy of Language in *The Scarlet Letter*" (*Imagining Language in America*, pp. 162–97), Michael P. Kramer counters those (beginning with Charles Feidelson) who cite Hawthorne's indeterminate symbolism and offers a fresh look at the complex ways that language constitutes political and social life. Kramer takes his cue from the "double language" of Dimmesdale's election sermon (chapter 22), which he uses to interrogate "The Devil in Manuscript," "The Minister's Black Veil," as well as Hawthorne's love letters and *The Scarlet Letter*. Briefly, Kramer's Hawthorne understood that "words distort something else, an emotional, unverbalized supplement to the text," and he struggled repeatedly at the boundary of those linguistic realms. Kramer's most provocative move is comparing Hawthorne to Rousseau (and to Winthrop), finding parallels between the "undertone" in Dimmesdale's sermon and the "pure expressivity" in Rousseau's "cry of nature" (prelinguistic "man's first language"). Kramer contrasts the languages of "The Custom-House" and *The Scarlet Letter* in terms of the "discontinuous" (public-private) aspects of American experience, but the novel, he argues, "takes us back to the very origins of American society" and to a world of potential linguistic intimacy in which public and private languages, like natural and civil liberty, were not so separate.

Laurie A. Sterling's "Paternal Gold: Translating Inheritance in *The Scarlet Letter*" (*ATQ* 6:17–30) offers a highly intelligent analysis of the economy (various forms of exchange and valuation) at work in the novel, and it features many interesting connections—for example, between Hawthorne, Pearl, and the issue of legitimacy, between biological and literary paternity, and especially between paternal and maternally speculative notions of value. Well worth reading with earlier studies by Michael Gilmore and Michael Ragussis, Sterling's essay represents an important "economic" reading of *The Scarlet Letter*.

In "*The Scarlet Letter* as Icon" (*ATQ* 6:251–62) Samuel Coale focuses on Hawthorne's fascination with objects, images, and icons—his interest in a "psychology of idolatry"—and particularly on the way such "things" exceed or "outlast" their narratives. Implicitly countering those who see Hawthorne as proto-deconstructionist, Coale posits a quasireligious Hawthorne for whom "deep meaning," or "metaphysical radiance," resides in and beyond objective, iconic realities. The scarlet letter, Coale reminds us, does not merely signify an absence; it is a "mystic symbol." In this provocative revisionist essay Coale ranges widely from studies of Puritan iconography to more recent theories of the gaze, finally grounding Hawthorne in his subculture of mediums, magnetism, and mesmerism.

In "Paradigm and Paramour: Role Reversal in *The Scarlet Letter*" (Scharnhorst, *Critical Response,* pp. 220–32), Marilyn Mueller Wilton argues for a simple reversal in which Hester plays the "hero" and Dimmesdale the "heroine" of the novel. Wilton relies wholly on stereotypical ideas of male and female characterization in making her case that Dimmesdale embodies " 'pure unattainable love'—the heroine." In contrast, James Barszcz's "Hawthorne, Emerson and the Forms of the Frontier" (*Desert, Garden, Margin, Range,* pp. 44–54) collapses the dichotomy between wilderness and civilization. Hawthorne emphasizes the continuity between those realms (in "Main-Street") and the impossibility of escaping "acculturated circumstances" for an "unmediated world or frontier" in the forest scene of *The Scarlet Letter.* Barszcz thus reclaims Hawthorne for an Emersonian tradition of skepticism from which he is "usually excluded."

The Nathaniel Hawthorne Review (18.1) includes three short pieces on "The Custom-House." In "Seized by the Button: Rhetorical Positioning at 'The Custom-House' Door" (pp. 1, 3–5), Thomas R. Moore employs rhetorical and reader-response theory to analyze Hawthorne's "opaque style," particularly the way he blurs the fiction/nonfiction distinction and negotiates the ambiguous narrator-narratee relationship in the opening section of the Preface. Citing the Preface's "double nature" (as autobiographical sketch and "Kunstlererzählung"), Alfred Weber, "The Framing Functions of Hawthorne's 'The Custom-House' Sketch" (pp. 5–8), insightfully links "The Custom-House" and the "Conclusion" (chapter 24) of the novel, which together transform the narrative into a "framed romance." And Richard R. O'Keefe wonders if there is "An Echo of Emerson in Hawthorne's 'The Custom-House'?" (pp. 9–11). The answer of course is "Yes": Hawthorne's list of proper names ("Pingree, Phillips, Shepard, Upton, Kimball, Bertram, Hunt") in the next-to-last paragraph of the Preface echoes Emerson's similar list in "Hamatreya."

Another trio of minor pieces rounds out the year's activity. In "Hester Prynne and the Folk Art of Embroidery" (*UMSE* n.s. 10:80–85), Haipeng Li simply establishes that Hester is often identified with that folk art. Alfred Kazin's "The Opera of 'The Scarlet Letter'" (*NYRB*, 8 October: 53–55) emphasizes the dark, brooding, but also intensely emotional and sexual—the operatic—characteristics of the novel. And Charles Swann in "A Hardy Debt to Hawthorne?" (*N&Q* 39:188–89) compares Dimmesdale's experience "in a maze" (chapter 20) to Angel Clare's demoniacal mood in Thomas Hardy's *Tess of the d'Urbervilles*.

b. *The House of the Seven Gables* Two studies of Hawthorne's representation of the self highlight criticism on *The House of the Seven Gables*. H. L. Gable, Jr., "Kaleidoscopic Visions: Images of the Self in *The House of the Seven Gables*" (*ArQ* 48, i:109–35), analyzes ontology through symbolism in order to uncover Hawthorne's "basic message": the Pyncheons have lost the "vivifying fluid of the true spirit by their worship of Mammon," while the Maules have become alienated from materiality by fixing on the "abstract creativity of the spiritual." Gable's analysis of imagery is compelling, although his conclusion that Holgrave and Phoebe sanctify "Nature's balance between flesh and spirit" will seem very familiar. Gable's optimistic view of personal identity can be contrasted with William J. Scheick's in "The Author's Corpse and the Humean Problem of Personal Identity in Hawthorne's *The House of the Seven Gables*" (*SNNTS* 24:131–53). Scheick closes the gap between Hawthorne's 18th-century empiricism and 19th-century Romanticism by "annotating" the presence of "Humean skeptical empiricism" in the novel. Citing Hume's characterization of identity as a *"fictitious* belief" (*A Treatise of Human Nature*), Scheick finds many analogs—in Hawthorne's descriptions of the five major characters, in the self-effacing and unreliable narrator, in the unstable romance form, in the equivocation of the ending, and in Hawthorne's own authorial ambivalence.

Michael Dunne, "The Narrative Authority of History in Hawthorne's *The Seven Gables*" (*TPB* 29:6–14), also discovers a skeptical Hawthorne. Elaborating on Susan Mizruchi's 1988 study, Dunne examines the narrative devices—the mixing of documentary history, "traditionary lore," dream, mesmeric testimony, "metadiegetic narrative" (Holgrave's legend of Alice Pyncheon)—that Hawthorne uses to "subvert historical authority." Another historical study, *Salem Witchcraft and Hawthorne's* House of the Seven Gables (Heritage) by Enders A. Robinson, is misleadingly titled. Focusing on the witchcraft trials of 1692 and aiming at the general reader, Enders uses numerous passages from Hawthorne's fiction to shed light on that subject, but he does not engage critical issues. Where he does mention *Gables* he identifies the "real-life counterparts" of the characters—Jaffrey Pyncheon as John Hathorne, Matthew Maule as Samuel Wardwell, Phoebe as Sophia Hawthorne, Holgrave as Nathaniel.

Two reprintings in *The Nathaniel Hawthorne Review* offer interesting glimpses into the effects of Hawthorne's novel. Richard S. Kennedy's "E. E. Cummings' Analysis of *The House of the Seven Gables*" (*NHR* 18, ii:1, 3–4) prints Cummings's meditative 6 June 1944 journal entry, which emphasizes various character pairs (Holgrave-Phoebe, Holgrave-Hepzibah, Judge Pyncheon-Uncle Venner) in terms of their power to do good or evil. N. Luanne Jenkins Hurst's "Sophia Hawthorne as Literary Critic and Educator: A Letter" (*NHR* 18, ii:5–8) reprints Sophia's long 16 February 1851 letter to Elizabeth Peabody, including the novel's first reader/listener's rhapsodic response.

c. *The Blithedale Romance* Besides Millington's chapter, only three essays were published on *Blithedale* this year, but all three merit some attention. Addressing Foucauldian issues about literary complicity in the "vast network of invasive social control," Richard Hull argues provocatively in "Critique of Characterization: It Was in Not Knowing That He Loved Her" (*Style* 26:33–49) that Hawthorne resists characterizing, or policing, his characters by anticipating a "postmodern episteme" of "not knowing" them. Where many critics fault Coverdale for preferring his own fantastical version of Priscilla, Hull claims that Coverdale's lack of interest in Priscilla's "realities" reflects the novel's refusal of "panoptic" knowledge of others. Covering some of the same issues from a very different perspective, Roberta F. Weldon's "Tyrant King and Accused Queen: Father and Daughter in Nathaniel Hawthorne's *The Blithedale Romance*" (*ATQ* 6:31–45) focuses on the Old Moodie-Zenobia relationship as a "subconscious" variation on the innocent woman wrongly accused (by her father) motif. Moodie hates Zenobia because she threatens his "patriarchal status," Weldon argues, and she asks whether the novel represents a "subversive revision from the cultural margins or a cautionary tale told from the culture's center." Weldon opts for the latter, because instead of empowering Zenobia to rescue herself Hawthorne kills her to restore patriarchal power—even if he feels "conflicted" about it. Ffrangcon Lewis's "Women, Death and Theatricality in *The Blithedale Romance*" (*JAmS* 26:75–94) tracks theatrical metaphors in the novel and discusses Zenobia's death in relation to Shakespeare's Ophelia, especially as portrayed on the stage by the pre-Raphaelite Sir John Millais the year before Hawthorne published *Blithedale*.

d. *The Marble Faun*   Besides Carton's tour de force, relatively little of note was published on Hawthorne's last completed novel. Peter M. McCluskey, in " 'The Recovery of the Sacred Candlestick': Jewish Imagery and the Problem of Allegory in *The Marble Faun*" (*PAPA* 18, ii:15–27), examines Jewish references in the novel to illustrate Hawthorne's contrast of Old and New Testament values and his meditation on the illegibility of history and the failure of allegory. Focusing on the "Postscript" Hawthorne added to second editions, Patricia Marks, "Romance and the 'Beer-Sodden English Beefeaters': Hawthorne's 'Postscript' to *The Marble Faun*" (*NHR* 18, i:12–14), finds Hawthorne illegible—deliberately so in this "modernist device before its time," a "refictionalizing," or metafictional, postscript that underlines the work's indeterminacy and open-endedness. In a superficial essay, "The Role of Rome in Hawthorne's *The Marble Faun* and Henry James's *Daisy Miller*" (*RSItal* 9:43–52), George Bisztray contrasts Hawthorne's depiction of an "anachronistic baroque city" and papal state and James's twenty-years-later portrayal of a secular, increasingly modern metropolis. Using Freud, Peter Brooks (*Reading for the Plot*), and René Girard (*Violence and the Sacred*) in "Hawthorne's Monstrous Doubles: Metonymic Links Between *The House of the Seven Gables* and *The Marble Faun*" (*NHR* 18, ii:15–19), Elzbieta H. Olesky asserts more than proves her claim that the deaths of

Judge Pyncheon and the Model enact ritual sacrifices keyed to Hawthorne's unresolved Oedipal conflict.

v Essays on Tales and Sketches

Hawthorne wrote a remarkable number of fascinating short stories, and their variety and excellence are confirmed by the number of tales receiving scholarly attention. In one of the year's best essays, "Thomas Hutchinson and Robin's Molineux Problem" (*SAR:* 177–94), Robert C. Grayson expands on earlier work by Michael Colacurcio, James Franzosa, James Duban, and others to analyze the interrelationship between Irish philosopher William Molyneux and Thomas Hutchinson. Identifying Robin with the Royalist Hutchinson and the blind man in the "Problem" that Molyneux posed to John Locke, Grayson details the controversy surrounding Massachusetts' resistance to England's Acts of Trade. Like Hutchinson and Molyneux's blind man, Robin cannot initially perceive the "people's determination to rule themselves." When like Molyneux's blind man he stops relying on his senses and begins using his imagination, however, Robin achieves historical understanding through identification with the townspeople. From a different point of view but with equal dexterity, Janet Carey Eldred, in "Narratives of Socialization: Literacy in the Short Story" (*CE* 53 [1991]:686–700), compares "My Kinsman" to Faulkner's "Barn Burning" and Toni Cade Bambara's "The Lesson" as a "literacy narrative," "a fiction that dramatizes the collision between competing discourse communities." While the rural Robin expects "honest language," he encounters deceptive "multivocal languages" in the city. The ending does not reflect Robin's maturation but leaves him seeking a language between a "monologic, whole, unified rural discourse and the urban polyphonic rhetoric that communicates subversion, power, and violence."

Another interesting study of a Revolutionary War tale is "Mimetic Desire and the American Revolution: Hawthorne's 'Lady Eleanore's Mantle'" (*HSL* 22, ii–iii[1990]:23–43), in which Richard Boyd profitably employs René Girard's theory of triangular, mimetic desire and the role of the scapegoat to illuminate psychological and historical meanings—the "communal function of private desire." Boyd zeroes in on the "reciprocal desire" between Lady Eleanore and her obsessively deferential admirer, Jervase Helwyse, to explain Hawthorne's uncanny insights into the psychology of revolutionary behavior. In showing how all parties share "moral culpability" for ritualistic violence against Lady Eleanore, Hawthorne "deconstructs" Revolutionary mythology. Using Edmund Quincy's 1837 *Atlantic Monthly* essay on "Old Houses" as a "point of departure" for Hawthorne's *Democratic Review* tales, "Legends of the Province-House," Geoffrey D. Smith, in "The Reluctant Democrat and the Amiable Whig: Nathaniel Hawthorne, Edmund Quincy and the Politics of History" (*NHR* 18, ii:9–14), is able to contrast Hawthorne's comparatively democratic attitudes with Quincy's Whig biases but also to reveal the dimensions of Hawthorne's conservative nostalgia.

Allene Cooper's "The Discourse of Romance: Truth and Fantasy in Hawthorne's Point of View" (*SSF* 28 [1991]:497–507) clarifies Hawthorne's narrative method by analyzing his "neutral territory" of "discourse that could be read as either the voice of the narrator or the thoughts of a character." Her examination of "Rappaccini's Daughter," "The Artist of the Beautiful," and "Alice Doane's Appeal" confirms Hawthorne's notorious ambiguity.

In a comparative study, "The Artist and the Tailor: Parallels between Carlyle's *Sartor Resartus* and Hawthorne's 'The Artist of the Beautiful' " (*PAPA* 18, ii:29–43), W. Dale Hearell cites several similar passages to prove Thomas Carlyle's direct influence on Hawthorne. Hearell sees similarities in the authors' use of light and dark imagery and in their attitudes toward industrialism and the spiritual quest ("the spiritual conception of the soul's limitless creativity"). William Freedman's "The Artist's Symbol and Hawthorne's Veil: 'The Minister's Black Veil' *Resartus*" (*SSF* 29:353–62) shows Carlyle's influence on another tale. Freedman convincingly extends W. B. Carnochan's 1969 reading of the tale as an experiment in symbolism, adds Carlyle's views on the indeterminacy of symbols, and discovers Hawthorne's "message": that the only truth is "the artistic symbol's boundless resonance and evocative force." In "Community and Interpretive Communities in Stories by Hawthorne, Kafka and García Márquez" (*SSF* 29:551–59), Ronald E. McFarland insightfully compares "The Minister's Black Veil" to "A Hunger Artist" and "A Very Old Man with Enormous Wings" as three metafictional accounts of "interpretive communities" and their epistemological and ethical problems in "reading" anomalous individuals.

In "Julien Green's Black Veil" (*PLL* 27 [1991]:371–80) Kathryn E. Wildgren discusses the frightening, explosive impact of "Veil" on Julien Green (and his veiled homosexuality). Green first read the tale in 1919 and subsequently used a black veil in several novels, particularly to represent a hidden creative power. Similarly, George Toles's "The Mystery of Crinkle's Nose" (*Raritan* 11, iii:80–97), an interesting example of subjective criticism, places "The Birthmark" within a context of other stories about physical transformations (from Kathryn and Byron Jackson's "The Mystery of Crinkle's Nose" to Anne Tyler's *Celestial Navigation*) and his own imaginatively embodied relation to such "bodily conscious" texts. The result is an illuminating, meditative account of how readers interact with literature.

Barbara Fass Leavy, *To Blight with Plague*, pp. 168–83, relies on Carol Bensick's 1984 argument about syphilis in "Rappaccini's Daughter," and by emphasizing the language of disease (with help from Eugene Brieux's play, *Damaged Goods*, and other works of "plague literature") she considers Beatrice a "case study of the crisis experienced by one struggling to free herself of an identity that *equals* her disease." In a pair of notes, "Two Potential Sources for Pietro Baglioni in Nathaniel Hawthorne's 'Rappaccini's Daughter' " (*SSF* 28 [1991]:557–64), and "The Probable Etymological Roots of Hawthorne's Pietro Baglioni in 'Rappaccini's Daughter' " (*Names* 40:167–72), Ronald J. Nelson proposes a civil architect named Pietro Baglioni (1629–1705) and a doctor of law also named Pietro Baglioni as sources for Hawthorne's character, and then pursues the Italian words "*baglio/bailo*" (foster father, tutor, guardian), "*baglio*" (nautical beam), and "*abbaglio/abbagliare*" (mistake, dazzling) as alternate sources.

In an insightful note, Joan Elizabeth Easterly, "Lachrymal Imagery in Hawthorne's 'Young Goodman Brown' " (*SSF* 28 [1991]:339–43), interprets dewdrops on Goodman Brown's cheek in the witches' Sabbath scene as an "absence of tears" signaling the character's failure to weep or demonstrate "deep and redemptive human feelings"—condemning him to an "anguished life that is spiritually and emotionally dessicated." In "Cultural Fate and Social Freedom in Three American Short Stories" (*SSF* 29:543–49), Walter Shear astutely compares the same tale to "Rip Van Winkle" and "The Jolly Corner" through their structural similarities: leave-takings, fabulous experiences, and returns to society. Stressing the social dimensions of this tale and the others, as Shear does, represents a suggestive turn of the critical screw.

For Raymond Benoit, "Fault-Lines in Kierkegaard and Hawthorne: *The Sickness unto Death* and 'Ethan Brand' " (*Thought* 66 [1991]:196–205), the two works published about the same time exemplify important cultural changes: threatened individualism, increasing mechanization,

estrangement from being, scientific subversion of faith, excessive intel-
lectualism, the emergence of "Homo Economicus" and extinction of
"Homo Religiosus" ("Ethan"). In another intertextual study, "The Tragi-
cal History of Ethan Brand" (*ELWIU* 19:55–60), Kurt Eisen briefly
examines the character's roots in Marlowe's and Shakespeare's tragic
heroes, especially Doctor Faustus.

Sylvie L. F. Richards, "Nathaniel Hawthorne's 'Monsieur du Miroir'
Through Jacques Lacan's Looking Glass" (*NHR* 18, i:15–20), perceptively
reads the tale and Lacan's "Le Stade du Miroir" as mirror texts. Like *The
Scarlet Letter* in Mellard's hands, Hawthorne's tale reveals uncanny anticipations of Lacan's insights into the constitution of selfhood and subjectivity. In another careful work of scholarship, John F. Birk, "New Roots
for 'Merry Mount': Barking Up the Wrong Tree?" (*SSF* 28 [1991]:345–
54), persuasively shows that Milton's "L'Allegro" and "Il Penseroso"
compose "an out-and-out blueprint" for Hawthorne's story, which divides into comparable parts. Birk finds many parallels in language,
setting, characters, imagery, and structure. "The Wives of the Living?:
Absence of Dreams in Hawthorne's 'The Wives of the Dead'" (*SSF*
29:323–29) by Mark Harris answers the question of whether Hawthorne
represents dreams or reality in the story by arguing that, although neither
"wife" actually dreams events, Hawthorne cautions against "ignorance of
the distinction between dreams and reality."

Elizabeth Goodenough has developed some of the territory that Laura
Laffrado's study of the children's books leaves open. In *"Grandfather's Chair:* Hawthorne's 'Deeper History' of New England" (*L&U* 15
[1991]:27–42), she explores Hawthorne's attitude toward children in the
context of conflicted (Puritan vs. Romantic) 19th-century attitudes. The
different ages, genders, and temperaments of the children reflect "contrasting ideologies of the nineteenth-century child" and child-rearing,
and Goodenough connects those contrasts to Hawthorne's complex
representation of a "deeper history" that questions patriotic and progressive myths.

vi **Essays on Other Works**

Thomas R. Moore's "Hawthorne as Essayist: *Our Old Home* and 'Chiefly
About War Matters'" (*ATQ* 6:263–78) advances the modest claim that
critics have insufficiently appreciated Hawthorne's talents as essayist, and

Moore performs a rhetorical analysis of two works to demonstrate the point. In "Meeting the Dark: Autobiography in Hawthorne's Unfinished Tales" (*Gerontologist* 32:726–32), Celeste Loughman argues the obvious point that Hawthorne's emphasis on old age and quests for immortality in these "literary false starts," especially the *Elixir of Life* manuscripts, reflects his ambivalence about death and mortality.

Southern Illinois University at Carbondale

3 Poe

Benjamin F. Fisher

More books about Poe arrived this year than for some time past. Diverse approaches are evident, sometimes within a single book. Provocative readings of tales like "Liegia" and "Usher" (shades of Leslie Fiedler) will doubtless elicit rejoinders and revaluations. The overall drift in what is surveyed below indicates the continuing move away from biographical connections. Source and influence study continues to hold a major place.

i Books, Parts of Books

Louis J. Budd and Edwin H. Cady add *On Poe* (Duke) to their series reprinting the "best" from *American Literature,* which makes handy 17 good articles from the journal's early years to the present. Jeffrey Meyers's contribution to the already ample ranks of Poe biography in *Edgar Allan Poe: His Life and Legacy* (Scribner's) features a generally straightforward chronological narrative style, albeit the book holds out little that is new. Meyers treats Poe's problems with women and alcohol in interesting terms, and his work on the legacy gathers a considerable body of information into manageable compass. Much more might be said on several subjects, and Meyers's book lays foundations for future building—on Poe and Arthur Conan Doyle, Poe and detection, Poe's influence on 20th-century figures. Some unevenness occurs elsewhere (e.g., in the critiques of "Cask" and "Usher") because Poe's texts do not supply what Meyers offers as facts. The assertion that Poe turned out an "enormous quantity of critical hackwork and trashy stories during his short career" does not seem to be borne out in the remainder of the book. (Had we a complete gathering of Poe's critical writings, we might better evaluate such comments. Oh editor, come forth!) One also wearies of the excessive reference to premature burial in Poe's era. Poe biography remains better served by *The Poe Log* and the work of Kenneth Silverman and A. H. Quinn.

Michael L. Burduck's *Grim Phantasms: Fear in Poe's Short Fiction* (Garland) reassesses a hallmark in Poe's work, arguing from the premise of "phobic pressure points" set forth by the horror novelist Stephen King in *Danse Macabre,* King's critique of horror fiction and films. Burduck uses 21 tales as the bases of his evaluation. Thus, he expands on what we find, for example, in David R. Saliba's *A Psychology of Fear* (1980), a book that drew caveats from one of my predecessors (see *ALS 1980,* pp. 51–52). Burduck adds to our knowledge of Poe's familiarity with theories about and treatment of mental disorders, especially those inspired by Dr. Benjamin Rush (thereby supplementing work by David E. E. Sloane, David Butler, I. M. Walker, and others). In sum, writes Burduck, Poe's concepts of fear "were not visions of dangerous fancy but images of reality," and his fiction of fear was a vital segment of his canon. Lest one begin to think that this book considers a strictly gloomy body of fiction, I note that Poe's humor also figures prominently in Burduck's critiques. His wide but relevant ranging over Poe scholarship adds usefulness and strength to the book, as does the good index.

Lois Davis Vines expands her thoughts already on record in *Valéry and Poe: A Literary Legacy* (NYU). Vines reminds us that Poe's impact on Valéry has not gotten such attention as have lines extending from Poe to Baudelaire and Mallarmé. Her own convincing—and eminently read-able—study takes us from Poe's tales, such as "MS. Found" and the Dupin works, to *Eureka,* to poetic theory. Ironically, she notes, Poe's ideas ultimately turned Valéry from literature "toward the quest of pure intellectual power." Vines's command of relevant primary and secondary materials and her original critical perceptions are most impressive.

ii Brief General Studies

Mami Hild's "The Quest for a Sense of Security—An Undercurrent of E. A. Poe's Works" (*Doshisha Literature* 35:67–85) presents us with a Poe whose theme of home as the center of security establishes what I see as his literary kinship with Hawthorne's domestic myth, a commonality not customarily noticed. Terence Whalen's "Edgar Allan Poe and the Horrid Laws of Political Economy" (*AQ* 44:381–417) marshals economic factors in the literary marketplace during Poe's era to support an argument that, among other accomplishments, Poe invented the detective story to appeal to a mass audience. Although well-written, this piece in its critical overview will not surprise many Poe scholars. In addition to invoking Marx, Whalen might pay greater respect to work by such predecessors as Howard Mumford Jones (*Ideas in America*) and Bruce I. Weiner on Poe's sensitivity to his marketplace. Marty Roth's "The Unquenchable Thirst of Edgar Allan Poe" (*Dionysos* 3, iii:3–16) investigates Poe's alcoholism and his use of alcohol and opium addiction in the writings, concluding that the pervasive perversity in the canon may devolve from Poe's own condition. Roth is not the innovator in assessing liquorishness in Poe as his study might suggest: he neglects pertinent work by Alexander Hammond (see below under *Pym*), Curtis Dahl, James W. Christie, and my *The Very Spirit of Cordiality* (1978).

iii Pym

The most substantial contribution this year to work on Poe's tantalizing novel may be found in *Poe's* Pym: *Critical Explorations,* ed. Richard Kopley (Duke), which emanates from a 1988 conference. Following Kopley's brief introduction—on literary-historical and critical contexts for *Pym*—16 essays are grouped categorically. The first seven are source studies. Susan F. Beegel's " 'Mutiny and Atrocious Butchery': The *Globe* Mutiny as a Source for *Pym*" (pp. 7–19) convincingly links events of an 1824 debacle involving a Nantucket whale ship with Poe's book. Equally persuasive, Joan Tyler Mead follows a lead proffered back in 1895 by G. E. Woodberry in the Stone and Kimball edition of Poe, in "Poe's 'Manual of Seamanship' " (pp. 20–32), to connect Poe's novel with William Falconer's *A New Universal Dictionary of the Marine* (1769). J. Lasley Dameron in "*Pym's* Polar Episode: Conclusion or Beginning?" (pp. 33–43) is no less compelling in unearthing *Pym* origins in a well-known inspiration for *Moby-Dick,* William Scoresby's *Journal of a Voyage to the Northern Whale-Fishery* (1823). Bruce I. Weiner supplements his previous thoughts on Poe's narrative methods in comparing those in *Pym* with techniques pervasive in *Blackwood's Magazine* terror fiction: "Novels, Tales, and Problems of Form in *The Narrative of Arthur Gordon Pym*" (pp. 44–56). Poe did not emerge from his work on *Pym* as a novelist, but his efforts assisted in shaping and strengthening his short-story writing. New vistas on Poe's roots are opened by Carol Pierce and Alexander G. Rose III in their demonstration of Arthurian elements in *Pym* and possibly other Poe works—"Poe's Reading of Myth: The White Vision of

Arthur Gordon Pym" (pp. 57–74). Most striking is their view that the shrouded human figure devolves from Guinivere legendry, although it is by no means the sole correspondence with Arthurian lore to be considered. (To be read in tandem with the Pierce-Rose essay is Alan Lupack's "American Arthurian Authors: A Declaration of Independence" in *The Arthurian Revival,* ed. Debra N. Mancoff [Garland], pp. 155–73, especially the passage on Lambert A. Wilmer's 1827 play, *Merlin,* which drew on Poe's unhappy fate in relation to Sarah Elmira Royster.) Joseph J. Moldenhauer in "*Pym,* the Dighton Rock, and the Matter of Vinland" (pp. 75–94) shows how Vinland sagas and their derivatives influenced Poe's handling of hieroglyphic language. Finally, Burton R. Pollin assesses motivation and method in Poe's absorption of inspirations: "Poe's Life Reflected through the Sources of *Pym*" (pp. 95–103).

Moving to broader critical studies in the collection, we find Poe's awareness of death lore and ritual intriguingly elaborated by Grace Farrell in "Mourning in Poe's *Pym*" (pp. 107–16). More sensational aspects of death as figuratively and symbolically related to concepts of writing are illuminated in J. Gerald Kennedy's "*Pym* Pourri: Decomposing the Textual Body" (pp. 167–74). David H. Hirsch " 'Postmodern' or Post-Auschwitz: The Case of Poe" (pp. 141–52) also centers on Poe's death-intentness, most particularly in terms of death of the conscience in the 20th century. Hirsch's argument, which includes existentialism, Adorno, Bloom, and de Man, should stimulate new readings of many Poe texts.

The subject of *Pym* and race continues to enliven scholars, as John Carlos Rowe's essay, "Poe, Antebellum Slavery, and Modern Criticism" (pp. 117–40), in the Kopley volume demonstrates. Poe's pro-slavery stance, as it underlies thematics in *Pym,* is revaluated through a Derridean-Lacanian lens. Rowe concludes that the antebellum and the postmodern Poe are much more intricately intertwined than others have admitted. Rowe's observations regarding G. R. Thompson's selections and apparatus for the Library of America volume of Poe's criticism should probably be modified in light of disparities between Thompson's original preparation of all of Poe's known critical writings and the final editorial mandate for a selective volume. Rowe might also revamp his views regarding the Paulding-Drayton review of *Pym* after reading Joseph V. Ridgely's essay on the matter, mentioned below; Poe did not always have such editorial authority in the *Southern Literary Messenger,* which published the review, as Rowe suggests. Alexander Hammond's

"Consumption, Exchange, and the Literary Marketplace: From the Folio Club Tales to *Pym*" (pp. 153–66) supplements work by Michael T. Gilmore and Nina Baym. The topic is Poe's scripting into *Pym,* when working on the Harper book version, tropes involving food and cannibalism (of an author) derivative from his earlier tales, most particularly as *Pym* reflects Poe's anxieties about his new literary marketplace. Hammond's ideas invite further exploration. Another patterning is discerned by John T. Irwin, who argues for Poe's subtle handling of a theme emanating from Sir Thomas Browne, to intensify Pym's unwittingness in interpreting the shrouded white figure—his own shadow reflection—in contrast to a reader's comprehension: "The Quincuncial Network in *Pym*" (pp. 175–87). A companion reading appears in G. R. Thompson's "The Arabesque Design of *Arthur Gordon Pym*" (pp. 188–213), a condensation of Thompson's keynote address at the 1988 conference, already published in greatly expanded form in *ESQ* 38 (1989) (see *ALS 1990,* p. 51).

Two very different pieces conclude Kopley's gathering. John Barth's " 'Still Farther South': Some Notes on Poe's *Pym*" (pp. 217–30) tenders a "writer's view" of how the novel betrays repeated inconsistencies, how it does not embody a coherent myth of the wanderer, how Pym is no genuine "dramatic" character, and, finally, how *Pym* is no "counterfeit" novel, "but an isomorph; not a hoax but a mimicry." Refreshingly, Barth, who admits that *Pym* was an influence on his own novel, *Sabbatical: A Romance* (1982), unabashedly concludes that Poe's book may not be its creator's finest accomplishment. David Ketterer, in a final one-essay section headed "A Bibliographer's View," gives us "Tracing Shadows: *Pym* Criticism, 1980–1990" (pp. 233–74), eight pages of citations introduced by lengthy commentary. As Ketterer points out, deconstructive readings faced off by visionary readings constitute the mainstay in Poe criticism during the period covered, and much repetition is evident.

Relevant to John Carlos Rowe's essay in the Kopley collection is the argument in Dana Nelson's chapter on Poe in *The World in Black and White,* "Ethnocentrism Decentered: Colonial Motives in *The Narrative of Arthur Gordon Pym*" (pp. 90–108). Nelson again raises the question of Poe's authorship of the Paulding-Drayton review, a discussion that must yield, as other like-spirited arguments must, to Joseph V. Ridgely's evaluation, "The Authorship of the 'Paulding-Drayton Review' " (*PSA Newsletter* (20, ii:1–3, 6), which convincingly establishes that Poe did not write the piece. Nelson's central idea, that in *Pym* racist and counterracist texts commingle, is interesting, but one comes away not sure whether he has clarified matters. Yet another reading fixing on some of these same interpretive issues is that of Thomas Gustafson in *Representative Words* (Cambridge), pp. 329–30, 345–47. Gustafson asserts that *Pym* and "The Gold-Bug" represent an antebellum literature that expresses ambiguities in language and the "obtuseness" of most readers about decoding signs. Emerson and Poe share a suspicion of the mob and related decay of language (as is evident, in Poe's case, in "Some Words with a Mummy" and "The Gold-Bug"), so they seek "more transcendent language" that would give "purer meaning to the language of the tribe."

iv Poems

Poe's bond with song composition is the topic in Burton R. Pollin's "Poe as a Writer of Songs" (*ARLR* 6:58–66), which concludes that Poe's emphasis on "repetition in prosody" and a possible comic intent are perceptible in such ventures. Pollin lists the titles of what he categorizes as Poe's song poems and tabulates the numbers of musical compositions based on Poe's creations. Oddly, in surveying scholarship on Poe and song, what Pollin calls Sara E. Selby's "untitled" study should be "The Music of Mr. Poe"; it was properly identified in *ALS 1985*, p. 51.

v Tales

Like Barth on *Pym*, Yaohua Shi is unafraid to state that the much plowed-over "Ligeia" remains decidedly ambiguous, baffling those who champion its supernaturalism and those who would accept a natural explanation—a Todorovian approach. Shi's survey of divergent viewpoints is useful: "The Enigmatic Ligeia/'Ligeia'" (*SSF* 28 [1991]:485–96). This perennial favorite among Poe's tales also gets a new look in Grace McEntee's provocative "Remembering 'Ligeia'" (*SAF* 20:75–83). The narrator, we learn, "becomes his own reader-response critic." He turns to Gothicism and creates "an account of how [he] became the artist who could tell this tale," a twofold story of Ligeia and her strong will and of the narrator's struggle for artistic maturity. Ligeia, his muse, instructs him in Gothicism by forcing him to endure horrific experiences. Diane Long Hoveler's "The Hidden God and the Abjected Woman in 'The Fall of the House of Usher'" (*SSF* 29:385–95), pivoting on Derrida, Lacan, and Kristeva, provides a panorama of mythic underpinnings connecting the gods Mogon and Apollo, plus Christ and Roderick (and their female doubles) in a "continual metatextual dialogue"—although, Hoveler concludes, readers who become caught up in attempted excavations of the deities' and characters' significance may be merely exercising their own imaginations.

Tracy Ware's sensible overview of divergent opinions makes "'A Descent into the Maelstrom': The Status of Scientific Rhetoric in a Perverse Romance" (*SSF* 22:77–84) refreshing reading. Ware finds religion and science at cross-purposes within the narrator, and thus she argues that his escape, and not the scientific dubiety of his story, is paramount. The tale is perverse because it permits one to disagree with both the visionary and the ironic readings of others. Ware's argument should be read in conjunction with William J. Scheick's essay, cited below.

Several essays deal with Poe's crime tales. Harold Schweizer's "Nothing and Narrative 'Twilighting' in 'The Purloined Letter'" (*L&P* 37, iv [1991]:63–69) posits that the Minister D—— ultimately assumes the Queen's role, in which his body will be exposed and the letter returned to its rightful owner. Slâvis Zizek's earlier "The Detective and the Analyst" (*L&P* 36, iv [1990]:27–46), by way of moving from Doyle's *The Hound of the Baskervilles* as Gothic novel to hard-boiled detective fiction, notes how, receiving payment for his services, Dupin "forestalls the 'curse'— the place in the symbolic network—resting upon those who come into possession of the letter." John T. Irwin brings us another of his splendid critiques in "Reading Poe's Mind: Politics, Mathematics, and the Association of Ideas in 'The Murders in the Rue Morgue'" (*AmLH* 4:187– 206); he locates a new prototype for Poe's Dupin in Baron Charles Dupin, mathematician brother to André Dupin, who is usually credited with being in the sleuth's background. Ingeniously arguing points connected with other aspects of the Dupin tales, Irwin constructs a combination of 19th-century French politics and mathematics in Poe's education as foundations for the ratiocinative fiction.

vi Sources, Influences, Affinities

William J. Scheick's "An Intrinsic Luminosity: Poe's Use of Platonic and Newtonian Optics" (*SLJ* 24, ii:90–105), a top-flight source study, sights keenly on wellsprings of Poe's scientific knowledge and the uses of it in poems and prose, especially *Eureka* and "Marginalia." Scheick is especially revealing when he addresses "a critically neglected feature of [Poe's] work: how his notions of human perception relate to his ideas about optics." His information on Sir David Brewster supplements work by Burton R. Pollin and Roberta Sharp. Scheick's conception might be brought to bear on the late Maureen C. Mabbott's idea that an exploration of the sidelong glances in Poe's writings might yield fruitful results.

A superb gloss on *Pym* sources in sea writings (see citations above) is William E. Lenz's "Narratives of Exploration, Sea Fiction, Mariner's Chronicles, and the Rise of American Nationalism: 'To Cast Anchor on That Point Where All Meridians Terminate'" (*AmerS* 32, ii [1991]:41–61). Conversely, Poe's treatment of the city receives brief, but telling, attention at several points in Sidney H. Bremer's *Urban Intersections* (Illinois). Poe did not perceive cities as altogether negative locales. Poe as poet and short-story writer in the marketplace figures in Ezra Greenspan's "Evert Duyckinck and the History of Wiley and Putnam's Library of American Books, 1845–1847" (*AL* 64:677–93). The selections of his works published there brought the "best hearing" Poe had in his lifetime.

A zealous argument for an important source of "Usher" in John Hardman's *Blackwood's* tale, "The Robber's Tower," a translation from H. Claurens's German "The Robber's Castle," informs Thomas S. Hansen's "Poe's 'German' Source for 'The Fall of the House of Usher': The Arno Schmidt Connection" (*SHR* 26:101–12), a follow-up to Thomas Ringmayr's 1988 *SHR* essay (see *ALS 1990*, pp. 53–54). Hansen apparently inclines toward the view that will have Poe's tale altogether serious, which may minimize his findings (he might profit from the spirit in Yaohua Shi's and Tracy Ware's kinds of latitudinarian interpretations, cited above). If one agrees that Hardman's story is a source for "Usher," or even *the* major source, of which I remain unconvinced, such belief does not preclude finding comedy in Poe's story. What Hansen seems to overlook is that Hardman's piece, like Poe's, might strike some readers as typical of manifold Gothic conventions and therefore that each story or both stories may have no single major source. Hansen would be more convincing were he to present his findings as a straightforward source study instead of showing condescension to critical ideas offered by others. His observations about Poe's knowledge of the German language, however, will be far more readily accepted. A reprint of Hardman's story appears in the same issue of *SHR* (pp. 113–32).

Turning to influences, we find Poe and 1890s British decadence scrutinized—in addition to what Jeffrey Meyers, cited above, supplies in the way of information and speculation—by Susan J. Navarette in "The Soul of the Plot: The Aesthetics of Fin de Siècle Literature of Horror" (*Styles of Creation,* pp. 88–113). Navarette highlights Poesqueness in the fiction of Oscar Wilde (*The Portrait of Dorian Gray*), Arthur Machen, and M. P. Shiel, who created what H. P. Lovecraft later termed "the actual anatomy of the terrible or the physiology of fear." Shiel's story "Xélucha," Navarette thinks, is a decadent reworking of "Ligeia."

Several other items have 1890s contexts. No overriding influence study, Carol de Dobay Rifelj's *Reading the Other: Novels and the Problem of Other Minds* (Michigan) nonetheless contains interesting asides about Stanley Cavell's exploration of Poe via Wittgenstein, the Poe-Doyle similarities in technique, and the shared themes of love for a dead woman or a statue in "Ligeia" and Villiers de l'Isle Adam's *Tomorrow's Eve* (1886). I wonder if the dismemberment episode in *Tomorrow's Eve* owes something as well to "The Tell-Tale Heart." Robert F. Fleissner's "The Cask in the Catacomb: Poe and Conan Doyle Again" (*A.C.D.* 3:116–22) plausibly treats "Cask" as background for "The New Catacomb," a non-Holmesian horror story. More about Poe-Conan Doyle, most of it concerned with detective fiction and the Holmes stories, appears in *Sir Arthur Conan Doyle: Interviews and Recollections,* ed. Harold Orel (St. Martin's, 1991).

Moving into the 20th century, we may accept the methodological affinities between Poe's tales—the Dupin pieces, "Masque," "Usher," and "Cask," with possible distillations through Nabokov's *Lolita*—and Raymond Chandler's story "Pearls Are a Nuisance," discerned by J. O. Tate in "Raymond Chandler's Pearl" (*Clues* 13:177–96). Poe, Lovecraft, and Stephen King (the first two influential on the third) write horror fiction in which, pervasively, ideological clashes take center stage; so argues Karen A. Hohne in "The Voice of Cthulhu: Language Interaction in Contemporary Horror Fiction" (*Styles of Creation,* pp. 79–87). In Poe "unofficiality" centers in the content that obsesses his narrators and their actions—"madmen and murderers"; Lovecraft moves unofficiality more directly into technique; King, in whose work unofficiality is even more accessible than in writings by the previous two, portrays officiality as pretending "to know everything." Anthony Magistrale's *Stephen King: The Second Decade* (Twayne) contains scattered information on the Poe-King relationship. King's Bachman books, to Magistrale, are more Kafkaesque than Poesque. He draws on some, but not all, recent scholarship on Poe's impact on King. Poe, advocate of the short poem, is a forerunner of the concretist movement in poetry during the 1950s and 1960s, says

Augusto de Campos, an exponent of concretism, in "From Dante to the Post-Concrete: An Interview with Augusto de Campos" (*HLB* n.s. 3, ii:19–35).

vii Textual, Bibliographic Studies

The four-volume *Edgar Allan Poe: Critical Assessments,* ed. Graham Clarke (Routledge, 1991), should not be neglected despite any of its inaccuracies or high price ($499). In particular, it reprints many contemporaneous notices that would otherwise be inconvenient to consult. Kent P. Ljungquist's "Poe's 'Autography': A New Exchange of Reviews" (*American Periodicals* 2:51–63) enlarges our information on the press reception of a work often overlooked, even by specialists, highlighting E. P. Whipple's hostile viewpoints. More work like Ljungquist's article would contribute significantly to Poe studies. Burton R. Pollin covers reception of another kind in "A Posthumous Assessment: The 1849–1850 Periodical Press Response to Edgar Allan Poe" (*American Periodicals* 2:6–50). He treats obituary notices of Poe, giving special attention to printings of "Annabel Lee" and "The Bells," along with other information regarding Poe the poet, reminiscences, and further-ranging cultural attitudes.

University of Mississippi

4 Melville

John Wenke

Major studies appeared this year on Melville's family and his applications of rhetoric, law, and English painter J. M. W. Turner. Once again, *Moby-Dick* attracted the broadest range of efforts on issues substantial, idiosyncratic, and trite.

i Biographical Contexts

In *Herman Melville's Malcolm Letter: Man's Final Lore* (Fordham), Hennig Cohen and Donald Yannella transcribe and annotate Melville's 20 February 1849 letter to brother Allan. They examine Melville's sense of paternity as well as his life within the family sphere. The playful, hyperbolic, and heavily allusive letter clarifies personal and genealogical dimensions of masculinity—Melville's status as son, brother, and, suddenly, father. In marshaling extensive archival evidence, the book elucidates the tangled web of immediate and extended family relations, especially those imperatives associated with "family authority and filial duty." Following a trenchant account of child-rearing practices in the Gansevoort-Melville and Shaw households, Cohen and Yannella speculate on how family duty may have contributed to Malcomb's suicide. Insistently, they link documentary evidence with Melville's literary works. Notes and appendices complement the critical narrative. Twelve appendices treat such specific persons and related topics as "Kate Gansevoort and the Melvilles." *Melville's Malcomb Letter* offers a prescient minibiography of tense family lives.

Lynn Horth's "Richard Bentley's Place in Melville's Literary Career" (*SAR:* 229–45) focuses on the public life, arguing convincingly that much of Melville's career turned on the publisher's timely "presence as an external pressure on Melville's development." Horth reprints two recent

discoveries—Martha Jones's reports on *Mardi*. Within a week, despite
Jones's decidedly negative evaluation, Bentley accepted *Mardi*. In a
second report, she is severe regarding the work's "irreligious" aspect.
Horth notes, "Bentley was well aware of the risk he was taking . . . and
one about which his awareness and even fears must have been 'frankly'
stated in his letter to Melville." Despite unrealized hopes for profit,
Bentley retained an abiding regard for Melville's genius.

ii General

In " 'The Flower of Fame': A Centennial Tribute to Herman Melville
(1819–1891)" (*ESQ* 38:89–117), Merton M. Sealts, Jr., illuminates Melville's "reputation," his wavering status before contemporary readers and
reviewers, as well as his posthumous popularization and canonization.
Eventually, Melville softened his contempt for publicity, allowing his
portrait to be published: "But in the language of his late verse . . . true
fame cannot be induced through any mere artifice; it must grow organ-
ically." Sealts wryly considers various 20th-century attempts to improve
Melville via abridgement. He argues that 40 years ago neither Melville,
Thoreau, Dickinson, Whitman, nor Faulkner were canonical; in fact,
they were perceived as threats to established hierarchies. Melville will
remain "not as a merely parochial figure in the changing canon of a single
national literature but as an author of world importance." Similarly,
Marc Dolan in "The 'Wholeness' of the Whale: Melville, Matthiessen,
and the Semiotics of Critical Revisionism" (*ArQ* 48, iii:27–58) investigates Melville's centrality to American studies and its relation to "the
process of canon formation and the semiotics of critical rediscovery."
Dolan applauds Melville's canonical status as a "structural necessity" that
"reflects a larger movement of critical historiography." Drawing from
Roland Barthes, Dolan views canonicity as emerging from texts that
engage mythic concepts and perform useful "sign-functions." He compares the rediscovery of Zora Neale Hurston to the dynamics of the
Melville revival: both writers were transfigured, so to speak, according to
perceptions of genre and companion writers. In 1919 Melville was a
minor New York writer of sea tales in the tradition of Dana. Once *Moby-
Dick* was ordained a masterwork with Shakespearean resonations, however, Melville rose from footnote to headline. Then followed the work of
F. O. Matthiessen, a particularly crucial figure who saw Melville's work in
terms of "metaphysical symbolism." Matthiessen was able to guarantee

Melville literary immortality because his work was both "assimilable and unique." Dolan rehabilitates Matthiessen and his sense of "wholeness," seeking to reverse "fifty years of meta-critical revisionism [that] obliterated the truly radical nature of Matthiessen's interpretation."

Bryan C. Short's *Cast by Means of Figures: Herman Melville's Rhetorical Development* (Mass.) weds sophisticated rhetorical theory and deft literary exegesis. Short delineates Melville's conscious employment of rhetorical tropes. In seeking to bridge the gap between a biographical author and his lingual presence in literary works, Short contends that the "problematic nature of Melville's narrators, narrative perspectives, and authorial identity reflects an art which conceives and responds to itself in rhetorical rather than philosophical or representational terms." "Tropological" departures inevitably manifest technical responses to artistic crises. A foundation chapter proposes 18th-century rhetorician Hugh Blair and his "association of figurative language with the passions and the imagination" as a seminal aesthetic influence. In *Typee* Melville accommodates and transforms elements of Blair's neoclassical rhetoric: Tommo moves from metaphor to metonymy, from "logical comparisons" to "associations justified by contiguity within a uniform, static field." The predominant trope of *Omoo* is synecdoche, which is extended in *Mardi*: "What the synecdochic and hyperbolic rhetoric of *Mardi* represses is Melville's investment in the ironic and metaleptic structures of *Typee*, the tragic impossibility of his voice finally achieving freedom from the past." Before *Moby-Dick*, Melville employed such "Romantic tropes" as "irony, metaphor, synecdoche, metalepsis, [and] hyperbole/litotes." The achievement of *Moby-Dick* resides in its realization of a "symbolic rhetoric." Ishmael is freed "from the project of troping and redeeming [his] origins," Melville's central concern in earlier works. Then in *Pierre*, with its "parodic critique of the rhetoric of selfhood," Melville appropriates such "post-Romantic" tropes as "tautology, repetition, nominalization, [and] anasemia." These forms characterize the later fiction. Throughout his impressive study, Short links a dominant trope with an attending thematic complex—metalepsis and identity, metaphor and death. There are times, however, when Short's own terms seem brusquely synecdochic. In *White-Jacket*, "Salvation by the sea, central theme of *Moby-Dick*, begins a corresponding alternation in and return to figures of metaleptic enablement and a swerve away from the synecdochic and metaphoric orders which have characterized the sea since *Typee*." His rhetoric, at times, thickens: "The catachrestic concatenation of metonymy and synecdoche gives a false appearance of metaleptic resolution, of a circularity which enables rather than paralyzes." Still, Short's demanding book successfully recasts Melville's aesthetic and breaks new ground. His argument will repay close reading and occasion dispute, especially regarding his fundamental insistence on the "intentionality of rhetorical figures."

Earl Rovit's "Melville and the Discovery of America" (*SR* 100:583–98) considers the political implications of rhetorical tropes. The paradigm of Columbus suffuses Melville's work as dialectical myth and antimyth, "a ready-to-hand fictional formula" of paradoxical dimensions—the "hidden is in plainest sight"—and thus highlights the millennial seeker's culturally based and biased blindness. Rovit finds that "the metonymic process of Discovery and the metaphoric revelation of Apocalypse" stand in polarized tension, with each term complicated both by the ensuing "process of *un*discovery, of a masking" and the "metaphor of Creation," the emergence of "something radically new." In *Law in Art: Melville's Major Fiction and Nineteenth-Century American Law* (Peter Lang), Susan Weiner more narrowly examines Melville's preoccupation with legal issues as they derive from personal and cultural contexts and infiltrate (and often dominate) his work. After discussing the Preface to *Typee* as a possible reply to future father-in-law Judge Lemuel Shaw, Weiner argues that Melville uses "aspects of legal reasoning in order to subvert . . . objective methodology, the reliability of facts, and the ideal of the impartiality of judicial decision-making." Thus, literature and law become alternative "systems of truth-seeking." *Typee* depicts both the erosion of common sense and natural law traditions and their replacement by a highly technical "instrumental concept of legalism." In such works as *White-Jacket,* "Benito Cereno," and *Billy Budd,* ship life functions as a repressive legal microcosm wherein Melville examines the relations of labor and race to the hierarchies of power. Consistently, Melville emphasizes "the authority of the imagination over the authority of the law." Judge Shaw is a presiding contrapuntal presence, a touchstone for situating Melville's stand on crucial legal issues. At times, Melville's works are made to seem direct replies to Shaw's legal opinions. Consequently, Weiner occasionally overdetermines legal cause and aesthetic effect: "Melville's disillusionment with the law may have contributed to his method of disrupting the plot, thereby hindering its goal-oriented thrust toward resolution of conflict." Her argument that "Bartleby" depicts the "interconnection of representation, reproduction, and law" is strenuous but unconvincing, and her own similes occasionally serve as evidence—the lawyer's "portrait" of Bartleby "is more like a photographic image than a verbal one." Her strongest chapters treat "Benito Cereno" and *Billy Budd*. Delano's "legal reasoning operates as a mode of perception" that is "political and thus morally deficient in nature." *Billy Budd*'s "legal plot" generates "the complexities and limitations of interpretation and judgment."

Lawrence Buell situates Melville within a postcolonial framework. In "Melville and the Question of American Decolonization" (*AL* 64:215–37), he wonders what happens when "an American autodidact . . . enters the arena of cosmopolitan culture." Buell enlarges on the cultural possibilities attending free speech and action when promulgated within the repressive domain of formal codes. Given this fall into history, "insinuation" replaces "direct statement." While *Billy Budd* epitomizes America's "postcolonial anxiety," Melville's earlier works dramatize multiple configurations whereby innocence is assailed and qualified by the imposition of "imperial forms." Buell illuminates the antebellum writer's conflicted sense of a "bicontinental audience." *Typee, Redburn,* "Benito Cereno," and *Clarel* dramatize the entanglement—rather than the dissociation—of European-American styles and cultural affiliations. By the time he wrote *Clarel,* Melville had achieved a complex cosmopolitanism, a "magisterial casualness about an American subject." Like Buell, André Kaenel in *"Words Are Things": Herman Melville and the Invention of Authorship in Nineteenth-Century America* (Peter Lang) explores the intricacies of an emerging national literature, but he contends with the writer's struggle to *be* an author within a marketplace, "the duality of authorship as figurative construction and as material practice." Kaenel builds on Pierre Bourdieu's model of "the literary field," a "mediatory space" between a text's composition and its marketing, between "discourse and institution." The first three chapters examine issues affecting market, culture, and authorial identity; the remaining chapters pair specific texts, for example, *Typee* and *Pierre, White-Jacket* and *Billy Budd*. Kaenel draws Melville insistently seeking to modify his own authorial story, especially in his "yearning for anonymous authorship."

In *L'Imaginaire-Melville* Viola Sachs offers a collection of essays by French critics devoted to "mythic texts . . . that overtly or not, center around the myth of America as a New World." Sachs's authors practice something called "mythocritical minutious analysis," the close examination of specific words as revealing "webs woven by association, analogies, correspondences." Buried beneath these "realistic details" supposedly lies a "holistic sacred world." *MSEx* (89) devotes the entire issue to "over 90 newly discovered reviews, notices, and mentions of Melville and his works from dozens of nineteenth-century periodicals." New findings are reported by Gary Scharnhorst, Richard E. Winslow III, Lynn Horth, Burton R. Pollin, and Kent P. Ljungquist. In "More Evidence of H. M. Tomlinson's Role in the Melville Revival" (*SAF* 20:111–13), Mary A. Taylor reprints and discusses Christopher Morley's 1921 published version of a private letter attesting to Tomlinson's "tireless propagandizing for Melville at home and abroad." Joyce Sparer Adler in *Dramatization of Three Melville Novels* (Mellen) reveals in her adaptations of *Moby-Dick,* "Benito Cereno," and *Billy Budd* "that dramatic interpretation is a form of literary criticism." Her introduction situates earlier adaptations in relation to her fine work.

iii Source, Influence, Affinity

Robert K. Wallace's *Melville and Turner: Spheres of Love and Fright* (Georgia) proposes J. M. W. Turner as an indirect but formative influence on the early works and as *the* major influence on *Moby-Dick.* In this lavishly produced and beautifully illustrated tome, Wallace describes how "the imaginative unfolding that culminated in the creation of *Moby-Dick* drew upon a painterly self-education that culminated in the appropriation of Turner's powerful aesthetic of the indistinct." Part One, "Turner Before Melville, 1775–1845," explores Turner's life and reputation. To exemplify the evolution of the artist, Wallace examines 21 engravings of works by Turner that Melville acquired later in life. Part Two, "Melville Before *Moby-Dick,* 1845–1849," contends that the art criticism of William Hazlitt and John Ruskin put Turner before Melville's eyes and that he consciously adapts Turner's aesthetic. Melville's style changes from the "linear, picturesque . . . world of *Typee* (1846) and *Omoo* (1847) to a visual world reaching toward the vortex, the sublime, and the visionary. This stylistic transition compressed into three years the kind of transition Turner had made in three decades." In such an analogical case, terms are bound to get slippery: "The subtlety with which these scenes are rendered in light and shade corresponds in a general stylistic sense to the optical precision that distinguishes *Mardi* from Melville's earlier books." Part Three, "Composing *The Whale,* 1850–1851," centers the book. Wallace's *Moby-Dick* evolves directly from "Melville's imaginative appropriation of Turner" and becomes reflected in the continuing influence of art criticism by Hazlitt, Ruskin, and Charles Lock Eastlake. The argument involves contortions. By marshaling a host of circumstantial collateral citations, Wallace wrenches virtual impossibilities into ostensible plausibility. With a tapestry of might-have-beens, for example, he answers the good question: "How did Melville so powerfully adapt to his own use another writer's review of a painting he had probably never seen with his own eyes?" Wallace convincingly argues for Turner's influence on the Spouter Inn painting, but some readers will doubt that this is the culminating moment of Melville's creative life. Part Four, "*Moby-Dick* and Turner's Vision," offers a lucid parallel study of "liquid spheres," "solar spheres," and "psychic spheres."

There is much to admire in Wallace's book, most notably his sensitivity to the pictorial dimensions of Melville's art. While the case for parallel visions seems incontrovertible, the case for Turner's determinant influence seems a deduction that precedes and shapes much of the evidence: "Without England's greatest modern painter in his mind's eye, Young America's leading novelist could hardly have conceived, much less so eloquently expressed, the dazzling vision of the truth of nature that he achieved while composing his *Whale*."

John M. J. Gretchko's *Melvillean Loomings: Essays on* Moby-Dick (Falk and Bright) is a lively collection of notes on sources, allusions, hidden references, etymologies, and slang. Gretchko links "Call me Ishmael" to Welsh hero Taliesin. He uncovers buried excremental references, puns, and jokes. His association of sailor dog lore with a "stellar motif" is eccentric and farfetched: he sees Jack Bunger and Captain De Deer as "companion stars . . . each a dog, a phallus, and a first-magnitude star." But Gretchko does enlarge our understanding of Melville's debt to Hindu sources and the science of Egyptology. In "The Moose and the Whale: Thoreau's 'Chesuncook' as a Terrestrial *Moby-Dick*" (*ATQ* 6:77–94), Gregory M. Pfitzer associates the mythic dimensions of whaling with Thoreau's version of the hunter myth, leveling differences and finding unity through self-generated metaphors: Ishmael and Thoreau "are time travellers of sorts who begin their journeys as spiritual innocents in a pre-Adamic or pre-discovery condition." Later, he compares and contrasts both authors' adaptations of mythic materials. In "Melville's *Moby-Dick*" (*Expl* 50:148–50) Naoki Onishi plausibly argues that Cotton Mather's *Magnalia Christi Americana* inspires the "bird imagery" evoked during the catastrophe of the novel.

In " 'Turkey on His Back': 'Bartleby' and New York Words" (*MSEx*

90:16–19), Hans Bergmann deftly argues that Melville adapts "a complex formal convention whose settings often include New York offices and clerks, whose action often includes an encounter between the 'ordinary' lawyer or merchant and an extra/ordinary 'other' . . . from the streets." The New York story seeks to explain the city through the depiction of idiosyncratic language, places, and individuals; by refusing to supply explanatory closure, Melville departs from convention. The absence of direct documentary evidence does not impede Stan Goldman from making a well-argued case in "A Source for *Clarel* and 'Fruit of Travel Long Ago': Bellows' *The Old World in Its New Face*" (*MSEx* 90:14–16). Goldman juxtaposes related passages and demonstrates that Melville derived *Clarel*'s Syrian monk and various representations of the Parthenon from Henry Whitney Bellows, the Melvilles' pastor from 1863 to 1882. Melville's appropriation of specific reading material serves as a "genetic moment," an inspiration for successive recastings. Martin Bidney in "Thinking about Walt and Melville in a Sherwood Anderson Tale: An Independent Woman's Transcendental Quest" (*SSF* 29:517–29) discusses how Anderson's "Out of Nowhere and into Nothing" depicts Rosalind Wescott's emotional struggle between the gentle but married Walter Stoner and the bold, reclusive bachelor, Melville Sayer.

iv Early Works

The year's least convincing case comes from John Evelev's " 'Made in the Marquesas': *Typee,* Tattooing and Melville's Critique of the Literary Marketplace" (*ArQ* 48, iv:19–45). Evelev imbues the tyro author with an uneasy awareness of how his audience objectifies "any act of representation." Thus, *Typee* stands as "a critique of the practices and requirements of the literary profession in the United States in the 1840s." Tommo's shifting attitude toward tattooing constitutes "a textualization of Melville's critical consciousness." This "representation of representation" connotes Melville's "conflicted reaction toward writing written across the narrative." Tommo's disinclination for becoming scarred for life is at one with "Melville's conflicted attitude toward writing itself." A shaky analogy makes a wobbly premise: "Tattooing is a form of writing which seems a threat of violence, a violence to identity, and thus Tommo's rejection seems a rejection of writing as a recuperation or re-assertion of identity." Even if the biographical and genetic record refutes "the critiques which seem implicit in [Tommo's] textualized rejection," Evelev asserts his premise by way of repression: "Tommo's rejection of Typee culture . . . is the sublimated and displaced textualization of Melville's own concern for being inscribed within the marketplace's demand for objectified exchange." Assertion grounds discussion, and "repression" explains what more assertion and fallacious analogy cannot. Nor is *Typee* well-served by David Bergman in "Cannibals and Queers: Man-Eating" (*Gaiety Transfigured,* pp. 139–62), an anxious meditation on Melville's ambivalence toward homosexual inter/discourse, male identity, and power. Bergman counts *Typee* among a number of gay narratives in which the protagonist seeks out cannibals. Tommo *desires* to meet the cannibals and thus secretly wishes to be eaten. His obsession with allaying hunger—with eating—actually reflects a repressed desire to be eaten: "the intensity of the desire may be measured by the intensity of the need to deny it." What is not, must be. Bergman makes a necessary tactical exclusion, insisting that Tommo's fear is irrational: his Tommo never encounters "physical" evidence of cannibalism; thus his delusional "cannibalistic phobia" covers his "anxiety about the desire for egalitarian sexual relations with Mehevi." Most readers will find indisputable evidence of cannibalism at the end of chapter 32.

Beverly Hume Thorne in "Taji's Yillah: Transcending the Fates in Melville's *Mardi*" (*ELWIU* 19:61–72) argues that "the narrator is not so much searching for the transcendentalist's 'All' as he is for a world or an identity beyond the confining male hierarchies of Mardi." Failed kings like Peepi and Donjalolo provide impetus for Taji's repudiation of diachronic time and the American patriarchal order. He seeks a " 'universe-old truth' that is intimately related to his eternal self." In " 'To Tell Over Again the Story Just Told': The Composition of Melville's *Redburn:* (*ESQ* 37:311–20), Stephen Mathewson identifies scenic replication as a compositional principle and tends to level psychological hills and valleys. Mathewson might have distinguished between instances of obvious padding and creative reinvention. It is not sufficient to see Harry Bolton as a mere redaction of Redburn, especially in light of Bolton's failure to enter the world of work.

Sam Whitsitt in "The Fall Before the Fall: The Game of Identity, Language, and Voice in Melville's *White-Jacket*" (*ArQ* 48, ii:57–79) concocts the following problem: "To examine Melville's sense of the identity which he felt ought to have held between language and self is to examine Melville's struggle with his flesh—his materiality—and his desire to be at one with, identical to, his skin." After refuting claims that

Melville plagiarized White Jacket's fall from the mast, he goes on to deconstruct the relationship between the narrator's identity and the "identity of the novel itself," especially the alleged parallel between "the textual body of the character White Jacket, who will be read by other characters in the novel, and the body of the text, *White-Jacket,* being read by the reader holding it in hand." This exercise in the reading of reading being read often defies readability. This year we find not only that tattooing is like writing (see Evelev above), but so is flogging: "Part of what makes flogging violent is that it, like writing, resorts to prosthetics: to artificial devices, tools. The very gesture announces that in the flogger/writer there is a certain lack." With such strokes, Whitsitt flogs on, attacking alleged dislocations between modes of rhetoric and modes of being. In "Revolution and Identity in Melville's *White-Jacket* and *Israel Potter*" (*L'Imaginaire-Melville,* pp. 53–64), Dominique Marcais explores Melville's "revolutionary spirit" as manifest "in pun, in words inscribed within others, in strange names and curious episodes, in errors and mistakes."

v Moby-Dick

In *Critical Essays on Herman Melville's* Moby-Dick (Hall), editors Brian Higgins and Hershel Parker provide a rich compendium of materials from 1851 to the present. Their introduction surveys the biographical record and describes how Melville's earlier books, travels, and literary researches prepare for the composition of the novel. Of special note is their history of its critical reception—its lukewarm, perplexed reviews, the gradual accumulation of tributes, and the evolution of modern commentary. Higgins and Parker distinguish between critical and scholarly approaches, arguments that derive from theory or assumption and arguments generated from documentary evidence. They reprint significant British and American reviews from 1851, extracts from contemporary articles and essays on the status of Melville's career in the mid-1850s, "commentary from 1874 to 1919 . . . and several of the most rhapsodic pieces of the Melville Revival." The editors classify contributions from modern scholarship according to "Literary Influences and Affinities," "The Whale, Ahab, and Ishmael," "Genesis," and "New Essays" by John Wenke, David S. Reynolds, and Hershel Parker, which focus, respectively, on intellectual, cultural, and domestic contexts. In "*Moby-Dick* and the Impress of Melville's Learning" (pp. 507–22), I examine how a host of sources—in Bayle, De Quincey, Mary Shelley, Carlyle, and Emerson—figure in the genesis of *Moby-Dick,* especially regarding Melville's fusion of vestigial and reformulated materials. I view "The Mat-Maker" chapter as "an exemplary paradigm for speculating on ways in which the vestigial narrative provided direction and clues for his reconstruction." In " 'Its wood could only be American!': *Moby-Dick* and Antebellum Popular Culture" (pp. 523–47), Reynolds disputes the view of Melville as an alienated Titan and elucidates his intense interest in "the ephemeral literature of his time and culture. . . . it was precisely Melville's *openness* to images from various contemporary cultural arenas . . . that accounts for the special complexity of *Moby-Dick.*" As the period's "most broadly absorptive fiction," the narrative transforms elements from "Romantic Adventure, reform literature, radical-democrat fiction, and subversive humor." In "*Moby-Dick* and Domesticity" (pp. 545–62) Parker examines "the rival—and incompatible—claims of creativity and marriage" and "explores the possibility that Melville embodied some of his domestic comforts, compromises, and tensions in *Moby-Dick.*" Parker elucidates Melville's conflicting motives for his 1849 trip to Europe. His periods of work, vacation, and moving greatly affected the compositional process. Melville wrote this most masculine of books in the company of many women.

Among the year's most accomplished essays is Geoffrey Sanborn's "The Name of the Devil: Melville's Other 'Extracts' for *Moby-Dick*" (*NCF* 47:212–35). After assuming that Melville's notes on white magic and black magic in his seventh volume of Shakespeare expressed his own insights, Charles Olson pointed the way for subsequent genetic arguments. Sanborn proves that "Melville did not invent these notes. All but one of the sentences . . . were extracted from . . . an essay called 'Superstition and Knowledge' in the July 1823 issue of the *Quarterly Review.*" These extracts from Sir Francis Palgrave depict "continuities within inversions" and possibly inspired Melville's presentation of the "radical identity" of ostensibly contradictory "modes of being and behavior." This discovery redefines an aspect of the critical history of *Moby-Dick* and illuminates, while further complicating, its genesis. In "Melvilla" (*MSEx* 91:1–10) Douglas Darden offers an engrossing imaginative adventure, his demonstration "that a novel could more directly *in-form* architecture. . . . In this manner [Melvilla] was to be a corresponding, parallel work to *Moby-Dick* defined in architectural terms." Melvilla rises on Manhattan's Lower East Side, "isolated as an island within the island." Darden describes an "archive, a common room, and vaults for solitary reading," and relates them to "prime movers" of the novel's action. John J. Staud's lucid "*Moby-Dick* and Melville's Vexed Romanticism" (*ATQ* 6:279–93) argues that Ishmael does not polarize Nature and consciousness. Rather, both aspects of Romantic transcendental possibility are "equally seductive prescriptions for self-fulfillment that delude and threaten individual identity and, finally, the larger community."

Questions of gender and sexuality continue to excite argument and rhapsody. In "Ishmael's (m)Other: Gender, Jesus, and God in Melville's *Moby-Dick*" (*Journal of Religion* 72:325–50), Mark Lloyd Taylor closely examines "The Tail" chapter and fashions a paradigm linking theology and gender. God the Father reflects masculine power, while God the Son embodies "feminine negativity" or the "lack of power." Taylor explores enigmas associated with the absence and presence of divine power, especially as reflected in Ishmael's scant depictions of Jesus, the masculine-feminine polarity, familial bonds, "inversions of the self," and predestination. Within this mix, Taylor finds that the dialectical presence of Hebraic and Platonic materials leads Ishmael to subsume and then blur distinctions between Calvinism and Transcendentalism. Though Terry Roberts's "Ishmael as Phallic Narrator" (*SAF* 20:99–109) reads like a joke, it is perfectly serious. Roberts decides that Melville "used the phallus in *Moby-Dick* to represent Ishmael's penetrating sensibility." His "cycle of voices . . . suggests in turn phallic erection, intercourse, climax, and diffusion." Roberts sprinkles the essay with his own descriptive analogies—"impotent Ahab," "erect self-consciousness," "metaphysical intercourse," "quiescent, post-coital tone." Roberts even asserts that through "metaphysical intercourse . . . a narrative sensibility . . . can literally penetrate the boundaries of its world." In a similar vein, Kim Long in "Ahab's Narcissistic Quest: The Failure of the Masculine American Dream in *Moby-Dick*" (*CCTEP* 57:42–50) degrades Melville's masterwork into a trite sexual allegory about the horrors of phallic power. Long makes the absurd claim "that a feminine presence pervades the novel and gives it its most important theme: the battle of male against female in the ongoing search for the American Dream." Gone are Ahab's theological and philosophical self-justifications; he is simply out for rape. Melville's supreme embodiment of brute masculinity—the white whale himself—is not He but She: an "ambiguous symbol of femininity. . . . the whale could . . . be viewed as feminine because Ahab seeks to pierce it with his harpoon, to force his masculinity into the inner regions of Moby Dick."

In "'Defamiliarization' and the Ideology of Race" (*CLAJ* 35:325–38), Marsha C. Vick incisively draws on Russian formalist Viktor Shklovsky to demonstrate that Melville makes "the familiar look unfamiliar." To undermine the received ideology of white Eurocentric superiority, Melville "defamiliarizes" slavery through tropes of whiteness and blackness. He replaces self-serving cultural hierarchies with the subversive—but radically democratic—ethos of ontological equality. Hilda Urén Stubbings in *The Magic Glass: The Individual and Society as Seen in the Gams of Herman Melville's* Moby-Dick (Rubena) dusts off and publishes a revised master's thesis. She marches lockstep from gam to gam, discussing the "interrelationship of persons" as well as "wider themes." Her argument lacks critical clarity, and she propagates at least one gross distortion: a "naive" Melville "reasoned that because American democracy was the hope of the world the United States was justified in seizing the lands of the Indians . . . who would eventually benefit from their civilizing alliance with the usurpers."

Agnès Derail in "Melville's Leviathan: *Moby-Dick; or, The Whale* and the Body Politic" (*L'Imaginaire-Melville*, pp. 23–31) examines Melville's references to Hobbs's *Leviathan* and argues that "the novel consists in an anatomy of the new nation, an inquiry into the body politics of a dawning democracy." Derail identifies contradictions and failures of democracy aboard the *Pequod*. In "American Identity and the Counterfeit Whale" (*L'Imaginaire-Melville*, pp. 33–45), Viola Sachs complements Lawrence Buell's essay (see above). In *Moby-Dick* Melville questions the United States' "claim to be essentially different and new in relation to England and the Old World." The novel is "symbol and sign . . . of a counterfeit nation pretending to be something that it is not." Sachs explicates topographical features, errors in the first American edition, and other potential "clues" to Melville's subversion of the American ethos. Sina Vatanpour's "Of Money, Cash and Writing in *Moby-Dick; or, The Whale*" (*L'Imaginaire-Melville*, pp. 47–52) finds that money "structures a hidden text within the text," then elaborates on various configurations of the word "cash."

vi From *Pierre* to *The Confidence-Man*

In "Genre and Ideology: The French Sensational Romance and Melville's *Pierre*" (*JA Cult* 15, iii:1–8), Sheila Post-Lauria contends that "Melville consciously shaped his work in accordance" with a genre that "combined social analysis with sentiment, sensation, and erotic in-trigue." She illuminates Melville's attraction to popular low-brow forms, especially his tendency to transform convention for subversive (and high-brow) intentions. In making her case, Post-Lauria slights the narra-tor's intermittent satire of the very form he adapts. According to Bev-erly A. Hume in "Of Krakens and Other Monsters: Melville's *Pierre*" (*ATQ* 6:95–108), Melville's "highly self-conscious narrative strategy" employs a detached third-person narrator who critiques Pierre's "blind reliance upon feminine stereotypes and upon the failure of western literary culture . . . to create a viable intellectual atmosphere for young American authors." Hume explores Melville's conflicted attitudes toward both high canonical resources and popular forms, and she deftly links Melville's attack on "feminine monstrosities" not simply to his "Krakens" reference but to an intertextual array of coiled mythic monsters. Melville seeks to "transcend . . . the negative constraints of a culture and tradition which he . . . most oppressively felt." Hume's essay clearly stands among the strongest accounts of Melville's response to "a gender-biased literary tradition" that translates women into angels and monsters. Clark Davis in "Asceticism and the Fictive in *Pierre*" (*ESQ* 38:143–59) offers a discern-ing account of Melville's movement away from "the primal, mythopoeic ocean" and his compensatory creation of a self-consciously artificial landscape, a "world without flesh." Pierre's grandfather and father are bodiless conceptions that burden Pierre with an enervating "mixture of phallic anxiety and ambition." The discovery of his father's ostensible sin leads him to renounce his own body, and he plunges into asceticism.

Ronald Wesley Hoag's "The Corpse in the Office: Mortality, Muta-bility and Salvation in 'Bartleby, the Scrivener'" (*ESQ* 38:119–42) expli-cates Bartleby as a "functional memento mori" and the lawyer as "a man compelled to share his office with a figurative corpse." Hoag makes a strong case for seeing Bartleby and the lawyer as secret sharers of a pained and inscrutable humanity. Bartleby is "not particular," or unique, though he is "'deranged' . . . beyond the range of human consola-tion." In "Melville's Bartleby as an Archetypal Shadow" (*JEP* 13:318–21), Michael C. Brennan views the pallid man as a projection of the lawyer's repressed inner life. In this Jungian reading, the lawyer fails to grow and "conjoin his public *persona* with his compensating private *shadow*."

Alide Cagidemetrio's *Fictions of the Past* provides a clear and sophisti-cated assessment of an often confused subject. Verisimilitude depends not "upon the representation of events of history, but . . . upon referen-

tiality to history." *Israel Potter* is an experiment "in writing the past
'anew.'" Melville reads and then rewrites the past through "the sources
that define it." History, then, constitutes a politically charged rhetoric
and interpretation. Melville's departure from his source becomes "increasingly ordered by a symbolic logic that revolves around the paradigms of escape and revolutionary action, verses imprisonment and
delayed release." He qualifies the myth of American exceptionalism in
favor of a new universality.

In his lucid introduction to *Critical Essays on Herman Melville's "Benito
Cereno"* (Hall), Robert E. Burkholder examines knotty problems related
to the narrative's sources, contexts, politics, and interpretations, and he
surveys its evolving reception from sparse reviews through new essays by
Sterling Stuckey, Carolyn L. Karcher, and H. Bruce Franklin. Burkholder identifies the failure of Formalists to contain the energies of the
story within an articulated unity. He summarizes Historicist readings
that illuminate "particulars rather than universals": more recent criticism
explores the "intersection of its history and recent attitudes, events, and
movements," especially in relation to Melville's depictions of slavery and
rebellion and his strategies of disclosure and nondisclosure. Stuckey's
"'Follow Your Leader': The Theme of Cannibalism in Melville's 'Benito
Cereno'" (pp. 182–95) focuses on Aranda's skeleton and disputes the
received notion that the African slaves cannibalized their deposed master. Stuckey suggests that, according to an Ashantee custom of war,
Aranda's body was shaved "down to its skeleton" and symbolically reflects
"a white historical act." Stuckey offers as source T. Edward Bowdich's
Mission from Cape Coast Castle to Ashantee, though he does not indicate
how or when Melville might have had access to it. In "The Riddle of the
Sphinx: Melville's 'Benito Cereno' and the *Amistad* Case" (pp. 196–229),
Karcher reads the tale not from the "perspective . . . of the masters, but of
the slaves" and contends that Melville plants multiple "clues" that displace Delano's racist stereotypes in favor of "an alternative reality, rooted
in a very different understanding of African culture." Less convincing is
her fully researched and provocative argument that the *Amistad* slave
uprising in 1839 constitutes Melville's "primary inspiration," though not
his primary source, for the 1855 tale. Attenuated suppositions undermine
the plausibility of the case "simmering in his consciousness for so many
years." She conflates the *Amistad* case with Melville's first voyage to
England, his fictionalization of it ten years later, and the composition of
"Benito Cereno" six years after that. H. Bruce Franklin in "Past, Present,

and Future Seemed One" (pp. 230–46) examines the "snarled knots" of Melville's multiple stories and traces their "historical, rather than just their narrative, chronology." The march of time portrays Christopher Columbus, Charles V, and Dominican Friars: "amid these emblems of monasticism and the Inquisition . . . Babo [in the shaving scene] carries out his most audacious reversal of imperial power." The pervasive historicity of "Benito Cereno" focuses Melville's "cryptic show of symbols staged to confront, perplex, hoodwink, and even pillory at least some of its readers."

Of the two final pieces in *L'Imaginaire-Melville*, Janine Dove-Rumé's "Melville's *Encantadas:* Harmony or False Note?" (pp. 65–76) reveals in "translinguistic" and numerological games; and Michel Imbert in "Cash, Cant and Confidence: Of Paper-money and Scriptures in *The Confidence-Man*" (pp. 77–93) explores the signs and tokens that make money and faith equally dependent on spurious confidences.

vii Late Works

Nathaniel Philbrick in "Hawthorne, Maria Mitchell, and Melville's 'After the Pleasure Party' " (*ESQ* 37:291–308) discusses how astronomer Maria Mitchell, whom Melville met in Nantucket in 1852, makes her way into the poem. In 1872 Melville read Hawthorne's *Passages from the French and Italian Notebooks* and found that Mitchell visited the garden of Rospigliosi Palace with the Hawthornes: "This connection of the unmarried stargazer to Hawthorne . . . must have incited a welter of conflicting memories and associations." It was Melville, not Hawthorne, who appreciated Mitchell's "Zenobia-like passions that lurked beneath her Victorian proprieties." In "After the Pleasure Party" the ostentatious speaker projects Hawthorne's platitudinous aspect. Philbrick argues that the *Notebook* inspired both the creation of "a Mitchell-like character" and the poem's story line. The poem exposes Melville's "tangled and wounded psyche still wrestling with his childlike feelings of loss and betrayal."

Two essays explore Renaissance influences on *Billy Budd*. In "Melville's Marvell and Vere's Fairfax" (*ESQ* 38:59–70), Charles Larson discusses Melville's affinity with Marvell's protomodern "sense of ambiguity, of the doubleness of the world." Marvell's portrait of Fairfax in "Upon Appleton House" parallels Vere's moral dilemma over Billy. Unlike Fairfax, Vere does not shirk his duty; like Fairfax, he wrestles with a tortured conscience. Beginning with the dubious premise that "Billy in the Darbies" is "essential to any understanding of Melville's rhetoric and figures of captivity," Michael C. Berthold in "'Billy in the Darbies,' 'Lycidas,' and Melville's Figures of Captivity" (*ATQ* 6:109–19) argues that Melville's poem "becomes . . . an exercise in the practice of a special respectful narratization of the story and person of captive Billy." The "provisionality" of *Billy Budd* reflects Melville's alleged "fears of commodifying the subjects of his own captivity narratives." Not everyone will find the "similarities" between "Billy" and "Lycidas" so "striking"; somehow, the distance between the narrative proper and the coda poem impugn the narrator's reliability. This year in Melville studies concludes with R. W. Desai's preposterous "Truth's 'Ragged Edges': A Phenomenological Inquiry into the Captain Vere-Billy Budd Relationship in Melville's *Billy Budd, Sailor*" (*StHum* 19:11–26). Desai grants interpretive priority to the passage in which Vere recalls a fellow student's stutter; Desai then claims that Vere had—and has—"resentment towards 'the bright young schoolmate of his.'" Vere executes Billy not because of the Articles of War, but because of his "latent and long-nurtured envy of his boyhood rival." To hang Billy is finally to "establish [Vere's] superiority over" his stuttering schoolmate.

Salisbury State University

5 Whitman and Dickinson

Gary Lee Stonum

i Walt Whitman

Three questions currently dominate Whitman criticism, each responding to Whitman's unusual insistence on his own body. One derives from
deconstruction and related speculations: how can the body be presented
or represented in a text? Another worries the nature of Whitman's
selfhood, especially as it is caught up in issues of gender and sexuality.
And a third asks how or in what circumstances Whitman's embodied
poetic self sponsors a democratic political vision. All three questions
contribute to the intensified interest in "Crossing Brooklyn Ferry,"
which seems to be displacing "Song of Myself," "The Sleepers," "Out of
the Cradle," and other candidates as the quintessential Whitman poem.

a. Bibliography, Editing; Biography The indispensable guide to current items pertaining to Whitman remains the annotated quarterly
listings by Ed Folsom, "Whitman: A Current Bibliography" (*WWR*
10:42–51, 91–98, 162–69, 224–31). The only primary source to appear in
print this year is the seventh volume (of a projected nine) of Horace
Traubel's notes, *With Walt Whitman in Camden, July 7, 1890-February 10,
1891* (So. Ill), ed. Jeanne Chapman and Robert MacIsaac.

   The late Michael Lynch's "Walt Whitman in Ontario," pp. 141–52 in
The Continuing Presence of Walt Whitman, expands on an earlier, less
accessible piece describing Whitman's 1880 visit to Canada.

b. General Criticism Byrne R. S. Fone in *Masculine Landscapes: Walt
Whitman and the Homoerotic Text* (So. Ill.) develops a strong version of
the gay studies approach to Whitman, namely, that as a writer Whitman

My thanks to Sarah Turner for help in researching this article.

is constitutively homosexual. By contrast to biographical arguments or
those based on Whitman's place in Victorian sexual discourse, Fone reads
a homosexual literary identity directly out of Whitman's published and
unpublished writings. In other words, he offers exegesis, not history.

As the core of Whitman's imagination, Fone identifies a few clearly
homoerotic scenes and images, linking them across the time between
Whitman's first publications and the 1855 *Leaves of Grass*. The ur-text is
the Fierce Wrestler passage in the notebooks, the basis of section 28 of
"Song of Myself." Not only does the passage give us an especially striking
moment in Whitman's mythography, but that moment is the one that
generates Whitman's sense of poetic power. Indeed, the Wrestler is
Whitman's muse, Fone declares, and the encounter with this figure one
that organizes and underwrites the whole of his work.

Fone reads arguably homoerotic scenes powerfully but perhaps not
conclusively. On the one hand, his close attention to the early writings,
the notebooks, and the 1855 edition delineates a clear, unequivocal
homoerotic reading of Whitman. On the other hand, everything depends on the exegesis of a few passages, and the test of those readings
seems ultimately a questionably dogmatic appeal to experience. Fone
refers occasionally to the historical and theoretical scholarship on sexual
identity, to be sure, but the burden of his argument rests on a declaration
that "homosexual" and "heterosexual" pursuits are mutually exclusive,
that they divide between them the entire field of the erotic, and that the
critic can always and easily distinguish them. Fone repeatedly admon-
ishes us to distinguish sex from sexuality and acts from discourse,
although for him the body and its desires stand so plainly at the origin of
everything that discourse can only be something that happens to a body
already in place.

By contrast, in *Whitman's Presence: Body, Voice, and Writing in* Leaves
of Grass (NYU), Tenney Nathanson writes at length against any such
uncomplicatedly prelinguistic origin. Arguing on semiotic rather than
referential grounds, Nathanson sees Whitman's sexuality and his politics
as having their basis in an essentially literary problematic, rather than the
other way round. The most ambitious of this year's Whitman studies,
Nathanson's book takes up a number of topics without always clearly
relating them. Primarily, he seeks to reconcile Whitman's overt claims
with those of modern accounts of discourse. How, he asks, can a post-
structuralist take seriously Whitman's insistence on an unmediated rela-

tion to his audience and to the objects of his experience? One answer is to take Whitman's poetry as more performative than constative. The poet's frequent claims to be corporeally present to the reader or to transcend merely literary representation are not reports, but enactments.

Following Jonathan Culler, Nathanson pays particularly close attention to the details of Whitman's apostrophes, his addresses to the reader, and to the objects that his poems contemplate. These frequently produce what Nathanson calls an image of voice, one that invokes the natural experience of speech issuing from a body sufficiently nearby for the voice to be audible. At the same time, Whitman's addresses regularly and uncannily make the voice bodiless, its source invisible, and its location mysterious. The result is that voicing calls forth a presence that is just out of reach, just about to be there before us. And from such a performative invocation comes, Nathanson argues, the peculiar intimacy and power of Whitman's best poetry, the 1855 and 1856 editions of *Leaves of Grass*.

Such poetry is also said to mobilize archaic traces of a precultural self and of the body before it has been conscripted into the symbolic order. Nathanson cites Julia Kristeva's distinction of the precultural semiotic she calls *chora* from signification proper, that is, the cultural order as we now inhabit it. The appeal is like Fone's, but from the other direction. Whereas Fone grounds his argument in the certainty that referential experience gives rise to poetic language, Nathanson bases his on an equally dogmatic proposition that a kind of semiotic locale can exist beneath, beyond, or before the otherwise ubiquitous space of representation. The appeal, in other words, is to a textualist theory that, unlike most, already believes along with Whitman that communication can be unmediated.

Whitman most convincingly uses a performative mode to redeem representational discourse in "Crossing Brooklyn Ferry," a poem Nathanson returns to repeatedly. By 1860, however, and especially in the "Calamus" poems, Whitman's performative poetics fades, and he seeks instead to ground his poems directly in nature, an attempt that he recognizes is tantamount to accepting the representational order within which nature is available to us. Whereas he had initially viewed created nature as an array of carapaces, sometimes indicating but often misrepresenting the animating forces within, now his poems about sexually desirable bodies presuppose that such bodies dwell within history and within the symbolic order. Sexuality precedes sex, after all. In further contrast to Fone, who emphasizes the single and singular objects of desire in writings before 1860, Nathanson insists that such objects are represented as belonging to groups and hence as traversed by the social codes linking the members and affording them group identity.

In both the title and the text of Leaves of Grass: *America's Lyric-Epic of Self and Democracy* (Twayne), James E. Miller, Jr., summarizes views he has developed over his long, illustrious career; scholars would be advised to consult the earlier, richer versions.

Parts of James Dougherty's *Walt Whitman and the Citizen's Eye* (LSU) also rehearse a firmly established view: Whitman as undertaking a largely Emersonian errand of consciousness. However, Dougherty's most interesting chapters celebrate a different poet from the one busily apprehending and incorporating the Not-Me. Identifying "Crossing Brooklyn Ferry," *Drum-Taps,* and a number of post-1860 lyrics as crucially "visualist" poems, Dougherty sees them as naturalizing Whitman's otherwise free-floating omnivorousness by basing it in the mystery of eyesight. As a shared, partly learned capacity, eyesight gives Whitman's "I" a way of connecting with the "You" it seeks. In practice, this means that Dougherty reads Whitman's poems as if they were pictures, helpfully noting their relation to both the popular illustrations and the high art that Whitman would have seen. In addition, Dougherty attends closely to the duration of seeing, arguing with the help of 19th- and 20th-century accounts of vision that some Whitman poems mime the activity of visual perception.

Where Nathanson sees Whitman inhabiting a single space, namely, that of representation, Dougherty sees two regions, a visualist or pictorial one in addition to one caught up in the coils of language and consciousness. Explicating the second region, he sounds the received wisdom of 30 years ago, a Coleridgean esthetics of the imagination. But on the possibilities of vision he has a great deal to say, explicitly recognizing that his approach challenges other attempts to ground Whitman's work in physicality, particularly those attempts arising from gender studies or gay studies. Such studies "have gone wrong insofar as they have attended only to sexual and specifically genital physicality," he declares in the course of showing how eyesight can construct a democratic objectivity and thus do the work that Fone and others have ascribed to homosexuality. The visible is political in that it is there for all to see, and for all to see in largely the same ways; it makes possible a connection between viewers who each might otherwise be imprisoned in the self. Visualism thus offers a solution to a traditional question in Whitman criticism, the link between the "I" and the "En Masse."

In "Whitman's Political Vision" (*Raritan* 12, i:98–111), Charles Molesworth sees Whitman's politics in a more familiar way, albeit one also based on the voluntary association of free individuals. Molesworth celebrates Whitman's anticipation of both John Dewey's sense of democracy and Jürgen Habermas's notion of communicative action, two political theories that minimize the importance of belonging to races, classes, genders, and so on.

By contrast to Dougherty's and Molesworth's individualism, M. Jimmie Killingsworth measures Whitman against communitarian standards and in doing so opens the way to a fresh political reading of the poetry. In the brief, tantalizing "Tropes of Selfhood: Whitman's 'Expressive Individualism'" (*The Continuing Presence of Walt Whitman*, pp. 39–52), Killingsworth notes that both Robert Bellah and Charles Taylor cite Whitman as a prophet of expressive individualism, the belief in doing your own thing which they see as the enemy of community. Against their familiar understanding of Whitman and his influence, however, Killingsworth asks if the naively referential view of language they presume might not underestimate the "protopolitical" resources of Whitman's writing.

Despite its topical title, Michael Moon's "Rereading Whitman under Pressure of AIDS: His Sex Radicalism and Ours" (*The Continuing Presence of Walt Whitman*, pp. 53–66) dwells on Whitman's time more than on his uses or resonances today. Moon argues that Whitman's concern with death is inextricable from his thematics of sexuality and the body, not a separate concern or one only added as Whitman aged.

Concentrating on syntactic details, John Schwiebert in *The Frailest Leaves: Whitman's Poetic Technique and Style in the Short Poem* (Peter Lang) offers a number of useful observations about particular texts while admirably refusing to inflate his subject beyond its explicit bounds. Among the techniques he singles out are sonnetlike turns in a poem's argument, a pictorial technique somewhat anticipating Imagism, and various elaborations on traditional meters and stanza forms.

Graham Clarke's not especially scholarly *Walt Whitman: The Poem as Private History* (St. Martin's) seems aimed toward British students only superficially acquainted with Whitman. As such, it regularly presents as triumphant conclusions what critics on this side of the pond would take as starting points, such as the idea that "The Sleepers" is a sort of antitext to "Song of Myself." On the other hand, this drawback for scholars would be a virtue to someone seeking an up-to-date introduction to Whitman's poetry.

c. Criticism: Individual Works   Alan Helms's "Whitman's 'Live Oak with Moss'" (*The Continuing Presence of Walt Whitman,* pp. 185–205) conveniently reprints and comments in detail on the original 12-poem sequence that became "Calamus." Helms is especially interesting on stylistic politics—Whitman's difficulties writing freshly about homosexual love in the shadow of Shakespeare's sonnets, and also on the more frequently discussed question of the cost to Whitman in broaching such a theme at all.

Carol Zapata Whelan, in "'Do I Contradict Myself?': Progression Through Contraries in Walt Whitman's 'The Sleepers'" (*WWR* 10:25–39) draws on Kristevan psychoanalysis to claim that "The Sleepers" is a less troubled and uneasy poem than others have seen. Gayle L. Smith's "Reading 'Song of Myself': Assuming What Whitman Assumes" (*ATQ* 6:151–61) looks at aspects of Whitman's grammar in order to examine how the author limits the reader's freedom of response.

Applying a Derridean theme to Whitman's political thinking, Robert Leigh Davis in "Whitman's Tympanum: A Reading of *Drum-Taps*" (*ATQ* 6:163–75) suggests that at key points in Whitman a membrane in the ear or on a drum helps unite seemingly opposed terms. This keeps alive throughout and after the Civil War the possibility of "intermingled states," one of Whitman's ideals in early editions of *Leaves of Grass* and one that has been seen as threatened by the war. Noting the same threats, Burton Hatlen in "The Many and/or The One: Poetics Versus Ideology in Whitman's 'Our Old Feuillage' and 'Song of the Banner at Daybreak'" (*ATQ* 6:189–211) evaluates two poems according to a familiar scheme, whereby the younger, better Whitman poetically allows phenomena to speak their diverse meanings, but the older, ideological writer works to dictate unified meaning, especially under the pressure of sectionalism and the Civil War.

In "Whitman's *Specimen Days* and the Theatricality of 'Semirenewal'" (*ATQ* 6:177–87), Glenn Cummings mixes a conventional thematic claim—that Whitman experiences only a partial renewal in the Timber Oak episode—with some de Manian ruminations on the symbol and on autobiography. In "'Act Poems of Eyes, Hands, Hips and Bosoms':

Women's Sexuality in Walt Whitman's *Children of Adam*" (*ATQ* 6:213–31), Maire Mullins seeks to defend Whitman's portrayal of female sexuality but seems unhelpfully fixed on the question of whether Whitman's views were conventional.

d. Affinities and Influences   Another defense of Whitman against feminist objections appears in Alicia Ostriker's "Loving Walt Whitman and the Problem of America" (*The Continuing Presence of Walt Whitman*, pp. 217–31). Ostriker flatly asserts that "the phallic economy of which feminist theorists complain has no place in [Whitman's] diffuse polymorphous eroticism."

Something of a defense against another charge appears in Ed Folsom's "Culturing White Anxiety: Walt Whitman and American Indians" (*EA* 45:286–98). Folsom reads Whitman's portrayal of Native Americans against Simon Ortiz's poem, *From Sand Creek,* seeking partly to protect Whitman from the angry dismissals offered by Maurice Kenny, most recently in "Whitman's Indifference to Indians" (*The Continuing Presence of Walt Whitman,* pp. 28–38).

Most of this centennial year's studies of Whitman's influence predictably regard it as positive or at least neutral. As predictably, most of the studies bear less on Whitman than on those he influenced, and so they can be omitted here. An exception is Amitai Avi-Ram's "Free Verse in Whitman and Ginsberg: The Body and the Simulacrum" (*The Continuing Presence of Walt Whitman,* pp. 93–114). Avi-Ram develops the significance of Allen Ginsberg's poetically encountering Whitman in a California supermarket, one locus classicus of the de-realized commodities that Baudrillard calls simulacra. Ginsberg's poem opens up the reversibility of one of Whitman's key assertions: "this is no book,/Who touches this touches a man." Avi-Ram then argues that the "line can work both ways, to vivify the book or, more likely, to suggest that there can be no man to touch, only the simulacrum of the man to be found in the book." Prosody is a crucial issue here. Avi-Ram claims that, as the most conspicuously nonrepresentational features of verse, rhyme and meter are the least likely to be simply caught up in the chain of signifying substitutions poststructuralism calls the symbolic order. The claim is then provocatively deployed to reject Whitman's otherwise widely accepted defense of free verse, namely, that it is less artificial than traditional forms and therefore a better vehicle for liberating the authentic and the organic.

Whereas meters have an arguably natural link to biological rhythms, however, free verse attaches more to an *idea* of the body and hence remains a captive of signification. In other words, because free verse is representational rather than, say, iconic, and although it even seeks to represent the body's ideal freedom from culture, it cannot help reinscribing the cultural discipline it would free us from.

ii Emily Dickinson

The most noteworthy trend in this year's comparatively scanty work on Dickinson is the revival of textual scholarship. The problem of how Dickinson's poems are to be edited has in recent years become increasingly central to many ostensibly exegetical and biographical issues.

a. Bibliography and Editing For this year Barbara Kelly has continued to provide a "Current Bibliography" (*DicS* 81:3–20), but the pending demise of this periodical gives these listings of secondary material an uncertain future. Not included in Kelly but worth mentioning is the acquisition by Amherst College of two previously unknown manuscripts, a letter to Susan Dickinson and a new version of "The feet of people walking home," also sent to Susan and tentatively dated 1858.

In "Fading Ratios: Johnson's Variorum Edition of Emily Dickinson's Poetry" (*Emily Dickinson Journal* 1, ii:100–120), Jo-Anne Cappeluti discusses the conflicting appeal of "original" and "final" versions of the poems, examining in detail cases in which Thomas Johnson violates his avowed preference for letter copies over packet copies.

Recent critiques of Johnson's editorial principles and practices owe a great deal to Susan Howe. In lectures for several years she has persuaded many scholars to take much more seriously the verbal and visual arrangements on the pages of Dickinson's manuscripts. Much of her argument is now available in "These Flames and Generosities of the Heart: Emily Dickinson and the Illogic of Sumptuary Values" (*Sulphur* 28 [1991]:134–55). Paula Bennett in " 'By a Mouth That Cannot Speak': Spectral Presence in Emily Dickinson's Letters" (*Emily Dickinson Journal* 1, ii:76–99) fervently radicalizes Howe's already bold arguments, proposing not only that letters and poems often can hardly be distinguished but apparently that virtually all of Dickinson's art is a form of erotic correspondence that disrupts the boundaries between private communication and public document.

b. Biography   Biography from the beginning has been central to Dickinson scholarship, and if anything it is increasing in importance. This year, for example, a number of studies combine literary and biographical interpretation or base the literary on the biographical. The most wide-ranging is Martha Nell Smith's *Rowing in Eden: Rereading Emily Dickinson* (Texas), which also more than any other study links biographical and interpretive issues with bibliographical ones. Without directly advancing a singular thesis about how Dickinson should be reread, Smith suggests that we need to attend more closely to how Dickinson composed her poems and especially to how she circulated many of them in letters. Smith's boldest suggestion is that we consider as a kind of generic unit the correspondence Dickinson had with various persons, both the letters she wrote them and the poems she sent them.

Smith's central contribution is to examine closely the relation between the poet and Susan Dickinson and to argue for Susan's importance both as a beloved and as a reader and editor of the poems. Smith at least touches in her study on nearly every other major critical, biographical, and bibliographical issue, but the price paid for the profuseness is diffuseness. Although she calls polemically for new readings, she is so unfailingly generous to other views that little more of a thesis emerges than the insistence on Sue's importance.

Like Smith's book, Judith Farr's *The Passion of Emily Dickinson* (Harvard) is not exclusively biographical, but it nevertheless centers on Dickinson's life and circumstances. Farr offers a "two loves" thesis, maintaining that during her most creative years Dickinson loved both Susan and Samuel Bowles, and that one can disentangle a "narrative" of poems for the one from a narrative of poems for the other. The case is plausible, but not evidently more or less so than other, divergent claims about the erotic origins of Dickinson's poetry.

Farr's more original contribution comes in studying Dickinson's sources. Dickinson was a learned poet, she asserts, claiming not only that the poet had a wider culture than is sometimes acknowledged but that many of her images, phrases, and scenarios derive from identifiable sources. Furthermore, in Dickinson's poems and letters these sources sometimes function as a code shared with the text's intended recipient or subject. Thus, documents said to be intended for Bowles (including the "Master" letters, Farr believes) draw minutely on the novels of Charlotte Brontë, one of his favorite authors, whereas texts to or about Susan draw on contemporary American painting, with which the poet's sister-in-law was especially well-acquainted.

Farr mostly notes already identified textual sources—*Aurora Leigh, Antony and Cleopatra,* Revelation, *Jane Eyre*—but she does a careful, perhaps definitive job charting how Dickinson uses them and how frequently she does so. Her more original claim is that Dickinson's poetry draws on painterly iconography or even specifically alludes to visual sources: Thomas Cole (especially the *Voyage of Life* series), other painters in the Hudson River Valley and Luminist tradition, and both the American and British Pre-Raphaelites.

Farr's readings can be brilliantly illuminating when the identification of the source is most persuasive. For example, she reads the "Master" letters as carefully and powerfully as anyone has done (and I say this even though unconvinced by her claim about Bowles). However, her interpretations can falter when the identification seems more dubious or tangential. She will, for instance, sometimes disregard a poem's specifics to dwell on some very broad iconographical and thematic nexus.

Despite the social and sexual issues she deals with, Farr seems notably uninfluenced by contemporary gender studies or indeed by the agenda of any other current school. By contrast, Betsy Erkkila in *The Wicked Sisters* responds primarily to what theory and criticism have had to say about woman poets. Her main concern is the debate about literary sisterhood, and in Dickinson's case she examines the issue biographically. Erkkila first insists on the importance to Dickinson of other women and then on how troubled these relations regularly were, not only with Susan but with Helen Hunt Jackson and Dickinson's circle of girlhood friends. The biographical claims are sometimes tendentious (she cites Mabel Loomis Todd as a character witness against her sexual rival, Susan), but in emphasizing discord and envy Erkkila sees some familiar matters freshly. For example, she notices that Dickinson persistently admired contemporary European women more than her American peers, a pattern that Erkkila sees as aligning Dickinson with Hawthorne's complaints against literary domesticity.

Erkkila is also the author of the already notorious "Emily Dickinson and Class" (*AmLH* 4:1–27), which limits to polemic the otherwise admirable idea of paying attention to class and class consciousness. More prosecutor's brief than critical study, the essay includes a denunciation of "I'm ceded—I've stopped being theirs" for its reactionary use of "the politically charged language of secession." The case seems to depend on confusing "cede" with "secede." Despite such flaws, however, the article is an effective gauntlet at the feet of those who would like to assume Dickinson's ideological rectitude.

In " 'The House Encore Me So': Emily Dickinson and Jenny Lind" (*Emily Dickinson Journal* 1, i:1–19), Judith Pascoe proposes that Jenny Lind's 1851 concert tour was as important an event in Dickinson's life as her encounter with Thomas Wentworth Higginson, providing her with a model of the woman artist in the marketplace. Pascoe argues also that Lind's white dress and famously childlike mien left their traces in Dickinson's life and work.

c. Criticism: General   Smith's, Farr's, and Erkkila's books all offer as much general criticism as biographical, but this year only one monograph largely ignores Dickinson's life. In *Choosing Not Choosing: Dickinson's Fascicles* (Chicago) Sharon Cameron argues for the importance of the fascicles as a formal device in Dickinson's poetry. Perhaps the most distinguished Dickinson scholar to adopt such an argument, Cameron more specifically proposes that Dickinson organized her fascicles according to the same principle by which she included variant readings on finished manuscripts, namely as a means of laying out alternatives without choosing among the possibilities arrayed.

Others have proposed that a poem's variants are less rejected phrasings than continuing contributions. Cameron goes further in claiming that subtle thematic or formal resonances one might find elsewhere in the same fascicle work the same way. The poem is not whole in itself, only in its relation to traces, echoes, and alternatives elsewhere. Such compositional practices thus amplify Dickinson's long-recognized penchant for multiplying semantic and syntactic possibilities.

Like UFOs, Dickinson's fascicles inspire more belief or scorn than reasoned argument. Cameron is no fanatic, but despite a provocative, intuitively appealing thesis and with the exception of a few powerful readings she has considerable difficulty making a coherent case. Her book is badly organized, so much so that one wonders if the University of Chicago Press any longer hires editors. Cameron's claims are compromised also by what seems to be lazy scholarship. She makes almost no reference to the considerable amount of textual and interpretive work of the last decade, although much of this is relevant and some directly supports or advances her position. Furthermore, although her claims are explicitly meant to apply to all of Dickinson's fascicles, she arbitrarily examines only three of them.

The year's other general studies can be divided into those chiefly addressing thematic concerns, those concerned with specific matters of form, and those broadly addressing Dickinson's poetics. The best of the first category is Roseanne Hoefel's examination of several Christological poems in "Emily Dickinson Fleshing Out a New Word" (*Emily Dickinson Journal* 1, i:54–75). Hoefel suggests, as others have, that Dickinson frequently prefers the Son's redemptive suffering to the Father's patriarchal authority. Not only does the poet imagine herself as imitating Christ, she understands this imitation as a way toward a nonphallogocentric position. Hoefel's argument is ambitious in confidently drawing analogies among theological, linguistic, and gender issues.

In "'Sweet Skepticism of the Heart': Science in the Poetry of Emily Dickinson" (*CollL* 19:121–28), Fred D. White offers a journeymanlike survey of Dickinson's uses of science and her attitude toward scientific inquiry. In "Emily Dickinson as Visionary" (*Raritan* 12, i:113–37) Paul Bray offers a deliberately footnote-free reading of Dickinson as a poet encountering the plenitude of being. One drawback is that Bray cannot then distinguish insights from platitudes, his phenomenological enterprise containing a number of both.

Among the studies of form and composition, Sarah Wider's "Corresponding Worlds: The Art of Emily Dickinson's Letters" (*Emily Dickinson Journal* 1, i:19–38) examines how Dickinson blends poetry and prose in many of her letters. In "Emily Dickinson, Homiletics, and Prophetic Power" (*Emily Dickinson Journal* 1, ii:54–75), Beth Maclay Doriani proposes that as many as half of Dickinson's poems are organized according to the rhetorical model governing Jonathan Edwards's sermons. She only demonstrates one clear-cut case, however, and although she defines the sermon model clearly, she does not attempt to show how or whether it differs from related models.

Drawing on Kristeva and Mikhail Bakhtin, Paul Crumbley in "Dickinson's Dashes and the Limits of Discourse" (*Emily Dickinson Journal* 1, ii:8–29) proposes that the dashes perform a hitherto unrecognized function: the emergence in the poem of other voices or views and hence the transformation of the univocal into the dialogical. Crumbley discusses only a few poems, which he reads from the Johnson edition rather than manuscript, so his article leaves unanswered some questions about how widely or deeply his claims apply. Nevertheless, he precisely distinguishes the emergent voices from related effects that others have noticed (lack of closure, syntactic doubling), and he shows persuasively that they can be found in at least some poems.

Cynthia Hogue's suggestive essay, "'I Didn't Be—Myself': Emily Dickinson's Semiotics of Presence" (*Emily Dickinson Journal* 1, ii:30–53) links the deferral of closure, presence, and mastery to the gendering of subject positions. More specifically, she argues that in circumventing a presence understood in visual terms—literally as the visibility of a physical body—Dickinson avoids both the positions that psychoanalysis derives from the gaze: the male viewer or the viewed female.

Claudia Yukman's "Breaking the Eschatological Frame: Dickinson's Narrative Acts" (*Emily Dickinson Journal* 1, i:76–94) argues subtly against reading Dickinson biographically and, indeed, even against too easily reading her referentially. Yukman shows instead that a range of poems are as much about the act of narrating as about the presumably referential story narrated. The Christian story of personal salvation, for example, can signify a crisis of subjectivity and not one of faith. More specifically, the speakers in "I heard a fly buzz" or "Life had stood a loaded gun" both move from being defined objects in a predetermined story, Christian in one case and patriarchal in the other, to being undefined, shifting subjects of a problematic enunciation. So also do the notorious poems spoken from beyond the grave, which Yukman reads as demonstrating how bodily presence interrupts Christian eschatology and issues a call for some apter narrative. Yukman's boldest move is to suggest that Dickinson appropriates the culturally dominant story of Christianity for narrowly literary rather than religious purposes. In particular, she establishes an analogy whereby life is to afterlife in Christianity as the events of the poem are to the text (or the reading of it).

d. Criticism: Individual Works In "'Goblin with a Gauge': Dickinson's Readerly Gothic" (*Emily Dickinson Journal* 1, i:39–53), Daneen Wardrop draws on Gothic fiction and the Freudian uncanny to investigate the reader's plight in "Twas like a maelstrom, with a notch." She argues that hesitation and repetition are the crucial features of Dickinson's Gothic and that a primary reference for both is the reader's word-by-word experience of the poem.

Case Western Reserve University

6 Mark Twain

Tom Quirk

This year was notable for three book-length biographical studies (the pick of the litter has to be Carl Dolmetsch's study of Twain in Vienna), two worthy collections of Twain's writings, and the third volume of Twain's *Letters*. *Huckleberry Finn* received a great deal of diverse and intelligent discussion, but solid critical studies were by no means confined to that novel. I am sorry to report that Walter Blair died 29 June 1992. If Blair's death marks the end of an era in Twain studies, Taylor Roberts's establishment of the *Mark Twain Forum,* a "discussion group" conducted through electronic mail, may mark the beginning of another.

i Editions

There is no need to sing the praises of the Library of America two-volume edition of *Mark Twain: Collected Tales, Sketches, Speeches, and Essays,* with the selections and notes prepared by Louis J. Budd, which appeared this year. Clive James has done so in the *New Yorker* (14 June 1993), placing this set at the top of the accumulating heap of Library of America volumes and contending that the whole project serves as so worthy a symbol of our culture that it upstages Mount Rushmore. James further celebrates Budd's edition as "a model of scholarship in service to literature," though he nowhere mentions the scholar by name who made the selections, chose the most reliable texts available, and prepared the notes. The selections in this edition are ample (270 in all), including some never collected before, such as "Barnum's First Speech to Congress," and resurrecting such choice items as "More Maxims of Mark," originally collected in 1927 by Merle Johnson. In any event, the volumes are a good deal cheaper than Mount Rushmore, and more portable too.

If Budd's collection richly conveys the diversity of Twain's writings over a 60-year period, Jim Zwick's collection, *Mark Twain's Weapons of Satire: Anti-Imperialist Writings on the Philippine-American War* (Syracuse), by tightening the focus considerably, reveals the fierceness of Twain's political commitments at the end of his life. Zwick gives a fuller account of Twain's sincere involvement in the Anti-Imperialist League than has hitherto appeared, and the gathered selections of his writings against the Philippine-American war (many never reprinted before and some previously unpublished) effectively demonstrate the depth of his opposition to individual figures (Generals Leonard Wood and Frederick Funston, particularly) and to American foreign policy and military practice. They disclose as well Twain's conviction that U.S. involvement in the Philippines was grounded in racist feelings and show the degree of the author's shame for his country and for the Anglo-Saxon race generally.

Written as a part of a "Great American Orators" series, Marlene Boyd Vallin's *Mark Twain: Protagonist for the Popular Culture* (Greenwood) follows a prescribed format—a discussion of Twain as speechmaker, along with analysis of the rhetorical methods he employed in particular speeches; a collection of Twain's speeches, some 16 in all; and back matter, including a chronology of significant speaking events and a bibliographic essay. Vallin's perceptions about Twain as an orator are hardly original. Likewise, her claim that Twain consistently spoke from the vantage point of the representative American and against the dominant culture—against pretense, humbug, and hypocrisy—and hence served as the "protagonist" for American culture must appear quaint in light of the several ways in which Twain has been reconstituted of late. Still, there is something attractive about the simplicity of a threadbare thesis that, though it has been virtually problematized out of existence, contains some germ of truth.

Volume 3, 1869, of *Mark Twain's Letters,* ed. Victor Fischer et al. (Calif.), continues the high standard set in volumes 1 and 2, printing 188 thoroughly annotated items, most of them previously unpublished; a revised "Guide to Editorial Practice" by Robert H. Hirst; extensive textual commentary; and six appendices, including a lecture schedule of Twain's two tours during 1868–70, facsimiles of enclosures with the letters, advertising circulars, and a calendar of Clemens's courtship letters, 1868–70. The 1869 correspondence details Twain's frustration at delays with the publication of *The Innocents Abroad* and his eventual satisfaction with reviews and sales; his casting about for a newspaper partnership and, on the advice and capital of Jervis Langdon, finally securing a one-third partnership in the Buffalo *Express;* and Twain's disgust with the annoyances and exhaustion of his lecture tours. Most importantly, it provides a record of Twain's ardent but never quite fatuous courtship of Livy, even after the announcement of their engagement in February 1869. These letters bristle with teasing good humor and fond hopes, and they are among the longest he ever wrote. If nothing else, this 700-plus page volume of the correspondence for a single year proves that the Mark Twain Project is in it for the long haul.

ii Biography

Resisting straight chronology, Carl Dolmetsch organizes *Our Famous Guest: Mark Twain in Vienna* (Georgia) topically in terms of the several contexts Twain inhabited in his stay in Vienna from September 1897 to May 1899. The result is a highly effective form of "literary cybernetics," in which we learn of Twain's reaction to Viennese journalism, politics, music, drama, high society, the Jewish question, pacificism, and technology and invention. What one gets, finally, is not only a picture of Twain during this period but of fin de siècle Vienna. Dolmetsch offers the possibility, without particularly insisting on it, that the dark quality of Twain's late writings may have stemmed from the stimulus of his intellectual environment rather than from a personal pessimism. Three special forms of that stimulus were literary impressionism, Phaeacianism (a brand of "aestheticism carried to excess"), and "therapeutic nihilism" (a "quasi-philosophical form of skepticism" in which existence had only those meanings one wished to give it). These intellectual currents may have contributed to Twain's literary methods and experimentation in dreams, solipsism, and impressionism. One could not say that Dolmetsch has demolished the "Bad Mood" theory of Twain's last years altogether, since one still has to ask whether he was responsive to these influences as an artist or as a personality whose cynicism found these mordant perspectives congenial. But from now on one will have to reconsider that theory.

Along with Dolmetsch's treatment of Twain's stay in Vienna and Jim Zwick's description of his involvement with the Anti-Imperialist League from 1901 to 1910, Nick Karanovich and Alan Gribben, eds., in *Overland with Mark Twain: James B. Pond's Photographs and Journal of the North American Lecture Tour of 1895* (Center for Mark Twain Studies at Quarry

Farm) have filled in a gap in late Twain biography—his lecture trip across the northern tier of the United States before he left from Vancouver for Australia on his round-the-world lecture tour to recoup his financial losses. Gribben's introduction, Twain's lecture manager Major James Pond's journal for that leg of the journey, and the 129 "Kodaks" Pond took on the trip and at Quarry Farm the following September effectively illustrate the forced good humor with which Twain undertook to relieve himself of his indebtedness. The handsomely produced volume has the look and feel of a coffee-table book, but it is substantive too—the text and photographs giving unretouched glimpses of Twain's discouragement alongside a certain determined resiliency.

Regrettably, Resa Willis's *Mark and Livy: The Love Story of Mark Twain and the Woman Who Almost Tamed Him* (Atheneum) is devoted too exclusively to the tenor of her subtitle. This biography of Olivia Langdon Clemens is ably written, and one will learn much about the Clemenses' travels, social engagements, purchases, domestic economies, and the like, and almost too much about the various and perennial ailments in the family and the means they might try to cure them. Willis convincingly conveys the undeniably strong and sincere quality of affection that obtained between Livy and her sometimes cantankerous husband for the duration of their life together. These are all virtues, but one learns little about the intellectual influences Livy had on Samuel Clemens or (apart from a few familiar anecdotes) how, precisely, she "edited" him and his often unruly imagination.

In "Literary Old Offenders: Mark Twain, John Quill, Max Adeler and Their Plagiarism Duels" (*MTJ* 29, ii[1991]:10–27), Horst Kruse rehearses the complicated and intriguing newspaper duel between Mark Twain and John Quill, both of whom made charges and countercharges of literary theft, and both, it appears, guilty of the crime. Kruse's account has less to do with the anxiety of influence than with common contemporaneous attempts to crowd out the competition. Kruse offers compelling circumstantial evidence that John Quill and Max Adeler were in fact pseudonyms for the same person, Charles Heber Clark, and that while Twain may have bested John Quill, Clark continued the duel under the name of Max Adeler. What makes the dispute interesting, and the problem particularly acute for Twain, is that it occurred at a time when Twain was attempting to achieve some social respectability and to move from being a newspaper humorist to a serious writer.

Lawrence Berkove in "Life after Twain: The Later Careers of the

Enterprise Staff" (*MTJ* 29, i[1991]:22–28) supplies miniature biographies of Dan De Quille, Charles Carroll Goodwin, Rollin Daggett, and Joseph Thompson Goodman, men who knew and worked with Twain, but whose own literary lives and achievements have been largely neglected. Each had literary aspirations and uneven talents and led lives of some interest before and after their association with Twain in the early 1860s.

iii General Interpretations

Henry B. Wonham's *Mark Twain and the Art of the Tall Tale* (Oxford) is an insightful and useful book—insightful because it traces with precision and intelligence Twain's appropriation and refinement of a tall-tale tradition from his earliest writings to its virtual disappearance in his later works, and useful because, while it does not propose a radically new reading of Twain, it does clarify and make precise a generally recognized feature of his art. According to Wonham, the tall tale was particularly popular in the United States because it affirmed collective experience and cultural independence. The tall narrative cultivates and thrives on a simultaneous address to separate audiences—insiders and outsiders. Wonham traces the development of this inherited narrative mode in several of Twain's writings— *The Innocents Abroad, Roughing It* (Twain's western "*Bildungsroman*"), "Old Times on the Mississippi" (the "test" of the yarn is the river itself), *Tom Sawyer,* and *Huckleberry Finn* (readers must reach beyond Huck's story in order to seek participation in a community of knowing readers whose understanding quite surpasses the narrator's). After *Huck Finn,* the tall narrative remains only an "echo" in Twain's work; the ideal of communal understanding gives way to feelings of collective guilt.

In *Mark Twain and the Feminine Aesthetic* (Cambridge), Peter Stoneley undertakes to explore how the feminine aesthetic, as an "ideological process that involved men and women, both in its creation and its effects," operated in Mark Twain as a writer who was both personally ambivalent about the feminine ideal and at the same time often representative of men who "decried the artificiality of feminine values, and yet supported the imposition of the artificial conditions that had produced them." Stoneley accomplishes this in a broad-ranging and densely textured survey of Twain's writings, both early and late, that, among other things, localizes notions of the masculine and the feminine in the robust West and the genteel East and, later, in the progressive and busy North and the enfeebled and nostalgic South. He observes from a different perspective the same paradoxical tensions operating in *The Prince and the Pauper* and *Joan of Arc,* arguing that these "feminine" texts actually served Twain's masculinist prerogatives. By considering a group of late writings, Stoneley further argues that Twain's fascination with a feminine aesthetic survived a personal cynicism that had demolished his faith in a masculine ideal of progress. The net result of his inquiry is a somewhat uneven but always interesting account of Twain's shifting attitudes toward the feminine, a perspective that allows Stoneley to take up several neglected texts alongside familiar works and to shed light on both.

Influence and the anxiety that flows therefrom seem to have been a particularly popular topic this year. One example is James Hirsh's "Samuel Clemens and the Ghost of Shakespeare," (*SSNTS* 24:251–72). In sketches, burlesques, the philosophical dialogue *What Is Man?,* and most extensively in *Huckleberry Finn,* Hirsh detects in plain statements and verbal echoes an abiding Shakespearean influence on Twain and an attendant anxiety over this influence. Twain's essay "Is Shakespeare Dead?" is an attempt to dethrone the bard and at the same time to extenuate himself as the product of a rural village whose own literary achievements do not measure up to the master. Hirsh's parallels are sometimes strained, and his conclusions often exceed his evidence, but the piece is informed and informative. Another example of influence study is Wesley Britton's brief note, "Carlyle, Clemens, and Dickens: Mark Twain's Francophobia, the French Revolution, and Determinism" (*SAF* 20:197–204). He persuasively connects Twain's reading of *The French Revolution* and *A Tale of Two Cities* to Twain's natural antipathy to the French, arguing that Twain read and reread these two texts, drawing from them what he needed at the time to solidify his contempt for French character. Eventually, he yoked the incipient deterministic elements in Carlyle and Dickens to the overt literary naturalism of Zola and applied his disgust to the whole of the "damned human race."

Everett Emerson and Lawrence Berkove supply two fine thematic treatments of Twain. In "Mark Twain and Humiliation" (*MTJ* 29, i[1991]:2–7) Emerson briefly explores Twain's long-standing feelings of social and moral vulnerability and the resulting humiliation he felt in his life and dramatized in his fiction, early and late, and he includes nice analyses of the theme of humiliation in "The Man That Corrupted Hadleyburg" and in the last version of "Jim Wolf and the Tom-Cats." That Twain was able to treat such feelings with humor and sympathy in his fiction is to his credit, but when he described man's "sole impulse" in *What Is Man?,* his emphasis on shame as a dominant force in human life was anything but funny. Berkove in "Mark Twain's Mind and the Illusion of Freedom" (*JH* special issue: 1–23) notes that Twain never outgrew his early Calvinistic view of the impossibility of human freedom. Though he adopted several religious perspectives during his lifetime, at its deepest level Twain's writing always displays a Calvinist perspective. Berkove argues his thesis through the analysis of *Roughing It, Huckleberry Finn,* and *Connecticut Yankee*—the first coheres by virtue of its underlying theme of disappointment and the inability to be free of Adam's curse; the second dramatizes the false notion of freedom and the temptation to believe in it; and the last shows Hank Morgan's dream of a democratic republic destroyed not so much by feudalism as by Hank's own tainted human nature.

Finally, Frederick Crews's *The Critics Bear It Away: American Fiction and the Academy* (Random House) contains two chapters ("The Parting of the Twains," pp. 47–72, and "A Yankee in the Court of Criticism," pp. 73–88) not on Twain as such, but on Twain criticism. These chapters figure in the prevailing argument of the book, largely conducted earlier in the *New York Review of Books,* that the most illuminating way to identify the camps of current critical controversy is not as a debate between formalists and poststructuralists but as one between the "Apriorists" and "Empiricists." Crews clearly favors the latter, whose capacity to tolerate "indeterminacy" marks them (and Crews himself) as unreconstructed liberal humanists. He maintains that the empiricist's attachment to positive evidence and responsibility to reasonable inference (and, among Twainians, Crews finds James M. Cox and Howard Baetzhold particularly admirable in this regard) is alive and well in the academy and still worthy of attention and practice.

iv Individual Works Through 1885

Roberta Seelinger Trites's "Narrative Inconsistencies in Clemens' *The Innocents Abroad*" (*JASAT* 23:1–16) is a capable but hardly eye-opening essay that argues that *Innocents Abroad* is "consistently inconsistent" but nevertheless reflects the conflicting values inherent in postbellum American culture. Twain shared with Bancroft, Henry Adams, and Frederick Jackson Turner a deep ambivalence toward a typically American innocence and an Old World experience. Thus, Twain's text "controverts" itself because by its very nature innocence cannot be explored. *Innocents Abroad* attempts to "center itself around an 'undecidable' concept," but because those same contradictions were pervasive in American culture, the book's popularity derived from its capacity to express sentiments shared by the public. In this connection, perhaps it is worth mentioning that David Levin's fine 1985 piece, "Innocents Abroad: From Mark Twain and Henry James to Bellow, Malamud, and Baldwin," is reprinted in the 1992 collection of his essays, *Forms of Uncertainty: Essays in Historical Criticism* (Virginia), pp. 289–310.

Christopher Holcomb's "Nodal Humor in Comic Narrative: A Semantic Analysis of Two Stories by Twain and Wodehouse" (*Humor* 5:233–50) is likely of greater interest to semanticists than Twainians. Holcomb undertakes to show that humor may be located not merely in a series of jokes but in "joke-like constructions"; these constructions he terms "nodal points of humor," and they may be identified when certain semantic scripts in the text come into opposition. The advantage of his theory, which he demonstrates in an analysis of Twain's "Journalism in Tennessee," is that it enables one to see how humor is fully integrated into the whole of a narrative and is often inseparable from it.

Seeking to extend Howard Baetzhold's earlier observation that the Colonel Sellers of *The Gilded Age* is in part modeled after Mr. Micawber of *David Copperfield,* Malcolm M. Marsden instances in "Dickens's Mr. Micawber and Mark Twain's Colonel Sellers" (*DSA* 21:63–77) the several parallels that exist between the two characters—their resiliency and dramatic flair: their reliance on language to relieve or transform their dire circumstance; and their capacity to serve their creators as means to satirize capitalism. Marsden sees Twain's creation not as derivative but as the translation of an English literary model into an authentic American character.

Carl Dolmetsch proposes in "Cowardice and Courage: Mark Twain, Stephen Crane and the Civil War" (*Profils Américains: Les Écrivains Américains Face à la Guerre de Sécession* [Montpellier] no. 3:39–50) that Stephen Crane in his readings in the four-volume *Battles & Leaders of the Civil War* was particularly influenced by Twain's "Private History of the Campaign that Failed." Specifically, he argues that *The Red Badge of Courage,* in its initiation theme, in the particular characterizations of several characters (including Henry Fleming), and in tone and metaphor bear unmistakable resemblances to Twain's fictionalized memoir.

v Adventures of Huckleberry Finn

As is usual, *Huckleberry Finn* received the most and the most varied attention this year. In *Satire or Evasion?: Black Perspectives on* Huckleberry Finn (Duke), the editors, James S. Leonard et al., have collected 15 essays by African American scholars and educators on the vexed question of the racist qualities in *Huckleberry Finn*. Nine of the essays first appeared in the *Mark Twain Journal*—the essays by Richard K. Barksdale, Rhett S. Jones, Julius Lester, Charles H. Nichols, Charles H. Nilon, Arnold Rampersad, David L. Smith, and Kenny J. Williams were published in the special issue of the journal for fall 1984, and an essay by Bernard W. Bell was published in spring 1985—and are reprinted here with some revisions. The six new essays prepared for this volume round out the multiple perspectives on Twain's novel.

John H. Wallace in "The Case Against *Huck Finn*" (pp. 16–24) formalizes the complaints against the novel he has made for several years, that it is "the most grotesque example of racist trash ever written." Wallace may overstate his case at times, but that should not divert us from the fact that he does have a case to make. Peaches Henry also believes that the novel may be a pernicious presence in the public school curriculum. The question, as she poses it in "The Struggle for Tolerance: Race and Censorship in *Huckleberry Finn*" (pp. 25–48), is not whether to introduce it into the classroom, but at what point and how. Ninth-grade students as a rule do not possess the literary sophistication to discern the book's ironies, but in the hands of capable and enlightened teachers, Twain's novel may prove of positive value in the high school curriculum. In any event, Henry is right to point out that high-culture interpretive "acrobatics" or First Amendment pleadings that serve to exonerate or extenuate Twain and his novel are beside the point. The cult of the expert is doing enough damage to higher education, and we need not inflict such arcane sophistication on the young.

Frederick Woodard and Donnarae MacCann in "Minstrel Shackles and Nineteenth-Century 'Liberality' in *Huckleberry Finn*" (pp. 141–53) likewise dispute interpretive ingenuity which attempts to get round the unmistakable traces of black minstrelsy, and the assumption of white supremacy it dramatizes, in all of the Huck and Jim narratives. Twain's novel may subvert several myths concerning the racial inferiority of blacks, but it leaves others intact, and these are particularly observable in his depiction of Jim. Betty H. Jones, by contrast, argues in "Huck and Jim: A Reconsideration" (pp. 154–72) that these comic aspects of Jim's character are superficial compared to his archetypal function as Huck's mentor and surrogate father. Twain's intent is to elevate Jim, not denigrate him, and through his tutoring of Huck, Jim urges the boy and, symbolically, the nation to move beyond its innocence and toward its own best promise.

Mary Kemp Davis in "The Veil Rent in Twain: Degradation and Revelation in *Adventures of Huckleberry Finn*" (pp. 77–90) examines the parallels between the Wilks episode and Jim's recapture on Spanish Island and his subsequent mistreatment as forms of "degradation ceremonies." The first episode, she contends, is a "comic treatment of degradation ritual," but the second "veers away from a tragic denouement." Unlike the tarring and feathering of the King and the Duke, which is typical of communal acts of degradation of those subversive to the dominant culture, Jim's "freedom" at the end adds to "the deeper meaning of Jim's 'Calvary.'" Carmen Subryan's "Mark Twain and the Black Challenge" (pp. 91–102) surveys Twain's lifelong progress in recognizing the "moral challenge" of the situation of blacks and describes a man who had transcended his own racial bias. "If Twain failed to escape completely from his own times," she observes, "he was well in advance of them; he still has much to say to those in our own time who have not learned." Obviously, black perspectives on Twain's novel are multiple, but James Leonard and Thomas Tenney's introduction and their instructive headnotes to each section of the collection frame the terms of the debate and give them thematic coherence. An annotated bibliography of further readings completes the collection.

Four essays take different approaches in attempting to "place" this novel in broad historical and literary terms. In his intricate and ingenious essay, "Nationalism, Hypercanonization, *Huckleberry Finn*" (*Boundary 2* 19, i:14–33), Jonathan Arac explores the "hypercanonicity" of *Huckleberry Finn*, which is to say, how it has come, along with a very few other works, to monopolize curricular and critical attention and command a certain cultural idolatry. In an extended comparison between *Huck Finn* (a specimen of the local narrative) and Cooper's *The Pioneers* (a specimen of an earlier national narrative), Arac maintains that Twain has displaced Cooper in the minds of most literary historians but that, in fact, it may be Cooper's novel that is the more "fundamentally multifocal" and "uncentered" work because it is not insulated from the historical contradictions and competing forces of public institutions that constitute our national life. *Huck Finn* is so insulated because it locates its tensions in the psyche of its marginalized protagonist—ignorant of history, law, custom, and the like—and seeks no cultural sanction beyond the ability of the individual to feel right about his or her local behavior.

Gorman Beauchamp's "*Ragged Dick* and the Fate of Respectability" (*MQR* 31:324–45) is a ranging and eminently readable essay. Beauchamp explores the inversion of respectability from the appearance in 1868 of Alger's *Ragged Dick* to our own time, when a white rap performer like Vanilla Ice serves as his current equivalent. Along the way, Gorman pauses to put *Huckleberry Finn* up against what may be considered another, though greatly different, national narrative, Alger's story of rags to riches. His conclusions, inevitably, are very different from Arac's: in an age that no longer respects respectability, Huck is far more respectable now than he was when he appeared before the public in 1884. By contrast, J. T. Barbarese does not see character (literary or other) as particularly significant. He argues in "Landscapes of the American Psyche" (*SR* 100:599–626), through a panoramic survey of the relation to the American landscape of Rip Van Winkle, Nick Carraway, Roderick Usher, Holden Caulfield, and others, that in American fiction character is fairly constant, whereas the landscape itself is dynamic. Huck Finn's experience forecloses on the possibility of recovering a romantic landscape, and his flight to the Territory is an altogether ambiguous ambition. In Huck, American character seems finally to have "taken measure of itself and found the interior of the human heart as unknowable and revelatory as whatever stretches before it."

The most provocative of these broad-ranging essays is William R. Everdell's "Monologues of the Mad: Paris Cabaret and Modernist Narrative From Twain to Eliot" (*SAF* 20:177–96). By assuming that *Huckleberry Finn* is primarily a comic monologue and only secondarily an autobiography, Everdell is able to trace a comprehensive line of influence that reaches back to Dickens's platform lectures and to later comic performances in the Paris cabaret in the early 1880s and forward to "Prufrock" and 20th-century stand-up comics. In an astute analysis of this form of comedy as a means of increasing a sense of presentational "immediacy," Everdell argues that in *Huck Finn* Twain took "one of the larger steps in post-Romantic American literature toward immediacy." He does not insist on a demonstrable line of influence, but he is convincing in his disclaimer: "Just because J. Alfred Prufrock wore the bottoms of his trousers rolled, while Huckleberry Finn usually stripped and swam, does not mean that they did not both put their feet in the same river." Their particular forms of literary confession rescue both figures from the dismissiveness of readers through a "new rhetorical posture" that largely derives from spoken comedy.

Three other essays explore resemblances and influences. For Philip V. Allingham in "Patterns of Deception in *Huckleberry Finn* and *Great Expectations*" (*NCF* 46:447–72) these two novels share patterns of deception perpetrated both on the fictional characters and on us as readers. The differences between them are important, however. While Dickens retains a faith in the capacity of a culture to reform, a "Scroogian change of heart and a general awakening of social conscience," Twain constructs on the raft "the idyll of a classless, racially equal 'community of saints' " that is shattered by the social community on shore. Pip is allowed to grow and mature socially and spiritually, but Huck's deceptions are largely defensive gestures, acts of self-protection against the prevailing social order. Gretchen M. Beidler in "Huck Finn as Tourist: Mark Twain's Parody Travelogue" (*SAF* 20:155–67) reads the novel as the account of a domestic tourist, Huck, and against the accounts of America provided by foreign visitors, particularly those of Mrs. Trollope and Basil Hall, which Twain had read when he was writing *Life on the Mississippi*. This angle of vision enables Beidler to identify the too often neglected acts of generosity and hospitality performed by all manner of characters along the river while at the same time acknowledging the vulgarity, intolerance, and crudity that infect the river communities. *Huckleberry Finn*, by this reading, serves as parody and mild corrective to foreign travelogues which depicted America as uncivilized, while at the same time having a young domestic tourist reject becoming so barbarously "sivilized."

Another influence study is Jon Powell's "Trouble and Joy From 'A True Story' to *Adventures of Huckleberry Finn:* Mark Twain and the Book of Jeremiah" (*SAF* 20:145–54). In this strained attempt to link two texts by way of the book of Jeremiah, Jim's prophecies in the novel, and a rather managed emphasis on the words *trouble* and *joy,* Powell reads the novel as both deterministic, in the biblical sense that the people are deaf to the pleas of the Prophets, and morally affirmative in Huck's withdrawal from a wicked, racist society. A more successful treatment of the question of what sort of morality Twain is recommending in and through Huck is Gregg Camfield's " 'I Wouldn't Be as Ignorant as You for Wages': Huck Talks Back to His Conscience" (*SAF* 20:169–75). Supplying a previously untranscribed passage from Twain's notebooks in which Huck rebukes his conscience and which may have been a regular part of Twain's lectures in Australia, Camfield notes that this late statement on Huck's bouts with his conscience sheds light on the question of whether Twain was recommending a utilitarian or intuitive romantic notion of morality in the novel. Twain in the 1890s is endorsing, and probably on stage, a "sentimental morality," a moral sense activated and strengthened by felt experience rather than by precept, training, or even reason. In his later writings, however, Twain despaired of the capacity of the moral sense to do much except produce human misery.

Another retrospective commentary on *Huckleberry Finn* is Axel Knoenagel's "Mark Twain's Further Use of Huck and Tom" (*IFR* 19:96–102). Knoenagel speculates on the possible explanations for why the later Huck and Tom narratives represent such a disappointing falling off from the novel. Among those reasons are Twain's identifiably commercial motives in writing them, the largely derivative plots that he borrowed and, even so, seemed unable to control, and the degradation of Tom from a romantic innocent to an amoral and arrogant adolescent and of Jim from a dignified human being to a wholly comic character. If nothing more, the "flawed character of the sequels also reflects upon the quality of the original."

Four essays dealing with particular features of the novel round out this year's offerings on *Huck Finn*. Walter Kokernot in " 'The Burning Shame' Broadside" (*MTJ* 29, ii[1991]:33–35) discusses an 18th-century broadside that reveals that the "Royal Nonesuch" swindle has a long and indecent history, one that may have been a part of English folklore tradition. In " 'Fawkes' Identified: A New Source for *Huckleberry Finn*" (*ELN* 29, iii:54–60), Peter Beidler offers the persuasive explanation that the book Twain requested from his publisher James Osgood in 1882 as one by "Fawkes" was in all likelihood a misspelling of Faux and that the book in question was William Faux's *Memorable Days in America* (1823). Although this book seems not to have served Twain in any detectable way in his preparation of *Life on the Mississippi*, Biedler does note some parallels between it and certain passages or episodes in *Huckleberry Finn*.

Alan and Carol Hunt in "The Practical Joke in *Huckleberry Finn*" (*WF* 51:197–202) contend that Twain "transforms a folkloric device into a literary form" that fortifies the novel's themes. They distinguish between the practical jokes Tom and Huck play on Jim. Both are malicious in intent, but Tom's succeed and reinforce his place as an insider in a white racist society, whereas Huck's backfire and eventually contribute to his sense of community with Jim. Donald A. Barclay's "Interpreted Well Enough: Two Illustrators' Visions of *Adventures of Huckleberry Finn*" (*The Horn Book* 68:311–19) compares Kemble's illustrations of the first edition of the novel with, among others, Barry Moser's illustrations of the centennial edition. Later illustrators of *Huckleberry Finn* have never enjoyed the advantages Kemble had when he illustrated the book, for Kemble achieved an "intimacy" with the text that others could not. This occurred for several reasons: illustrations were placed at the head of every chapter, intertwining the hand-drawn first word of the chapter before it yields to the printed text; the large number of illustrations (174 as opposed to Moser's 49) allowed Kemble to depict episodes within the book pretty much where they occur in the text; and the format permitted the drawings to run alongside the texts instead of being inserted as plates. Illustrators after Kemble had to settle for bringing an "atmospheric" quality to the novel, whereas Kemble's were integrated into the narrative itself.

vi Individual Works After 1885

Predictably, attention to post-*Huck Finn* texts tended to collect around *A Connecticut Yankee* and *Pudd'nhead Willson,* though there were some notable exceptions.

In his illuminating essay, "The Bound Apprentice" (*MTJ* 29, i[1991]: 13–21), David Barrow compares the speech Twain actually gave in 1886 to the association of printers known as the New York Typothetae with the one he had originally prepared for them, in order to shed light on Twain's problematic position with regard to labor and a decaying apprentice system from which he had himself risen, on the one hand, and the rise of capital investment and new technology with which Twain was deeply involved through his overly confident involvement with the Paige type-setter, on the other. Understood in these terms, *A Connecticut Yankee* dramatizes Twain's concerns with the social consequences of a new industrial order rather than solely reflecting his personal financial anxieties. The novel itself may be understood as a "cautionary tale," and Twain's actions, as opposed to those of other sorts of venture capitalists, may be seen as relatively "benign."

An analogous treatment of *A Connecticut Yankee* is H. Bruce Franklin's "Traveling in Time with Mark Twain" (pp. 157–71 in *American Literature and Science*). In a provocative and sometimes rather ingenious reading of the *Yankee* through the later tale, "From the 'London Times' of 1904," Franklin sees the novel as "probably the first fiction to explore philosophical and political paradoxes inherent both in the very conception of time travel and in Anglo-European perceptions of time relationships in nineteenth- and twentieth-century history." Twain involves himself in a number of historical and factual paradoxes, among them creating an alternative future for the 6th century, which correspondingly contradicts the present and the past for the 19th. Then he plays out the implications of his premise by having Hank's industrial republic destroyed by the church, finance capitalism, and modern warfare. Not only does Twain interrogate the notion of time as marked by progress, but he demonstrates that this forward movement as it approaches the 20th century may "transform the future into a prehuman primeval past."

David Ketterer, who in 1986 proposed that Max Adeler's story "The Fortunate Island" served as inspiration for *A Connecticut Yankee* (thus justifying Adeler's accusation of Twain's plagiarism), notes in " 'The Fortunate Island' by Max Adeler: Its Publication History and *A Connecticut Yankee*" (*MTJ* 29, ii[1991]:28–32) that Adeler's tale first appeared in 1880 as "Professor Baffin's Adventures," and he identifies at least four printings of the tale that Twain might have read. More specifically, he speculates that Twain may have at least scanned the piece in Montreal in December 1881. A contrast to this sort of sleuthing is to be found in Donald L. Hoffman's "Mark's Merlin: Magic vs. Technology in *A Connecticut Yankee in King Arthur's Court*," pp. 46–55 in Sally K. Slocum, ed., *Popular Arthurian Legends* (Bowling Green). In yet another essay that takes on the intentionalist reading of "Everett Carter and his fellow positivists," Hoffman sees the novel as an "Oedipal contest for world domination," in which Hank Morgan and Merlin share more than they suspect. The only thing that separates Hank from the primitive society of Arthur's England is TNT, a technologically efficient means of magic and coercion. Hank's "amnesia of origin," which is to say his inability to recognize that his nature is inscribed on him by an ancient, murderous past, reveals to us as readers that, ultimately, he is not "the shaper of Camelot, but that he was shaped by it." Such ponderous themes, combined with the burlesque of the novel, lead Hoffman to observe that Morgan is essentially a "charming, naive Kurtz, hollow at the core, and prancing about in circus tights to celebrate 'the Horror.' "

Thomas D. Zlatic examines Twain's deep ambivalence toward things

medieval in "The 'Seeing Eye' and the 'Creating Mouth': Literacy and
Orality in Mark Twain's *Joan of Arc*" (*ClioI* 21:285–304). Progress, for
Twain, required a textually literate culture, but he admired an oral
culture that provided an immediate, participatory, and communal relation to the world. Joan of Arc, as opposed to de Conte, was, for Twain,
the "epitome" of eloquence. Her preliterate consciousness gave her an
intuitive vision of reality beneath the surfaces of language, and her
simple heart enabled her to speak convincing truths; but her rhetorical
power derives from her place in an essentially oral world, and her
peculiar heroism was no longer possible in the 19th century.

Lawrence Howe gives an interesting if questionable twist to the
current fascination with Twain and "doubling" in "Race, Genealogy and
Genre in Mark Twain's *Pudd'nhead Wilson*" (*NCF* 46:495–516). The
doubleness in the novel can "only" be understood in terms of history and
genealogy; for this theme is not a "Twainian quirk" but inherent in the
reversible stereotypes of the Negro and aristocrat that Tom Driscoll
embodies. Moreover, because of its pervasive ironies, the novel as a
specimen of detective fiction violates the very genre it follows because
irony multiplies signifiers, whereas detective fiction depletes them until
there is a "stable" relation between the signifier and the signified—that is,
a solution to the crime. So far so good. But Howe also claims that
Pudd'nhead Wilson is a "mongrel," a deliberate parody of detective fiction
that, in part, allowed Twain to call into question institutions of law and
custom and to "negrify" and thus "punish" the father of the genre, Edgar
Allan Poe. Even Howe admits that his claim that the novel is a "metanar-
rative mystery" in which the mulatto murderer is a fictional embodiment
of a despised literary father, Poe himself, may at first glance appear "out-
landish." For me, even after closer inspection, the claim remains so.

If Howe's essay is too ingenious and intricate, Virginia Hale's "Mark
Twain, Detective" (*Connecticut Review* 14, i:79–84) relies too heavily on
plot summary. She recapitulates the substance of Twain's several detective tales, identifying the author's impulse to satirize and mock the genre
itself. But in *Pudd'nhead Wilson,* she proposes, Twain employed the
devices of detective fiction to inquire into the "ultimate mystery: 'What
is man? What does he mean?' " Finally, Susan Gillman devotes about
a quarter of her essay, "The Mulatto, Tragic or Triumphant? The
Nineteenth-Century American Race Melodrama" (*The Culture of Sentiment,* pp. 221–43) to *Pudd'nhead Wilson* and two related unfinished
race narratives to demonstrate that for Twain the concept of race was

grounded in institutional power relations and that he failed to consider questions of race as they pertain to gender. For this reason, he could not write in the mode of the "race melodrama," which begins with a kinship-based model of race.

Mary Boewe, in "Smouching towards Bedlam; or, Mark Twain's Creative Use of Some Acknowledged Sources" (*MTJ* 29, i[1991]:8–12) takes on the problem of sources, influences, plagiarism, and the neutral territory between. For Twain, there were permissible smouches (as in borrowing a watermelon) and reprehensible ones (as in out-and-out plagiarism), but there were problematic smouches as well, such as Twain's own borrowings from other writers to whom he gives due credit but also takes some liberties in modifying the acquired property. Boewe examines in particular Twain's borrowings from John Hay's *Castillian Days* for the bullfighting scene in *A Horse's Tale* to show how Twain adapted, improved on, and sometimes censored his sources.

Pavel Balditzin's "Mark Twain's *Autobiography* as an Aesthetic Problem" (*Russian Eyes on American Literature,* pp. 71–84) argues that the originality and aesthetic achievement of Twain's autobiography lies in its deliberate violation of the rules of the genre. Though he was well-acquainted with other autobiographies and the conventions of the genre, Twain opted to follow the "law of creative free play" in his *Autobiography,* parodying the form at times, presenting himself through others' eyes, introducing a deliberate layering of several voices in the narrative and attendant incongruities, indulging in political satire, and stringing the episodes of his life together almost at random. The result, for Balditzin, is not the summing up of a life but the impression of a life still in the making. Twain committed himself to an open-ended form and chose "not to draw a 'diagram of his fate' "; instead, he wrote "a cardiogram that must still be interpreted."

In "Theodor's Imperfect Creation: A New Reading of Mark Twain's *The Mysterious Stranger*" (*Cithara* 31, ii:30–37), Mark Harris argues for his "new" reading with apparent indifference to or ignorance of any textual difficulties with "The Mysterious Stranger" (he cites De Voto's 1946 text from *The Portable Mark Twain*). His insistence that Theodor is simply working out ideas through his own dreams and that Satan is a figure of Theodor's dream life is therefore invalidated before it ever begins—especially so since the emphasis of his argument falls on the problematic final chapter.

University of Missouri-Columbia

7 Henry James

Richard A. Hocks

James scholarship in 1992 differs from that of the past several years in one important respect: although criticism remains plentiful as ever, the major works are not critical books but splendid editorial work and an important biography. Ignas Skrupskelis and Elizabeth Berkeley have produced a magnificent volume of William and Henry's *Correspondence,* John Auchard a superb edition of *Italian Hours,* and George Monteiro a good collection of the Henry James/Henry Adams letters. Fred Kaplan has published his important biography of the novelist, the first since Leon Edel. There is much worthy criticism by Jonathan Auerbach, Ian Bell, John Kimmey, and Priscilla Walton, as well as stellar essays by Helen Killoran, Jerome McGann, Henry McDonald, William Macnaughton, Susan Mizruchi, Beth Newman, Margaret Scanlan, Andrew Scheiber, Meili Steele, Donald Wolff, and numerous others. At least one ideological issue raised by this mix of criticism—and therefore addressed by me as well—is the present status of Henry James as an imaginative realist writer; that is, has postmodernism been successful in its strenuous effort to eviscerate the idea of realism in James? Both sides of that dispute can be found here.

i Editions, Biographical Studies

The major publication of the year besides Kaplan's biography is *The Correspondence of William James,* Volume 1: *William and Henry, 1861–84,* ed. Ignas K. Skrupskelis and Elizabeth M. Berkeley (Virginia), the first of three volumes printing the correspondence between the brothers. Part of a projected 12-volume edition of William's correspondence to be selected from some 9,000 extant letters, volumes 1–3 will include all 737 of William and Henry's surviving letters. Jamesians will know certain familiar passages (such as Henry's self-consolation that Minny Temple's death "translated [her] from this changing realm of fact to the steady realm of thought"), but to read the entire contents of the first volume is to be stunned anew by the greatness of and relation between the elder James siblings. These letters are rich and impressive, as the two subjects develop and articulate their respective geniuses. There are actually more letters by Henry (94) than William (69) here, yet the personalities, intellects, and moral qualities of both shine by the end of this first install-ment. Henry's compassion and affection for William and the other chil-dren, Alice, Robertson, and Wilky, is striking despite our prior knowl-edge of it. His array of salutations, "Beloved Bill," "Willy," "Brother Bill," "Beloved Brother," captures the tone throughout. It does not, how-ever, capture the range and steady intelligence of the younger brother, especially when he proffers criticism of art and culture, and in effect writes "travel sketches" of Oxfordshire, Rome, Lucerne, London, and elsewhere. Henry seems morally impressive when, in an exchange of roles and residences with William, he ably and charitably renegotiates his father's will so that all share equally and Wilky is not disinher-ited. William's brilliance is stylistically energized by his slang—"brain-fag," "moonshiny"—and even by his inveterate contractions—"Beloved H'ry"—for which reproduction and exquisite general editing Skrupskelis and Berkeley deserve our great thanks. This publication obviously raises again the issue of psychic rivalry, a position set forth forty years ago by Edel in the first volume of his biography. One has to say, however, that the correspondence—admittedly only one kind of evidence, though a major one—leads the reader away from the Edel theme, or at least mitigates it. Meanwhile, the obverse view, regarding Henry's homoerotic "twinship" feelings for William, a view Edel himself incorporated into his own last revision, is likewise not nearly so apparent as one might expect, not even with the news of William's marriage to Alice Gibbens. One may be thus tempted to side with Gerald Meyers, who in his introduction to this volume contests Edel's thesis. A fascinating aspect of these letters, however, does bear on the question: William feels free to comment on literature, from George Eliot to George Sand, and he never hesitates to critique Henry's work. If we consider that, by 1884, where this volume closes, Henry is the well-published novelist, critic, and short-story writer, and William still struggles with his eyesight and *Psychology* project, perhaps William's "literary criticism" of Henry is psychically necessary to protect himself at that stage against his inferior career. But the greater irony is that William's commentary on Henry's work is usually very astute! And Henry is by no means cowed by it—indeed, he seems to like it. The letters do, however, provide "symptoms" of their anxieties, especially the endless discussion of their respective "bowels." But even here, one gets the sense of two people less hypochondriacal than sympathetic, although admittedly that became more complex after 1884. Bowels aside, the correspondence of William and Henry will make the scales drop from one's eyes in recognition that these giants of American literature and thought were brothers.

Another collection, carefully edited by George Monteiro, is *The Correspondence of Henry James and Henry Adams: 1877–1914* (LSU), the first volume to print all surviving letters between the two men. Although the letters read a bit lopsidedly, 25 by James and only seven by Adams, the collection is helpfully augmented by four letters from James to his longtime friend Marian "Clover" Hooper Adams, all written in the 1880s, at the time he was drawing on her wit and liveliness in pieces like "Pandora" and "The Point of View." Monteiro newly transcribes all letters from manuscript and provides copious annotation as well as an appendix calendar of unlocated letters. His introduction provides a detailed record of the comments to be found elsewhere of each man about the other and of other people about the two of them. As a result, it supplements the very different sort of analysis of James/Adams found in earlier critics like R. P. Blackmur. Though Monteiro makes no comment, I was startled to discover that James alluded to Mrs. James Russell Lowell's unexpected death, its shock to her husband, but also their "precarious" relationship caused by her "insanity" in his last letter to Clover Adams the same year she too committed suicide.

Finally, John Auchard has produced the finest edition of a James nonfiction work I have seen in his *Italian Hours* (Penn. State), the first since the Horizon Press volume of 1968 and far superior in every respect. To begin with, Auchard's timing is propitious, for Bonney McDonald and James Tuttleton/Agostino Lombardo have spurred important new interest in James's complex response to Italy (see *ALS 1989*, p. 104; *ALS 1990*, p. 118). Auchard provides copious annotation of the corrected 1909 Houghton Mifflin edition which is his copy-text, a collation of that version with the first English Edition, an appendix which reprints James's reviews of Italian travel books by Howells, Taine, Hawthorne, and others, and an extended textual note. The note is for understanding the evolution of this crucial collection of essays composed over some 40

years and on the basis of 14 visits to Italy, the essays arranged un-
chronologically and textually revised like the fiction in the New York
Edition. Auchard's introduction is almost a Jamesian travel essay in its
own right, a blue-ribbon guide not only to the major Italian cities but to
the different temporal Italys, before, during, and after James's lifetime. It
is rare to see an editor so aesthetically attuned to his subject. As for James,
his decision to begin the 1909 *Italian Hours* with Venice and end with
Naples makes one realize that, like Yeats, he probably evolved from a
"Byzantium" sensibility toward the "rag and bone shop" of humanity.

Of equal importance with the William/Henry *Correspondence* is Fred
Kaplan's major new biography, *Henry James: The Imagination of Genius*
(Morrow), the first on the novelist since Edel's five-volume Pulitzer Prize
biography (1953–72) and its most recent re-incarnation (1985). The appearance last year of R. W. B. Lewis's *Family Narrative* and over the last 15
years of volumes on William by Howard Feinstein, on Wilky and Bob by
Jane Maher, and on Alice by Jean Strouse make Kaplan's new work welcome and timely. R. W. B. Lewis last year "added" nothing save his own
graceful narrative style and a slight retreat from Edel's neo-Freudianism.
Kaplan, although he has no great revelations to offer, gives us a very
different kind of biography from Edel's. He emphasizes more than Edel
the relationship between James's homoeroticism and his fiction, while on
the other hand he insists more than Edel originally did on James's
lifelong physical celibacy—"verbal passion did not imply physical action." A major biographer of Dickens and Carlyle, Kaplan provides fine
vignettes conveying the ethos of James's Victorian-Edwardian milieu.
This work is more conventionally organized than Edel, with none of
Edel's trademark "retrospective" structures. Other interesting features:
Kaplan's different handling of William's resignation from the Academy
of Arts and Letters, emphasizing public politics, not personal animosity;
James's response to immigrant Jews in 1905, a position Kaplan finds less
anti-Semitic than have other commentators and more consistent with
James's lifelong views, that is, he had more Zolaesque passion about the
Dreyfus affair than he sometimes let on; and Constance Fenimore
Woolson's suicide, which Kaplan treats less romantically than does Edel
(in line with recent scholarship, perhaps), although he does conclude
that James still felt vaguely responsible.

In light of the new publication of their correspondence, Kaplan's view
of the Henry/William relationship is interesting. He writes of their

"consanguinities and their rivalries [as] strong" and proposes that "the brothers could hardly conceive of a world without one another." If Edel saw them a bit too much as "Jacob and Esau," Kaplan perhaps over-argues the psychosexual passion of Henry for William, especially in his attempt to reread a brilliant novel like *Portrait* into a confusing sexual narrative with Henry as Isabel, William as Osmond, and Goodwood somewhere between. Having granted Henry James his celibacy, so to speak, Kaplan tries to compensate by emphasizing his homoeroticism, enumerating his successive (verbal) "loves" of William, Paul Joukowsky, Morton Fullerton, Hendrik Anderson, and Jocelyn Persse, and by read-ing a good bit of the fiction as expressive of his troubled sexuality. The method does not always work; for example, "The Pupil," "The Aspern Papers," and "The Turn of the Screw" are not well explained by James's homosexual panic. However, I find the psychological interpretation of William's need to return to Cambridge at the time of his father's death a very convincing example of Kaplan's method at its best. He has consulted the ten thousand letters of James which remain unpublished, and this important biography points to the need someday for a full collection of those letters.

In *Testamentary Acts* (Oxford) Michael Millgate explores the "pattern of conscious career conclusion" of Victorian writers Browning, Tenny-son, James, and Hardy. In the James chapter (pp. 73–109), he recounts James's reliance on memory to "reassert control of his past and present life" by establishing an "invented" mode of biography in *William Wet-more Story,* then extends the same principle into the New York Prefaces and James's "imperialistic retouchings" of the texts, as well as his burning of private documents and doctoring autobiographical memoirs. This is very familiar content, yet Millgate nicely assesses James's Shakespearean *Tempest*-like aura in the late years. Virginia Allen in "Ethos and Margin-alization in the Henry James/H. H. Wells Affair" (*Extrapolation* 33:317–32) states that Edel is mistaken about James's never having considered collaboration. She argues that letters published by Edel himself imply he wished to collaborate with Wells, but Wells rejected the offer. Finally, donning the persona of Detective Dupine in "Dupine Tracks J.J." (*SoR* 27 [1991]:803–25), Alfred Habagger tracks the ghosts in James's fiction and discovers that James Barber, "J.J.," a brother of Henry, Sr., com-mitted suicide, a tragedy that taught 13-year-old Henry, Jr., that "Amer-ica undid its gentlemen," so it was safer to keep one's distance and settle into British life and art. "Dupine" thus determines that an "obscure suicide" shaped the young nephew into James the novelist.

ii Sources, Background, Influences, Parallels

John Kimmey has been publishing solid and informative articles on James's use of London in his fiction for almost 15 years. His *Henry James and London: The City in His Fiction* (Peter Lang, 1991) integrates these separate studies nicely into a whole and supplements them at strategic points. Although the approach is structured thematically and chronologically by decades rather than by individual novels or tales, my favorite analysis remains *The Princess,* first, because it shows Kimmey's method at its best in combining background study with James's creative use of these geographical resources, and, second, because *The Princess* is itself the richest of James's London books, the equal of anything by Dickens or Gissing. Kimmey's book not only fills an obvious void in James studies but is indispensable for American academics who teach—as they sometimes do—Henry James in an academic exchange program in London. Two signature pieces by Adeline Tintner, "Vernon Lee's 'Oke of Okehurst; or the Phantom Lover' and James's 'The Way it Came' " (*SSF* 28 [1991]:355–62) and "Cora Crane and James's 'The Great Condition': A Biblio-Biographical Note" (*HJR* 13:192–97), point out connections between other writers and James. In the first, Tintner shows that the theme of "The Way It Came" is very close to Vernon Lee's ghost story, but that James's is a masterpiece of concision while Lee's is "redundant" and "overdrawn." In the second, Tintner tells of a volume of *The Anglo-Saxon Review* inscribed to Stephen Crane as a gift from James. Tintner discovered that Cora Crane added to the inscription that it was a gift to herself as well, but that the story "The Great Condition" had been "neatly excised." Tintner speculates that Cora removed these "offending pages" from the *Review* because its protagonist was a woman with a checkered past, much like Cora herself, who had been the "one-time madam of Hotel de Dream, a whorehouse in Jacksonville."

Henry McDonald has penned another fine treatment of James's philosophical ties to Nietzsche (although not Stephen Donadio's "Emersonian" Nietzsche) in "Nietzsche, Wittgenstein, and the Tragic Henry James" (*TSLL* 34:403–49). His wide-ranging, loose-and-baggy-monster essay portrays James as "subverting" the dominant continental and Anglo-American philosophical traditions and thus critiquing modernist epistemology itself in the same way as do Nietzsche and Wittgenstein. McDonald associates James with Nietzschean "joyful/tragic bewilderment," with performative art, and with "master morality" as opposed to "slave-essentialist resentment." The later Wittgenstein contributes a critique of "private" language divorced from its social, cultural, and historical reality. McDonald is very powerful in what he affirms but mistaken in what he rejects: for example, he wrongly claims that criticism has followed Percy Lubbock up to the present, simplistically equates Hume, Locke, and William James, even misrepresents the context of Eliot's famous "mind so fine" locution. McDonald rightly points out, *pace* postmodernists, that James critiques romance in his Preface to *The American,* yet throughout the essay James's own views about other important matters—like the nature of consciousness—are glided past. One of McDonald's key concepts is Nietzschean "excess," and this essay itself gains greatly but suffers some from that quality. "The Double Trajectory: Ambiguity in Brahms and Henry James" (*19th-Century Music* 13, 2 [1989]:129–44) by Roland Jordan and Emma Kafalenos will interest Jamesians who are also trained musicians with an interest in structuralism! The authors show with rigor that "Owen Wingrave" and Intermezzo, op. 119, no. 1, both written in 1892, similarly illustrate principles expounded in the work of Greimas and Todorov. In James's case, the "trajectory of events" and the "trajectory of the perception of events" create ambiguity while avoiding 20th-century discontinuity; in other words, structuralist thought confirms that, like Brahms's piece, James's tale is a fin de siècle work. Oddly, this technical essay never mentions that "Wingrave" has been the basis for an opera.

In her study *Rich and Strange: Gender, History, Modernism* (Princeton, 1991), pp. 38–63, Marianne DeKoven reads "The Turn of the Screw" and Charlotte Perkins Gilman's "The Yellow Wallpaper" together as 1890s "incipiently modernist" texts which exhibit "profound ambivalence" at the prospect of eroticized feminine will to power. Dekoven's Irigaray-based analysis contains nuanced psychoanalytic interpretation of water in both tales, but her main point is that these texts "damn" their protagonists on obverse grounds: for Gilman female capitulation is damnation and for James female victory is damnation—which both authors desire and fear. Dekoven's close reading strengthens her theme that "to repudiate the conventional feminine is not at all to be free of it; quite the contrary." Gian Balsamo in "Henry James and Emma Bovary" (*CRCL* 18 [1991]:547–56) reiterates that James's ambiguous view

of Emma prompted him to create in Isabel Archer a female consciousness able to stand both the aesthetic and moral test he applied in his
critique of Flaubert. Connections between Charles Demuth the painter
and James are posed by Mary Cappello's deconstructive piece "Governing the Master('s) Plot: Frames of Desire in Demuth and James" (*W&I*
8:154–70). Demuth, a "gay American painter," created illustrations for
"The Turn of the Screw" that show he identified with both the Governess and the master behind the tale. In "Henry James' 'Longstaff's
Marriage' and 'Barbara Allan'" (*ALR* 24, ii:81–87), W. R. Martin and
Warren U. Ober exhibit parallels between James's story and this ballad,
which he probably became familiar with during conversations with
Francis J. Child, the collector of English and Scottish ballads and a
longtime family friend. Readers aware of such borrowings can better
understand the tale's "whimsically ironic tone."

Playing detective, Elizabeth Steele in "Chaucer and Henry James:
Surprising Bedfellows" (*HJR* 13:126–42) displays parallels in characters,
action, and diction between *Troilus and Criseyde* and *The American*.
Steele's thesis reechoes T. S. Eliot's earlier argument that art copying art is
no different from art copying life. "Henry James and Ford Madox Ford:
A Troubled Relationship" (*HJR* 13:172–91) by Joseph Wiesenfarth states
that even though Ford claimed to have an intimate friendship with
James, the evidence from letters and biographers shows that it suffered a
breach when Ford left his wife for Violet Hunt. Yet Wiesenfarth points
out that Ford's critical study of James has brilliant insights into James's
literary method and style, while Ford's war novel dramatizes "the value of
James's fiction." In "Caught Between Canons: James, Pound, and Eliot,"
pp. 101–19 in *Rewriting the Dream: Reflections on the Changing American
Literary Canon*, ed. W. M. Verhoeven (Rodopi), C. C. Barfoot argues for
reading these three writers of mixed nationalities as a unified whole
rather than with the artificial split between the two canons, an academic movement of fairly recent history. He suggests that such "putative
boundaries" should be regarded instead as "a revelatory configuration,
emitting patterns of meaning and significance." Finally, "James and
Dostoevsky: The Heiress and the Idiot" (*HJR* 13:67–77) by John Kimmey argues for the influence of *Don Quixote* on both James and Dostoyevsky. Each writer, intrigued with the Christlike figure of Quixote,
creates a saintly picaro—Cervantes to make a comedy, Dostoyevsky's
Prince Fedor to make a Christian drama, and James's Milly Theale to
make a female tragedy-melodrama.

iii Critical Books

Postmodernism has had time now to insist that, of all the many things James is, the one thing he is not is what he himself most of the time thought he was, a realist. Priscilla L. Walton's *The Disruption of the Feminine in Henry James* (Toronto) brings this theme almost to its boiling point. Her feminist/deconstructive thesis is that in James, recurrences of feminine "absence" and "otherness" demolish the position that he is a realist, which view, she opines, is hopelessly wedded to "referentiality," "knowability," and "humanism," assuming wrongly that author and reader may share some knowledge of truth and reality. Walton's chief mentors besides Derrida are Althusser, Macherey, Cixous, and Kristeva. Some of her readings are creative and fresh, despite an ideological relentlessness. For example, the exploration of absent elements in *Wings,* Maggie's feminine textuality through "revision" in *Golden Bowl* (see also below), and the Governess's paradigmatic "disruptions" of Douglas's, the narrator's, and her own attempts at "control"—these are argued with energy and acumen. What I take issue with, however, are less Walton's philosophical mentors than her unremitting claim that "realist/referentialists" have always read James "univocally" and have not responded to his elasticity. Walton knows her French theory well enough, but she does not know—or at least does not want to believe—that for years a stupendous amount of James criticism and interpretation has explored his plurality, "self-reflexivity," and open-endedness within the framework of realism—or at least in contexts consonant with the historical movement and aims of realism. Walton needs to realize, too, that such a thesis-driven study unwittingly invalidates its own claims and seems more "univocal" than realism on its worst days. There *is* a most valuable point to be made about James's feminine core as a writer implicit in Walton's study, but it never shines because of her misconceived bashing of allegedly "masculinist" realism, humanism, and the like. Walton's Derrideanism is far more satisfying, however, in " 'There Had to Be Some Way to Show the Difference': Authorial Presence and Supplementarity in James's 'The Private Life' " (*VRev* 18:12–23) because, like, say, "The Figure in the Carpet" vis-à-vis Wolfgang Iser, "The Private Life," with its endlessly deferred and displaced authors and sources, seems a "natural" for Derrida's traces and constant supplementarity. Walton is in her element here as she dissects the story as a virtuoso piece of "textual production," without reductive attacks on realism. A "Derridean" level is almost always present in James, but only in metafictional tales like "The Private Life" is it likely to dominate and become the (decentered) center of the work.

Another critical work, Ian F. A. Bell's *Henry James and the Past: Readings into Time* (St. Martin's, 1991), applies not to deconstructionism or feminism but New Historicism to emphasize how the fiction of the late '70s and '80s is sensitive to the emergence of consumer culture by its strategies of "performativeness, desire, and surface," employing techniques of the marketplace "which create the illusion of the fixity of goods in order to sell them." Like John Kimmey, Bell has presented segments of his argument for several years, but unlike Kimmey he has not fully revealed his philosophical foundation until this book. His Frankfurt School orientation separates him, of course, from Priscilla Walton in all but one respect, the finding that James deploys a Romance of "surface and performance" rather than a "totalising" realism of opposition between exterior and interior. With textual nuance and historical context, Bell gives long intertextual readings of *Washington Square, The Bostonians,* and *The Europeans.* High points include a rereading of Morris Townsend as "less obvious victim," a coupling of Matthias Pardon and Basil Ransom, and positive features of "surface" in the character of Eugenia. Ultimately, James aestheticizes "the commercial object in the late 1870s within the earlier history of the 1840s."

But again, as with Walton, a question should be raised about Bell's postmodernist assumptions regarding realism. First of all, that rich interweaving between surface and depth that he stresses is an epistemological concept found foremost in the novelist's brother's philosophy and in some subsequent phenomenological schools, and it should not require commentators like Theodor Adorno or Mikhail Bakhtin, much less Leo Bersani, to supposedly "discover" this Jamesian core. Second, critics are now too swift to celebrate James's definition of "Romance" in his Preface to *The American,* when in fact it was a definition of "the romantic" and proposed as a flaw (see McDonald, above). Third, they are swift to criticize with James's approval "the hegemony of the centre," yet "centre" was exactly James's own favorite term and idea. Overriding all these matters, once more, is the dismissive caricaturing of late-19th-century realism as some rigid doctrine, when James himself knew it opened things up. "Essentialism" and absence of "closure" are the heart of William James, whose mature definition of self—*pace* Ross Posnock and

Bell—was a permeable function, not an entity (for the issue of James and realism, see also Anthony Hilfer, below).

Finally, in *The Romance of Failure: First-Person Fictions of Poe, Hawthorne, and James* (Oxford, 1989), Jonathan Auerbach explores in James some of the same territory as William Goetz (see *ALS 1986*, p. 96) and, to a far lesser extent, Sergio Perosa (see *ALS 1978*, p. 100). He is concerned with the "peculiar duplicity" of first-person narrators who simultaneously act in and retrospectively tell their tales, but also with "the psychology of the form, what it says about an author's relation to his work." In James's case, as seen in "The Aspern Papers," "The Figure in the Carpet," and *The Sacred Fount,* first-person form, though it may putatively constitute personal identity, in fact progressively constricts it, until the Newmarch narrator becomes a ghost who is "virtually obliterated." Yet James's experiment is a "servicable nightmare," for the author thereby emerges with his own sanity while leaving behind the "disengaged experience" James later criticized as "the romantic" in his Preface to *The American.* A fine complement to Goetz's study, Auerbach combines perceptive narratology with frequent illuminating analogy—as, for example, his terrific comparison of the "Aspern" narrator to Milton's Satan.

iv Criticism: General Essays

"Henry James and Ethical Reality: An Introduction" (*TSLL* 34:377–79) by Anthony Hilfer introduces the essays by McDonald (see above) and Scanlan (see below) with a brief but eloquent plea to see James and "realists of the past acknowledged on something like their own terms." He suggests that American realist fiction has begun to displace postmodern fiction in the 1980s, and with this shift ethics may reemerge as an issue in literary studies, once "mezmerized" critics awake from their "postmodernist dogma" and "take note."

Robert Dawidoff has a long discussion of *The Ambassadors* in *The Genteel Tradition and the Sacred Rage: High Culture Vs. Democracy in Adams, James, and Santayana* (No. Car.), pp. 75–141, an old-fashioned culture study. Dawidoff addresses an enduring cultural dialogue between Tocquevillian and Jeffersonian interpretations of democracy, how "cosmopolitan aristocrats" like James renegotiate their allegiance to the genteel tradition in the wake of repudiating the sacred rage of Puritan morality. *The Ambassadors* exhibits the "dilemma of a traditionalist sensibility confronted with American capitalist, democratic culture." This chapter is a sort of academic meditation, with Strether an everyman figure for American Studies.

M. Giulia Fabi's analysis of female friendship in "The Reluctant Patriarch: A Study of *The Portrait of a Lady, The Bostonians,* and *The Awkward Age*" (*HJR* 13:1–18) offers detailed Jamesian illustrations of the increasing deterioration of female relationships in these three novels. Fabi feels that such societal deteriorations anticipate those James later rendered in *The American Scene.* "Henry James in *The Bookman* of New York" (*HJR* 13:315–27) by Arthur Sherbo offers a bibliographical sampler of entries in *The Bookman,* which contains comments on James's letters, style, and influence on other writers like Wharton and Conrad. J. F. Burrows in "Not Unless You Ask Nicely: The Interpretative Nexus Between Analysis and Information" (*L&LC* 7, ii:91–109) offers textual analysis done with a sophisticated computer word search of narrative segments from the 1877 version of *The American, The Portrait of a Lady,* Jane Austen's *Mansfield Park,* and James's 1907 revision of *The American.* Burrows's point is to demonstrate the outcome of predictive comparisons between James and Austen and between James's earlier work and his later revision of it.

Discussing the supernatural forces in several James tales, Leonard Heldreath's "The Ghost and the Self: The Supernatural Fiction of Henry James," pp. 133–40 in *The Celebration of the Fantastic: Selected Papers from the Tenth Anniversary International Conference on the Fantastic in the Arts,* ed. Donald Morse et al. (Greenwood), claims that these ghosts are often a cultural or family past, or even a subliminal part of the character revisiting the present. Such visitation forces characters to reexamine and come to terms with their lives and themselves. Ross Posnock's "The Politics of Nonidentity: A Genealogy" (*BoundaryII* 19:34–68) reprises last year's *The Trial of Curiosity* (see *ALS 1991,* p. 107). Posnock challenges negative pronouncements on *The American Scene* by contending that James adopts a "pragmatic cultural criticism" anticipating John Dewey's. Posnock conceives "nonidentity" as at once a "challenge to a fixed identity" and engagement in public life and responsibility while resisting conventional modes of such engagement.

In "Henry James and the *Atlantic Monthly:* Editorial Perspectives on James's 'Friction with the Market'" (*SB* 45:311–32), Ellery Sedgwick explains that unlike his father's dilettantism Henry saw himself as a literary professional from his first publications and made a high percentage of his income in journals like the *Atlantic*. However, when in the 1890s the *Atlantic* tried to attract a broader middle-class audience, editors began to reject James as a highbrow writer of introspective realism, preferring third-raters and action-filled romances. Sara Blair's New Historicist analysis, "Changing the Subject: Henry James, *Dred Scott*, and Fictions of Identity" (*AmLH* 4:28–55), argues that the "Trollope" essay read against the Scott case reveals James reevaluating the "American sources of literary modernity." Blair believes that by the end of this essay James ironically resembles the historical figure of Dred Scott, who, covered with legal discourse, stands beyond the law. James seeks this privileged position in order to effect his mastery in his own sphere of influence.

v Criticism: Individual Novels

In "James's *The American:* A (New) man is being beaten" (*AL* 64:475–95) Eric Haralson demonstrates skillfully that Christopher Newman exhibits that "muscular system of morality" promoted by John Henry Newman, Christopher's namesake. Haralson's Freudian reading also claims that James defeats Newman's desire for fatherhood, because this prototype of the new American man sought "to seize the power of the father." Michael Hobbs in "Reading Newman Reading: Textuality and Possession in *The American*" (*HJR* 13:115–25) contends that Newman, as naive reader, fails to re-create Claire in his own image, thereby experiencing the death of his "commercial imagination" but the birth of "psychological insight." In "Forsaking the Bridal Veil: Henry James's Allusion to Correggio's *The Marriage of St. Catherine* in *The American*" (*HJR* 13:78–81), Lynne Shakelford argues that this painting of St. Catherine, a learned aristocrat who rejected an emperor's offer of marriage and was martyred, foreshadows Claire de Cintré, who rejects Newman to enter the Carmelite order—and is thus figuratively martyred in Newman's eyes.

Craig Howard White in "The House of Interest: A Keyword in *The Portrait of a Lady*" (*MLQ* 52 [1991]:191–207) analyzes the novel through the refracting lens of James's term of many uses, "interesting," the keyword connecting the growth of his aesthetic with the increase of his "economy." White points out that James's leisured class "drew" from interesting women like Isabel as if they were capital in a bank, a more than punning transference of people and events into money. In "The

Lady or the Scholar? 'Contending Lights' in James's Portrait of Isabel Archer" (*HUSL* 18 [1990]:48–80), Sharon Deykin Baris reveals James's "pyrotechnic display" in showing the conflicting portraits of lady Isabel; yet Baris also emphasizes that by the novel's end the portrait is as partial and multivalent as the American text/telegram that announces Isabel's arrival. Baris draws on many famous visual portraits of ladies to analyze James's "double-lighted method." Following William Stafford and Sharon Beth Ash, William Sayres in "The Proud Penitent: Madame Merle's Quiet Triumph in Henry James's *The Portrait of a Lady*" (*ELWIU* 19:231–45) reargues the case for Merle as the energizing force in this novel who is later resurrected in such figures as Kate Croy and Charlotte Stant. Sayres stresses the image of the "proud" victor with "her mission accomplished" rather than the beaten "penitent" who slinks away. An object-relations study by Carole Vopat, "Becoming a Lady: The Origins and Development of Isabel Archer's Ideal Self" (*L&P* 38, i–ii:38–56) locates Isabel's idealized self not in the happy childhood she describes but in a lonely life with a father who both spoiled and neglected her. This psychological background, says Vopat, explains why Isabel rejects Goodwood, a sexual suitor who offers his hard manhood, and accepts Osmond, a father figure who mirrors her ideal self. This also seems to be a year for *Portrait*-related reprints. Roger Gard's 1986 *Penguin Critical Study of* The Portrait of a Lady (Penguin) is conveniently divided into "Introduction," "Before Marriage," and "After Marriage," and remains an accessible overview for college students. A bit more sophisticated "case" study collection is *Major Literary Characters: Isabel Archer,* ed. Harold Bloom (Chelsea), which combines critical abstracts going back to Horace Scudder and Yvor Winters with contemporary approaches like those of Jonathan Freedman, Stephanie Smith, and William Veeder—all reviewed previously in *ALS.*

In "The Representations of Nature in Henry James's *The Europeans*" (*IFR* 19:1–7), Christine Raguet-Bouvart explains that James offers the reader his interpretation of the images of nature from his own youth. The word "sketch" from the title suggests that James uses the novel as his canvas, making the reader become "the visitor in a museum or spectator at a play."

Brook Thomas's historicist essay "The Construction of Privacy in and Around *The Bostonians*" (*AL* 64:719–47) ponders the difference between legal and metaphorical possession of works of art, as suggested in copyright law, and the difference between possession of works of art and people, as embodied in slavery laws. Thomas's point is that in James's novel of the Reconstruction period, Verena enters into a relationship covered by marriage law, not copyright law, and thus her tears at the end will not be her last, as the narrator fears. Using Hawthorne's *Scarlet Letter* as a prism through which to view "The Politics of Hysteria in *The Bostonians*" (*SCRev* 8, ii [1991]:57–72), Judith Sensibar affirms that James demystifies the image of the silent and idealized 19th-century woman and transforms that "comforting and familiar" sign into the modern equivalent of the scarlet *A*. Sensibar proposes that Olive, whose hysterical silence has been transferred to Verena, henceforth will speak with power to "reinvent and reshape" language. Jane Wolf Bowen in "Architectural Envy: 'A Figure Is Nothing Without a Setting' in Henry James's *The Bostonians*" (*NEQ* 65:3–23) explores the theme-motif of Boston buildings recording the history of homelessness at the root of American culture. Throughout the novel James uses architectural metaphors— outsides—to render the collapse of the inner life of his characters. Only the text itself is not destabilized. In "Eros, Art, and Ideology in *The Bostonians*" (*HJR* 13:235–52) Andrew Scheiber argues skillfully that readers of the text are, like Verena, asked to choose between "two interpretive frameworks"; yet James's ending exposes the "savior prince" as more evil than the "wicked witch herself." His "muffled endorsement," then, gives a slight nod to the liberal lesbian's will to power over the reactionary heterosexual's—the former leads to "a moral wilderness," while the latter ends in "cynicism, stasis, and, finally, silence."

Margaret Scanlan's excellent "Terrorism and the Realistic Novel: Henry James and *The Princess Casamassima*" (*TSLL* 34:380–402) claims that the deep terror James uncovers in the book is that no matter how carefully one plots, whether one be novelist or revolutionary, one cannot change the world. By examining the novel's structure of repetition throughout the strata of society, Scanlan shows convincingly that James was demonstrating how completely the romantic dream of originality was collapsing in *The Princess*'s "richer model of the possibilities of realism" (see also Anthony Hilfer, above).

With ample illustration from James's textual revisions and a persuasive conclusion demonstrating the superiority of James's decision to divide the 1908 version of the novel into books, William R. Macnaughton in "The New York Edition of Henry James's *The Tragic Muse*" (*HJR* 13:19–26) argues for the superiority of the revised text of *Tragic Muse* because of these improvements. In "Sins of Omission: What Henry James Left Out

of the Preface to *The Tragic Muse* and Why" (*ALR* 25 i:38–53), Gregory M. Pfitzer states that James's claim in the Preface that he does not
recall its origins is false, because, when it was published he was involved
with three women: Mrs. Humphrey Ward, the novelist; Mme. Elisa Felix
Rachel, the French actress; and Constance Fenimore Woolson, the writer
and critic. James's sin of omission was his failure to acknowledge their
connection to his novel.

Jonathan Havey's "Kleinian Developmental Narrative and James'
What Maisie Knew" (*HSL* 23: i [1991]:34–47) claims that Melanie Klein's
account of developmental "defensive splitting" offers a theoretical lens
for understanding this novel with its many opposites and doubles. Havey
traces Kleinian psychic fragmentation, maintained through splitting and
idealization, through Maisie's concealment and secrecy as she forms a
series of attachments to surrogate parents.

Susan L. Mizruchi's "Reproducing Women in *The Awkward Age*"
(*Representations* 38:101–30) surveys in much detail James's implicit cultural critique in 1899 of turn-of-the-century social science doctrine—
born of anxiety and a need for the "structural transformation of the
public sphere"—that reifies women as "objects for human reproduction."
Mizruchi's intertextual approach to the novel cites considerable scholarship exposing the paradox of "science" in James's time. Not only does
James emerge as an astute critic of contemporary scientific ideology, but
to a lesser extent Mrs. Brook, surprisingly, joins him by her tacit resistance to Nanda's future as a fertile mother employed to replenish
English stock.

Jerome McGann's tour de force essay, "Revision, Rewriting, Rereading; or, 'An Error [Not] in *The Ambassadors*'" (*AL* 64:95–110), slyly
proposes that the alleged reversal of chapters 28 and 29 "discovered" in
1950 was itself the mistake; that is, the Methuen English edition has the
incorrect order, not the Harper edition from which James revised for
Scribner. McGann's cleverness in dealing with all the internal chronological problems identified by Robert Young and followed by scholars ever
since can remind us that linearity is never the whole case in late James
fiction. All Jamesians should read McGann's lively dialogue between
"Henry" and "James." "Value and Subjectivity: The Dynamics of the
Sentence in James's *The Ambassadors*" (*CL* 43 [1991]:113–33) by Meili
Steele is an ambitious philosophical attempt to go beyond deconstruction and reconnect semantics (not merely semiotics) with subjectivity
and value in late James. Building on the work of Lyotard and Searle,

Steele argues the "incommensurability" between Strether's aesthetic and ethical categories. The interpretation of Strether and Gostrey's final scene is especially good. Elizabeth Dalton in "Recognition and Renunciation in *The Ambassadors*" (*PR* 59:457–68) identifies a pattern that links James and Strether with the reader's experience of recognition in the novel and shows that the "cost of seeing" for Strether is a recognition of his own incapacity, a loss James himself experienced as a child looking into the confectioner's window. Least illuminating and all too familiar is Kyung-woo Yeo's " 'Virtuous Attachment' As a Basic Structure in *The Ambassadors*" *JELL* (18 [1991]:929–38), which argues that Bilham's phrase motivates Strether's and the reader's confusion until, with the aid of clues and "nonverbal gestures," the enigma is dispelled in the boat scene.

In a needlessly turbid and often jargon-ridden essay, "*The Wings of the Dove:* 'Not Knowing, But Only Guessing' " (*HJR* 13:292–305), Kumkum Sangari asserts that the "famous polysemy" of this late James novel still offers its readers not only a plurality of plot interpretations but a plurality of sociocultural relationships and stylistic perspectives. Yet this openness can be a form of "enclosure" because "the actual reading of the text becomes almost identical with the reader postulated by the text."

Employing Irigaray's post-structuralist feminist theory, Priscilla Walton's " 'Mistress of Shades': Maggie as Reviser in *The Golden Bowl*" (*HJR* 13:143–53) reargues a theme in her book (see above), that Maggie's revisions in Book II are liberating because they feminize the rigidity of and introduce plurality into the male discourse. However, Walton claims that these actions do not change the oppressive social structure in the text, suggesting that a method that lacks agency continues to leave women "leashed and reduced."

vi Criticism: Tales

In "Mary Codman Peabody, Boston Conscientiousness, and 'An International Episode' " (*HJR* 13:231–34), Alfred Habegger corrects the "factual error" of confusing Elizabeth Palmer Peabody with Mary Codman Peabody. Leon Edel identified the former as James's model for Miss Birdseye in *The Bostonians*, while Habegger proposes that the latter, because of her "constant scraping against moral problems," bears a striking resemblance to the heroine Bessie of "An International Episode." J. M. Wilkinson-Dekhuijzen in " 'Nothing Is My *Last* Word on Anything': Henry James's 'Lady Barberina' " (*ES* 73:324–36) believes that the comparison of James's handling of the international theme in this long tale to a ballet is richly justified because James's organization of plot and characters remains fluid and balanced, like dancers in a ballet who never "harden into types."

Although "The Patagonia" is not James at "his dramatic best," writes Stanley Tick in "Sailing Again on 'The Patagonia'" (*JAmS* 26:84–90), the story does teach us to read James in all his complexity because of the ambiguity of the tale's first-person narrator and the engagement of the observers. Such narrative techniques challenge the reader not only by "the story of the hero," but " 'the story of the story itself' "—to use James's words.

Agreeing generally with interpretations by Adeline Tintner and others of sexual secrets in the story, Robert White's "The Figure in the Carpet of James's Temple of Delight" (*HJR* 13:27–49) adds to that carpet an Indian phallic symbol that James uses to represent the divine life force and to celebrate "the vital dimension of human sexuality as seen in Oriental temple art." James's knowledge of Oriental sexuality aside, White's identification of the figure as phallic icon may strike readers as less than unexpected.

Janet Gabler-Hover in "The Ethics of Determinism in Henry James's 'In the Cage' " (*HJR* 13:253–75) shows that Henry's title and his central concerns in this story come from William's "The Dilemma of Determinism." William's definition of "soft determinist"—setting the caged bird free with one hand while tying its feet with the other—is the ethical theme of chance that James couples with allusions otherwise to classical fate to give this story its dense fictional language. Although the protagonist does not gain freedom, James's art "gives her the space to try."

With a dialectical analysis that twists and turns like the tale itself, John H. Pearson's "Repetition and Subversion in Henry James's *Turn of the Screw*" (*HJR* 13:276–91) identifies two types of repetition centering on the debate of male vs. female authority: Platonic repetition in the patriarchical power of the absent Uncle and the other males, Miles and Quint, who represent the Uncle; Nietzschean repetition in the subversion of the "established" authority as practiced by the Governess and the other female characters. In his double frame for the tale, James too asserts and subverts his own as well as the Governess's authority over the story; yet the very existence of the female discourse denies the exclusivity of patriarchical authority. Using Lacan's multifaceted theory of the gaze, Beth Newman in "Getting Fixed: Feminine Identity and Scopic Crisis in

The Turn of the Screw" (*Novel* 26:43–63) states that the 19th-century woman was caught in a "complex knot of visual relations." In this tale the gaze, which can be identified as part of the patriarchy, is not necessarily evil because, however problematic, it does create subjectivity and identity. However, the Governess is caught between two definitions of the ideal woman: the inconspicuous but vigilant watcher and the "desirable woman" who is the object of visual pleasure. She consciously chooses the former but unconsciously desires the latter, all of which shapes the content of what she sees.

Esther Rashkin's detective exercise, "In the Mind's I: The Jolly Corner of Henry James," pp. 93–122 in *Family Secrets and the Psychoanalysis of Narrative* (Princeton), proposes that Spencer Brydon reenacts his entire family drama, playing the role of Spencer who haunts the grandfather, the grandfather who searches out the adulterer, and the grandfather "who envisions the bastard born of the cuckolding." Rashkin thinks that this tale is not psychoanalytic allegory but a drama of haunting that calls on the reader to decode what the character cannot decipher for himself. Using a historical approach, Russell J. Reising in " 'Doing Good by Stealth': Alice Staverton and Women's Politics in 'The Jolly Corner' " (*HJR* 13:50–66) contends that although Alice is "too patient and too passive"—marks of the traditional female—she does represent by her actions and her creative response to the new economic and social order the attitude of a "New Woman." In his analysis of this urban woman, Reising seeks to correct critical feminist commonplaces of James as "sexist," "reactionary," or "aloof from social/cultural concerns." Comparing the protagonists of "The Jolly Corner," "Rip Van Winkle," and "Young Goodman Brown," Walter Shear's "Cultural Fate and Social Freedom in Three American Short Stories" (*SSF* 29:543–49) shows that each character is alienated from his society because each experiences the flow of past into present. Such change creates a rift between personal and social identity, creating in turn a gap between the private and public histories of each character, which occasions "the disappearance and emergence of the private self."

Finally, after closely reading James's "Crapy Cornelia" and his "rather sour comedy" "Fordham Castle," N. H. Reeve in "Matches and Mismatches in Two Late James Stories" (*CO* 21:322–29) proposes that James's principal interest in marriage was the value of that relationship, when aborted, to reveal the reasons why people took it on in the first place! Reeve's essay examines aging men in midlife crises who expect their women "to launch their schemes," keep them afloat, but not get in their way.

vii Criticism: Nonfiction

Benjamin Goluboff's "The Problems of the Picturesque: Nineteenth-Century American Travelers in Britain" (*NOR* 18, ii [1991]:5–16) poses the problem of how travel writers like James and predecessors Harriet Beecher Stowe and Hawthorne could deal with the picturesque without reducing British reality to sentimentality. Hence, in *English Hours* James is constantly aware of grimy and poor British children "hovering about one's knees."

In "The Swiftian Journey of Henry James: Genre and Epistemology in *The American Scene*" (*HJR* 13:306–14), Helen Killoran presents a tidy and provocative argument that James's travel book is de facto a novel of manners wherein buildings are supporting characters and that the grotesque inversion of American culture gradually clarifies itself as the "fractured" protagonist travels from "Arcadia" north to Florida. Killoran makes a fine case for James's "Brobdignagian nightmare" vision in a work that extends 18th-century satire into modernist irony. Almost as good, "Jamesian Historiography and *The American Scene*" (*HJR* 13:154–71) by Donald Wolff draws on views from Hegel, Tocqueville, Schlegel, and Bakhtin to present James's "dialogical repression," which combines a conservative Tocquevillian sense of tragedy and decline with a more transcendental Hegelian sense of irony. Wolff denominates James's theory "Rhetorical Historiography," because such opposing views evince a "ghostly presence" holding together James's impressions of America. Finally, "Henry James and 'Vulgarity' " (*English* 170:113–25) by Andrew Cutting defines James's use of "vulgarity" in *American Scene* as an absence of taste that constitutes a "lack of appreciation, carelessness to the point of crassness," even "coarseness" about the grounds of human dignity. Cutting seems unaware of James's often positive etymological use of "vulgar."

University of Missouri

8   Pound and Eliot

George Kearns and Cleo McNelly Kearns

Pound's extraordinary productivity and range continue to generate scholarship and criticism of a quality varying from very high (Scott Hamilton) to sometimes shockingly slight (mostly unmentioned below). Politic issues seem less dominant than in recent years, while an interest in influences continues. Eliot studies, on the other hand, were meager, with books rather narrow in focus and articles for the most part thin. Exceptions, of course, are noted, especially Ted Hughes's gathered encomia. The commentary on Pound is by G.K., that on Eliot by C.M.K.

i   Pound

a. Text, Biography, and Bibliography   The outstanding achievement of 1992 is the 11-volume gathering of *Ezra Pound's Poetry and Prose: Contributions to Periodicals* (Garland), ed. Lea Baechler, A. Walton Litz, and James Longenbach. (Volume 11 contains addenda and index.) Here are the more than 2,000 entries in Section C of the 1983 Gallup bibliography, and more, reaching from youthful pieces of 1902 through Pound's old age and beyond, for the final volumes include articles as late as 1981 that reprint many letters. Among the pleasures allowed by the oversized format is the same-size photographic reproduction of each piece in its original layout and typefaces. Familiar articles, poems, and cantos are presented as they first appeared, with riches for the Poundian in such rarities as the lovely 16-line elegy, "Prayer for a Dead Brother," in the style of the lyrical passages of *Rock-Drill* and *Thrones;* written in 1954, it was published in 1972. If the entry "A Note on Danny Kaye" in Gallup's bibliography ever made you wonder what Pound had to say on that subject, you can now discover it, a two-line enthusiasm. The volumes are irresistible for browsing through Pound both cracked and sublime.

Pound spent the summer of 1912 on a walking tour of Provence, keeping a notebook as he went. The prose—"I am a lover of strange & exquisite emotions"—still touched at times by the fin-de-siècle glow of the early poems, often breaks into drafts of translations of troubadour verse as well as free sketches of original poems. The unguarded jottings have a spontaneity to them, responding to a dialectic of a past now gone, now present. Richard Sieburth has beautifully introduced and annotated what remains of the notebooks in *A Walking Tour in Southern France: Ezra Pound Among the Troubadours* (New Directions). As a preliminary, Sieburth followed in the poet's footsteps, "discovering in the process that in almost every case the actual details of observed geography clarified the most puzzling cruxes of the manuscript." The notes reflect this experience, and they report fully on Pound's reading and subsequent use of troubadour materials.

In "Ezra Pound's Ezperiment for *Esquire*" (*YULG* 67:37–46) Donald Gallup reprints an unpublished article in which Pound attempted a lively chatter and banter he thought appropriate for a popular magazine. It is not of much interest, but it makes clear that "our Brother Percy" in Canto 16 is indeed Shelley, not, as the *Companion* has it, a naval officer. *Paideuma* (21, i–ii:199–220) reproduces Lawrence S. Rainey's monograph, *A Poem Including History:* The Cantos *of Ezra Pound,* a concise, fresh introduction accompanying a 1989 exhibition at Yale.

William McNaughton's "Kingdoms of the Earp: Carpenter and Criticism (*Paideuma* 21, iii:9–40) supplies 30 pages of convincing corrections to fact, anecdote, and taste in Humphrey Carpenter's massive biography of Pound, *Serious Character: The Life of Ezra Pound* (1988), which, with its "pervasive pusillanimity," was produced "without scholarly standards, literary standards, and critical standards . . . and raises once again the vexatious question of good will."

b. General Studies Scott Hamilton's *Ezra Pound and the Symbolist Inheritance* (Princeton) is a critical study of the first importance. Experienced Poundians will find much to learn, including a cornucopia of stimulating critical suggestions. Hamilton's book is by no means a narrow study of sources and intertextuality, although he does trace Pound's fairly thorough, if idiosyncratic, responses to 19th- and early-20th-century French poetry in detail, revealing many references and resonances. Hamilton is sensitive to differences among the French poets—between Gautier and Laforgue in particular—allowing him to see the contradictory impulses they brought to, or reinforced, in Pound. Extensive knowledge of the French poets serves Hamilton as a useful hermeneutic leading to original readings of the *Lustra* poems, *Propertius, Mauberley,* and the *Cantos.* A brief notice can hardly suggest the richness of this study, which embraces considerations of Michel Foucault's *Les Mots et Les Choses* as a "veritable compendium of Poundian themes" and of the "central drama" of the *Cantos* as a "tension between the immediate presence of sign-as-signature and the absence inscribed in language with the passing of time." Hamilton's independence of judgment often reminds me of that of Donald Davie. The book concludes with a chapter on Robert Duncan's revisionary rewriting of *The Spirit of Romance.*

Making use of "Benveniste, Peirce, and Jakobson; Compagnon's investigation of citations; and recent text theory," Laszlo K. Géfin casts a cold eye on the opening lines of Canto 2 in "So-Shu and Picasso: Semiotic/Semantic Aspects of the Poundian Ideogram" (*PLL* 28:185–205). Géfin sardonically reviews the contradictory guesswork of critics and annotators of the So-Shu/Picasso ideogram, concludes that it is beyond legitimate interpretation, and seriously calls into question Pound's claims for the precision of the ideogrammic method.

Jacqueline Kaye has edited *Ezra Pound and America* (St. Martin's), a collection of essays based on papers read at a 1989 Pound Conference at Essex. Among the essays are Maria Luisa Ardizzone's additions and corrections to her *Ezra Pound e la scienza* (1987), with considerations of Modernist "machine art" (pp. 1–17); L. S. C. Bristow's study of rhetoric and polemic in the radio broadcasts (pp. 18–42); E. P. Walkiewicz and Hugh Witemeyer's research into Pound's involvement with popular-radical American politics in the '30s, through his contacts with Senator Bronson Cutting (pp. 166–80); and Eric Mottram's unusual approach to Pound through the phenomenology of Merleau-Ponty (pp. 93–113). Of particular interest is A. D. Moody's close reading (pp. 79–92) of passages from the Adams cantos, based on a study of Pound's notebooks, showing the careful "music" Pound created from documentary sources, a "formidably controlled writing, with nothing of the rag-bag about it."

Michael Faherty's "The Third Dimension: Ezra Pound and Wassily Kandinsky" (*Paideuma* 21, iii:63–77) thoughtfully examines the influence of the painter's 1912 *Über das Geistige in der Kunst,* about which Pound wrote enthusiastically in his vorticist days. Faherty draws attention to the conflicting claims of Kandinskian abstraction and early imagist theory. In an unusual approach to imagism, Daniel Tiffany's

"The Cryptic Image" (*Paideuma* 21, iii:79–92) closely examines the text of *Gaudier-Brzeska,* with its mixture of elegy and polemic. Pound was haunted by the phantoms of his friends Gaudier-Brzeska and Will Smith, who died young, and who are figured in Elpenor and Mauberley. Tiffany connects Pound's haunting with his "doctrine of the Image." The piece is marred for me—but many will find it *à la page*—by a trendy psychoanalytic prestidigitation leading to discovery of "the unspeakable pleasure which Pound takes (but cannot acknowledge) in assuming the feminine role [!?] of the one who is haunted by memories and images . . . [and] of cross-dressing."

Philip Kuberski's *A Calculus of Ezra Pound: Vocations of the American Sign* (Florida) is an encyclopedic display of poststructuralist *cum* Lacanian psychoanalytic *cum* Frankfurt School vocabulary. The critic lays relentless siege to Pound, surrounding him with catapults and towers derived from Derrida, Foucault, Adorno, Baudrillard, and the like. Had those theorists written earlier, or had Pound written later, might he have sophisticated himself with their help, or would he have remained stubbornly attached to his "conceptually reactionary" faith in natural signs, his "resolute opposition to the modernist conception of the sign's *necessary* difference with itself"? Kuberski's elaborate worrying of "the crisis of representation that characterizes modernity" has come to sound a bit *déjà écrit* (many of his concerns are more maturely considered by Scott Hamilton).

c. Relation to Other Writers   In *ABC of Influence: Ezra Pound and the Remaking of American Poetic Tradition* (Calif.), Christopher Beach studies a "Pound tradition" as manifested in the work of Charles Olson, Robert Duncan, Denise Levertov, Gary Snyder, and Edward Dorn in particular, but also extending widely, as one would expect, to number Robert Creeley, Allen Ginsberg, and many others. Problematics of influence are examined, and the book concludes with a consideration of the poetics and practice of Charles Bernstein and the Language poets.

Bruce Clarke's "Dora Marsden and Ezra Pound: *The New Freewoman* and 'The Serious Artist'" (*ConL* 33:91–112) provides a sketch of Marsden's strength and individualism, as corrective to the now "canonical misreading" of events leading up to the name change from *The New Freewoman* to *The Egoist.* Clarke demonstrates that Marsden "controlled and supervised" her journals in ways that do not support the story of Pound steamrollering "the frail, reclusive, and cranky Marsden into submission." Clarke's work is supplemented in a well-researched piece by Charles Ferrall on "Suffragists, Egoists, and the Politics of Early Modernism" (*ESC* 18:432–46).

Pound "read a good deal of Kipling—and continued to read him, however fitfully." Paul Skinner has commented on the poet's varied responses in "Pounding, Hoofing, Kipling: Attitudes to Rudyard Kipling in the Writings of Ezra Pound and Ford Madox Ford" (*Paideuma* 21, i–ii:29–43). Robert Spoo has edited "The Letters of Ezra Pound and Vladimir Dixon" (*JJQ* 29:533–56), a 1924 exchange. Dixon, a Russian-American businessman whose interests in writing and music placed him on the fringes of the Paris avant-garde, contributed one of the "litters" to the *Exagmination* of *Work in Progress*. In "Reading Ernesto Cardenal Reading Ezra Pound: Radical Inclusiveness, Epic Reconstruction and Textual Praxis" (*Chasqui* 21, ii:43–52), Tamara Williams records the Sandinista's claim that Pound was the greatest influence on his poetry of *exteriorismo*. The title of Lesley Higgins's "Making 'Connections': Medieval Master-Narratives and Ezra Pound's Fascism" (*ESC* 18:447–60) promises much, but in what sounds like an escaped seminar paper Higgins delivers little more than that Pound's "realm is a prison of cunning artifice and hate" in which his Dante "was the consummate phallic hero/poet."

d. The Shorter Poems and Translations   Selections from Ernest Fenollosa's notebooks and Pound's translations from them are examined in Steven Yao's " 'And With You Especially, There Was Nothing at Cross-Purpose': Pound's Treatment of Women in *Cathay*" (*Paideuma* 21, i–ii:101–19). Yao does not attempt to erase aspects of the poet that make him a fair target of feminist attack, yet the "actual poetic practice in *Cathay* . . . contradicts the sexism inherent in his simple equivalence between poetry and masculinity." The female speaker of "The River-Merchant's Wife," for example, "is more assertive both intellectually and emotionally" than in Li Po's original poem. Quite apart from the anti-misogynist argument, Yao's article is of interest to students of *Cathay*, especially since he works closely with some of the ideograms.

In "Ezra Pound's 'Meditatio': Two Notes" (*Paideuma* 21, i–ii:161–66) K. Narayana Chandran gives what is surely the most extended commentary that five-line poem has received. His concern is with the poem as logopoeia and as a truly remarkable "metaphorical echo" of a short poem by John Wilmot, Earl of Rochester, whom Pound had mentioned in

connection with logopoeia in *How to Read*. Sylvan Esh finds an echo
from Arnaut Daniel's "Doutz brais e critz" in the "Metro" poem, in " 'In
a Station': Provence, London" (*Paideuma* 21, i–ii:173–74); and Jyan-
Lung Lin suggests that we see "Pound's 'In a Station of the Metro' as a
Yugen Haiku" (*Paideuma* 21, i–ii:175–83).

e. The Cantos   In "Empedocles's Golden Age of Aphrodite in Pound's
Later Cantos" (*Paideuma* 21, i–ii:151–59), Elizabeth Bruce supplies valu-
able contributions to a reading of those cantos through a study of John
Burnet's *Early Greek Philosophy* (1892), which Pound had used in his early
London years, then returned to at St. Elizabeths. Robert Casillo gives a
detailed reading, with English translations, of Cantos 72 and 73, the
"Italian" cantos, in "Fascists of the Final Hour," included in a collection
of essays, *Fascism, Aesthetics, and Culture*, ed. Richard J. Golsan (New
England). There have been other excellent readings and translations of
these cantos, notably Massimo Bacigalupo's (*Paideuma* 20, iii:9–41), but
Casillo's piece is valuable for the richness of the literary, historical, and
biographical contexts it provides.

Walter Baumann, wearing his learning lightly, has searched the text for
every trace of his native and adopted lands in "The German-Speaking
World in *The Cantos*" (*Paideuma* 21, iii:41–61) and "Yeats and Ireland in
The Cantos" (*Paideuma* 21, i–ii:7–27). The references are accompanied
with a lively, informative commentary.

The title of Norman Wacker's excellent "The Subject Repositioned/
The Subject Repossessed: Authority and the Ethos of Performance in
The Pisan Cantos" (*Paideuma* 21, i–ii:81–100) suggests its concerns: the
problematics of the poetic subject's "*écriture* of his material condition,"
writing himself "into the place of his production." The Pisan cantos
become Pound's "archaeology of how individual subjects come to be
organized within economies formed by multiple overlapping representational fields . . . suggesting alternatives to the modernist cultural dominant of the post-war period."

In "Pound's Language in *Rock-Drill*: Two Theses for a Genealogy"
(*Paideuma* 21, i–ii:121–48), Maria Luisa Ardizzone has studied some
obscurely published Pound texts; books in his library; and unpublished
manuscripts, letters and notes, among them a document written in
Italian, probably in 1940, for George Santayana, which Ardizzone translates as *Pragmatic Aesthetics by Ezra Pound*. Hers is a densely learned

article, too rich to summarize briefly; the central argument is that, in continuation of his lifelong attack on metaphysics and abstraction, Pound formulated a concept of poetry as "pragmatic," as he had come to understand the term, a concept that informs the language of the later cantos.

I cannot decide whether Teresa Winterhalter's "Eyeless in Siena, or Ezra Pound's Vision Through History" (*Paideuma* 21, iii:109–22) restates in a convoluted way what I always took to be the case, or whether it is just too clever. Her subject is the Sienese cantos (42–44) and the famous *Usura* Canto 45. Winterhalter wants us to see Canto 45 not as a moment of unmediated lyric grandeur, but as Pound "standing in ironic relation to his own delivery." The Sienese cantos appear worthless as history, but they are poetic if read as a "baffling image of history . . . that calls upon us to perpetually monitor the performances of our interpretations, rather than a static moral-laden past. . . . [T]hus we are led, nearly eyeless, in grand confusion into the dramatic present of these cantos." Have we an avatar of New Criticism, a return of the repressed?

Tim Dean's "How Long Is the Pound Era?" (*Paideuma* 21, i–ii:45–63) is principally a thoughtful reading of Canto 49, the "Seven Lakes" canto, but it extends into a consideration of the canto's influence, especially on Gary Snyder, and a claim that the *Cantos* are "not just a component of High Modernism but *always already postmodern* too." Now that we have had postmodern considerations of Yeats and Woolf, and of course Joyce and Stein, are there any Modernist texts left which are not postmodern (too) (after all)?

ii Eliot

a. Text, Biography and Bibliography *T. S. Eliot's Drama: A Research and Production Sourcebook* (Greenwood) by Randy Malamud meets and exceeds the promise of its title, offering not only a copious and useful textual and production history of Eliot's plays and associated performances (including *Cats*) but a summary of Eliot's career and an informative and critical canvass of each of his major works. Also to be noted in this category is Tony Sharpe's brief biography, *T. S. Eliot: A Literary Life* (Macmillan), which emphasizes Eliot's public identity. Sharpe admits that he has uncovered little new, but anyone wanting a sound book on Eliot's life and career will not go astray with this one.

b. General Studies. In *Myth, Rhetoric, and the Voice of Authority: A Critique of Frazer, Eliot, Frye, and Campbell* (Yale), Marc Manganaro has delineated an interesting conjunction of texts and broached a potentially rich subject: the rhetoric of anthropology and its influence on certain major literary figures. He notes that anthropology was moving in Eliot's day from dependence on textual sources—and hence on a wide range of voices and points of view—to the study of a single culture mediated through the voice of one (and only one) ethnographer. Manganaro draws a parallel between this methodological shift and tendencies Eliot helped to crystallize in literature. He takes a dim view of this move, arguing that Eliot, whom he calls a "crowd pleaser" at heart, sought a master discourse that would "protect and privilege" his role as the comparatist author whose panoptic vision sees and judges all. Manganaro thus participates in a currently fashionable rhetoric of aspersion on Eliot, aspersion cast often on procedures the critic seems oblivious to in his or her own work. (See also the comments on Badenhausen and Jeffreys, below.)

A good corrective to Manganaro's argument is Manju Jain's *T. S. Eliot and American Philosophy: The Harvard Years* (Cambridge), which situates Eliot far more clearly in the anthropological and philosophical discourse of his day. Jain is especially cognizant of the importance to Eliot's work of American pragmatism, continental sociology, and comparative religion as well as British anthropology. She argues that Eliot consistently held a totalizing perspective to be impossible; with each shift in comprehension of any object, he thought, something was lost as well as gained. Any synthesizing moment was based on a forcing together of perspectives, proving sooner or later untenable. Jain extends her argument to draw parallels between the views of Heidegger and Hans-Georg Gadamer and those of Eliot, and she argues that Eliot is subject to similar blindnesses, including that of an overidealized sense of tradition. Eliot's poetry, she concludes, qualifies this idealism, giving it the dark tones his theory lacks.

With Ted Hughes's *A Dancer to God* (Faber) we leave behind the world of academic scholarship and enter the more expanded universe of poetic response. Hughes's book had its genesis in three honorific occasions. These pieces, however, are not mere pontifications; they are the record of a profound engagement with Eliot's work by a poet of very different temperament. Hughes argues that Eliot was unique in understanding the modernist sense of crisis as in fact a global phenomenon, a "spiritual catastrophe" extending beyond Western elites to the world economy as a whole. Hughes celebrates Eliot's ability to render this catastrophe and to do so in ways that have moved not only the urban sophisticate but the ordinary reader. The major resource Eliot brought to this task was his understanding of the role of shaman in the psychological exploration of the occult or hidden side of the soul, for Hughes the true locus of unconscious energy, eros, and poetic inspiration. Hughes takes a somewhat more sanguine view of the healing properties of unleashing this daimon than Eliot did. Nonetheless, he brings something to the understanding of Eliot's work without which all else is straw.

All three of the books discussed above touch in various ways on Eliot's relation to alternative and deep-seated sources of inspiration stemming from outside the usual compass of the white Western male ego. Robert Fleissner's *T. S. Eliot and the Heritage of Africa: The Magus and the Moor as Metaphor* (Peter Lang) both literalizes and extends this concern by taking up in detail the question of Eliot's debt to African and African American cultures. Fleissner's book is often difficult to follow in its hermetic tangle of cross-references, hidden allusions, and multiple linkages, but there is much valuable material and a deep engagement with the impact of Eliot's work on an actual African American readership as well as on prominent African American writers such as Ralph Ellison and Melvin Tolson. Likewise, in a study more interesting than its purview might suggest, *The Refining Fire: Herakles and Other Heroes in T. S. Eliot's Works* (Peter Lang), Laura Elizabeth Niesen de Abruña seeks to weave around the thread of interest in the Herakles myth running through Eliot's work an extended study of his attempt to envision a modern hero who would be at once "heroic, decisive, sexually potent, and spiritually alive."

c. Relation to Other Writers   In his "In Search of 'Native Moments': T. S. Eliot (Re)Reads Walt Whitman" (*SoAR* 57, iv:77–91), Richard Badenhausen traces Eliot's changing view of Whitman, a view which moved from disapprobation through reestimation to admiration. Badenhausen associates this change with Eliot's attempt to reposition himself late in his career as poet in the American tradition. For reasons unclear to me, he manages to make a perfectly comprehensible change of taste and stance sound faintly reprehensible, as if Eliot were no more than a literary pollster. Badenhausen has written straightforwardly about Eliot

in " 'When the Poet Speaks Only for Himself': The Chorus as 'First
Voice' in *Murder in the Cathedral*" (*YER* 11, iv:79–84) as well as in the
thoughtful essay on Eliot's sense of audience reviewed below.

d. The Poems and the Plays   Clare Regan Kinney's *Strategies of Poetic
Narrative: Chaucer, Spenser, Milton, Eliot* (Cambridge) is a highly theoretical but lucid study of the form and practice of the narrative poem, a
study in which Eliot's *The Waste Land* plays a role in part as counter-
example or challenge to her dominant paradigm. Kinney argues that the
narrative poem has its own poetic and problems, among these the
tendency of the lyric mode to undercut or work against its strongest
impulses and effects. Her theory is too complex to summarize here, but
when it comes to Eliot, in spite of the fact that *The Waste Land,* which
she calls "a poetic anti-narrative," does not quite meet her case, she has
deft and felicitous points to make, such as that the poem gives the effect
of "an unhappy copia," an uneasy simultaneity which defies teleology.

Stefan Hawlin in "Eliot Reads *The Waste Land: Text and Recording*"
(*MLR* 87:544–54) brings to that poem a deep immersion in the problems of the relationship of voice and performance to the written text.
Hawlin argues that there is a "special relationship between personality,
physical voice, and poetic voice" in a poet's reading of his or her own
work that makes a valuable, though not definitive, contribution to its
interpretation. He validates this view with a close study of one of Eliot's
recorded performances of *The Waste Land* (item no. 309, T6117-19, side
A, in *Literary Readings: A Checklist of the Archive of Recorded Poetry and
Literature in the Library of Congress*).

As Eliot's dissertation in philosophy has come to be better understood,
often in the light of post-structuralist theory and criticism, several critics
have made attempts to link it more closely to his poetry. Donald Childs,
in his "Metamorphoses, Metaphysics and Mysticism from 'The Death of
Saint Narcissus' to 'Burnt Norton'" (*CML* 13:15–28), has provided an
excellent example of how this might be done. Childs argues that the
figure of Narcissus is a symbol of the Bradleyan solipsism that Eliot had
undertaken to critique in *Knowledge and Experience*. He goes on to show
connections between the radically antifoundationalist critique of logo-
centrism in "Burnt Norton" and Eliot's early critique of metaphysics,
and he concludes with an interesting analysis of the modulation of
Narcissus into the figure of Echo.

N. Eakambaram's "An Indian Reading of *Murder in the Cathedral*"

(*CLS* 29, i:172–81) is an attempt to locate Hindu philosophical insights and values in the play without displacing its explicitly Christian dimensions. Eakambaram is particularly good at registering the way in which the significant moment in the hero's spiritual life occurs offstage, during one of those absences from the scene that are so strongly felt in the theater and so easy to forget on the page. His comparative points are perhaps too little qualified, as when he associates Eliot's still point unequivocally with the Advaitin absolute, or the dark night of the soul with the Upanishadic negative dialectic. Nonetheless, this reading of *Murder in the Cathedral* is of interest for its multicultural perspective.

e. Criticism In "The Shaman's Secret Heart: T. S. Eliot as Visionary, Critic and Humorist" (*TLS*, 2 Oct.:10–12), Stephen Medcalf provides an overview of much recent Eliot criticism, including a number of books already discussed in this essay. Medcalf is sympathetic enough to Eliot's own vision to find apt and pointed criticisms of those who do not see things the same way, as for instance in his strictures on Ted Hughes's *A Dancer to God*. At times too academic by half, Medcalf prefers the verbal pyrotechnician to the shaman in Eliot, but he recognizes both dimensions, and his review strikes a welcome note of civility and balance in Eliot criticism.

A similar civility is manifest in Harvey Teres's "Remaking Marxist Criticism: *Partisan Review*'s Eliotic Leftism, 1934–1936" (*AL* 64:127–153). Teres traces the *Partisan*'s critique of Marxist orthodoxy during the mid-1930s, especially in the work of William Phillips and Philip Rahv. He sees Eliot's contribution to that critique in an insistence on the relative (although never complete) autonomy of literature; on attention to general sensibility rather than to localized ideological formulation as a basis for political criticism; and on the dialectical relationship between individual and tradition. It was neither "coincidental nor capricious," Teres concludes, that two young critics who allied themselves with the proletariat in that period seized on Eliot's criticism as a valuable resource in their attempt to develop an engaged, responsible, but supple and open left criticism.

Odd and oblique but charming confirmation of this link between Eliot and left-liberal discourse is provided by the personal essay "My Kinsman, T. S. Eliot" by Frank Lentricchia (*Raritan* 11, iv:1–23). Lentricchia's engaging piece describes his own coming of age as an Italian-American kid from upper New York state whose first positive engagement with Culture leads to a life of letters, an exuberant practice of literary criticism, and eventually to the café in Soho where he composes this particular essay. Lentricchia's comic description of the denizens of that café on that day (a Chinese couple who speak an idiomatic Italian dialect, a hefty Italian man with "an important body" who has an exchange with a waiter requiring pages to decode) is informed by years of textual study—not least, as he tells us, the study of Eliot himself.

In "'Communal Pleasure' in a Uniform Culture: T. S. Eliot's Search for an Audience" (*ELN* 29, iii:61–69), Richard Badenhausen speaks to the problem of spanning classes, also invoked by Lentricchia, by arguing that Eliot's search for a unified audience that would transcend without suppressing class divisions motivated his advocacy, later in his career, of a "homogeneous" culture. In such troubling essays as those in *After Strange Gods* and *Notes Toward a Definition of Culture,* Eliot seems to wish to deny or erase all forms of difference, including ethnic and religious ones. Badenhausen argues that this wish is fueled by a desire for a unified but still disparate audience, in which the equally valid claims of the populace and the elites might both be reflected and met.

Buried somewhere in Mark Jeffreys's "The Rhetoric of Authority in T. S. Eliot's *Athenaeum* Reviews" (*SoAR* 57, iv:93–107) are a number of reasonable points about the sometimes rather contrived quality of Eliot's stance as a mandarin in matters of art and letters. Jeffreys, however, seems stunned by his own revelations. He notes with shocked distaste Eliot's use of "imposing words" and words borrowed from other disciplines. He is particularly offended by Eliot's use of *big* words, such as "irrefragable," "equipoise," and "narthekophoroi" (the last is admittedly something of a facer, although funny enough in context). Jeffrey's queasy rhetoric of vilification is not only ill-judged but distracting from otherwise viable points.

Michael North avoids these and other pitfalls in his somewhat recherché but always interesting article on Eliot's use of African American dialect, vulgar slang, and popular minstrelsy, "The Dialect In/Of Modernism: Pound and Eliot's Racial Masquerade" (*AmLH* 4:56–76). North argues that Eliot assumes the African American mask, both in private in his letters and in public in his poetry, to explore the role of the "class outlaw," the *metic,* or foreigner, whose difference from the dominant culture and linguistic practice is an occasion both for self-doubt and for self-affirmation. Using the theories of Gilles DeLeuze and Félix Guattari on deterritorialization, estrangement, and the literature of the margin,

North seeks to show, among other things, how modernism makes a strange but understandable alliance with a minority position in the arts. "Transatlantic modernism" of the kind explored and embodied by Pound and Eliot, North argues, which is "notoriously the work of exiles and émigrés," may in fact be *the* "literature of this emerging world minority."

Rutgers University
New Jersey Institute of Technology

Alexander J. Marshall, III

Faulkner criticism remains alive and well, holding steady around last year's numbers, though still down from years past. I review here 75 articles and nine book-length studies that offer a range of critical approaches and ideological perspectives. Bakhtinian and marginalist studies take the vanguard, but the most notable feature of this year's scholarship is the focus on the short story, led by the publication of *Faulkner and the Short Story,* a volume growing out of the 1990 Faulkner and Yoknapatawpha Conference.

i Bibliography, Editions, Manuscripts, and Biography

The Faulkner Newsletter & Yoknapatawpha Review continues as a source of interesting reading on Faulkner, and its checklists are useful. The April–June issue (12, ii) contains Faulkner's 1925 letters to reviewer Monte Cooper on the subject of literary criticism in which he asks her to look over some of his recent work. In terms of editions, there is good news for those of us who miss the "fifth section" of *The Sound and the Fury;* Modern Library (Random House) has issued "The Corrected Text with Appendix."

As Lawrence Wells states in his prefatory eulogy on the late Carvel Collins in *Faulkner and the Short Story,* "It was his custom in papers and articles . . . to reveal some previously unpublished fact about William Faulkner. . . . his paper which I read today—entitled ' "Ad Astra" through New Haven: Some Biographical Sources of Faulkner's War Fiction'—is no exception." What Collins reveals in this posthumously published essay (pp. 108–27) is both the importance of Faulkner's 1918 New Haven experience for "more of his fiction than 'Ad Astra'" and the fact, "not described in his biographies," that he returned to Connecticut in 1921. In

1918 Faulkner met a "shellshocked" officer named Bland who became both the RAF pilot of "Ad Astra" and Quentin Compson's foe in *The Sound and the Fury*. Faulkner also became acquainted with an American veteran of the German army, the model for the German prisoner in the story and a source for stories of fraternization in both "Ad Astra" and *A Fable*. W. Kenneth Holditch's "The Brooding Air of the Past: William Faulkner" (*Literary New Orleans,* pp. 38–50) is based on interviews with "famous Creoles" who knew Faulkner, and it considers the relation between Faulkner the young artist and the city of New Orleans. Charles A. Peek brings us "An Interview with Malcolm Cowley" (*FJ* 5, i [1989]:51–59) that took place during the First Annual Faulkner Conference in 1974. "The Falkners and the University, Mississippi, Post Office" (*FJ* 5, i [1989]:49–50) interest Gerald W. Walton: when Murray Falkner wrote the university chancellor recommending his son for the new postmaster opening, he was writing about Jack, not William. And Arthur F. Kinney enlightens us on "Ben Wasson and the Republication of Faulkner's *Marionettes*" (*FJ* 5, i [1989]:67–72) and "*Count No 'Count:* Ben Wasson's Long Homage to Faulkner" (*FJ* 5, i [1989]:73–80).

The single book-length entry in this category is James G. Watson's *Thinking of Home* (Norton), a collection of Faulkner's letters to his parents from the early period of his career, 1918–25. These "letters of a young man coming of age" provide a unique look at Faulkner's attitudes toward his family, his home, and his art. Watson has also mined this vein in " 'My Father's Unfailing Kindness': William Faulkner and the Idea of Home" (*AL* 64:749–61). His "Faulkner's 'What Is the Matter with Marriage' " (*FJ* 5, ii [1990]:69–72) reprints the 250-word piece Faulkner wrote for the New Orleans *Item-Tribune* in 1925. Also of biographical interest is Joan Williams's "Faulkner's Advice to a Young Writer" (*Faulkner and the Short Story,* pp. 253–62).

ii Criticism: General

"Mo Yan and William Faulkner: Influences and Confluences" (*FJ* 6, i [1990]: 15–24), by my predecessor at this chapter, M. Thomas Inge, looks at the way one of China's leading authors "reflects the influence of Faulkner through his narrative techniques and structural principles, his portrayal of tragic figures trapped in a nostalgia for the past, and the tendency of his narrators to create out of the histories of their own families powerful fictional interpretations of that past." Inge has also gathered three previously published essays on Faulkner into *Faulkner, Sut, and Other South-erners* (Locust Hill). Sergei Chakovsky's " 'The Whole History of the Human Heart on the Head of a Pin': Toward Faulkner's Philosophy of Composition" (*Russian Eyes on American Literature,* pp. 161–72) examines Faulkner's various comments on artistic craft. Russian eyes of a disdainful sort interest Edward A. Malone in "Nabokov on Faulkner" (*FJ* 5, ii [1990]: 63–67), and the eyes of the critical community are dealt with by Frederick Crews in "Faulkner Methodized" (*The Critics Bear it Away,* pp. 113–42).

Donald P. Duclos tells us that the source for "William Faulkner's 'A Song' for Estelle" was the French lyric "Obstination" (*FJ* 5, i [1989]:61–65). In "Horace Benbow and the Myth of Narcissa" (*AL* 64:543–66), John T. Irwin examines incest and doubling in the recurrences of the Quentin/Horace/Gavin character type. And Jean Mullin Yonke writes that "Faulkner's Civil War Women" (*FJ* 5, ii [1990]:39–62) "rise above traditional female roles" and "stand in stark contrast to his Confederate soldiers who miserably fail to protect women or defend their homeland."

iii Criticism: Special Studies

A fascinatingly complex study is Philip M. Weinstein's *Faulkner's Subject: A Cosmos No One Owns* (Cambridge). Drawing on a range of theoretical and ideological perspectives (especially Althusser, Bakhtin, and Foucault), Weinstein argues that "Faulkner's major novels are the ones in which [his] desire (imperial or beleaguered) for self-ratifying clashes most urgently with the differential forces—shaped by politics, race, and gender—that would unseat the coherence of the struggling male subject. In theme and form these novels enact the invasion of the unknown into the precincts of the familiar, and they suggest that such acts of self-constitution produce a selfhood not sutured but splintered—a subjectivity irreparably fissured, a cosmos no one owns." A difficult work, it is nonetheless rewarding in revealing the ways social norms and cultural codes shape both character and narrative. Faulkner's evolving attitude toward women is Claire Crabtree's subject in "Plots of Punishment and Faulkner's Injured Women: Charlotte Rittenmeyer and Linda Snopes" (*MichA* 24:527–39). However, Crabtree argues that "Faulkner's steps toward a more positive, inclusive paradigm for femininity are faltering ones," subverted by the tragic fates of these characters: "Simply, when his women characters become threateningly independent, he eliminates them, Charlotte through a botched abortion and Linda through exile

from the South." Faulkner's dysfunctional families receive a rather sociological treatment in Rosalie Murphy Baum's "Family Dramas: Spouse
and Child Abuse in Faulkner's Fiction" (*The Aching Hearth*, pp. 221–40).
Baum notes "the complexity and multicausal nature" of abuse in Faulkner, pointing out that "his dramatizations of intrafamilial violence support all four of the theories most favored today in explanations of spouse
and child abuse."

Peter Nicolaisen examines "'The dark land talking the voiceless
speech': Faulkner and 'Native Soil'" (*MissQ* 45:253–76) and finds that
"the tensions so often found characteristic of his works also determine his
attitude to the land." Nicolaisen argues that those "very basic tensions"
indicate "that his writing resisted the kind of ideological commitment"
that we find in his contemporary European and Nashville Agrarians; for
Faulkner, "the land could never be contained in any one ideological view,
but . . . would always have to compete with others." An "antidote to the
conspiracy theory in Professor [Lawrence] Schwartz's essentially New
Historicist account [*Creating Faulkner's Reputation* (1988)]," William
Bedford Clark's "Where Ideology Leaves Off: Cowley, Warren, and
Faulkner Revisited" (*SNNTS* 24:298–308) argues that "Faulkner's art
was from first to last inductive and mimetic, a determined effort to
reflect a world in which the particularized and specific took precedence
over the generalized and abstract. It stands by its very nature as an anti-
ideological mode of cognition." Howard C. Horsford looks at facts,
fallacies, and anachronisms in "Faulkner's (Mostly) Unreal Indians in
Early Mississippi History" (*AL* 64:311–30), noting Faulkner's "Vague-
ness—or indifference—regarding the actualities of the early history of his
state" and his preference for "imaginative reconceptions of history and
"ahistorical conflations of chronology and event." While Gabriele Gut-
ting's *Yoknapatawpha: The Function of Geographical and Historical Facts
in William Faulkner's Fictional Picture of the Deep South* (Peter Lang)
makes some interesting comments about "the space-time network of
[Faulkner's] narrative design," the book is more interesting and useful as
a reference for cross-checking Faulkner's real and fictional worlds.

iv **Individual Works to 1929**

Lothar Hönnighausen examines parallels in "Thomas Mann's *Bud-
denbrooks* and William Faulkner's *Sartoris* as Family Novels" (*FJ* 6, i
[1990]:33–45). The original work, not finally published until 1973, is the

subject of "Medicine—Faulkner's Guide to the Future of Humanity" (*UMSE* n.s. 10:177–80); Teri Lucas shows how Will Falls, Miss Jenny, and Doctors Peabody, Alford, and Brandt of *Flags in the Dust* provide "a comparative study of humanity's past, present, and future within the story line of old Bayard's medical problem." Faulkner warns us, Lucas argues, that "the knowledge of the future must always be tempered with the values of the past." Philip Cohen studies some differences between Faulkner's vision and Ben Wasson's revision in "*Flags in the Dust, Sartoris,* and the Unforeseen Consequences of Editorial Surgery" (*FJ* 5, i [1989]:25–43).

As usual, there was a lot of interest this year in *The Sound and the Fury.* Sanae Tokizane considers Faulkner's revisions of the "Anecdote of the Vase: The Introduction to *The Sound and the Fury*" (*Faulkner Studies* 2:53–70). Margaret D. Bauer's "The Evolution of Caddy: An Intertextual Reading of *The Sound and the Fury* and Ellen Gilchrist's *The Annunciation*" (*SLJ* 25, i:40–51) contains some interesting reflections on the question of incest between Caddy and Quentin. Robert E. Fleming suggests "James Weldon Johnson's *God's Trombones* as a Source for Faulkner's Rev'un Shegog" (*CLAJ* 36:24–30). And Philip Dubuisson Castille examines "Dilsey's Easter Conversion in Faulkner's *The Sound and the Fury*" (*SNNTS* 24:423–33), finding "that she turns away from the Compsons after the Easter Sunday service"; Shegog's sermon motivates her "to break free . . . and renounce her years of resignation and denial." But perhaps the most interesting essay of the year is Kevin Railey's "Cavalier Ideology and History: The Significance of Quentin's Section in *The Sound and the Fury*" (*ArQ* 48, iii:77–94). Examining the history of both the region in general and Faulkner's family in particular, Railey argues that Quentin "embodies an ideological orientation within Faulkner's socio-historical milieu, one losing the social power it once possessed." This "orientation" explains his obsession with Caddy's virginity—"the very cornerstone of Cavalier ideology was the 'purity' or 'honor' of white women within the upper class"—and his suicide in 1910 "may be seen as the symbolic embodiment" of the Cavaliers' loss of status that was signaled historically by the 1911 political defeat of Leroy Percy, "the last Delta planter to hold a major political office in Mississippi."

v Individual Works, 1930–1939

There were a number of good works on *As I Lay Dying* this year, including Warwick Wadlington's As I Lay Dying: *Stories out of Stories*

(Twayne). Elizabeth Hayes examines the "Tension Between Darl and Jewel" (*SLJ* 24, ii:49–61), calling it "absolutely necessary" for both Darl's identity and the novel's structure. Hayes considers Darl "the single most important character in *As I Lay Dying*," and the essential issues Darl's central preoccupation with Jewel and Jewel's relationship with Addie. Relationships with Addie and her relation to language concern Paul S. Nielsen in "What Does Addie Bundren Mean, and How Does She Mean It?" (*SLJ* 25, i:33–39). For a psychoanalytic approach from the scientific perspective, see "Faulkner's *As I Lay Dying:* Issues of Method in Applied Analysis" (*PsychQ* 61:65–84), by Francis Baudry, M.D. Parallels with Augustine's *Confessions* form the subject of Patrick Samway's "Faulkner's *As I Lay Dying* and St. Augustine" (*Faulkner Studies* 2:21–34). And feminist insights are offered by Deborah Clarke and Christiane P. Makward in "Camus, Faulkner, Dead Mothers: A Dialogue" (*Camus's L'Étranger: Fifty Years On*, ed. Adele King [St. Martin's], pp. 194–208). Iorgos Galanos studies "The Metaphoricity of Memory in Faulkner's *As I Lay Dying*" (*FJ* 5, ii [1990]:3–13) and concludes that "By inverting the oppositional hierarchy of memory and movement within metaphor, Faulkner offers a vehicle with which modernism can more successfully carry out its project to modernize language and render it capable of registering space and movement." A most intriguing and complex analysis is presented by John T. Matthews in "*As I Lay Dying* in the Machine Age" (*Boundary II* 19, i:69–94). Matthews contends that "the Bundrens have already been *constituted* by the dialectical history of capitalist agriculture, commodified economic and social relations, and the homogenizations of mass culture in the nineteenth-century South," and that "Faulkner's modernist treatment of the social reality indicated by the Bundrens' predicament is not entirely absorbed into the aesthetic of modernist abstraction that universalizes their story. Rather, the traces of very specific historical conditions appear in the novel, and they appear in such a way as to suggest that modernization is part of a dialectic internal to the workings of the novel and of the history it reflects upon."

Pamela E. Knights focuses on Horace Benbow in "The Cost of Single-Mindedness: Consciousness in *Sanctuary*" (*FJ* 5, i [1989]:3–10), arguing that "Faulkner uses Horace to give a hearing to voices sensed only at the edges of previous works." Jay Watson, on the other hand, suggests that "The Failure of Forensic Storytelling in *Sanctuary*" (*FJ* 6, i [1990]:147–66) may have "proved cathartic for Faulkner" by purging Yoknapatawpha County of the ineffectual Horace Benbow and "paving the way for later, sunnier versions of forensic telling" in the form of Gavin Stevens.

Twayne's Masterwork Studies has brought out Alwyn Berland's *Light in August: A Study in Black and White,* a good general guide to one of Faulkner's more difficult and problematic works. Martin Bidney studies influences and parallels in "*The Ring and the Book* and *Light in August:* Faulkner's Response to Browning" (*VN* 81:51–59), arguing that "Like Browning, Faulkner seeks to show how the exercise of visionary power makes possible a penetrating moral psychology of crime and punishment." Bidney calls the novel "Faulkner's most comprehensive attempt to reassess and refashion, in his own terms, the poetic legacy of the nineteenth century." And our perceptions of Joe Christmas and his existential identity form the subject of Irene Gammel's "'Because He Is Watching Me': Spectatorship and Power in Faulkner's *Light in August*" (*FJ* 5, i [1989]:11–23).

The appendices to *Absalom, Absalom!* are examined from two perspectives. Daniel Ferrer questions "Editorial Changes in the Chronology of *Absalom, Absalom!:* A Matter of Life and Death?" (*FJ* 5, i [1989]:45–48); and Pamela Dalziel finds three additional narrative voices in the Chronology, the Genealogy, and the map in her "*Absalom, Absalom!:* The Extension of Dialogic Form" (*MissQ* 45:277–94), arguing that, far from providing resolution or closure, these additions maintain the polyphonic play. Another Bakhtinian study of polyphony is Minghan Xiao's "The Fundamental Unfinalizability of *Absalom, Absalom!*" (*NOR* 18 [1991]:34–47). Heberden W. Ryan's "Behind Closed Doors: The Unknowable and the Unknowing in *Absalom, Absalom!*" (*MissQ* 45:295–312) examines the various images of doors that block understanding for both characters within the novel and the reader who "is destined to remain outside the door (text), knocking (reading) again and again in a futile attempt to gain entry." In "Through Rosa's Looking-glass: Narcissism and Identification in Faulkner's *Absalom, Absalom!*" (*MissQ* 45:313–21), Alain Geoffroy psychoanalyzes Rosa's motives in conducting her "decisive raid on Sutpen's Hundred, which eventually leads the Sutpen story to its conclusion." And parallels between Sutpen and Flem Snopes form the subject of Corinne Dale's "*Absalom, Absalom!* and the Snopes Trilogy: Southern Patriarchy in Revision" (*MissQ* 45:323–37). Dale argues that "Both serve to acknowledge the financial basis of Southern paternalism and to suggest the kinship of Old South planter and New South businessman. Moreover, by exposing the contradictions inherent in economic systems justified by paternalism, Faulkner also more radically challenges patriarchy itself."

In *"Absalom, Absalom!* and the Ripple-Effect of the Past" (*UMSE* n.s. 10:56–66), Robert Dunne presents "a critical overview of the major characters' conception of time and history, via their tellings of the Sutpen story." Tim Poland suggests that Quentin's visit to "the Sutpen burial plot offers up the plot" of "Faulkner's *Absalom, Absalom!"* (*Expl* 50:239–41). And an excellent study is Robert Dale Parker's Absalom, Absalom!: *The Questioning of Fictions* (Twayne [1991]), enlightening both as an introduction for new readers and as a critical reading in its own right.

Faulkner's ambivalent relation to the past is the subject of two very different essays on two very different works. In "A Precarious Pedestal: The Confederate Woman in Faulkner's *Unvanquished"* (*JAmS* 26:233–246), Diane Roberts argues that "She becomes, for him, a figure in crisis, both a nostalgic evocation of some epic or Edenic past and a critique of plantation pieties." And Patrick McHugh's "William Faulkner and the American New Jerusalem" (*ArQ* 48:24–43) studies *The Wild Palms* as an example of Faulkner's criticism and support of "the Edenic tradition."

vi Individual Works, 1940–1949

The relationship between narrator and material is the subject of William J. Mistichelli's "Perception Is a Sacred Cow: The Narrator and Ike Snopes in William Faulkner's *The Hamlet"* (*FJ* 5, ii [1990]:15–33). But most of the critical interest in the works of this period focused on *Go Down, Moses.*

Is *Go Down, Moses* a novel, a collection of stories, or a short story cycle? The short answer is "Yes." In her study of "Contending Narratives: *Go Down, Moses* and the Short Story Cycle" (*Faulkner and the Short Story,* pp. 128–48), Susan V. Donaldson finds "a battlefield . . . , an unyielding contest between individual stories of resistance and discontinuity and the all-encompassing narrative of the McCaslins." Robert H. Brinkmeyer, Jr., examines "striking parallels between the early Christian ascetics" and Isaac McCaslin in *"Go Down, Moses* and the Ascetic Imperative" (*Faulkner and the Short Story,* pp. 206–28). To what extent did Faulkner's discovery of Columbus affect Part Four of "The Bear"? That is the subject of Nancy Dew Taylor's *"Go Down, Moses* and the Literature of the New World Commemoration" (*FJ* 6, i [1990]:25–32), an interesting argument that Faulkner's reading of "Columbus-related materials" in

1942 helped shape the style and substance of that section of the novel. One of the more intriguing connections seems to be related not so much to Columbus himself as to Jacob Wasserman's biography ("For the past is only apparently past. Everything is, and persists").

Lucas Beauchamp receives critical attention in two interesting essays. In "Man on the Margin: Lucas Beauchamp and the Limitations of Space" (*FJ* 6, i [1990]: 67–79), Keith Clark argues that Faulkner "not only cuts Lucas off from his own people, but he denies him a language and a voice through which he can communicate *his* story." Clark sees this "major defect" of *Intruder in the Dust* as resulting from Faulkner's inability "to cut the umbilical cord linking him to his native homeland— a South with a cancerous racial history and a proclivity to confine the blackman to the space of a nigger." Philip M. Weinstein is a bit more generous, tracing the evolution of Lucas Beauchamp from the 1940 stories "A Point of Law" and "Gold Is Not Always" through *Go Down, Moses* and *Intruder in the Dust*. In " 'He Come and Spoke for Me': Scripting Lucas Beauchamp's Three Lives" (*Faulkner and the Short Story*, pp. 229–52), Weinstein comments that "To say who Lucas Beauchamp is involves, irreducibly, charting the racial identity of William Faulkner."

vii Individual Works, 1950–1962

In "Conceiving the Enemy: The Rituals of War in Faulkner's *A Fable*" (*Faulkner Studies* 2:1–19), Joseph R. Urgo argues that the novel "is not a war story. Rather, it is a novel about the creation of narrative out of formalized (or perhaps bureaucratic) human sacrifice. Like much of what Faulkner wrote in his apocrypha, *A Fable* seeks to undermine the stories we tell about war and warmaking." Kevin I. Eyster's "The Personal Narrative in Fiction: Faulkner's *The Reivers*" (*WF* 51:11–21) notes that "the fictive world of Lucius Priest, with his grandson as audience, consistently exhibits characteristics identified, examined, and discussed by folklorists collecting personal narratives in their fieldwork."

viii The Stories

The shopworn phrase "relatively neglected" may no longer be applicable to Faulkner's short stories, thanks largely to the publication of *Faulkner and the Short Story*. John T. Matthews leads off with "Shortened Stories: Faulkner and the Market" (pp. 3–37), examining "how a body of Faulk-

ner's short fiction internalizes the conditions of the literary marketplace,"
how his stories "incorporate formally and thematically the sense of
curtailment or abbreviation, the processes of aesthetic commodification,
and the nature of mass cultural consumption." James B. Carothers adds
to his fine work on the genre and expounds upon Faulkner's references to
"whoring" in "Faulkner's Short Story Writing and the Oldest Profession"
(pp. 38–61). Hans H. Skei's "Beyond Genre? Existential Experience in
Faulkner's Short Fiction" (pp. 62–77) argues that a handful of Faulkner's
best stories transcend the limits of the form by "present[ing] experience,
episodes, critical situations, which are not of the everyday type, which
are not controlled and tempered by society, rules, and conventions,
which somehow elude us in normal daily life, but which may be seen as
more basic, more primitive, and perhaps more *genuine* than the experience relayed in stories of action and event in a society of men and
women, at a given time and in a specific place, from which the stories
never take off." David Minter examines resistance to and attempts at
reconciliation in " 'Carcassone,' 'Wash,' and the Voices of Faulkner's
Fiction" (pp. 78–107). John T. Irwin's "*Knight's Gambit:* Poe, Faulkner,
and the Tradition of the Detective Story" (pp. 149–73) shows how
"Faulkner interprets or inflects various conventions and images" associated with the genre. Tao Jie surveys the history of "Faulkner's Short
Stories and Novels in China" (pp. 174–205). And the collection ends
with a section on "Soviet Perceptions of Faulkner's Short Stories." Sergei
Chakovsky's "William Faulkner's Short Stories in the USSR: An Intro-
duction" (pp. 263–68), Maya Koreneva's "Faulkner's Short Stories in
Russian" (pp. 269–71), and Ekaterina Stetsenko's "Soviet Criticism of
Faulkner's Short Stories" (pp. 272–76) cover much of the same ground in
terms of publication history and critical reception, while Tatiana Mo-
rozova is more analytical in "Between God and Satan: Vision of the
Human Predicament in Short Stories By Faulkner and Russian Authors"
(pp. 277–81), arguing that "The invisible conflict between God and
Satan lies at the core of all visible conflicts: social, political, national,
personal, and so on"—a point we certainly would not have expected from
that international quarter but a few years ago. Finally, Tamara Denisova
notes the affinities between Faulkner's South and her own world in
"Faulkner and the Ukraine" (pp. 282–85).

Allen Ramsey's " 'Spotted Horses' and Spotted Pups" (*FJ* 5, ii [1990]:
35–38) suggests that Faulkner's title may derive from and allude to a

regionalism, "spotted pups," and "could be an analogue not only for the mongrel horses but for the Snopes clan as well."

Gene M. Moore's study "Of Time and Its Mathematical Progression: Problems of Chronology in Faulkner's 'A Rose For Emily' " (*SSF* 29:195–204) argues that "evidence from the [original] manuscript makes it possible to solve some of the problems of Miss Emily's chronology by fixing the date of her father's death." Moore briefly summarizes eight previous chronologies before offering his own version of Emily's life, 1856–1930. James M. Wallace addresses the question of Homer's homosexuality in "Faulkner's 'A Rose for Emily' " (*Expl* 50:105–7), saying that the question is somewhat moot, the evidence coming strictly from the narrator who is involved in "a sloppy bucket-brigade of gossip" and therefore unreliable. In "A Good Rose Is Hard to Find: Southern Gothic as Signs of Social Dislocation in Faulkner and O'Connor" (*Image and Ideology*, pp. 105–23), Margie Burns contends "that the Southern gothic is a literary technique which both enacts and conceals the dehumanization of response *to* the South, by representing it as a dehumanization of response *in* the South."

Jacques Pothier's "Of Rats and Uncles: Time Out of Joint in 'Uncle Willy' 's Jefferson" (*Faulkner Studies* 2:35–52) finds the story "a crucible of a great deal that is in previous or later fiction, from *Sartoris* to *The Reivers*," and suggests that it "may be considered a working through of the conflict" with authority that was "disguised" in "A Rose for Emily." And Raymond Benoit compares two works which "Americanize" the mythological "magnetism" of the World Tree in "Archetypes and Ecotones: The Tree in Faulkner's 'The Bear' and Irving's 'Rip Van Winkle' " (*NConL* 22, i:4–5).

Randolph-Macon College

Albert J. DeFazio III

Fitzgerald attracted no full-length studies and only two dozen articles this year, but an otherwise humdrum year was revived by the appearance of a four-volume anthology of criticism and the "First International F. Scott Fitzgerald Conference," hosted by Hofstra University and attended by scholars from several countries. Read the details, along with professional news and notes, reviews, and bibliography, in the second and third volumes of the *F. Scott Fitzgerald Society Newsletter,* coedited by Jackson R. Bryer, Alan Margolies, and Ruth Prigozy.

Hemingway scholarship finds itself burgeoning with biography and waist-deep in gender studies but sadly devoid of much-needed critical editions. Conferences celebrating the 50th anniversary of *For Whom the Bell Tolls* yielded two valuable collections. Other notable events included the discovery of 20 additional *Toronto Star* articles, the appearance of three biographies, and the swelling of the available archive at the John F. Kennedy and Princeton University libraries. Charles Oliver's distinguished tenure as editor of the semiannual *Hemingway Review* came to a close; his successor, Susan F. Beegel, has already made strides to ensure that it will continue to include the rigorous scholarship that makes it one of the finest of author journals. She has modified the format, expanded the book reviews, and included a "letters" section designed to encourage lively debate (indeed it has) in an already thriving industry.

i   Textual Studies, the Archives, and Bibliography

Matthew J. Bruccoli's "Getting It Right: The Publishing Process and the Correction of Factual Errors—with Reference to *The Great Gatsby,*" pp. 40–59 in Dave Oliphant, ed., *Essays in Honor of William B. Todd* (Austin: Harry Ransom Humanities Research Center, 1991), argues that editors of "documents of social history," such as Fitzgerald's works, are obliged to emend "obvious factual blunders that can be corrected by simple substitution" and provides numerous examples of "external" and "internal" errors (i.e., inconsistencies) that merit emendation in *Gatsby*. Failure to do so, he wryly concludes, leaves us "to beat on, goats against the current. . . ." If you missed the illustrated brochure of the same title, "Celestial Eyes: From Metamorphosis to Masterpiece" (see *ALS 1991*, pp. 153–54), you have a second chance to read Charles Scribner III's discussion of Fitzgerald's indebtedness to Francis Cugat and learn of Matthew J. Bruccoli's discovery of eight other sketches of the *Gatsby* dust jacket (*PULC* 53, ii:140–55).

Douglas LaPrade gives us a bilingual edition of Hemingway's *The Spanish Earth/Tierra de España* (*Archivos de la Filmoteca* [Valencia, Spain] 13:9–21) and an accompanying preface, "Introducción a *Tierra de España*" (pp. 6–8). To my knowledge, LaPrade's edition represents the only English-language publication of Hemingway's narrative since its first appearance. Susan Seitz adds "A Final (?) Note on the Textual Errors of Ernest Hemingway's 'Summer People'" (*HN* 11, ii:2–5); she consults the manuscript and discovers a "transcriptual error, a reinserted scene, and some more significant changes in punctuation." Thus, we have another voice in the chorus of pleas for a critical edition of the Hemingway canon. Scrutinizing the University of Texas manuscript, Max Westbrook, in "Text, Ritual, and Memory: Hemingway's 'Big Two-Hearted River'" (*NDQ* 60, iii:14–25), hails its importance, identifying variants and proposing that the story is a ritual of restoration.

"News from the Hemingway Collection" (*HN* 11, ii:58–60; 12, i:106–108), by Megan Floyd Desnoyers et al., continues to keep scholars abreast of new acquisitions, openings, and research grants at the John F. Kennedy Library. The *Hemingway Review* notes that Princeton University Library has opened the archives of Charles Scribner's Sons, a trove including more than 400 of Hemingway's letters and 30 boxes of film, publicity materials, and copies of manuscripts. And the *Toronto Star* has scooped William White's *Ernest Hemingway Dateline: Toronto* (1985) in announcing William McGeary and William Burrill's discovery of "20 definite and five probable 'new' stories" by Hemingway in the *Star*'s archives (1 Mar. 1992: F1–F8).

I continue to contribute the "Current Bibliography" to the *Hemingway Review* (*HN* 11, ii:64–72; 12, i:99–105) as well as the *Fitzgerald Newsletter* (2, i:9–13).

ii Biography

Jeffrey Meyers provides the most significant biographical study of Fitzgerald of the year: "Scott Fitzgerald and Edmund Wilson: A Troubled Friendship" (*ASch* 61:375–88) notes that Wilson's criticism of his friend's work seemed to have a supportive/destructive nature and that Wilson sometimes appeared more interested in destroying Fitzgerald's talent than in encouraging it. Alfred Meyer adds "The Fitzgerald Syndrome" (*Psychology Today* 25:73–74+), which considers the inner and outer forces that snatched the arrows of F. Scott and John F. Kennedy in midflight.

Hemingway's biographers fasted last year, serving up only Michael Reynolds's *Hemingway: An Annotated Chronology* (Manly/Omnigraphics, 1991), which whetted appetites for this year's feast. Now appears the third volume of James R. Mellow's "Lost Generation" trilogy, *Hemingway: A Life Without Consequences* (Houghton Mifflin), complete with an engaging prose style and a thoughtful commentary, which is sympathetic without being uncritical. It tells the whole life but focuses largely on Hemingway's Paris years, an indulgence that readers might grant Mellow, given the temporal bent of his previous biographies on Stein and the Fitzgeralds. *Hemingway* is unencumbered by a lockstep thesis: neither war nor love nor mother is isolated for praise or blame. But the question of gender receives special attention, and so do Hemingway's numerous relationships with other men. Here, Mellow sees a pattern: Hemingway often chose male friends who were older and willing to be instructed. Picking nits, I would quarrel with the stipulation "older," because Hemingway had many friends who were younger: Leicester Hemingway noted that Ernest liked to have a spiritual kid brother around, and men such as Arnold Samuelson and A. E. Hotchner served this purpose. And Hemingway did not reserve for males alone his penchant for "teaching": he shared his travels with Hadley, his safari with Pauline, his fishing with Mary. But Mellow rightly emphasizes the importance of camaraderie, especially in conjunction with *place;* for the combination of these two elements during Hemingway's youth brought him "incredibly close to the still point of the world"—a world, even an Eden, that he would again and again try to re-create in his fiction. Mellow deftly sculpts a meaningful context for Hemingway's friendships, particularly during his adolescence and the fascinating years of his artistic growth in Paris; the journey down, post-World War II, seems to gain its own momentum, and we are through so quickly that the aged Hemingway does not entirely over-shadow his youthful self. Mellow seems well aware that his is but one biography among dozens, and he consciously reveals his methodology as he presents his case. Such reflexivity has miffed a few reviewers, but I find his occasional admission regarding biographical cruxes—"there is noth-ing conclusive to say, either way"—a refreshingly honest statement. Well-documented and eminently readable, Mellow's biography is a welcome addition to a laden shelf.

Michael Reynolds has published the third installment, *Hemingway: The American Homecoming* (Blackwell), of what was scheduled to be a five-volume biography. He takes us to the spring of 1929, and I suspect that his concluding volumes will be hefty if he intends to engage his considerable investigative talents on the relatively little-known period of Hemingway's decline. Reynolds's strengths remain his critical acumen, his stylistic grace, and his tireless excavation of the archive. But while his opus answers many questions, his methodology raises a few, too. His attention to detail is universally praised; but his penchant for dramatiz-ing these details, both in his italicized headnotes and in his periodic forays into Hemingway's thoughts, prompt reviewers to condemn his "flair for fiction" and his "creative pictorialism." True, these are nonstan-dard features, but biography of Hemingway has grown beyond the standard, and Reynolds, like Mellow, seems to realize that he is writing not *the* story but *his* story of Hemingway's life. So long as his scholarship meets the rigorous standards that he has established for himself and other biographers, I say we should allow him to dress his facts as he pleases.

Gioia Diliberto's *Hadley* (Ticknor and Fields) improves on Alice Hunt Sokoloff's *Hadley: The First Mrs. Hemingway* (1973). The new biography owes much of its richness to Sokoloff's taped interviews with Hadley Mowrer, and it charts the courtship, marriage, divorce, and parenting of the Hemingways. Its strength lies in its expanded descriptions of bio-graphical cruxes; for example, contrary to allegations that Hadley inten-tionally lost her husband's "complete works," Diliberto cogently argues, in concert with Hadley's consistent account, that the suitcase was indeed stolen. The biography's weakness is its incomplete understanding of Hemingway and his art; too often Diliberto relies on others to comment on the relationship between the Hemingways' lives and Ernest's work. At one juncture, she scolds Hemingway for encouraging Hadley to play the piano at parties: "Like all egotists, Ernest assumed that anything he was interested in was inherently important and fascinating." Her observation seems valid, but I wonder if Hemingway's "assumption" isn't one of the qualities of his character that made him think that readers would be spellbound by a description of a bullfight or a fishing trip.

Lighter biographical fare includes a contemporary account of Hemingway's role in the liberation of Paris, found in Nelson D. Lankford, ed., *OSS Against the Reich: The World War II Diaries of Colonel David K. E. Bruce* (Kent State, 1991); some readers will be surprised to learn that Hemingway had help in accomplishing this feat. James R. Corey adds "An Encounter with Hemingway" (*HN* 12, i:77–79), a vignette about seeing, but not approaching, the author in a roadside café in Montana four days before his death. And Megan Floyd Desnoyers draws on the Kennedy Library's rich archives for her "Ernest Hemingway: A Storyteller's Legacy" (*Prologue—Quarterly of the National Archives* 24:335–50), which includes wonderful photography and excerpts from unpublished works.

iii Influences, Sources, Parallels

Tracing Fitzgerald's influence, T. Jeff Evans in "A Cultural Confluence: Ross Macdonald and F. Scott Fitzgerald" (*Clues* 13:21–43) notes how Macdonald's *The Barbarous Coast* incorporates sources from *The Last Tycoon* and claims that the authors share "a similar moral vision of our urban existence, a vision in whose articulation Macdonald consciously turned to Fitzgerald for subject matter, structure, technique and theme." Paul Giles explores Fitzgerald's religious themes and images in "Conformity and Parody: Scott Fitzgerald and *The Great Gatsby*," pp. 169–87 in *American Catholic Arts and Fictions* (Cambridge), concentrating on the "Catholic cultural inheritance" which manifests itself in *The Great Gatsby*, his "most profound yet, at the same time, most enigmatic meditation upon the mythologies of Catholicism." Timothy M. Rivinus, M.D., gives us "Euphoria and Despair: Youthful Addiction in *This Side of Paradise* and *Novel with Cocaine* [M. Ageyer]" (*Dionysos: The Literature and Addiction TriQuarterly* 4, ii:15–29), a critical-biographical study that looks at two works that "graphically depict youthful addiction in a way that older, nonaddicted people seldom comprehend" and traces Armory Blaine's budding alcoholism and Vadim Maslennikov's dependence on cocaine.

Examining Hemingway's journalism as a source for his fiction, Elizabeth Dewberry Vaughn in " 'Truer Than Anything True': *In Our Time* and Journalism" (*HN* 11, ii:11–18) shows how Hemingway's interest in the relationship between journalism and fiction allowed him to question the nature of reality in both kinds of texts. Natalia Yakimenko's "Ernest Hemingway: The Road to Literary Craft" (*Russian Eyes on American Literature*, pp. 142–60) also explores the journalism and the "textual dialogue" between it and "Soldier's Home" and "Big Two-Hearted River," concluding, perhaps too quickly, that the aesthetic theories of Anderson, Pound, Stein, and Eliot were more important to Hemingway's development than his own life experiences—including journalism.

Several articles contemplate the role of works and artists who helped to shape Hemingway's artistic vision. Charles L. Ross, " 'The Saddest Story' Part Two: *The Good Soldier* and *The Sun Also Rises*" (*HN* 12, i:26–34), remarks the similarities between Jake Barnes and John Dowell and characterizes Hemingway's first novel as his "finest Fordian performance." The influence of Homer is the subject of Kathleen Morgan and Luis Losada's "Santiago in *The Old Man and the Sea:* A Homeric Hero" (*HN* 12, i:35–51), where Santiago is compared with heroes from the *Iliad* and *Odyssey*. J. Gerald Kennedy and Kirk Curnutt explore Gertrude Stein's influence in "Out of the Picture: Mrs. Krebs, Mother Stein, and 'Soldier's Home' " (*HN* 12, i:1–11) and suggest that Hemingway may be pushing her "out of the picture" just as the Rhine "does not show" in the story. Robert Gajdusek, in "A Brief Safari into the Religious Terrain of *Green Hills of Africa*" (*NDQ* 60, iii:26–40), examines the "multi-leveled Joycean structure and technique," particularly the pattern of Christian iconography. Tracing Hemingway's use of the story of "Bluebeard," Steven C. Roe's "Opening Bluebeard's Closet: Writing and Aggression in Hemingway's *The Garden of Eden* Manuscript" (*HN* 12, i:52–66) discovers "disturbing psychological truths" about David, who is "self-absorbed, prideful, detached, and compulsive." Hildy Coleman's note, " 'Cat' and 'Hills': Two Hemingway Fairy Tales" (*HN* 12, i:67–72) posits "Rapunzel" and "Clever Hans" as possible sources.

Exploring parallels, Richard S. Pressman gives us "Individualists or Collectivists?: Steinbeck's *In Dubious Battle* and Hemingway's *To Have and Have Not*" (*StQ* 25:119–33), suggesting that both novels are "simultaneously engagements with the Depression and evasions of it." And Joseph M. Flora compares the short story collections *Collected Stories* and *In Our Time* in "Stegner and Hemingway as Short Story Writers: Some Parallels and Contrasts in Two Masters" (*SDR* 30, i:104–19).

Two articles help to account for the technical skills and accurate details of Hemingway's fiction. William Braasch Watson consults the experts about Robert Jordan's knowledge of demolition in "Investigating Hemingway" (*NDQ* 60, i:1–27) and points readers to the people, places, and texts that Hemingway drew on while writing *Bell*. Guy Stern's "Comrades-in-Arms: Models for Fiction. Hemingway and the Exiles from Nazi Germany," pp. 108–27 in Luis Costa et al., eds., *German and International Perspectives on the Spanish Civil War: The Aesthetics of Partisanship* (Camden House), documents Hemingway's interaction with numerous exiles, especially while producing *The Spanish Earth.*

iv Criticism

a. Full-length Studies: Fitzgerald   Do not be misled by the title: *Gatsby's Party: The System and the List in Contemporary Narrative* (Purdue), by Patti White, is not about Gatsby's tribulations in composing his guest list. Rather, she uses that list to frame her discussion of systems-theoretical methodology, which turns out to be an incredibly fast-moving train, despite bearing its freight of jargon. Readers uninitiated in systems theory receive no aid from White and will likely find that this book speeds beyond their ken.

b. Full-length Studies: Hemingway   This year three studies on Hemingway appeared: one monograph, part of the "modern novelists" series; a study of the lyrical pattern of *In Our Time;* and an allusion specialist's view of *The Sun Also Rises.* The best of these is Peter Messent's *Ernest Hemingway* (St. Martin's), which examines Hemingway's "response to modernity and its conditions," treating style, the themes of identity and gender, and place. Although it claims to be for all readers, Messent's text develops themes and discusses techniques that novices will have to meet in some other companion volume. He focuses, for example, on the ramifications of Hemingway's style—one that he describes as filtering the narrative through a character's consciousness before revealing that a "larger political and institutional frame had invalidated the meaning of that individual response." In his chapter on identity he argues that Hemingway's best effects occur early in his career "when he is charting the uncertainties and instabilities of the subject's position"; later, a protagonist like Colonel Cantwell will act with authority which leads to a loss of Hemingway's fictional power (although some of this power returns with *Islands* and *Eden*). Messent's discussion of gender leads him to conclude that Hemingway's constant dwelling on the subject of gender role and sexual identity suggests "his awareness of the uncertainty of the traditional gender hierarchies." Provocative and compact, Messent's study will guide advanced students and teachers alike.

In *Hemingway's* In Our Time: *Lyrical Dimensions* (Bucknell) Wendolyn E. Tetlow aims to demonstrate that "*In Our Time* is a coherent and integral work," something that others have accomplished and that she reaffirms through close readings which are especially good in relating the vignettes to their surrounding stories. She means to prove her point by characterizing the "emotive structure or tonal patterns," yet these essential terms remain insufficiently defined. Less satisfactory is Wolfgang E. H. Rudat's *Alchemy in* The Sun Also Rises: *Hidden Gold in Hemingway's Narrative* (Mellen): this study of allusions unearths a few nuggets, but Rudat's speculations seem incredible to me.

c. Collections: Fitzgerald   A two-year lull in the publication of collections has come to a close with editor Henry Claridge's four-volume *F. Scott Fitzgerald: Critical Assessments* (Robertsbridge, U.K.: Helm Information). This anthology has eluded me: only 600 sets, costing about $500 apiece, were published. But Jackson R. Bryer's laudatory review (*Fitzgerald Newsletter* 3 [1993]:12–13) indicates that the 226 selections are well-chosen and sensibly arranged. Volume 1 includes "Fitzgerald in Context" and "Memories and Reminiscences"; volumes 2 and 3 treat the major publications; and the final volume houses "General Perspectives" and "Fitzgerald and Other Writers." The most recent essays date from the mid-1980s, assuring more work for anthologists in the near-term.

d. Collections: Hemingway   Rena Sanderson has gathered nine fine essays presented originally at the "Hemingway in Idaho" conference (June 1989). To *Blowing the Bridge: Essays on Hemingway and* For Whom the Bell Tolls (Greenwood), she adds two previously published essays and her own introduction succinctly summarizing the history of the novel's composition, critical reception, and current reassessment. Kurt Vonnegut's keynote talk on Hemingway struck me as uninspired, and the edited transcript presented here, "Kurt Vonnegut on Ernest Hemingway" (pp. 19–25), reads like informal recollections of a writer who simultaneously recognizes that Hemingway had an "admirable soul the size of Kilimanjaro" and disdains the long shadow that the soul cast. Michael Reynolds's "Hemingway's West: Another Country of the Heart" (pp. 27–35) demonstrates how Hemingway's visit to the American West in 1928 changed the author and his fiction; the early protagonists, "victims of outside forces," had little in common with "the violent, confident, self-reliant" men of the West who served as models for Morgan, Jordan, Cantwell, and Hudson—"Westerners at their core." William Braasch Watson's spadework in "Joris Ivens and the Communists: Bringing Hemingway into the Spanish Civil War" (pp. 37–57) uncovers some interesting documents which suggest that Ivens acted as Hemingway's "case officer"—his guide "in order that the recruited person will produce the desired ends" for the organization—during the filming of *The Spanish Earth*. Especially interesting to textual scholars is Thomas Gould's " 'A Tiny Operation with Great Effect': Authorial Revision in the Manuscript of Hemingway's *For Whom the Bell Tolls*" (pp. 67–81); Gould documents Hemingway's editorial revisions of obscene words and love scenes designed to circumvent "the limiting cultural standards of the period." Exploring Hemingway's growing impatience with "a superficial leftist vision of brotherhood," H. R. Stoneback's " 'The Priest Did Not Answer': Hemingway, the Church, the Party, and *For Whom the Bell Tolls*" (pp. 99–112) accounts for Hemingway's subsequent attraction to "the core Christian vision of the oneness of humankind" represented by the church. Robert E. Gajdusek's "Pilar's Tale: The Myth and the Message" (pp. 113–30) concentrates on Pilar's story of the slaughter of the Fascists, wherein Hemingway depicts a ritual out of which comes renewed life; in this way absolutes are restored through cycles. Gerry Brenner stages "Once a Rabbit, Always? A Feminist Interview with María" (pp. 131–42), a fictional interview between a feminist and a marginalized woman who asks as many questions as she answers—challenging not only the methodology but traditional characterizations of her. She views Jordan as a latent homosexual, Hemingway as a not-quite-comprehending creator. Mark C. Van Guten in "The Polemics of Narrative and Difference in *For Whom the Bell Tolls*" (pp. 143–57) finds "a subversive text," one that cannot be read in purely historical or fictional terms and that questions the authority of writing, difference, and truth. Dean Rehberger concludes the volume with " 'I Don't Know Buffalo Bill'; or, Hemingway and the Rhetoric of the Western" (pp. 159–84), an examination of Hemingway's use of the "adventure ethos" with special reference to Owen Wister that focuses on the western at the turn of the century.

In their capacity as guest editors for the *North Dakota Quarterly*,

John J. Michalczyk and Sergio Villani present a special issue, "Malraux, Hemingway, and Embattled Spain" (60, ii), which bears the name of the conference where the papers were originally presented in 1990. Sixteen of the issue's 23 articles treat either both authors or Hemingway's *For Whom the Bell Tolls,* which celebrated its 50th anniversary of publication. Covering film, journalism, and fiction, this interdisciplinary issue provides historical, biographical, and critical commentary that could have been complemented by an introductory essay on the writers and their milieu.

The volume opens with four essays that explore the artistic and political commitment of the two men. In a slight essay, "Behind *For Whom the Bell Tolls* and *L'Espoir:* Propaganda Rumble and Closet Journalists" (pp. 1–7), Bernard Wilhelm briefly sketches the reception and reputation of both authors and remarks that their works, unlike most of the 15,000 others on the Spanish Civil War, escape categorization as "raw propaganda." John Garrick's "Two Bulls Locked Horn in Horn in Fight: The Rivalry of Hemingway and Malraux in Spain" (pp. 8–18) considers their animosity and concludes that Malraux's writing may have been more eloquent and historically accurate, but that Hemingway is recognized by Spaniards as being more "human." Blending biography and criticism, Bickford Sylvester in "The Writer as *l'homme engagé:* Persona as Literary Device in Hemingway and Malraux" (pp. 19–39) explores the artistic goals of the writers and the ways in which they "manipulated the public into identifying their successive plots with stages in their personal lives." Scrutinizing their war films in "*The Spanish Earth* and *Sierra de Teruel:* The Human Condition as Political Message" (pp. 40–49), John J. Michalczyk applauds their rare blending of documentary film with artistic and ideological depth.

The remaining essays, diverse in their methodologies, fall under the generous rubric of "Ernest Hemingway: Literary Warrior." The depth of Hemingway's "Anglo-Saxon or modern Western values" is called into question by Allen Josephs's "In Another Country: Hemingway and Spain" (pp. 50–57). Josephs suggests that the author's work is "inconceivable without Spain and without Spanish values"; "Where," he asks, "is Hemingway's American novel?" Citing Robert Jordan as "a paragon," Robert W. Lewis, in "Hemingway, Malraux, and the Warrior-Writer" (pp. 58–71) traces Hemingway's attraction to war and soldiers and its implications for his art, arguing that *For Whom the Bell Tolls* rises above charges of historical or political inaccuracy because it is "a kind of mythic story" in which truth to fact becomes largely irrelevant. What is more, claims Gunther Schmigalle in "Seven Ambiguities in Ernest Hemingway's *For Whom the Bell Tolls*" (pp. 72–82), it is "facts" straining against one another, creating a work "profoundly contradictory and ambivalent," that seem to make the novel attractive to a reading public not always able to maintain political credos and personal convictions. Asking why Jordan fails to kill Pablo, Wolfgang E. H. Rudat's "Hamlet in Spain: Oedipal Dilemmas in *For Whom the Bell Tolls*" (pp. 83–101) suggests that Hemingway has rewritten *Hamlet* "into a story where a morally cleansed Claudius and Jocasta-figure Gertrude survive an oedipal onslaught because cooperation between father and son [Jordan] resolves the oedipal dilemma." Cognizant that the complex politics of a half-century ago puzzle contemporary readers, William Braasch Watson accounts for the "contextual realities, both personal and historic" in "Hemingway's Attacks on the Soviets and the Communists in *For Whom the Bell Tolls*" (pp. 103–18); understanding these realities, alleges Watson, prevents us from relegating the politics and history of the novel to an intricate footnote and allows them to occupy "the political and moral center of the novel." Similarly, Robert E. Fleming's "Communism vs. Community in *For Whom the Bell Tolls*" (pp. 144–58) sees Jordan's belief in communism as a philosophical concept replaced by "a less sophisticated notion of the unity of the individual with humankind—unified by a primitive, tribal sense of community." E. San Juan, Jr., in "Ideological Form, Symbolic Exchange, Textual Production: A Symptomatic Reading of *For Whom the Bell Tolls*" (pp. 119–42) eschews normative and hermeneutic approaches in favor of one that seeks a text's ideology by examining "the lived relations of humans, their imaginary linkage to their 'real' conditions." San Juan views the novel "as the textual fabrication of an internally complex ideology unsynchronized by multiple contradictions"; that is, Jordan's comment, for example, about "the planes [being] beautiful whether they are ours or theirs" is undercut by his following comment, "The hell they are, he thought." Unless readers privilege one of these thoughts, they are left to judge Jordan as "dispersed or fissured." The prose of the "symptomatic reading," which San Juan claims allows us to open the text and articulate its radical otherness, is dense, but his remarks about the gaps and silences in the text are insightful.

Treating Hemingway's play, Erik Nakjavani's "Hemingway's *The Fifth Column* and the Question of Ideology" (pp. 159–84) concentrates on the differences between ideology and politics, finding a rift in the play that is not unlike the human psyche. In "Hemingway's German Radio Address" (pp. 185–92) Wayne Kvam provides a transcript, concluding that Hemingway wrote it but not determining who translated or edited it. Criticizing Hemingway's journalism of the period for sometimes saying too little or too much, William E. Coté's "Hemingway's Spanish Civil War Dispatches: Literary Journalism, Fiction, or Propaganda?" (pp. 193–203) concludes that the works "cannot be held up as models of journalism of the highest order" and explains why. And closing the selections on Hemingway, Nora Ruth Roberts details his personal and professional relationship with Josephine Herbst in "Herbst and Hemingway in Spain" (pp. 204–16).

e. General Essays: Fitzgerald V. M. Tolmatchoff's "The Metaphor of History in the Work of F. Scott Fitzgerald" (*Russian Eyes on American Literature*, pp. 126–41) shows the unity of Fitzgerald's historical understanding of the world by focusing on biography, worldview, image, and composition. Familiar themes of *The Great Gatsby*—wealth, women, time, and unrealized possibilities—receive fresh treatment here, as do influences such as Keats and Conrad. Tolmatchoff concludes that Fitzgerald sensed a "decisive historical step" and "an imperceptible shift in time" when the ideal turned vulgar—and this was the main event of his artistic world.

James L. W. West III asks "Did F. Scott Fitzgerald Have the Right Publisher?" (*SR* 100:644–56). Was a "conservative" house the right place for the prophet of the Jazz Age? And what of Scribner's failure to "realize maximum or continuing" income from Scott's books—an oversight that forced the author to rely on commercial magazines for his income? West's answer: "Of course" Fitzgerald had the right publisher, and Scribner's became "an integral part of Fitzgerald's creative apparatus."

f. General Essays: Hemingway In "Hemingway's Senses of an Ending: *In Our Time* and After" (*HN* 12, i:12–18), Paul Smith discovers a pattern in Hemingway's conclusions. In most of the endings, he finds an inclusive element, a movement toward agreement or reconciliation; an exclusive element, an act of disagreement or separation; and a third element that predicts the character's future. The stories which follow this pattern document the rise and fall of Hemingway's mastery of the form.

Continuing the debate about narrative voice in *The Nick Adams*

Stories, Joseph Flora in "Saving Nick Adams for Another Day" (*SoAR* 58, ii:61–84) cogently argues against attributing all of the stories to Nick because this "might cause a misreading of narrative voice and lead readers to interpret stories too narrowly."

Kelli A. Larson's "Stepping Into the Labyrinth: Fifteen Years of Hemingway Scholarship" (*HN* 11, ii:19–24) laments the wealth of repetitive studies and remarks recent trends. Paul Miller's "French Criticism of Ernest Hemingway: A Brief Survey (1932–89)" (*Midamerica* 18 [1991]: 69–79) notes that, though Hemingway consistently outsells Faulkner by a wide margin, the latter remains "the darling of the intellectuals" while serious critical attention to the former has been "sparse, often condescending . . . devoted to the legend."

g. Essays on Specific Works: Fitzgerald   *The Great Gatsby* and *Tender is the Night* share honors as the most-discussed Fitzgerald works this year. Philip Sipiora's chapter, "Vampires of the Heart: Gender Trouble in *The Great Gatsby*" (*The Aching Hearth*, pp. 199–220), examines the abusive personalities in the novel, dividing them into two classes: the "hard abuse: blood and death" of Tom and Myrtle, abusive spouses; and the "soft abuse: deception and disillusion" of those who "slowly suck the life out of other characters." His reading reinforces the traditional notion that *Gatsby* captures the despair and shattered illusions that so many critics see as representative of the modern period in American literature. Yet Sipiora adds that the novel leaves an "affirmative residue" that the abusive personalities may spark a reading that is inherently ethical.

Philip Castille's "Jay Gatsby: The Smuggler as Frontier Hero" (*UMSE* n.s. 10:227–37) helps to explain Gatsby's magnetism, noting that his personal attractiveness and his publicly accepted profession as a bootlegger make him an antihero whose career is akin to that of Arnold Rothstein, one of the models for Meyer Wolfsheim, but whose faith in the future is unmatched by Nick. Gatsby is also the focus of Carmine Sarracino's "The Last Transcendentalist" (*CEA* 54, iii:37–46), where the bootlegger is characterized as a "doomed transcendentalist" whose freedom to define himself leads to the perils of counterfeit and self-deception. Gregory S. Jay in "From Emerson's Nature to Gatsby's Shirts," pp. 153–69 in his *America the Scrivener: Deconstruction and the Subject of Literary History* (Cornell, 1990), summarizes the response of several methodologies to *The Great Gatsby* (Marxist, psychoanalytical, deconstructionist) and suggests that Gatsby and Myrtle are victimized "by the economy of capitalist plagiarism" because they "struggle to fill up their lack of identity by inserting themselves into prescribed cultural plots"; thus, even their desires are "unoriginal, plagiarized." And Edward Wasiolek's "The Sexual Drama of Nick and Gatsby" (*IFR* 19:14–22) argues that Gatsby suffers from a "madonna complex" which uses "an idealized perfect woman to keep at bay, in the psyche, the . . . sexual woman." He revisits Keith Fraser's reading of Nick's encounter with Mr. McKee and the curious ellipsis that follows (see *ALS 1979*, p. 166) to suggest that both Gatsby and Nick are homosexual.

David Buehrer's "Diving into the Wreck, Again: The Psychological Fragmentation of Character in Fitzgerald's *Tender is the Night*" (*JEP* 13:281–95) proposes that psychology replaces the form of physical typology in *Gatsby* to represent the concerns of fragmented characterization in the postwar world. Catherine B. Burroughs in "Of 'Sheer Being': Fitzgerald's Aesthetic Typology and the Burden of Transcription" (*MLS* 22, i:102–09) observes that characters such as Nicole in *Tender is the Night* possess "sheer being," or emotional resilience, which enables them "to endure the world without much difficulty," while those who are "reflective and analytical . . . experience emotional annihilation." Taking another tack, Katherine Cummings in "Translation, Transference, and Other: *Tender is the Night*," pp. 230–78 in her *Telling Tales: The Hysteric's Seduction in Fiction and Theory* (Stanford, 1991), explores Fitzgerald's fascination with seconds and returns to the Melarky and Kelly drafts to document the pattern of seduction and transference in the novel. A deconstructionist reader of psychoanalysis, Cummings creates her own "tales" which engage with the fiction she discusses and suggest that psychoanalysis, itself, reads like a tale of seduction.

h. Essays on Specific Works: Hemingway   Nancy R. Comley and Robert Scholes in "Tribal Things: Hemingway's Erotics of Truth" (*Novel* 25:268–85) argue that "the bond between sexuality and truth for Hemingway was a matter of the primitive or primal" and that "sex across racial boundaries and sex that violates cultural taboos . . . are the warp and woof of sexuality" in *The Garden of Eden*. Toni Morrison notices a similar "disrupting darkness" in "Disturbing Nurses and the Kindness of Sharks" (*Playing in the Dark*, pp. 63–91), where she addresses Hemingway's "silencing" of Wesley from *To Have and Have Not:* he is a "nameless, sexless, nationless Africanist presence." But Morrison notes Hemingway's contrary movement in *The Garden of Eden;* here Catherine is depicted as "blackening up" her skin and "whitening out" her hair—acts that suggest the forbiddenness of the novel's actions.

Timothy D. O'Brien's "Allusion, Word-Play, and the Central Conflict in Hemingway's 'Hills Like White Elephants' " (*HN* 12, i:19–25) concludes that the tale is a "complex portrayal of woman's, not just Jig's, *final* compliance." Focusing on a neglected story, Robert Fleming's "Dismantling the Code: Hemingway's 'A Man of the World' " (*HN* 11, ii:6–10) asks if Hemingway reevaluated his "code" in light of his own failing health and advanced age. In "The Ambiguity of 'A Clean, Well-Lighted Place' " (*SSF* 29:561–74), David Kerner argues that the "purpose of the ambiguity" in the waiters' much-celebrated dialogue is to reveal "that the story is a tale of *two* 'nada's"—the younger waiter's and the old man's. Wolfgang E. H. Rudat in "Anti-Semitism in *The Sun Also Rises:* Traumas, Jealousies, and the Genesis of Cohn" (*AI* 49:263–75) argues that Hemingway, and not Jake alone, must take some responsibility for the anti-Semitic characterization of Cohn. David W. Ullrich's " 'What's in a Name?'—Krebs, Crabs, Kraut: The Multivalance of 'Krebs' in Hemingway's 'Soldier's Home' " (*SSF* 29:363–75) helps to explain why the story belongs to Krebs, who is "estranged, disaffected . . . alien," and not Nick Adams.

i. Miscellaneous   The ghost of Gatsby beats on in Jay Parini's "The Late Gatsby" (*Harper's* 285:37–39); Parini's sequel begins by having Nick encounter Wolfsheim and arranging to meet him for lunch where, presumably, they will conspire together about Nick's future. William McCranor Henderson helps to keep the Hemingway myth alive with his *I Killed Hemingway: A Novel* (St. Martin's): what if Hemingway had been assassinated by a rival from whom he had stolen writings in the '20s? Aficionados will delight in turning the pages of *Santiago: Saint of Two Worlds* by Marc Simmons et al. (New Mexico), with its three essays on the saint and pilgrimage and more than eighty black-and-white photographs by Joan Myers.

Part II

11 Literature to 1800

William J. Scheick

Scholarly activity in colonial studies was characteristically vigorous. Recent trends suggest that, with the possible exception of Anne Bradstreet, previous interest in colonial verse has given way to extensive analyses of Puritan prose. More than ever before, early histories now engage literary critics. The most substantial increase, however, has been in studies of captivity narratives. Mary Rowlandson is emerging as the author of critical choice during the early 1990s.

i Native Americans and the Colonial Imagination

In an issue of *WMQ* featuring essays on Columbian encounters, Patricia Seed's "Taking Possession and Reading Texts: Establishing the Authority of Overseas Empires" (49:183–209) illustrates that English legal documents used the form and substance of medieval papal bulls to legitimate control of territory, in contrast to Spanish emphasis on control of Native American people as a labor resource. And in "The Discursive Encounter of Spain and America: The Authority of Eyewitness Testimony in the Writing of History" (49:210–28), Rolena Adorno discloses that historical narration is an act of reinscription at once dependent on precedent models and reflective of personal agendas.

These encounters, seen from the other side, are recorded in two books. *Native American Testimony: A Chronicle of Indian-White Relations from Prophecy to the Present, 1492–1992*, ed. Peter Nabokov (Viking), presents a collection of records documenting especially the inability of New World inhabitants to refute their alleged wildness. James Axtell's *Beyond 1492: Encounters in Colonial North America* (Oxford) suggests that, within always mutating constraints, the fate of the indigenous peoples was in many ways a matter of the choices they made among their own culturally invented options. Axtell relatedly shows that the Jesuit missionaries, as agents of change, had a double impact insofar as they not only captured space through exploration and geography but also influenced European philosophic and social thought by means of their descriptions of Native American life.

An issue of *SAIL* includes " 'Honoratissimi Benefactores': Native American Students and Two Seventeenth-Century Texts in the University Tradition" (4, ii–iii:35–47), in which Wolfgang Hochbruck and Beatrix Dudensing-Reichel translate self-deprecating Greek and Latin literary exercises of dubious student authorship; " 'Pray Sir, Consider a Little': Rituals of Subordination and Strategies of Resistance in the Letters of Hezekiah Calvin and David Fowler to Eleazar Wheelock, 1764–1768" (4, ii–iii:48–74), in which Laura Murray points to the constraints that these authors determined to revise; and "Introduction: Samson Occom's *Sermon Preached by Samson Occom . . . at the Execution of Moses Paul, An Indian*" (4, ii–iii:75–105), in which A. LaVonne Brown Ruoff presents a complete edition of this discourse.

Annette Kolodny's "Letting Go Our Grand Obsessions: Notes Toward a New Literary History of the American Frontier" (*AL* 64:1–18) calls for the recovery of written and oral accounts reflecting first contacts with Otherness in the New World, suggesting landscape as an unstable locus, and recording patterns of mutable meanings. In "The Discourse of Abundance" (*AmLH* 4:369–85) Julio Ortega observes how the rhetoric of resemblance (the method of precedent discourse) was transformed into the rhetoric of difference (the method of New World description); this alteration signified a new model of developmental potentiality in both nature and culture. One metaphor of resemblance interests E. Thomson Shields, Jr., in "East Makes West: Images of the Orient in Early Spanish and English Literature of North America" (*M&H* 19:97–116); from the first encounter onward, the Americas were interpreted in terms of European ideas about Asia, and even well after this notion was exposed as erroneous, imagery drawn from this pattern of Orientalization often served William Byrd and others as a means of imparting definition to the New World.

Paul J. Lindholdt notes that people were lured to the New World by propaganda designed doubly to recruit and to entertain them, albeit the use of exaggeration and imagery sometimes conflicted with the goal of recruitment: "The Significance of the Colonial Promotion Tract" (*Early American Literature and Culture*, pp. 57–72). Among these recruits, the

Dutch should be reconsidered, especially Adriaen van der Donck's neglected *Description of New Netherlands,* urges Ada Van Gastel in "Ethnic Pluralism in Early American Literature: Incorporating Dutch-American Texts into the Canon" (*Early American Literature and Culture,* pp. 109–21). Raymond F. Dolle indicates that Smith seems to pit his own pragmatic method of New World settlement (defined as colonization and trade) against a predecessor's quest for adventure (defined as conquest and plunder): "Captain John Smith's Satire of Sir Walter Raleigh" (*Early American Literature and Culture,* pp. 73–83). Because old Virginians knew the story and Smith's adversaries never questioned the story, among other reasons, J. A. Leo Lemay answers in the affirmative the question posed by the title of his *Did Pocahontas Save Captain John Smith?* (Georgia).

ii Early Colonial Poetry

Both volumes of Raymond A. Craig's careful *A Concordance to the Minor Poetry of Edward Taylor (1642?–1729): American Colonial Poet* (Mellen) have appeared. In *A Reading of Edward Taylor* (Delaware) Thomas M. Davis scrutinizes the poet's manuscripts to raise questions about a number of generally held notions and determines that Taylor's meditations are essentially occasional, biographical, experimental, and developmental; they evidence the poet's change from concern with the quality of his verse to an obsession about the condition of his soul, a change accompanied by a diminishing of aesthetic attainment. Taylor among others appears in *Design in Puritan American Literature* (Kentucky), in which I focus on special literary moments (logogic cruxes defined by Renaissance and Reformed traditions) when Puritan authors and readers may hesitate to contemplate a central paradox of language—its dual capacity to conceal self-idolatry and to reveal deific scheme.

The connections between religious and medical beliefs, the correspondences between New and Old English therapeutic practices, the encounter of chemical (including alchemical) theories and Galenic humoral practice, and the differences between folk remedies and ministerial prescriptions are explored by Patricia Ann Watson, whose *The Angelical Conjunction: The Preacher-Physician of Colonial New England* (Tennessee, 1991) also identifies the key medical writings used by colonial doctors. One of these physicians is featured in Catherine Rainwater's reprinted " 'This Brazen Serpent Is a Doctors Shop': Edward Taylor's

Medical Vision" (*American Literature and Science,* pp. 18–38; see *ALS
1991*) and Randall A. Clack's "The Transmutation of Soul: The Opus
Alchymicum Celestial and Edward Taylor's 'Meditation 1:8'" (*SCN*
50:6–10), which discloses the poet's appropriation of an alchemical cycle
of regeneration pertaining to the self; Taylor especially alludes to the
transmutative powers of the Philosopher's Stone, which is created finally
not by the poet but by Christ. And "Taylor's Meditation 32" (*Expl* 51:13–
17) by Ann M. Cameron retraces the poet's progression from imagistic
confusion and tonal chaos to order and harmony as the remedial work of
grace.

Marjorie Hudson's "Among the Tuscarora: The Strange and Mysterious Death of John Lawson, Gentleman, Explorer, and Writer" (*NCLR*
1, i:62–82) details one southerner's encounter with Native Americans.
His encounter with landscape is discussed by E. Thomson Shields, Jr., in
"Paradise Regained, Again: The Literary Context of John Lawson's *A
New Voyage to Carolina*" (*NCLR* 1, i:83–97); whereas Robert Beverly
presents Virginia as a lost paradise and Ebenezer Cook(e) presents
Maryland as a false paradise, Lawson presents Carolina descriptively,
rather than narratively, in order to suggest its eternal nature as a true
paradise that no one can mar. "George Milligen, Colonial Carolina
Elegist" (*EAL* 27:101–16) presents James E. Kibler, Jr.'s edition of a poem
by a Loyalist; and "Thomas Teackle's 333 Books: A Great Library on
Virginia's Eastern Shore" (*WMQ* 49:449–91) is Jon Butler's catalogue of
the collection of a 17th-century Anglican minister.

iii Rowlandson and Early Colonial Prose

The sermonic use of typology, explains Deborah L. Madsen in "The
Sword or the Scroll: The Power of Rhetoric in Colonial New England"
(*AmerS* 33, ii:45–61) served Congregationalist clerics such as John Cotton
as a justification of their hierarchical social model. Consulting a manuscript fragment in order to undo Nathaniel Morton's editing, Mark L.
Sargent concludes that William Bradford's first dialogue responds directly to John Cotton's criticism of Separatism and, as well, registers
Bradford's effort to reconcile the present with the past by suggesting that
the political changes of the Protectorate were based on the values of
Elizabethan and Jacobean separatists: "William Bradford's 'Dialogue'
with History" (*NEQ* 65:389–421). Whereas retrospective Bradford saw
the saints in opposition to the world, prospective Winthrop saw them

attaining meaning within the world. Moreover, continues James Moseley in *John Winthrop's World: History as a Story; The Story as History* (Wisconsin), Winthrop's reflection on his written record of this struggle of the saints led him to interpret Puritan history as a designed story with a purpose. Design also interests Scott Michaelsen, whose "John Winthrop's 'Modell' Covenant and the Company Way" (*EAL* 27:85–100) discloses Winthrop's desire to bind the settlers of his colony by combining both a contractual flexibility based on the modern needs of people and the contractual rights of businessmen based on meeting economic requirements.

Increase Mather apparently adopted Whig discourse as a strategy to urge the restoration of the Bay Colony's charter without adopting Whig ideology as a historian; but, Stephen Carl Arch further explains in "The Glorious Revolution and the Rhetoric of Puritan History" (*EAL* 27:61–74), his son, Cotton, responded to a societal shift in authority by pointing to colonial historians like himself as exemplary to the community. Although Cotton was progressive in teaching his children to read and write, explains Jennifer E. Monaghan in "Family Literacy in Early 18th-Century Boston: Cotton Mather and His Children" (*RRQ* 26 [1991]:342–70), he restricted his daughter's range of education and gave them books suitable to their gender. Mather's attitude toward conjuration surfaces in Richard Godbeer's *The Devil's Dominion: Magic and Religion in Early New England* (Cambridge), and his millennial views are documented in Reiner Smolinski's reprinted *"Jehovah's Peculium: The New Jerusalem and the Jews in Puritan Eschatology"* (*Early American Literature and Culture*, pp. 84–108; see *ALS 1990*). *Forms of Uncertainty: Essays in Historical Criticism* (Virginia) includes reprints of several of David Levin's articles on Bradford (*ALS 1972*) and the Mathers (*ALS 1988; ALS 1990*) and an original essay, "Body and Soul in *The Angel of Bethesda:* Practical Advice with Literary and Spiritual Entertainment" (pp. 84–97), which identifies the homiletic features of Mather's medical book. And in "Damaging the Mathers: London Receives the News from Salem" (*NEQ* 65:302–08), Albert Cook reports that Mather's reputation was injured because the abridged second and third London editions of *Wonders of the Invisible World* stressed sensationalism over theology.

Entertainment of another sort emerges in Jeffrey Walker's " 'The War of the Words' in Harvard's Class of '54: Collegiate Literary Culture in Eighteenth-Century America" (*Early American Literature and Culture*, pp. 132–48), which presents several examples of verse expressing the often sophomoric attitudes and rivalries of colonial undergraduates, including Nathan Fiske. In their younger years, we may surmise from C. John Sommerville's *The Discovery of Childhood in Puritan England* (Georgia), these students possibly absorbed something of the emergent humanistic tradition from colonial reading matter for youth. This tradition interests Amanda Porterfield, whose *Female Piety in Puritan New England: The Emergence of Religious Humanism* (Oxford) indicates that John Cotton and Thomas Shepard, among others, relied on images of feminine humility to foster the self-control needed for the sway of their authority; indirectly they imparted real power to women, for whereas males used these images to transform human suffering into the hope of salvation, women used the same images to attain recognition as experts on female piety, which ideal was the cohesive of Puritan society.

Reviewing the spiritual confessions of the female members of Thomas Shepard's congregation, Kathleen Swaim's " 'Come and Hear': Women's Puritan Evidences" (*American Women's Autobiography*, pp. 32–56) shows that, contrary to male confessors, they chose biblical texts emphasizing familial relationships. The familial is featured in Margaret H. Davis's "Mary White Rowlandson's Self-Fashioning as Puritan Goodwife" (*EAL* 27:49–60), which reveals how the metaphor of the housewife not only imposed order over chaotic experience but also negotiated (without menace) the coalescence of self-effacement and self-assertion typical of colonial female authority.

Relatedly, in " 'My Own Credit': Strategies of (E)Valuation in Mary Rowlandson's Captivity Narrative" (*AL* 64:655–76), Teresa A. Toulouse perceptively explains how the sanctioned use of the various discourses of status, martyrdom, and providential signs credits the narrator; but Rowlandson's scripturally framed rhetoric of submission also registers an angry lack of acceptance that questions the established models for defining her value. Toulouse's "Mary Rowlandson and the 'Rhetoric of Ambiguity' " (*SPAS* 3:21–52) focuses on a rhetorical shift in the jeremiad (from action to passivity) as a typical disjunctive site where Puritanism both structured and inadvertently called into question religious beliefs. In "Mary Rowlandson's Narrative and the 'New' Theories of Early American Literature" (*Amst* 36 [1991]:249–63), Toulouse further explores the problems raised by the current critical tendency to equate culture with ideology, especially the designation of resistance as a form of collusion with the dominant cultural agenda.

Nancy Armstrong and Leonard Tennenhouse's "The American Origins of the English Novel" (*AmLH* 4:386–410) explores the influence of captivity narratives, such as Rowlandson's, on the trope of the abducted female body in 18th-century English fiction; this trope represents the mastery (especially through writing) of individual consciousness over everything. Eight 18th-century examples of these works are collected by Colin G. Calloway in *North Country Captives: Narratives of Indian Captivity from Vermont and New Hampshire* (New England).

Colonial concern with corporeal health as survival and growth informs "Violence and the Body Politic in Seventeenth-Century New England" (*ArQ* 48, ii:1–32), James Schramer and Timothy Sweet's exposé of the Puritan application of their religious discourse of the salvational process as warfare to their political discourse of the polis as a body; this combined ideological discourse justified their extermination of Native Americans. Likewise, claims Michael Warner in "New English Sodom" (*AL* 64:19–47), the coalescence of sodomy and national judgment is a source of anxiety for several male Puritan authors when treating the city-on-the-hill theme; Winthrop's erotization of social attraction is effectively based on a notion of the origins of love in resemblance, including the bond among members of the same gender.

Anxiety over contamination similarly informs the colonial disapproval of mining, especially in contrast to the self-renewing labor of agriculture; in "'Peculiar Soil': Mining the Early American Imagination" (*EAL* 27:151–69), Joseph M. Thomas excavates the Puritan concern with the sinful interior and the valuation of insular freedom that informs this repudiation. The antiauthoritarian pollution of Socinian trust in reasoned, negotiated, and consensual interpretation of the Bible is the subject of Michael Vella's introduction to a handy facsimile edition of William Pynchon's *The Meritorious Price of Our Redemption* (Peter Lang); although this book (possibly a subtextual component of *Gravity's Rainbow*, according to Louis Mackey) was burned in Boston and indeed reflects its author's high regard for civil liberties, the author's position within its dialogue—Vella reasonably cautions—is open to question. And the pollution of witches' speech is highlighted in Jane Kamensky's "Words, Witches, and Woman Trouble: Witchcraft, Disorderly Speech, and Gender Boundaries in Puritan New England" (*EIHC* 128:286–307), which suggests that this inversion of the ideal of feminine restraint represented the destructive potentiality of the unchecked colonial female voice.

Whereas the concept of marriage was pervasive in 17th-century Anglo-American sermons, explains Michael P. Winship in "Behold the Bride-

groom Cometh!: Marital Imagery in Massachusetts Preaching, 1630–
1730" (*EAL* 27:170–84), it eventually disappeared as a result of post-
Restoration changes in religious, social, and literary sensibility. Before the
Restoration, contends Francis J. Bremer in "To Live Exemplary Lives:
Puritans and Puritan Communities as Lofty Lights" (*SCen* 7:27–39),
John Winthrop and other New Englanders sought to reform England;
but their international perspective also encouraged them to see their role
as part of an international course that included evidence of divine truth
abroad.

The revised *Secret History*, A. James Wohlpart reports in "The Creation of the Ordered State: William Byrd's (Re)Vision in the History of
the Dividing Line" (*SLJ* 25, i:3–18), reveals a narrator who narrows his
perspective; no longer mediating law and anarchy, he becomes a traveler
concerned with separating chaos from social improvement (government,
economics, and religion). Kathryn Zabelle Derounian-Stodola considers
another traveler's use of several literary conventions to express a variety of
responses to the territory between New York and Boston: "The New
England Frontier and the Picaresque in Sarah Kemble Knight's Journal"
(*Early American Literature and Culture*, pp. 122–31). That English colonial literature relates less to regional geography than to Old World
history is noted in Ekaterina Stetsenko's "The Formation of the Secular
Literary Tradition in Colonial America" (*Russian Eyes on American Literature*, pp. 3–24).

The narratives of migration, Stephen Fender contends in *Sea Changes:
British Emigration and American Literature* (Cambridge), were fictions
about benevolent New World nature and decadent Old World culture
that tended to depict immigrants negatively and emigrants positively;
stressing material resources and natural process, this contradictory rhetoric of settlement (exemplified by Crèvecoeur's *Letters*) became the dominant mode of American descriptive discourse. However, Donald P.
Wharton's "Hudson's Mermaid: Symbol and Myth in Early American
Sea Literature" (*Early American Literature and Culture*, pp. 38–56) mentions that Renaissance sea literature archetypally exposes the limits of
human ability, especially in attempts to impose order over natural forces
or, as evident in 17th-century sea deliverance narratives, to resist divine
providence.

An encomium on a 20th-century interpreter of Puritan prose is featured in *SPAS* (3:1–164). An overview of Sacvan Bercovitch's career as
well as consideration of the place of Jonathan Edwards, the Jewish ques-

tion, and Perry Miller in his thought are provided by (among others) Emory Elliott, Mason I. Lowance, Jr., Michael P. Kramer, Rael Meyerowitz, and Ormond Seavey. And in "National Interest and the Genealogy of Early American Literature" (*Early American Literature and Culture,* pp. 23–37), Timothy K. Conley observes that the emergence of the United States as an imperialist power shaped and legitimated the fin de siècle professionalization of American literary studies, including colonial literature.

iv Edwards, the Great Awakening, and the New Divinity

The Works of Jonathan Edwards, Volume 10: Sermons and Discourses, 1720–23 (Yale), Wilson H. Kimnach's edition of previously unavailable writings, should make a significant difference in future studies of Edwards. Kimnach provides a detailed discussion, based on manuscript evidence, of Edwards's method of producing and revising sermons, which fall into three phases of development (1722–27, 1727–42, 1742–58). *Sinners in the Hands of an Angry God,* Kimnach contends convincingly, draws on the tradition of the "hands" execution sermon.

For Edwards, according to Linda Munk's "His Dazzling Absence: The Shekinah in Jonathan Edwards" (*EAL* 27:1–30), creation is a metonymic expression of divine superfluity; while not the Deity itself, creation is a surrogate communication of the divine. Pertinently, in "The Beginning of Time: Jonathan Edwards's *Original Sin*" (*Early American Literature and Culture,* pp. 149–64), Stephen R. Yarbrough ponders the difference between the prelapsarian singular absolute "now" and the postlapsarian sequential transient "now." *One Holy and Happy Society: The Public Theology of Jonathan Edwards* (Penn. State) is very much concerned with the "now," and Gerald R. McDermott discusses Edwards's advocacy of improvement in communal life despite the secondariness of his interest in civil liberties and his criticism of monarchical power. Edwards did not anticipate America's manifest destiny policy, however, but went against the grain of the emergent Revolutionary consciousness of his time by pessimistically prophesying the probable failure of New England.

v Franklin, Jefferson, Wheatley, and the Revolution

In the first colonial Methodist autobiography, explains Rodger M. Payne's "Metaphors of the Self and the Sacred: The Spiritual Autobiography of the Rev. Freeborn Garrettson" (*EAL* 27:31–48), self-expression mediates between history and myth, subjectivity and objectivity, and the ideal and the mundane. "The Spiritual Pilgrimage of Sarah Osborn (1714–1796)" (*ChH* 61:408–21) presents Charles E. Hambrick-Stowe's report on the anticipation of the Second Great Awakening in one woman's evangelical expression of the ideal of the new birth. That a southern poet, who found nature insufficient, supplemented fashionable beliefs with Christian tenets as a means of resolving spiritual tensions is the subject of "A Spiritual Pilgrimage through a Deistic Universe: Richard Lewis's 'A Journey from Patapsko to Annapolis, April 4, 1730' " (*EAL* 27:117–27), by Christopher D. Johnson.

Bereft of a cultural heritage, Houston A. Baker, Jr., argues in *Workings of the Spirit: The Poetics of African-American Women's Writing* (Chicago, 1991, pp. 39–41), Phillis Wheatley verifies herself in terms of a voiced autobiographical consciousness in "To Maecenas." Moreover, according to Phillip M. Richards's "Phillis Wheatley and Literary Americanization" (*AQ* 44:163–91), she combines the personae of the evangelist and the Whig patriot as a liminal identity of transformed social position that enables her to exult in spiritual equality and to castigate her audience. In "Phillis Wheatley's Appropriation of Isaiah" (*EAL* 27:135–40) I read the poet's "On Being Brought from Africa to America" as a subtle act of poetic appropriation that transforms biblical authorization into a form of exemplary self-authorization. Lucy K. Hayden's "Classical Tidings from the Afric Muse: Phillis Wheatley's Use of Greek and Roman Mythology" (*CLAJ* 35:432–47) discusses several borrowings and notes the poet's personal additions to her interpretation of Ovid.

That another poet, who wrote a verse tribute to Wheatley, urges equality by using Christian tenets to mediate between slave and master is the topic of Lonnell E. Johnson's "Dilemma of the Dutiful Servant: The Poetry of Jupiter Hammon" (*African American Imagination*, pp. 105–17). Other tensions—between religious and Enlightenment ideals, and familial and civic addressees—surface in "Spiritual and Rational Authority in Benjamin Rush's *Travels through Life*" (*TSLL* 34:284–300), Joseph Alkana's charting of one nationalist's anxious revisions of himself. Rush commences as a representative of inherited paternal authority, then questions this very authority in terms of empirical observations, and finally in an effort to align disparate grounds he retreats into the paternal authority of Christian tradition. Disclosing that Noah Webster's authoritative plan for a national language preserved the best features of a conservative tradition of linguistic pedagogy while at the same time it introduced changes based on the model of Thomas Paine's writings, Michael P. Kramer's *Imagining Language in America* (pp. 35–63, 119–36) concludes that Webster created a confused, if powerful, vision of America negotiated through competing rhetorical structures and enabling ambiguities, both of which anticipate the later manner of the Federalist.

Another occasion of ambiguity is identified in "Parasiting America: The Radical Function of Heterogeneity in Thomas Paine's Early Writings" (*ECS* 25:331–51), Molly Anne Rothenberg's identification of Paine's reliance on the figure of the parasite to convey a sense of America as at once visible and invisible, stable and unstable, systematic and dissolute; the image implicitly suggests the failure of Enlightenment liberalism to negotiate its internal contradictions and simultaneously points to the subversion of authoritarian structures and the formation of new alignments as an ongoing process. Authority also interests Mark L. Sargent, whose "Thomas Hutchinson, Ezra Stiles, and the Legend of the Regicides" (*WMQ* 49:431–48) discloses that whereas Hutchinson represented the judges of King Charles I as a Loyalist warning against insurrection, Stiles represented them as revolutionary martyrs of freedom.

One hero of the Revolution is featured in a special issue of *PMHB*. " 'Order, Discipline, and a Few Cannon': Benjamin Franklin, the Association, and the Rhetoric and Practice of Boosterism" (116:131–55) presents Sally F. Griffith's analysis of how Franklin's model of working behind the scenes while eschewing the appearance of leadership, and of proclaiming harmony while exploiting contention, influenced the emergent American tradition of collective voluntary action on behalf of communal development. In " 'Small Matters': Benjamin Franklin, Philadelphia, and the 'Progress of Cities' " (116:157–82), A. Michal McMahon scrutinizes a younger Franklin's domestic concern with environment, his admonition about unlimited urban development, and his attention to communal order and satisfying social relations. The similarities and differences between the almanacs of Franklin and his predecessors are assessed by William Pencak, whose "Politics and Ideology in *Poor Richard's Almanack*" (116:183–211) also clarifies who Franklin included and rejected as representatives of the new public sphere.

As assessed in Malini Johar Schueller's polemical *The Politics of Voice* (pp. 17–30), Franklin proffers a capitalist myth promising that success in the marketplace depends on autonomous individualism; and this hegemonic capitalist ideology fosters his marginalization of any dissenting voices. Typical of Franklin's duplicity, claims William H. Shurr's facilely trendy and factually inaccurate " 'Now, Gods, Stand Up for Bastards': Reinterpreting Benjamin Franklin's *Autobiography*" (*AL* 64:435–51), the first and very separate part of his memoir is an attempt by a seditious father to mollify his Loyalist illegitimate son, as a form of insurance should the older man fall captive to British forces.

Robert D. Habich explains, more reliably, that in Franklin's view certain absolutes are expressed within the transient, with the result that the stable replication of cause and effect informs his suggestion that readers should duplicate his exemplary behavior: "Franklin's Scientific Ethics: Exemplary Rhetoric in the *Autobiography*" (*Early American Literature and Culture*, pp. 184–91). That Franklin, who was skeptical of uniting science and metaphysics, held views more akin to Voltaire than to Newton interests A. Owen Aldridge in "Benjamin Franklin: The Fusion of Science and Letters" (*American Literature and Science*, pp. 39–57). Not Voltaire but French affairs are featured in *The Papers of Benjamin Franklin, Vol. 29: March 1 through June 30, 1779*, ed. Barbara B. Oberg (Yale). And the comments of the man whom Franklin urged to write a natural history of the New World are usefully, if not always reliably, edited by Edmund Berkeley and Dorothy Smith Berkeley in *The Correspondence of John Bartram, 1734–1777* (Florida).

Two rhetorical modes of colonial nature writers are identified in Pamela Regis's *Describing Early America: Bartram, Jefferson, Crèvecoeur, and the Rhetoric of Natural History* (No. Ill.)—description (emphasizing Linnean lists reflective of the timeless chain of being) and narration (emphasizing exotic or unknown individual moments reflective of temporal possibilities). As a result of this pattern, Regis indicates, Native Americans were "naturalized" in terms of the descriptive order of flora yet at the same time provided occasions for narrative disturbance. When early American spokesmen substituted natural history for antiquity, concludes Paul Semonin's " 'Nature's Nation': Natural History as Nationalism in the New Republic" (*NWR* 30:6–41), they used nature to legitimate the subordination of other races.

Relatedly, Dana D. Nelson's *The World in Black and White* (pp. 3–37) discloses that early representations of racial and cultural difference changed in emphasis from physical to moral origins; even when such authors as Cotton Mather and William Byrd assail racial tropes, their writings are compromised by the prevalent political and economic structures of colonial discourse, which normalizes the superiority of the white race in terms of the hierarchical metaphysics of the chain of being. Nor were women exempt from similar patterns of assignment, argues Kenneth A. Lockridge in *On the Sources of Patriarchal Rage: The Commonplace Books of William Byrd and Thomas Jefferson and the Gendering of Power in the Eighteenth Century* (NYU). Merging issues of political power and sexual power, Byrd and Jefferson both associate women with male extinction, but in actuality their idea of woman as a threat to order masks their male fear of chaos and self-rage over personal corruption. That Scottish Enlightenment thought informed the American understanding of the role of women in polity is the subject of "Morals, Manners, and the Republican Mother" (*AQ* 44:192–215), by Rosemarie Zagarri.

How the political agenda of egalitarianism informed resistance to emergent scientific specialization and language is the subject of Joseph W. Slade's "Thomas Jefferson" (*American Literature and Science,* pp. 58–76), which also argues that *Notes on the State of Virginia* demonstrates an original transformation of scientific principles into literary strategies for unfolding a chronicle of America. How we read the Declaration of Independence today is determined less by Jefferson's Revolutionary ideals than by the Gettysburg Address, Garry Wills controversially contends in *Lincoln at Gettysburg: The Words That Remade America* (Simon and Schuster). Trouble with Alexander Hamilton is a prime feature of *The Papers of Thomas Jefferson, Vol. 25: 1 January–10 May 1793,* ed. John Catanzariti (Princeton). And supplementing his earlier volume, Frank Shuffelton has contributed an equally valuable resource in *Thomas Jefferson, 1981–1990: An Annotated Bibliography* (Garland).

Embedded in Milton's epic, according to Lydia Dittler Schulman's *Paradise Lost and the Rise of the American Republic* (Northeastern), is a debate on republicanism that made the poem useful to early-republic leaders; this debate centered on the licitness of a just rebellion against tyranny and the danger of a people in bondage to their passions and private interests. The interests and politics of printers in relation to their audience are descriptively treated in Carol Sue Humphrey's *"This Popular Engine": New England Newspapers during the American Revolution, 1775–1789* (Delaware). Robert D. Arner shares two poems that raise questions about an episode of civil unrest: "The Muse of History: Robert Bolling's Verses on the Norfolk Inoculation Riots of 1768–1769" (*Early American Literature and Culture,* pp. 165–83). Edward W. Hanson identifies John Ingham in "J. I.'s *The Little Book Open*" (*ANQ* n.s. 5:19–29).

And a review of visual images, including political cartoons, in *Emblems of American Community in the Revolutionary Era: A Study in Rhetorical Iconology* (Smithsonian, 1991) suggests to Lester C. Olson that 1754 to 1800 was a period of ambiguity and mutability in America.

Concerning the early-national period, Terence Martin's instructive comparison of French, British, and American epics treating Columbus concludes that whereas Europeans perceived the New World as part of ongoing history, Americans like Joel Barlow emphasized a new begin-ning outside of history: "Three Columbiads, Three Versions of the Future" (*EAL* 27:128–34). Robert D. Arner details a life and career in *Dobson's Encyclopaedia: The Publisher, Text, and Publication of America's First Britannica, 1789–1803* (Penn., 1991), which emphasizes the impor-tance of print in furthering post-Revolution nationalism.

vi Brown, Rowson, and Contemporaries

A historical survey of slave-era drama in a part of the world with which mainland settlers had extensive contact is provided by Errol Hill in *The Jamaican Stage, 1655–1900: Profile of a Colonial Theatre* (Mass.). Cheryl Z. Oreovicz declares that certain dramatizations of lost liberties in Italy and Spain warned American youth to resist what was perceived as an early-national drift toward a diminishing of republican spirit: "Heroic Drama for an Uncertain Age: The Plays of Mercy Warren" (*Early American Literature and Culture,* pp. 192–210).

In "Sisterhood in a Separate Sphere: Female Friendship in Hannah Webster Foster's *The Coquette* and *The Boarding School*" (*EAL* 27:185–203), Claire C. Pettengill contends that close female interaction was a sacred bond that had become challenged by economic and social changes; accordingly, its representation in fiction was as contradictory as were expectations during the early republic. The ambiguity of Eliza's renunciation of coquetry (in which the sentimental signs of vision and virtue are exchanged) interests David Waldstreicher, whose "'Fallen under My Observation': Vision and Virtue in *The Coquette*" (*EAL* 27:204–18) concludes that women's subjectivity was at once permitted and closely scrutinized during the early republic.

In Susanna Rowson's *Charlotte Temple,* Susan K. Harris contends (*Nineteenth-Century American Women's Novels: Interpretative Strategies* [Cambridge, 1990], pp. 41–49) that the controlled narrator's interpreta-tive process is designed to teach female readers to do their duty and be safe by resisting their instinctive attraction to dissembling males, by surrendering their personal desire for immediate gratification, and by taking into account biological and cultural traps that apply only to women. And in her introduction to a welcome edition of *The Gleaner* (Union), Nina Baym carefully delineates the boundaries of Judith Sargent Murray's conflicted views concerning women.

Peter Kafer reasonably argues in "Charles Brockden Brown and Revolutionary Philadelphia: An Imagination in Context" (*PMHB* 116:467–98) that the emotional and moral complexities experienced during Brown's youth, specifically the conscientious refusal of his family to take sides during the war, influenced the absence of any single moral guide in his fiction. Jayne K. Kribbs's " 'Reserved for My Pen': John Davis's Place in American Literature" (*Early American Literature and Culture,* pp. 211–26) maintains that a writer whose American subject matter was recommended by Charles Brockden Brown should be reconsidered today.

"An Inexhaustible Abundance: The National Landscape Depicted in American Magazines, 1780–1820" (*JER* 12:303–30) offers Karol Ann Peard Lawson's survey of how land was approached as a patriotic inspiration for an independent people; self-conscious reflection on these images of cultural self-sufficiency, she concludes, conveyed to their viewers an idea of themselves. Paul Sorrentino's "Authority and Genealogy in Mason Locke Weems's *Life of Washington*" (*Early American Literature and Culture,* pp. 227–39) defends one biographer's metonymic portrait of the first president as a prescriptive attempt to define familial and political authority during the early-republic struggle to achieve a national identity.

I take my leave in the words of 16th-century traveler Anthony Jenkenson: "And here I cease for this time, entreating you to bear with this my large discourse, which by reason of the variety of matter I could make no shorter."

University of Texas at Austin

12   19th-Century Literature

Gary Scharnhorst

The universe of scholarship devoted to the so-called minor writers of the 19th century continues to expand at the speed of a reading light. In the past three years the number of books covered in this chapter has nearly doubled to 90, and not because I have begun to seine the bibliographical flood with a net of finer mesh. Included this year are such items as the edited letters of Civil War soldiers, several new anthologies of writings reclaimed from the margins, as well as the annual harvest of forgotten stories by women and ethnic writers. Critical essays covered by this chapter have so proliferated that the journals cannot contain them all: literally dozens of articles on such figures as Grace King, Lafcadio Hearn, Kate Chopin, Charlotte Perkins Gilman, and Constance Fenimore Woolson now appear in edited collections. Some of this scholarship follows the trends in popular culture, particularly with the release of the latest Hollywood adaptation of *The Last of the Mohicans* and the revival of interest in the Civil War in the wake of Ken Burns's PBS documentary and the movie *Glory*. Meanwhile, book-length critical monographs on single authors seem increasingly an endangered species.

i General Studies

This year, as for the past decade or so, the most important general studies germane to this chapter analyze texts by women writers from gendered perspectives. Nina Baym's *Woman's Fiction: A Guide to Novels by and about Women in America, 1820–70*, a trend-setter first published in 1978, has been reissued in a second edition with a new introduction (Illinois). Every teacher and scholar of the period should own a copy. Among the gynocritics indebted to Baym, if only indirectly: G. M. Goshgarian, whose meticulously researched *To Kiss the Chastening Rod: Domestic Fiction and Sexual Ideology in the American Renaissance* (Cornell) argues that such sentimental novels with presumably passionless heroines as Susan Warner's *The Wide, Wide World,* Augusta Jane Evans's *Beulah,* Maria Cummins's *The Lamplighter,* Mary Jane Holmes's *'Lena Rivers,* and Caroline Lee Hentz's *Ernest Linwood* were in fact psychodramas of incestuous sexuality; Elizabeth Moss, whose *Domestic Novelists in the Old South* (LSU) proposes that various works by Hentz, Evans, Caroline Gilman, Maria McIntosh, and Mary Virginia Terhune were written in defense of the South, its aristocracy, and the peculiar institution of slavery; Diane Lichtenstein, whose *Writing Their Nations: The Tradition of Nineteenth-Century American Jewish Women Writers* (Indiana) considers the writings of nearly 30 women, including Emma Lazarus, Rebekah Hyneman, and Annie Meyer; and Ann Romines, whose *The Home Plot: Women, Writing, and Domestic Ritual* (Mass.) focuses on the celebratory representation of housekeeping in the female-centered worlds of Stowe, Jewett, Freeman, Cather, and Welty. Similarly, Paula Bennett in "Late Nineteenth-Century American Women's Nature Poetry and the Evolution of the Imagist Poem" (*Legacy* 9:89–103) suggests that verse by such women as Anna Callender and Celia Thaxter lay the groundwork for the Imagist experiments of Pound, H. D., and Amy Lowell. A pair of new books participate in the same project of recovery and reclamation without restricting their analysis only to American women's writings. Susan Rubinow Gorsky's *Femininity to Feminism: Women and Literature in the Nineteenth Century* (Twayne) is a useful introduction to feminist readings of a wide variety of Anglo-American texts by both women and men, including Alcott, Gaskell, Phelps, Stowe, Austen, and George Eliot; and Laura Hapke in *Tales of the Working Girl: Wage-Earning Women in American Literature, 1890–1925* (Twayne) reviews the lively turn-of-the-century literary debate over women in the labor force joined by such writers as Freeman, Anzia Yezierska, Jacob Riis, and Abraham Cahan. Hapke also excerpts her argument in "The American Working Girl and the New York Tenement Tale of the 1890s" (*JACult* 15, ii:43–50).

As Margo Culley remarks in the introduction to her edited collection *American Women's Autobiography,* there is no more vibrant field of contemporary literary scholarship than autobiography studies, especially in feminist circles. Two general essays in Culley's collection germane to this chapter may illustrate the point: Sidonie Smith's highly theoretical "Resisting the Gaze of Embodiment: Women's Autobiography in the Nine-teenth Century" (pp. 75–110), which situates the life-writings of Eliz-abeth Cady Stanton and Harriet Jacobs "within the complexities and contradictions of patriarchal ideologies of gender"; and Ann D. Gordon's more accessible "The Political Is the Personal: Two Autobiographies of Woman Suffragists" (pp. 111–27), a historical analysis of the merger of public persona and private person in the writings of Stanton and Abigail Scott Duniway. In "Twice Other, Once Shy: Nineteenth-Century Black Women's Autobiographies and the American Literary Tradition of Self-Effacement" (*ABSt* 7:46–61), Joycelyn K. Moody considers a recur-ring rhetorical tool—the apparent withdrawal of the autobiographer from her narrative—that marks such 19th-century texts by African Amer-ican women as Jacobs's *Incidents in the Life of a Slave Girl, Memoir of Old Elizabeth,* and *Narrative of the Life and Travels of Mrs. Nancy Prince.* As modern literary theory reminds us, moreover, there is no neat distinc-tion, no essential difference, between published autobiographical texts and such unpublished writings as diaries and letters, which also presume an audience. Indeed, according to Jane H. Hunter in "Inscribing the Self in the Heart of the Family: Diaries and Girlhood in Late-Victorian America" (*AQ* 44:51–81), "the unviolated diary was rare." Hunter specu-lates about the function of diaries in the evolution of "Victorian girls into the New Women of the Progressive Era," with particular reference to the journal of Annie Winsor. In the review-essay "Heart's Expression: The Middle-Class Language of Love in Late Nineteenth-Century Correspon-dence" (*AmLH* 4:141–64), Susan Albertine approaches several collections of familiar letters as verbal, aesthetic, and/or literary artifacts.

This year, too, racial issues form the nexus of several general studies. In *The Word in Black and White: Reading 'Race' in American Literature, 1638–1867* (Oxford), Dana D. Nelson ponders the construction or de-ployment of racial codes in texts by mostly white authors of the period, among them Cooper's *The Last of the Mohicans,* Bird's *Nick of the Woods,* Simms's *The Yemassee,* Sedgwick's *Hope Leslie,* Child's *The Romance of the Republic,* and Jacobs's *Incidents.* Similarly, in "Inter(racial)textuality in Nineteenth-Century Southern Narrative" (*Influence and Intertextuality in Literary History* [Wisconsin], ed. Jay Clayton and Eric Rothstein, pp. 298–317), William L. Andrews maps the relationship between Nat Turner's "Confessions" and John Pendleton Kennedy's *Swallow Barn,* especially their competition to define "the Negro." Carla L. Peterson offers a Marxist-inflected analysis of the origins of the African American novel—with particular reference to William Wells Brown's *Clotel,* Frank J. Webb's *The Garies,* Harriet E. Wilson's *Our Nig,* Martin R. Delany's *Blake,* and Jacobs's *Incidents*—in "Capitalism, Black (Under)-development, and the Production of the African-American Novel in the 1850s" (*AmLH* 4:559–83). Shirley Samuels in "The Identity of Slavery" (*The Culture of Sentiment,* pp. 157–71) adopts a New Historicist approach to locate problems of personal, cultural, and national identity common to the pro-slavery epic *The Devil in America,* the antislavery magazine *The Slave's Friend,* and Child's *The Romance of the Republic.* In addition, four general studies this year are sited at the intersecting loci of gender and race: Kari J. Winter's *Subjects of Slavery, Agents of Change: Women and Power in Gothic Novels and Slave Narratives, 1790–1865* (Georgia), which compares the female gothicism of Ann Radcliffe and Mary Shelley to the antislavery feminism of Jacobs and Nancy Prince; Maggie Sale's "Critiques from Within: Antebellum Projects of Resistance" (*AL* 64:695–718), which argues that Douglass, Harper, and Jacobs challenge sexist and racist notions about African Americans by appropriating the rhetoric of the Revolutionary period; Harryette Mullen's "Runaway Tongue: Resistant Orality in *Uncle Tom's Cabin, Our Nig, Incidents in the Life of a Slave Girl,* and *Beloved*" (*The Culture of Sentiment,* pp. 245–64), on strategies of resistance inherent in the oral tradition appropriated by African American women; and Claudia Tate's *Domestic Allegories of Political Desire: The Black Heroine's Text at the Turn of the Century* (Oxford), which analyzes in detail 11 novels of "genteel domestic feminism" by African American women, including Harper's *Iola Leroy* and Pauline Hopkins's *Winona* and *Of One Blood.*

With the blurring of genre distinctions, the phrase "literary journalism" no longer seems oxymoronic. *A Sourcebook of American Literary Journalism* (Greenwood), ed. Thomas B. Connery, in fact contains biographical sketches of several figures covered in this chapter, including Richard Harding Davis, Stephen Crane, and Jacob Riis. In "The Making and Breaking of Chicago's *America*" (*American Periodicals,* 2:100–112), Guy Szuberla recounts the history of a short-lived, neglected literary weekly which heralded the Chicago Renaissance and resisted such "foreign" imports as Zolasque realism. In "Sentimental Figures: Reading *Godey's Lady's Book* in Antebellum America" (*The Culture of Sentiment,* pp. 73–91), Isabelle Lehuu discovers an unstable or equivocal relationship between the literary and visual texts in a popular late-19th-century magazine for women. Of related interest: Paul Lancaster's *Gentleman of the Press* (Syracuse), a biography of Julian Ralph of the *New York Sun,* which daily newspaper under the editorship of C. A. Dana was one of the most literate and literary in the late 19th century.

There is no new general study this year comparable to Michael T. Gilmore's *American Romanticism and the Marketplace* or R. Jackson Wilson's *Figures of Speech: American Writers and the Literary Marketplace.* However, *The Profession of Authorship in America, 1800–1870,* a collection of groundbreaking essays on literary-market forces by the late William Charvat, was reissued by Columbia University Press a quarter-century after its original publication. Ezra Greenspan's "Evert Duyckinck and the History of Wiley and Putnam's Library of American Books, 1845–1847" (*AL* 64:677–93), which chronicles Duyckinck's immersion in an early canon-forming project, neatly supplements the Charvat volume.

No fewer than five specialized classroom anthologies containing generous selections of 19th-century texts appear this year. *American Women Regionalists, 1850–1910* (Norton), ed. Judith Fetterley and Marjorie Pryse, reprints 64 stories and sketches by 14 writers, including Stowe, Jewett, Freeman, Sui Sin Far, and Zitkala-Sä. *American Women Writers: Diverse Voices in Prose Since 1845* (St. Martin's), ed. Eileen Barrett and Mary Cullinan, reprints texts by 57 writers, including Sojourner Truth, Alice Cary, and Rebecca Harding Davis. This volume neatly complements last year's *Meridian Anthology of Early American Women Writers,* ed. Katharine M. Rogers, which covers the period from 1650 to 1865. *African American Poetry of the Nineteenth Century* (Illinois), ed. Joan R. Sherman, contains 171 poems by 35 poets, among them Frances E. W. Harper, Adah Isaacs Menken, and Paul Laurence Dunbar. *The African-American Novel in the Age of Reaction* (Mentor), ed. William L. Andrews, neatly complements the poetry anthology by reprinting in an accessible paperback edition Harper's *Iola Leroy,* Chesnutt's *The Marrow of Tradition,* and Dunbar's *The Sport of the Gods.* Finally, *Anthology of Western Reserve Literature* (Kent State), ed. David R. Anderson and Gladys Haddad, contains a sheaf of early-19th-century letters by settlers as well as stories and verse by such figures as Howells, Chesnutt, Woolson, and John Hay.

By way of a coda to this section: Like the Anderson/Haddad and Fetterley/Pryse anthologies, two new monographs serve to remind us that—in addition to the firelines drawn in the canon wars around class, race, ethnicity, and gender—the factor of region or regional affiliation may also reconfigure the critical grid. James Hunt's *Writing Illinois* (Illinois) orbits around Bryant's poem "The Prairie" and literary representations of Lincoln; and Ronald Weber's *The Midwestern Ascendancy in American Writing* (Indiana) features such figures as Hamlin Garland and Robert Herrick.

ii Cooper, Irving, and Contemporaries

Like a Poe character or the monster in a Saturday morning serial, Cooper is often buried but never quite dead. This year is no exception, with the publication of 11 new articles on his work, five of them collected in *New Essays on* The Last of the Mohicans (Cambridge), edited with an expert introduction by H. Daniel Peck. As Wayne Franklin explains in "The Wilderness of Words in *The Last of the Mohicans*" (pp. 25–45), Cooper conceived the chaotic landscape around Glens Falls by an act of radical erasure of "history from nature" that enabled him to imagine the tumultuous events of 1757. The very language of the novel, with its rhetoric of "domestic affection" at war with forest codes, mirrors its frontier setting. In "From Atrocity to Requiem: History in *The Last of the Mohicans*" (pp. 47–65), Terence Martin provocatively juxtaposes the massacre at Fort Henry at the center of the book with the death of Uncas at its close to argue that Cooper takes the reader "from one kind of history to another," from "the savagery of fact" to "the tragedy of inexorable process." Robert Lawson-Peebles also focuses on the mayhem in chapter 17, "a synecdoche of American history" and "a dreadful portent" in Cooper's view of things to come, in "The Lesson of the Massacre at Fort William Henry" (pp. 115–38). Nina Baym situates Cooper's novel in an intertextual network of Indian tales by men and women, including Lydia Maria Child's *Hobomok* and Catharine Sedgwick's *Hope Leslie,* in "How Men and Women Wrote Indian Stories" (pp. 67–86). The women-centered narratives, Baym fairly concludes, challenge Cooper's claim to a superior realism as well as his assumptions about race and gender. (Baym also publishes a version of this piece under the title "Putting Women in Their Place: *The Last of the Mohicans* and Other Stories," pp. 19–35 in *Feminism and American Literary History* [Rutgers], a first-rate collection of 14 of her essays written over the past decade or so, many of them substantially revised for the book.) Crudely revising Leslie Fiedler's argument that miscegenation is the secret theme of the Leatherstocking series, Shirley Samuels contends in "Generation through Violence: Cooper and the Making of Americans" (pp. 87–114) that the third novel in the series "produces identities by a miscegenation of animal and human, natural and cultural." More problematically, in "Infanticide and Cultural Reproduction in Cooper's *The Last of the Mohicans*" (*CRevAS* 22:407–17), Mary Chapman discovers in the misogynist and racist violence of the novel "a fantasy of male parthenogenesis on the frontier that only men inhabit." Belaboring her thesis, Chapman asserts that the "infanticide trope" Cooper smuggles into the novel "simultaneously attempts to justify white genocide of native Americans and implicates white males in their culture's own sterility." This essay seems not so much to elucidate as to obfuscate the text or to mask it under an ideological veneer.

Nor is interest in Cooper this year devoted exclusively to a single novel. James E. Swearingen and Joanne Cutting-Gray's "Cooper's Pathfinder: Revising Historical Understanding" (*NLH* 23:267–80) forcefully disputes the myth-and-symbol reading of the Leatherstocking saga and recasts the fourth novel in the series as a type of meditation on history, Natty Bumppo as *Janus bifrons*. And according to Louise Barnett in "Speech in the Wilderness: The Ideal Discourse of *The Deerslayer*" (*Desert, Garden, Margin, Range*, pp. 19–28), the final novel in the series, rather than a mere adventure story, is "a speech-act drama in which speaking or withholding speech has profound consequences." In "The Fictions of Daniel Boone," another essay in the same volume (pp. 29–43), Mary Lawlor reviews Boone's various incarnations in the narratives of Cooper, John Filson, James Hall, and Timothy Flint. In "Cooper and Wordsworth" (*UMSE* n.s. 10:26–36) Lance Schachterle tallies the novelist's debt to the poet, chiefly his epigraphs to chapters and the Lake District setting of *The Deerslayer*. Fortunately, too, Cooper studies enjoy a vitality which extends beyond the Leatherstocking series, however central the tetralogy may be to the writer's modern reputation. In "James Fenimore Cooper's *The Spy* and the Neutral Ground" (*ATQ* n.s. 6:5–16), Bruce A. Rosenberg discursively relates some episodes in Cooper's early novel to the celebrated spy case of Major John André. Scott Michaelsen defends one of the most neglected novels in Cooper's oeuvre as an insightful satire on contract law in "Cooper's *Monikins:* Contracts, Construction, and Chaos" (*ArQ* 48, iii:1–26). And Kay Seymour House, editor in chief of the Cooper edition and a self-described reactionary in the present climate of literary studies, poignantly reminisces about her research in "The James Fenimore Cooper Collections at the American Antiquarian Society" (*PAAS* 102:317–27).

On the other hand, interest in Irving flags this year. William H. Shurr improves the occasion of the Columbian quincentenary in "Irving and Whitman: Re-Historicizing the Figure of Columbus in Nineteenth-Century America" (*ATQ* n.s. 6:237–50), which offers the unsurprising claim that both writers fashioned Columbus in their own images and appropriated historical fact for ulterior purposes. In "Cultural Fate and Social Freedom in Three American Short Stories" (*SSF* 29:543–49), Walter Shear adds to the voluminous scholarship on the Hawthorne-James connection, albeit with a twist, by suggesting that "Rip Van Winkle" is a type of paradigm text for "Young Goodman Brown" and "The Jolly Corner." William Collins Watterson attributes a portrait of Irving dating from the mid-1830s to the miniaturist James Vandyck in "Vandyck's Image of Washington Irving" (*SAR*, pp. 75–90). Irving also figures prominently in Bruce Greenfield's *The Romantic Explorer in American Literature, 1790–1855* (Columbia), in which he is characterized as the "historian of American discovery." According to Greenfield, Irving in his travel writings adopted "the discourse of national expansion" even while critiquing the policy and covertly revealing its contradictions. Unlike Irving, ironically, one of his friends and collaborators on *Salmagundi* is the subject of a monograph this year: in *James Kirke Paulding: The Last Republican* (Greenwood), Lorman Ratner usefully summarizes the events in Paulding's life and the circumstances of his career. Joel Myerson also sheds light on a neglected Knickerbocker poet and editor in "Willis Gaylord Clark: An Autobiographical Sketch" (*American Periodicals* 2:1–5).

The nascent Simms revival of recent years gets a boost this year with the publication of John Caldwell Guilds's monumental *Simms: A Literary Life* (Arkansas), the first critical biography of the writer in a century. According to Guilds, the author of *"Long Years of Neglect": The Work and Reputation of William Gilmore Simms* (see *ALS 1988*, p. 206), Simms's claim to "literary permanence" may be found in his fiction, especially his novels. Charles S. Watson supports this argument, if only indirectly, in "Simms and the Civil War: The Revolutionary Analogy" (*SLJ* 24, ii:76–89), which contends that Simms's last five novels about the American Revolution were topical commentary on the South's conflicted relations with the Union. Miriam J. Shillingsburg's "The Senior Simmes—Mississippi Unshrouded" (*UMSE* n.s. 10:250–55), a bit of genealogical history, is the stuff of informational footnotes.

Some of the most exciting scholarship in recent years has been devoted to the recovery of American Indian narratives of the antebellum period.

Barry O'Connell this year edits and introduces the complete writings of William Apess, a Pequot Indian, in a volume suitable for classroom adoption under the title *On Our Own Ground* (Mass.). This scholarly edition should go far in retrieving Apess from the black hole of critical neglect to which he has long been consigned. So too June Namias's new edition of *A Narrative of the Life of Mrs. Mary Jemison* (Okla.), an ostensible "captivity narrative" first published in 1824. The problem with such a text, as Namias and others recognize, is that every prior edition has been mediated or strained through the filter of white editors. In " 'With Them Was My Home': Native American Autobiography and *A Narrative of the Life of Mrs. Mary Jemison*" (*AL* 64:49–70), however, Susan Walsh recontextualizes the narrative within a Native American frame of self-disclosure; and in "Mary Jemison and the Domestication of the American Frontier" (*Desert, Garden, Margin, Range*, pp. 93–109), Susan Scheckel similarly distinguishes the narrative from more conventional stories of Indian cruelties. Rather than the expected ending—the restoration of the captive—Jemison's memoir concludes with her firmly settled in company with her mixed-blood children on the interstice between the Indian and white worlds. In addition, Neil Schmitz in "Captive Utterance: Black Hawk and Indian Irony" (*ArQ* 48, iv:1–18) strips away the editorial intrusions in *Black Hawk, An Autobiography* to reveal a dissident text that "is everywhere barbed, reproachful, scathing in its irony"; Barbara Juster Esbensen in "Retelling the Told Tales of Kah-ge-gah-ge-bowh and Arthur C. Parker," an essay in *Sitting at the Feet of the Past* (Greenwood), ed. Gary D. Schmidt and Donald R. Hettinga, pp. 21–24, recommends the oral legends recorded in 1850 by an Ojibway chief who took the name George Conway; Jonathan Bradford Brennan in "Speaking Cross Boundaries: A Nineteenth-Century African/Native American Autobiography" (*ABSt* 7:219–38) makes a strong case for the Native American origins of *A Sketch of the Life of Okah Tubbee;* and Elaine A. Jahner in "Transitional Narratives and Cultural Continuity" (*Boundary 2* 19, iii:148–79) reclaims some of the mythic texts of George Sword, an Oglala Sioux leader. Both Louis Owens in *Other Destinies: Understanding the American Indian Novel* (Okla.), pp. 32–40, and John Lowe in "Space and Freedom in the Golden Republic: Yellow Bird's *The Life and Adventures of Joaquin Murieta, the Celebrated California Bandit*" (*SAIL* 4, ii–iii:106–22) consider John Rollin Ridge's putative biography of Murieta a "subversive masquerade" (Owens's phrase). Rather than simply a blood-and-thunder potboiler, Ridge's novel is a "hybridized narrative" which dramatizes the Murieta legend to condemn American imperialism in California and the displacement of indigenous peoples. Ridge also figures prominently in Karl Kroeber's "American Indian Persistence and Resurgence" (*Boundary 2* 19, iii:1–25), which recommends the study of American Indian literature as an alternative to empty theoretical posturings.

I have reserved for special mention here several essays on neglected texts by white male writers of the period. In "Authority and Genealogy in Mason Locke Weems's *Life of Washington*" (*Early American Literature and Culture*, pp. 227–39), Paul Sorrentino seeks to rehabilitate the reputation of a writer usually derided as a glib mythmaker for juveniles. Even in his much-maligned biography of Washington, as Sorrentino persuasively demonstrates, Parson Weems was to some degree a purposeful artist: he adapted the "theme of filial rebellion to argue that the American Revolution was a family dispute that established a new genealogical line of authority." In "Robert Dale Owen's *Threading My Way* and Victorian Autobiography" (*Biography* 15:165–77), Clinton Machann favorably compares the conflicted father-son relations depicted in Owen's life-writing with those in John Stuart Mill's *Autobiography* and Edmund Gosse's *Father and Son*. In "Justified Bloodshed: Robert Montgomery Bird's *Nick of the Woods* and the Origins of the Vigilante Hero in American Literature and Culture" (*JACult* 15, ii:51–61), Gary Hoppenstand traces the vigilante archetype back to the character of Nathan Slaughter in Bird's novel, though the Indian-hater figure in American culture has an even longer history. Philip D. Beidler recounts the publication history, outlines the plot, and identifies sources of the early, pseudonymously published novel *The Lost Virgin of the South* in " 'The first production of the kind, in the South': A Backwoods Literary *Incognito* and His Attempt at the Great American Novel" (*SLJ* 24, ii:106–24).

A final note: *Kelroy,* a novel by Rebecca Rush of Philadelphia, is reprinted this year for the first time since 1812 in the Early American Women Writers series (Oxford), edited with a helpful introduction by Dana D. Nelson.

iii Popular Writers and Others at Midcentury

Stowe, Alcott, Douglass, and now Jacobs have become major compass points of critical attention. More than any other literary figure germane to this chapter, Stowe has been the beneficiary of the canon reformation of the past generation. Her star continues to ascend this year with the appearance of several major articles devoted to her writings. Predictably, *Uncle Tom's Cabin* inspires much of the discussion. In "Home as Heaven, Home as Hell: *Uncle Tom's* Canon," in *Rewriting the Dream* (Rodopi), ed. W. M. Verhoeven, pp. 22–42, Leslie Fiedler cries mea culpa for his qualified praise of Stowe's story some 30 years ago in *Love and Death in the American Novel* and proceeds to integrate its domestic mythology into his archetypal reading of the American psyche. Lynn Wardley's "Relic, Fetish, Femmage: The Aesthetics of Sentiment in the Work of Stowe" (*The Culture of Sentiment*, pp. 203–20) rehearses the now-familiar argument for Stowe's subversive strategies, her appropriation of the ideology of domesticity, particularly in *Uncle Tom's Cabin* and *Household Papers and Stories*. In "*Uncle Tom's Cabin* in *Frederick Douglass' Paper*: An Analysis of Reception" (*AL* 64:71–93), Robert S. Levine traces the sympathetic treatment given Stowe's novel in the pages of Douglass's abolitionist paper during the early 1850s; and in "Remodeling the Model Home in *Uncle Tom's Cabin* and *Beloved*" (*AL* 64:785–805), Lori Aske-land compares the ideology of domesticity celebrated in Stowe's and Morrison's novels. Both Jennifer L. Jenkins in "Failed Mothers and Fallen Homes: The Crisis of Domesticity in *Uncle Tom's Cabin*" (*ESQ* 38:161–87) and Winfried Fluck in "The Power and Failure of Representa-tion in Harriet Beecher Stowe's *Uncle Tom's Cabin*" (*NLH* 23:319–38) regard the novel as a type of noble failure, however. As Jenkins suggests in her revisionist essay, Stowe depicted not a process of salvation through maternal love (as Askeland, Jane Tompkins, and others have claimed) but unchecked matriarchal authority predicated on fear. "From Mrs. Shelby to Mrs. Legree," according to Jenkins, "Stowe's mothers neglect, deceive, or abuse their offspring." Marie St. Clare is the epitome of such mothers rather than the exception to them. On his part, Fluck attempts to transcend the cultural vs. aesthetic readings of the novel by theorizing on the effects of its melodramatic and sentimental strategy. The text abandons its pretense at representation, Fluck contends, because it must resort to sensationalism ("a permanent surplus of signification") to real-ize its moral and social purpose. This "failure of representation," para-doxically, "secures the novel's effectiveness." Fluck adds little to prior discussions of the novel; however, he expresses his points in more tortured language. Two other essays consider Stowe and the role of the female artist in the mid-19th century. In "Parlor Literature: Harriet Beecher Stowe and the Question of 'Great Women Artists'" (*Signs*

17:275–303), Joan D. Hedrick eloquently defends Stowe as a type of divine amateur who proved her mettle by writing parlor sketches for a mass audience; and in "The Artist's Craftiness: Miss Prissy in *The Minister's Wooing*" (*SAF* 20:33–45), Nancy Lusignan Schultz notes how, in her first domestic novel, Stowe subtly invested the character of the dressmaker-artist with a capacity to subvert authority.

Critical interest in Louisa May Alcott falls off ever so slightly this year, though I hardly presume to project a trend on this basis. As noted last year, Alcott sleuths still discover some surprising treasures, much as a sharp plow may turn up artifacts in fallow fields. Madeleine B. Stern reports the existence of yet another early Alcott sensation story, "Marion Earle," based in part on *Aurora Leigh* (*NCF* 47:91–98), and summarizes the record of Alcott's early contributions to a popular Boston weekly story-paper, the *Saturday Evening Gazette* (*American Periodicals* 2:64–78). Daniel Shealy collects and superbly introduces 38 of the author's short didactic writings for juveniles in *Louisa May Alcott's Fairy Tales and Fantasy Stories* (Tennessee). Jane E. Schultz discusses the extended domestic and military metaphors inscribed in another of the early, neglected works in "Embattled Care: Narrative Authority in Louisa May Alcott's *Hospital Sketches*" (*Legacy* 9:104–18). Less satisfactory is Frances Armstrong's "'Here Little, and Hereafter Bliss': *Little Women* and the Deferral of Greatness" (*AL* 64:453–74), a convoluted analysis of the novel's metaphors of expansion and diminishment which adds little to Alcott criticism. Harbour Winn's intertextual note, "Echoes of Literary Sisterhood: Louisa May Alcott and Kate Chopin" (*SAF* 20:205–08), spins out a fragile tissue of speculation that *Little Women* may have influenced a couple of Chopin's stories.

His critical stock on the rise, Frederick Douglass's autobiographies inspire three major journal articles this year. Unfortunately, each of these essays tends to blur the features of Douglass's subtle artistry with jargonological technospeak, the esoteric argot of latter-day gnostics. In "Heart Attacks: Frederick Douglass's Strategic Sentimentality" (*Criticism* 34:193–216), Stephanie A. Smith suggests that Douglass "manipulated antebellum sentimental ideology" in his successive autobiographical texts to "rescript a politics of community." Yet "Douglass's rescriptures do not always hold the balance between polarities; they oscillate uneasily"—whatever that may mean. Smith also uses "gender" as a verb. In "Frederick Douglass's Haven-Finding Art" (*ArQ* 48, iv:47–73), Barry Maxwell explores Douglass's complex wordplay, especially the geographical puns in *My Bondage and My Freedom,* to describe "how he authored his own subjectivity" or "evolve[d] a procedure of negative emulation"—whatever that may mean. Rereading the biblical typology (re-Scriptures?) of the 1845 *Narrative,* Sharon Carson enlists Douglass in the ranks of modern radical theologians in "Shaking the Foundation: Liberation Theology in *Narrative of the Life of Frederick Douglass*" (*R&L* 24, ii:19–34). Thomas Wortham's "Did Emerson Blackball Frederick Douglass from Membership in the Town and Country Club?" (*NEQ* 65:295–98) seems almost quaint by comparison. On the basis of extant manuscript evidence, Wortham casts doubt on the claim, now two generations old, that Emerson harbored a private antipathy toward Douglass.

Scholarship on Harriet Jacobs is a growth industry this year, with a half-dozen fine essays in print. In "Lydia Maria Child and the Endings to Harriet Jacobs's *Incidents in the Life of a Slave Girl*" (*AL* 64:255–72), Bruce Mills reviews the active editorial role Childs played in shaping the narrative, especially in foregrounding matriarchal themes to underscore its abolitionist message. The other Jacobs articles this year all echo or dispute the notion that a domestic ideology is inscribed in *Incidents.* In "Harriet Jacobs's Search for Home" (*CLAJ* 35:411–21), Elizabeth C. Becker suggests that the sentimental discourse of Jacobs's autobiography centers on her efforts to settle in a traditional home, and that thus her story resembles the plot of a popular domestic novel. In "Harriet Jacobs's Modest Proposals: Revising Southern Hospitality" (*SoQ* 30, ii–iii:22–28), Anne Bradford Warner focuses on the trope of feeding/eating in the text, arguing that Jacobs subverts the traditional perception of southern hospitality by establishing an analogy between the slave as flesh and the slaveowner as voracious carnivore. Both Franny Nudelman in "Harriet Jacobs and the Sentimental Politics of Female Suffering" (*ELH* 59:939–64) and Mary Vermillion in "Reembodying the Self: Representations of Rape in *Incidents in the Life of a Slave Girl* and *I Know Why the Caged Bird Sings*" (*Biography* 15:243–60) assume more radical stances. According to Nudelman, Jacobs narrates her (particularly sexual) experiences within the context of a domestic ideology disposed to condemn her behavior in order to reveal the rank hypocrisy of those genteel standards. Jacobs "exposes the assumptions of abolitionist discourse, and ancillary sentimental forms," Nudelman concludes, "not by definitively rejecting them" but by deconstructing them from within. Similarly, Vermillion explains how Jacobs subverts the seduction plot common in domestic fiction by countering the stereotype of the sexually exploited slave woman. In "The Changing Moral Discourse of Nineteenth-Century African American Women's Autobiography: Harriet Jacobs and Elizabeth Keckley" (*De/Colonizing the Subject*, pp. 225–41), William L. Andrews compares Jacobs's interrogation of sexual mores under the slave system in *Incidents* with Keckley's more circumspect and pragmatic critique in her postwar autobiography, *Behind the Scenes*. Of related interest: Frances Smith Foster discusses Keckley's memoir at length in "Autobiography after Emancipation: The Example of Elizabeth Keckley" (*Multicultural Autobiography*, pp. 32–63). Foster's claim that *Behind the Scenes* is "more assertive and more critical than those [African American autobiographies] published during slavery" seems just the sort of overstatement that Andrews's essay serves to correct. And in "Her Side of the Story: A Feminist Analysis of Two Nineteenth-Century Antebellum Novels" (*ALR* 24, iii:7–21), Angelyn Mitchell distinguishes between William Wells Brown's romantic strategy in *Clotel* and Harriet E. Wilson's sentimentalism in *Our Nig*.

Despite the slow ebb in their reputations, the Fireside Poets—or at least three of them—continue to interest scholars. Most significantly this year, Fordham issues the final two volumes (5 and 6) of *The Letters of William Cullen Bryant*, spanning the period from 1865 until the poet's death in 1878. This new edition supersedes in every way the Parke Godwin edition issued in 1883. Michael P. Kramer offers the most extended critical analysis of Longfellow's work in several years in " 'A Fine Ambiguity': Longfellow, Language, and Literary History," a chapter in his *Imagining Language in America* (pp. 64–89). Kramer contends that Longfellow was a sensitive if not always consistent or logical student of language whose academic writings betray "cultural ambiguity" or divided cultural loyalties. Julie A. Rechel-White marshals evidence that Whitman's poem "Excelsior" was a reply of sorts to Longfellow's popular poem of the same title in "Longfellow's Influence on Whitman's 'Rise' from Manhattan Island" (*ATQ* n.s. 6:121–29). For the record, *The Song of Hiawatha* is reprinted this year with an introduction by Daniel Aaron (Dent/Tuttle). Moreover, Jeanne Moskal prints a brief, hitherto unpublished Whittier letter in order to suggest, on rather slim grounds, that the poet enjoyed a wider popularity in the 1880s than commonly thought: "John Greenleaf Whittier and the Washington Territory" (*NEQ* 65:135–39).

Another pair of popular midcentury writers fare slightly better. Horatio Alger, Jr., a pale son of the genteel tradition, is the subject of three new articles this year. Hanley Kanar helpfully discusses Alger's ambivalence on racial issues in his first juvenile book in "Horatio Alger and *Frank's Campaign:* White Supremacy in a Northern Intellectual's Juvenile Novel" (*CLAQ* 17, i:36–40). Kanar's analysis is marred, however, by her repeated characterization of Alger as a typical abolitionist. (He was, more accurately, an antislavery liberal.) Carol Nackenoff emphasizes the antebellum and preindustrial standards by which Alger's heroes achieve middle-class respectability in "Of Factories and Failures: Exploring the Invisible Factory Gates of Horatio Alger, Jr." (*JPC* 25:63–80). Gorman Beauchamp reprises Alger's significance for modern cultural critics— adding little to the record, but summarizing it exceptionally well—in "*Ragged Dick* and the Fate of Respectability" (*MQR* 31:324–45). In "The Disappearance of Ik. Marvel" (*AmerS* 33, ii:5–20), a solid essay with sweeping implications, Arnold G. Tew and Allan Peskin trace the critical eclipse of Donald G. Mitchell, a.k.a. Marvel, whose esteemed 19th-century reputation was a casualty of 20th-century recanonizations that marginalized sentimental writers. Whereas the ongoing canon debate has led to the rediscovery of such writers as Fanny Fern and Susan B. Warner, however, it has scarcely touched Mitchell.

Whatever the truth of Whitman's assertion that "the real war will never get in the books," hundreds of Civil War narratives have been written, many of them by soldiers or survivors of the conflict. In "Genre Wars and the Rhetoric of Manhood in *Miss Ravenel's Conversion from Secession to Loyalty*" (*NCF* 46:473–94), Thomas H. Fick argues that De Forest's novel, with its various narrative modes, reenacts the very war it chronicles. The pioneering realism of the text, that is, deconstructed the genre of historical romance with its virile cavalier hero on which the South had based its claim to cultural superiority. Even more than the occasional De Forest or Crane scholar, Kathleen Diffley in *Where My Heart Is Turning Ever: Civil War Stories and Constitutional Reform, 1861– 1876* (Georgia) demolishes the critical commonplace that the war was largely "unwritten." Basing her analysis on some 300 stories published in magazines during the war and Reconstruction, Diffley discovers that not only did the "irrepressible conflict" become the stuff of popular fiction but that it disrupted the familiar form (especially on issues of race, region, and gender) that such tales had earlier assumed. Theoretically informed and eminently readable, Diffley's study is a virtuoso performance, a most valuable contribution to the literary history of the Civil

War. So too is Garry Wills's *Lincoln at Gettysburg: The Words That Remade America* (Simon and Schuster), which eruditely contends—as the subtitle suggests—that Honest Abe's three-minute speech reinvented the bases of constitutional government. More than any other scholarly work surveyed in this chapter, Wills's book proves the power of language to effect social change. For the record, the Gettysburg Address is one of the texts included in *The Portable Abraham Lincoln* (Viking), ed. Andrew Delbanco.

In addition to Wills's book, several literary-historical treatments of midcentury orations merit brief mention in this section. Steven A. Wartofsky in "Critique of the Upright Self" (*MR* 33:401–26) not only theorizes that oratory is typically a male project of dominance and "perhaps the most important means of sustaining popular consensus on important contemporary issues" but illustrates the point by reference to speeches on the national bank and slavery by Edward Everett, John C. Calhoun, and Daniel Webster. As if to reinforce Wartofsky's thesis, Robert Dunne sounds the anti-immigrant and anti-Catholic depths of Lyman Beecher's speeches in "A Plea for a *Protestant* American Dream" (*ON* 16:189–97). As if in deliberate counterpoint, however, Gail A. Hankins's "In the Beginning . . . Maria W. Stewart: Forerunner of American Women Orators" (*W&L* 15, ii:20–24) sketches the life and examines the rhetoric of a black Bostonian who was one of "the first women to challenge the taboo against female public speakers."

With the coming of age of a new generation of social historians who meticulously document the Civil War from the perspective of common folk rather than only the diplomats, politicians, and generals, the letters and diaries of foot soldiers in the conflict have acquired a certain cachet. Three such collections of documents appear in 1992: " 'The Rebs are thick about us': The Civil War Diary of Amos Stouffer of Chambersburg" (*Civil War History* 38:210–31), ed. William Garrett Piston; *When This Cruel War Is Over: The Civil War Letters of Charles Harvey Brewster* (Mass.), ed. David W. Blight; and *Blue-eyed Child of Fortune: The Civil War Letters of Robert Gould Shaw* (Georgia), ed. Russell Duncan. Shaw, the scion of a distinguished New England family, commanded the Massachusetts 54th Volunteers, the first regiment of black soldiers recruited in the North, whose exploits were dramatized in the movie *Glory*. Still, as Elizabeth C. Clark remarks in "Missing in Action: Confederate Females in Civil War Novels" (*L&U* 15, ii:15–26), southern white women are rarely portrayed realistically in war novels for young readers. Suzy Clarkson Holstein in effect proposes a corrective for such silence or neglect in " 'Offering Up Her Life': Confederate Women on the Altars of Sacrifice" (*SoSt* n.s. 2:113–30). Holstein explains that both Mary Chesnut's journals and Augusta Jane Evans's novel *Macaria* "provide a gloss for the role adopted by Southern womanhood during the Civil War." Coincidentally, Melissa Mentzer describes Chesnut's several attempts at revising or stylizing her journal for publication in "Rewriting Herself: Mary Chesnut's Narrative Strategies" (*Connecticut Review* 14:49–55); and the LSU Press reprints two of Evans's novels: *Macaria,* ed. with an introduction by Drew Gilpin Faust, and *Beulah,* ed. with an introduction by Elizabeth Fox-Genovese.

Just as critical interest in such newly canonized writers as Stowe and Alcott is no longer limited to *Uncle Tom's Cabin* and *Little Women,* Rebecca Harding Davis studies are no longer one-trick ponies. "Life in the Iron Mills" remains the central text in Davis's oeuvre, but none of the five essays on Davis this year is devoted entirely to it. Jane Atteridge Rose in "The Artist Manqué in the Fiction of Rebecca Harding Davis" (*Writing the Woman Artist,* pp. 155–74) traces the evolution of the artist figure in Davis's work, with sculptor-ironworker Hugh Wolfe only one of several points of discussion. In "Images of Self: The Example of Rebecca Harding Davis and Charlotte Perkins Gilman" (*ELN* 29, iv:70–78), Rose also juxtaposes Davis's "The Wife's Story," with its apparent tribute to maternal domesticity, and "The Yellow Wall-paper" to chart the sea change in the portrayal of women; and in "Class and the Strategies of Sympathy" (*The Culture of Sentiment,* pp. 128–42), Amy Schraeger Lang posits *Uncle Tom's Cabin* and "Iron Mills" as paradigm texts to demonstrate "that vocabularies of class, race, and gender"—the phrase has fast become a mantra in scholarship—"continually displace one another in midnineteenth-century sentimental fiction." On her part, Kristin Boudreau in " 'The Woman's Flesh of Me': Rebecca Harding Davis's Response to Self-Reliance" (*ATQ* n.s. 6:131–40) contends, albeit not always convincingly, that "The Wife's Story" represents a working-class critique of Emerson's dreamy idealism. Jean Pfaelzer's argument in "Domesticity and the Discourse of Slavery: 'John Lamar' and 'Blind Tom' by Rebecca Harding Davis" (*ESQ* 38:31–56) is also marred by a nettlesome assumption—that the Civil War was largely unwritten. As noted above, Kathleen Diffley adroitly challenges this premise in her new book. Thus,

Pfaelzer's major point—that Davis's Civil War stories are exceptional if not unique in their representation of slavery—pales in the context of Diffley's analysis.

Several other midcentury writers attract a modicum of attention this year. Joyce W. Warren painstakingly reconstructs the life of Sara Willis Parton, pioneering feminist writer and pseudonymous author of the novel *Ruth Hall,* in *Fanny Fern: An Independent Woman* (Rutgers), the most significant new biography of any figure covered in this chapter. *Gail Hamilton: Selected Writings,* a collection in the American Women Writers Series (Rutgers), ed. Susan Coultrap-McQuin, reprints some of the pseudonymous works of Mary Abigail Dodge, including excerpts from *A Battle of the Books,* an allegorical exposé of the accounting practices of midcentury Boston publishers. In "Catharine Maria Sedgwick's *Hope Leslie*" (*Desert, Garden, Margin, Range,* pp. 110–22), Carol J. Singley repeatedly contrasts Sedgwick's "frontier romance" with the Leatherstocking series to argue that its author "deserves as prominent a place in an American canon as Cooper." And as Susan Steinberg Danielson suggests in "Healing Women's Wrongs: Water-Cure as (Fictional) Autobiography" (*SAR,* pp. 247–60), Mary Gove Nichols's *Mary Lyndon* is organized according to a healing paradigm or reenacts in its structure and themes the parallels between writing and water cure.

iv Humorists

This category of scholarship, I worry, is liable to wither away. *Studies in American Humor,* founded in 1974 at Southwest Texas State University, announces this year its imminent suspension. The lead essay in the penultimate issue is "A Reading of Mr. Dooley" (7:5–31), in which John O. Rees contends that the humorist Finley Peter Dunne's comic persona, while uttering an occasional malapropism, voiced a sophisticated social satire. On a more positive note, scholarship on American humor is no longer limited basically to the writings of white males. The only two monographs in this category this year, in fact, are biographies of marginalized figures: Linda A. Morris chronicles the life of the dialect writer Frances Miriam Whitcher, the creator of the "Permilly Ruggles" and "Widow Bedott" personae, in *Women's Humor in the Age of Gentility* (Syracuse); and Daniel F. Littlefield, Jr., undertakes a similar recovery of the career of a Native American writer, the author of the "Fus Fixico" letters, in *Alex Posey: Creek Poet, Journalist, and Humorist* (Nebraska).

Littlefield also contributes a précis of his biography under the title "Evolution of Alex Posey's Fus Fixico Persona" to *SAIL* (4, ii–iii:136–44).

v **Post-Civil War Women Writers**

Among the figures in this category, Jewett, Freeman, Chopin, and Gilman continue to attract most of the attention. Ironically, while Jewett is no longer denigrated as a mere "local colorist," a label only the woefully uninformed nowadays would hang on her, Jewett scholarship has suffered "collateral damage" from recent attacks on the "New England tradition" of American literature. If Jewett's writings were marginalized under the terms of the traditional canon, that is, the danger today is that they will seem *too* familiar, too privileged by association, to pass muster with canon reformers. Few of the New Americanists, I suspect, will be impressed by the Jewett essays that have appeared in the *Colby Library Quarterly,* which occasionally resembles a trade magazine for the Jewett industry. For example, in "A Jewett Pharmacopoeia" (28:140–43) Ted Eden has compiled a list of some of the herbs and flowers Jewett mentions in her stories, and in "Unstable Narrative Voice in Sarah Orne Jewett's 'A White Heron'" (28:85–92), Heidi Kelchner offers a New Critical analysis of Jewett's story contra the gendered readings the text has inspired. Similarly, Michael Hobbs finds the Captain Littlepage episode an "ironic miniature" that reproduces the structure of Jewett's best book in "World Beyond the Ice: Narrative Structure in *The Country of the Pointed Firs*" (*SSF* 29:27–34); Randall Huff makes the case for a Russian influence on the writer in his intertextual note, "Sarah Orne Jewett's Tolstoyan Stories" (*IFR* 19:23–27); and Ellery Sedgwick recounts Jewett's star-crossed relations with her editor at Houghton Mifflin in "Horace Scudder and Sarah Orne Jewett: Market Forces in Publishing in the 1890s" (*American Periodicals* 2:79–88). On the other hand, modern gendered readings of Jewett situate her fiction in a feminist (as opposed to a privileged New England) tradition. In *Fiction of the Home Place* (Miss.), for example, Helen Fiddyment Levy includes Jewett as well as Cather, Glasgow, Porter, Welty, and Naylor in a cluster of women writers who imagine ideal female communities in didactic stories of "quasi-religious intent." Margaret Roman articulates an even more extreme position in *Sarah Orne Jewett: Reconstructing Gender* (Alabama), a thesis-ridden study that betrays its origins in the dissertation. According to Roman, almost "everything Jewett wrote" tells a single story: the subversion of "the male fixed social structure," the escape from the "sick, sexually divided society," the disruption of the "patriarchal society with its dual norms for men and for women." In Roman's view, "A White Heron" thus explores the symbolic hope for androgynous figures like the adolescent heroine Sylvy, who by story's end has "renounced imprisoning heterosexuality."

Freeman studies nowadays also boil with debate over the question of her feminism. On the one hand, Kate Gardner asserts that "it is now almost *de rigueur* to read Freeman as a feminist," and in "The Subversion of Genre in the Short Stories of Mary Wilkins Freeman" (*NEQ* 65:447–68), Gardner notes how Freeman revised conventional formulae to underscore the rebelliousness of her heroines. Similarly, according to Martha J. Cutter in "Beyond Stereotypes: Mary Wilkins Freeman's Radical Critique of Nineteenth-Century Cults of Femininity" (*WS* 21:383–95), Freeman's radicalism resides in her subversion of all "patriarchal images of femininity." Cutter explains how Freeman deconstructs the stereotypes of both "domestic saint" and "new woman" in her story "The Selfishness of Amelia Lamkin." One wonders, however, why Freeman's critique of both stereotypes does not simply make her an ideological moderate. Even Thomas A. Maik's "Mary Wilkins Freeman's 'Louisa': Liberation, Independence, or Madness?" (*NDQ* 60, iv:137–48), while raising the possibility that Freeman's protagonist is more insane than defiant, still reads the story through a modern feminist lens. On the other hand, Mary R. Reichardt has long argued that the feminist reading given some individual Freeman stories "falls flat" in the context of her entire body of work. Reichardt revisits this idea in *A Web of Relationship: Women in the Short Fiction of Mary Wilkins Freeman* (Miss.), which perceptively analyzes dozens of stories to demonstrate how Freeman's "turn-of-the-century New England women of every type struggled toward selfhood." Reichardt thus disputes the critical notion that Freeman's protagonists are all rebels like Sarah Penn in "The Revolt of 'Mother.'" Reichardt also edits *The Uncollected Stories of Mary Wilkins Freeman* (Miss.) which, its title notwithstanding, contains only 20 of the 100-plus tales listed in the bibliography of uncollected Freeman stories she compiled with Philip Eppard (see *ALS 1990*, p. 227). Still, this volume promises to introduce readers to a wider selection of Freeman's work than is commonly available in anthologies.

No other figure covered in this chapter this year is the subject of more published scholarship than Kate Chopin. Anne Rowe briefly sketches

Chopin's life in "New Orleans as Metaphor: Kate Chopin" (*Literary New Orleans*, pp. 29–37). *Perspectives on Kate Chopin* (Northwestern State University), ed. Grady Ballenger et al., prints nine of the papers delivered at the 1989 Chopin conference, which are unavailable elsewhere. Among the contributors are Phyllis Vanlandingham on Chopin's editors and Penelope A. LeFew on Chopin's response to Schopenhauer. A number of other papers read at Northwestern in 1989 as well as several read at the 1988 MLA in New Orleans are collected in *Kate Chopin Reconsidered: Beyond the Bayou* (LSU), ed. Lynda S. Boren and Sara deSaussure Davis. The 14 articles in this volume consolidate the advances in Chopin's reputation realized over the past generation. Chopin's biographer Emily Toth bolsters the argument of those critics who discern parallels between Chopin's stories and events in her life in "Kate Chopin Thinks Back Through Her Mothers" (pp. 15–25); Jean Bardot reports the discovery of new biographical data about the Chopin family in "French Creole Portraits" (pp. 26–35); and Heather Kirk Thomas challenges the myth that Chopin's last years were marred by an emotional depression that settled over her after the putative failure of *The Awakening* in " 'What Are the Prospects for the Book?': Rewriting a Woman's Life" (pp. 36–57). Among the essays on *The Awakening* in the volume, Deborah E. Barker's "The Awakening of Female Artistry" (pp. 61–79), Dorothy H. Jacobs's "*The Awakening:* A Recognition of Confinement" (pp. 80–94), and Lynda S. Boren's "Taming the Sirens: Self-Possession and the Strategies of Art in Kate Chopin's *The Awakening*" (pp. 180–96) foreground the problems Edna Pontellier confronts as a woman artist and her dissatisfaction with the restrictions placed on her; Martha Fodaski Black's "The Quintessence of Chopinism" (pp. 95–113) argues that the novel was influenced by the writings of George Bernard Shaw, although the case is complicated by the lack of firm evidence that Chopin read Shaw; both John Carlos Rowe's "The Economics of the Body in Kate Chopin's *The Awakening*" (pp. 118–42) and Doris Davis's "*The Awakening:* The Economics of Tension" (pp. 143–53) read the novel in terms of Edna's troubled negotiation of the economics of speculation epitomized by Léonce Pontellier; and Katherine Joslin's "Finding the Self at Home: Chopin's *The Awakening* and Cather's *The Professor's House*" (pp. 166–79) attempts to forge intertextual links between the two novels, not always successfully. Among the other essays in the book, Barbara C. Ewell in "Kate Chopin and the Dream of Female Selfhood" (pp. 157–65) places Chopin in a tradition of radical individualism, the oppositional canon of Emerson and Whitman; Sara deSaussure Davis in "Chopin's Movement Toward Universal Myth" (pp. 199–206) notes how the stories in *A Vocation and a Voice* point in the direction of *The Awakening;* Anne M. Blythe's "Kate Chopin's 'Charlie'" (pp. 207–15) corrects past misreadings of this little-known, late initiation story; and Nancy S. Ellis in "Insistent Refrains and Self-Discovery: Accompanied Awakenings in Three Stories by Kate Chopin" (pp. 216–29) highlights the musical tropes common to "After the Winter," "At Cheniere Caminada," and "A Vocation and a Voice."

Nor is most of the new scholarship on Chopin this year contained in the one volume. Perhaps the most instructive original essay on Chopin's novel is Anthony H. Harrison's "Swinburne and the Critique of Ideology in *The Awakening*," in *Gender and Discourse in Victorian Literature and Art* (No. Ill.), ed. Harrison and Beverly Taylor, pp. 185–203. Analyzing the heteroglossia or competing discourses of Chopin's text through a Bakhtinian lens, Harrison persuasively argues that Swinburne's poem "The Triumph of Time" is the "most influential pre-text" for the novel and that by appropriating the metaphors of Swinburne's verse Chopin exposes "the twin illusory ideologies of Christian religion and romantic love." Mylène Dressler refracts the novel through Lacan in "Edna Under the Sun: Throwing Light on the Subject of *The Awakening*" (*ArQ* 48, iii:59–75) to suggest that Edna is fundamentally an object of visual consumption. In "Edna Pontellier and the Myth of Passion" (*NOR* 19, iii:5–13), Lloyd M. Daigrepont contributes to the growing body of Chopin criticism that regards Edna as an ironic heroine or a target of satire. *The Awakening* is, in this reading, a critique of the courtly love tradition, a "forceful warning against the pernicious effects of erotic yearning." Marilyn Hoder-Salmon's *Kate Chopin's* The Awakening: *Screenplay as Interpretation* (Florida) contains a shooting script adapted from the novel, an elaborate genuflection to Chopin's new-canonical status. Nancy A. Walker also prepares a new edition of *The Awakening* (St. Martin's) that should rival the Norton Critical edition, with an informative historical introduction and critical history by Walker and reprinted essays by Elaine Showalter, Margit Stange, Cynthia Griffin Wolff, Patricia S. Yaeger, and Paula A. Treichler. Bert Bender, whose influential essay on Darwin and *The Awakening* appeared last year (see *ALS 1991*, p. 201), returns this year with a sort of prequel: "Kate Chopin's Quarrel with Darwin before *The Awakening*" (*JAmS* 26:185–204), which discusses her thoughts and misgivings about Darwin's theory of sexual selection in her early novel *At Fault* and a dozen or so early stories. For the record, too, 24 of Chopin's stories are reprinted this year with a serviceable introduction by Roxana Robinson in an inexpensive paper-back edition under the title *A Matter of Prejudice and Other Stories* (Bantam).

This year marks the centenary of the publication of "The Yellow Wall-paper" and, as I anticipated in this space last year, there was a bumper crop of Gilman studies. Barbara H. Solomon edits and introduces Herland *and Selected Stories by Charlotte Perkins Gilman* (Signet/NAL), a volume suitable for classroom adoption which by virtue of price and selection supersedes the Pantheon editions of *Herland* and *The Charlotte Perkins Gilman Reader.* Catherine Golden also edits *The Captive Imagination* (Feminist Press), a casebook on Gilman's best-known story, which includes a fine introduction by the editor ("One Hundred Years of Reading 'The Yellow Wallpaper,'" pp. 1–23), a solid bibliographical essay by Elaine R. Hedges ("'Out at Last'? 'The Yellow Wallpaper' after Two Decades of Feminist Criticism," pp. 319–33), as well as 14 reprinted essays by such eminent scholars as Annette Kolodny, Paula Treichler, and Judith Fetterley. In addition, Joanne B. Karpinski edits *Critical Essays on Charlotte Perkins Gilman* (Hall), which reprints several contemporary reviews and articles on Gilman by Hedges, Mary Hill, and others, plus five new critical essays: Lois N. Magner's "Darwinism and the Woman Question: The Evolving Views of Charlotte Perkins Gilman" (pp. 115–28), which locates her brand of reform Darwinism vis-à-vis both Herbert Spencer's social statics and Lester Ward's gynecocentric theory; Frank G. Kirkpatrick's "'Begin Again!': The Cutting Social Edge of Charlotte Perkins Gilman's Gentle Religious Optimism" (pp. 129–43), a study of the liberal theological views she expressed in her treatise *His Religion and Hers;* Catherine Golden's "'Overwriting' the Rest Cure: Charlotte Perkins Gilman's Literary Escape from S. Weir Mitchell's Fictionalization of Women" (pp. 144–58), an overview of Mitchell's rest-cure fiction; Shelley Fisher Fishkin's "'Making a Change': Strategies of Subversion in Gilman's Journalism and Short Fiction" (pp. 234–48), which considers her essays and stories complementary expressions of her progressive ideas; and my own "Reconstructing *Here Also:* On the Later Poetry of Charlotte Perkins Gilman" (pp. 249–68), which discusses her stillborn collection of late verse and prints several of her previously unpublished lyrics. Three major essays directly relevant to "The Yellow Wallpaper" also appear in journals this year. In "Exploring Lack and Absence in the Body/Text:

Charlotte Perkins Gilman Prewriting Irigaray" (*WS* 21:75–86), Georgia
Johnston asserts that Gilman's text anticipates Luce Irigaray's notions of
doubleness and the female body, as the narrator "becomes a multiple,
moving text within the wallpaper." On the other hand, in "Gilman's
'Interminable Grotesque': The Narrator of 'The Yellow Wallpaper'"
(*SSF* 28:477–84), Beverly A. Hume revises the consensus reading of the
story, with its feminist implication of patriarchy, by arguing that Gilman's
narrator is blind to the grotesque nature of her tale and transforms it into
a "darkly ironic" and black-humorous narrative. In "The Reincarnation
of Jane: 'Through This'—Gilman's Companion to 'The Yellow Wallpaper'" (*WS* 20:287–302), Denise D. Knight discusses Gilman's companion or sequel to the story, in which the narrator Jane reappears as a
type of Stepford wife. Knight, incidentally, has both an edition of Gilman's diaries and an annotated edition of her verse in preparation. Finally, Thomas Galt Peyser in "Reproducing Utopia: Charlotte Perkins
Gilman and *Herland*" (*SAF* 20:1–16) reads Gilman against the grain of
most recent scholarship to reveal the extent to which her utopia is not a
playful parody of the man-made world but its sinister mirror image.

   To judge from the stirrings on the critical fringe, the writings of Grace
King are ripe for revival despite their southern white-apologetic tone.
King's biographer Robert Bush briefly sketches the circumstances of her
life in "The Patrician Voice: Grace King" (*Literary New Orleans*, pp. 8–
15); and Zita Z. Dresner astutely notes the contradictions in the racial
and sexual codes inscribed in King's first story in "Irony and Ambiguity
in Grace King's 'Monsieur Motte'" (*New Perspectives on Women and
Comedy* [Gordon and Breach], ed. Regina Barreca, pp. 169–83). In "At
Odds: Race and Gender in Grace King's Short Fiction" (*Louisiana
Women Writers*, pp. 33–55), Linda S. Coleman performs a bit of alchemy,
turning the ideological defects of King's stories to advantage. Coleman
frankly acknowledges the racism of King's writings but argues for their
importance on the ground that they exhibit "the limitations that inter-
locking racism and sexism imposed on King and her representation of
Louisiana women." That is, while King claimed to be a literary realist,
she persisted in expressing a romantic or plantation mythology. Thus,
she was a type of unconscious victim of patriarchal southern culture who
was largely unaware of "her own part in the repressive racial structure of
postwar New Orleans." Similarly, Alice Parker recovers the neglected
novel *Les Quarteronnes de la Nouvelle-Orléans* by the upper-class Creole
author Sidonie de la Houssaye only to bury it again beneath the jargon-

ridden commentary of "Evangeline's Darker Daughters: Crossing Racial Boundaries in Postwar Louisiana" (*Louisiana Women Writers,* pp. 75–97); for example, "De la Houssaye's project is to gain access to a language of desire whose grammar and syntax are illicit by transposing libidinal energies, relocating sexual codes in stories of a marginal Other." Patricia Brady resurrects another forgotten (perhaps deservedly so, in this case) postwar woman writer from the footnote in "Mollie Moore Davis: A Literary Life" (*Louisiana Women Writers,* pp. 99–118).

Susan R. Gannon and Ruth Anne Thompson join forces on several projects related to Mary Mapes Dodge, author of *Hans Brinker* and editor of *St. Nicholas* from its inception in 1873 until her death in 1905. They collaborate on *Mary Mapes Dodge* (Twayne), a useful critical introduction to her career; "Mr. Scudder and Mrs. Dodge: An Editorial Correspondence and What It Tells Us" (*American Periodicals* 2:89–99), a summary and analysis of the letters Dodge sent Horace Scudder between 1866 and 1890; and "Mary Mapes Dodge and the Recasting of Saint Nicholas" (*Sitting at the Feet of the Past,* pp. 171–85), on Dodge's appropriation of the Knickerbocker traditions associated with St. Nicholas in the pages of her magazine.

Several late-century women writers of color are the subjects of articles which register their revival like blips on an oscilloscope. Elizabeth Young suggests in "Warring Fictions: *Iola Leroy* and the Color of Gender" (*AL* 64:273–97) that Frances E. W. Harper restaged the Civil War to depict black heroism on both the home front and battlefront—still more evidence that, hardly repressed, the war was written often, at least once from the perspective of an African American feminist. In "From Mysteries to Histories: Cultural Pedagogy in Frances E. W. Harper's *Iola Leroy*" (*AL* 64:497–518), John Ernest declares the novel "a study of discursive systems" which presumes "a specifically African American mode of understanding" that "resists cultural imperialism." Both Annette Van Dyke's "Introduction to *Wynema, A Child of the Forest,* by Sophia Alice Callahan" (*SAIL* 4, ii–iii:123–28) and A. LaVonne Brown Ruoff's "Justice for Indians and Women: The Protest Fiction of Alice Callahan and Pauline Johnson" (*WLT* 66:249–55) sketch the life of the first known Native American women novelist and summarize the plot of the novel. Both apply Nina Baym's formulation of the overplot common to popular women's fiction to their analyses, though they differ fundamentally in their conclusions. According to Van Dyck, *Wynema* "does not follow the pattern" Baym identifies; according to Ruoff, however, Callahan clearly subscribes to the formula. In "Race and Gender in the Early Works of Alice Dunbar-Nelson" (*Louisiana Women Writers,* pp. 121–38), Violet Harrington Bryan admirably outlines the major issues at stake in Dunbar-Nelson's fiction, from the emphasis on women's rights in her early New Orleans stories to the emphasis on race in her mature work. In "Pauline Hopkins and the Hidden Self of Race" (*ELH* 59:227–56), Thomas J. Otten brilliantly links the new psychologies to matters of racial identity and race-consciousness in *Of One Blood.* Hopkins's novel also figures as a case study in racialist fiction in Susan Gillman's "The Mulatto, Tragic or Triumphant? The Nineteenth-Century American Race Melodrama" (*The Culture of Sentiment,* pp. 221–43).

Other postwar women writers largely remain cottage industries. *Critical Essays on Constance Fenimore Woolson* (Twayne), ed. Cheryl B. Torsney, contains four pieces commissioned expressly for the volume: Sharon L. Dean's "Women as Daughters; Women as Mothers in the Fiction of Constance Woolson" (pp. 189–202), a taxonomy of parent-child relationships; Joan Myers Weimer's "The 'Admiring Aunt' and the 'Proud Salmon of the Pond': Constance Fenimore Woolson's Struggle with Henry James" (pp. 203–16), yet another exploration of the conflicted relations between the two novelists between their first meeting in 1880 and James's death in 1916; Caroline Gebhard's "Constance Fenimore Woolson Rewrites Bret Harte: The Sexual Politics of Intertextuality" (pp. 217–33), an intensive analysis of the "radical rewriting" of "The Luck of Roaring Camp" in "The Lady of Little Fishing"; and Carolyn VanBergen's "Getting Your Money's Worth: The Social Marketplace in *Horace Chase*" (pp. 234–44), which describes the vexed relations among character types, particularly between the sexes, in Woolson's final novel. Cheryl Walker also sketches the life and career of Rose Terry Cooke for *Legacy* (9:143–50), whose editors adopt a wider historical focus for the journal and unveil a new design.

vi The Howells Generation

Hardly the "dead cult" with its "statues cut down" he thought he had become near the end of his life, W. D. Howells continues to attract respectful and occasionally admiring notice. Three elegant volumes of *Selected Literary Criticism,* reprinting a total of 167 reviews and essays (including the complete text of *Criticism and Fiction*) from throughout his career, are issued this year in A Selected Edition of W. D. Howells

(Indiana) under the general editorship of David J. Nordloh and with introductions by Ulrich Halfmann, Donald Pizer, and Ronald Gottesman. As James W. Tuttleton remarks in "William Dean Howells and the Practice of Criticism" (*NewC* 10, x:28–37), to read these articles "is to discover how catholic and wide-ranging were Howells's literary interests and how perceptive and generous were his sympathies." In addition, Brenda Murphy edits and supplies an illuminating introduction to *A Realist in the American Theatre: Selected Drama Criticism of William Dean Howells* (Ohio), a collection of 29 pieces Howells published between 1875 and 1919 which includes reviews of Mark Twain's *The Gilded Age* and Ibsen's *Ghosts* as well as an article on the future of motion pictures. Both Sarah B. Daugherty in "The Ideology of Gender in Howells' Early Novels" (*ALR* 25, i:2–19) and Elizabeth S. Prioleau in "William Dean Howells and the Seductress: From *Femme Fatale* fo *Femme Vitale*" (*HLB* n.s. 3, i:53–72) defend the Dean from the charge that his female characters are mere pasteboard types, irrational and/or destructive, and both regard *Private Theatricals* a crucial or pivotal Howells text. Still, they approach the subject from slightly different angles with surprisingly different results. Daugherty examines Howells's depiction of gender conflict and the plight of women, especially in the novels in which his alter ego Basil March figures, concluding that in his later novels Howells frequently resorted to stereotypes and contrived episodes. On the other hand, Prioleau, a Freudian critic and the author of *The Circle of Eros: Sexuality in the Work of W. D. Howells* (see *ALS 1984*, p. 229), argues that Howells successfully eroticized the figure of the femme fatale in such late novels as *The Story of a Play*, which portray a "radiant, positive seductress" or "redemptive temptress" whose "strong, life-enhancing sexuality" empowers her "to defeat negative Eros." The other major essays on Howells this year: in "The Triumph of Irony in *The Rise of Silas Lapham*" (*SAF* 20:45–55), Arlene Young discusses (in a near-reversion to the New Criticism) the mocking tone that subverts class distinctions in Howells's best-known comedy of manners; in "Jays and Jags: Gender, Class, and Addiction in Howells' *Landlord at Lion's Head*" (*Dionysos* 3, iii:36–46), John W. Crowley teases out the metonymic implications of alcoholism among the refined Brahmins; and in "Those Other Selves: Consciousness in the 1890 Publications of Howells and the James Brothers" (*ALR* 25, i:20–37), Thomas Galt Peyser analyzes Howells's expression of the principles of the new psychology in *A Hazard of New Fortunes*.

A trio of postwar regionalists—Harris, Cable, and Harte—are the subjects of a spate of books and articles this year. Two essays in *Sitting at the Feet of the Past,* Hugh T. Keenan's "Joel Chandler Harris and the Legitimacy of the Reteller of Folktales" (pp. 81–91) and Anthony L. Manna's "Br'er Rabbit Redux" (pp. 93–108), defend Harris, albeit with reservations, from the charge that he skewed African American oral tradition in his Uncle Remus stories. Peggy A. Russo in "Uncle Walt's Uncle Remus: Disney's Distortion of Harris's Hero" (*SLJ* 25, i:19–32) blames the Disney movie *Song of the South* (1946) for the low esteem in which Harris is often held today. However, Michele Birnbaum's "Dark Dialects: Scientific and Literary Realism in Joel Chandler Harris's *Uncle Remus* Series" (*NOR* 19:36–45) builds a case on linguistic grounds against Harris, whose dialect stories "literally reinscrib[ed] an antebellum racial and social order." Alice Hall Petry fairly summarizes Cable's point of view toward his city of birth in "Native Outsider: George Washington Cable" (*Literary New Orleans,* pp. 1–7), and James Robert Payne discusses the original manuscript version of Cable's private treatise on civil rights in "George Washington Cable's 'My Politics': Context and Revision of a Southern Memoir" (*Multicultural Autobiography,* pp. 94–113). My own *Bret Harte* (Twayne) portrays Harte as a creature of the literary marketplace, a prototype of the modern man of letters as a man of business.

In addition, Lawrence J. Oliver recounts a fascinating though neglected chapter in literary history in *Brander Matthews, Theodore Roosevelt, and the Politics of American Literature, 1880–1920* (Tennessee), a timely reminder that literary studies were as ideologically colored a century ago as they are today.

vii Crane, Norris, Adams and the Fin de Siècle

Noteworthy Crane studies this year are ambitious in scope but few in number. Christopher Benfey's controversial new biography, *The Double Life of Stephen Crane* (Knopf), offers a provocative if problematical thesis: that Crane consciously "tried to live what he'd already written," that is, by becoming a war correspondent in Cuba after writing *The Red Badge of Courage.* Benfey overlooks the evidence, however, that in the case of *Maggie,* to cite but one example, Crane was writing about what he'd already lived. In *Stephen Crane: An Annotated Bibliography of Secondary Scholarship* (Hall), Patrick K. Dooley lists, describes, and organizes topically nearly 2,000 items published in English between 1901 and 1991. The volume should prove a boon to all Crane specialists. The most significant new critical essay on Crane is John Feaster's "Violence and the Ideology of Capitalism: A Reconsideration of Crane's 'The Blue Hotel' " (*ALR* 25, i:74–94), which foregrounds the story against the frontier culture in which it is set and the capitalist ethos that it critiques. In "Responding to Crane's 'The Monster' " (*SoAR* 57, ii:45–55), Ronald K. Giles maps some of the semantic indeterminacies and snares laid for the reader of the text, which betrays (in the now familiar formulation) a linguistic or rhetorical skepticism; and in "Reading, Writing, and the Risk of Entanglement in Crane's 'Octopush' " (*SSF* 29:341–46), Joseph Church contends that this early tale functions as a metafictional allegory of the writer at work. This year, too, the Crane Society launches *Stephen Crane Studies,* the first journal devoted exclusively to the author since the demise of the *Crane Newsletter.* Under the editorship of Paul Sorrentino, it is much more than a clearinghouse for society announcements. The first two issues include sprightly articles by such well-known Crane scholars as James B. Colvert, George Monteiro, Stanley Wertheim, and Milne Holton. A pair of notes in *Explicator* also merit passing notice here: George T. Novotny detects in a reference to "cloud-compelling Pete," the bartender-boyfriend in *Maggie,* an allusion to Jove (50:225–28); and Darryl Hattenhauer contends that Crane's revision of the last sentence of *Red Badge* retains the irony of the original version (50:160–61). For the record, too, Crane's novel is reissued this year with a new introduction by Malcolm Bradbury (Dent/Tuttle). Of related interest to Craneians: Arthur Lubow's exhaustively researched *The Reporter Who Would Be King* (Scribner's), the splendid new biography of Richard Harding Davis (who has recently been remembered, if at all, merely as the son of Rebecca Harding Davis). Like his friend Crane, Davis was an overnight literary sensation while still in his twenties; he later became a respected travel writer and war reporter in Cuba, though Lubow smartly characterizes him more as a flamboyant personality than a distinguished author.

Frank Norris is well-served this year, especially by the members of the Norris Society. The most tireless of Norrisians, Joseph R. McElrath, Jr., completes a hat trick with the publication of *Frank Norris Revisited* (Twayne), which deftly situates the author not in a reductive mechanistic or positivist tradition but in a humanist and humorous one; *Frank Norris: A Descriptive Bibliography* (Pittsburgh), which should prove to be the definitive compilation of Norris's writings; and "Edwin Markham in Frank Norris's *The Octopus*" (*FNS* 13:10–11), which notes that Markham, long thought to be a real-life model for the character of Presley, actually wrote a poem entitled "The Toilers." Similarly, Richard Allan Davison in "Frank Norris and William Cullen Bryant" (*FNS* 14:6–8) notes Norris's satirical reference to the Fireside poet in *The Octopus*. The other notable articles in *FNS* this year qualify or dispute the novelist's naturalism: Charles L. Crow's "Gnawing the File: Recent Trends in *McTeague* Scholarship" (13:1–4) divides Norris's modern critics into "anti-Naturalists" and "neo-Naturalists"; Nan Morelli-White's "The Damnation of *McTeague*: Frank Norris's Morality Play" (13:5–10) emphasizes the didacticism of the novel; and Charles Duncan's "Where Piggishness Flourishes: Contextualizing Strategies in Norris and London" (14:1–6) argues that the atavistic hero of *A Man's Woman* survives not because he is among the Darwinian fittest but because he returns to a primitive environment.

Despite Henry Adams's reputation as an aloof and alienated intellectual, scholars in recent years have been at pains to contextualize his life and work. That he was one of the wittiest letter writers of his generation we have learned for a certainty only within the past decade, with the publication of the definitive six-volume Harvard University Press edition of his correspondence. Ernest Samuels, one of the directors of that project and Adams's best biographer, has judiciously culled several hundred of the principal documents in *Henry Adams: Selected Letters* (Belknap). The indefatigable George Monteiro also edits, introduces, and annotates *The Correspondence of Henry James and Henry Adams, 1877–1914* (LSU), a sheaf of 36 letters the two writers exchanged over a period of 38 years. Joanne Jacobson theorizes in *Authority and Alliance in the Letters of Henry Adams* (Wisconsin) that the rhetorical strategies of private letters are perfectly suited to the negotiation of cultural conflict. Jacobson convincingly argues from this premise that Adams's letters silhouette radical changes in fin de siècle America as well as the writer's own conflicted cultural loyalties. Three other critics read Adams intertextually rather than as the great solitary he once seemed. Robert Dawidoff in *The Genteel Tradition and the Sacred Rage* (No. Car.) groups Adams with James and Santayana to analyze his wide-ranging attempts to attain a detached "Tocquevillian" perspective on democracy, especially in his *Education, History of the Administrations of Jefferson and Madison,* and novel *Democracy*. Keith R. Burich in "'Stable Equilibrium Is Death':

Henry Adams, Sir Charles Lyell, and the Paradox of Progress" (*NEQ* 65:631–47) considers Adams's early critique of Lyell's theory of uniformitarianism a harbinger of his later skepticism. Similarly, if more colloquially, Reed Whittemore in *Six Literary Lives* (Missouri) detects a "shared impiety" among Adams, London, Sinclair, Dos Passos, William Carlos Williams, and Allen Tate which acts as a precondition to modernism in the arts. Though Wittemore purports to emphasize "the books for which [Adams] is still best known" rather than his private life, his chapter on the writer is little more than a psychobiographical sketch.

The pulse of interest in Harold Frederic quickens slightly with the publication of three major essays on *The Damnation of Theron Ware*. With each passing year, Frederic's 1896 novel with its ambiguities, textual gaps, and shifting narrative stances seems more modern. As Bruce Michelson explains in "Theron Ware in the Wilderness of Ideas" (*ALR* 25, i:54–73), the novel dramatizes the intellectual exhaustion—"the degradation of ideas into poses and entertainments"—of the fin de siècle. Its "improvised incoherence" of empty talk and meaningless gesture is, in Michelson's astute analysis, well-suited to "a profoundly disordered time." In a similarly provocative rereading of the novel, Lisa Watt MacFarlane ("Resurrecting Man: Desire and the Damnation of Theron Ware," *SAF* 20:127–43) contends that the minister is lost precisely because he is trapped between "his professional 'feminized' self and the self socialized as a man," unable either to negotiate the contradictions of assigned gender roles or to discharge his clerical duties in a secular culture. Less challenging than either of these essays is Marcia Smith Marzec's "*The Damnation of Theron Ware:* Father Forbes as Structural Center" (*UDR* 21, iii:51–65), which asserts well past its midpoint its dubious claim about the novel: that only Forbes "stands amidst the extreme alternatives" Ware faces "without being baffled by them." Such a thesis presumes there is a site from which the tale may be read drained of its irony and ambiguity—reduces it, that is, to a less complex and textured novel. To tap the new market of Civil War buffs, apparently, Syracuse also reprints a collection first issued 26 years ago, albeit with its title changed from *Harold Frederic's Stories of York State* to *The Civil War Stories of Harold Frederic,* ed. Thomas F. O'Donnell.

No Anglo author better illustrates the 19th-century interest in what we today call multiculturalism than Lafcadio Hearn, who lived perhaps the most exotic life of any American writer of the day. Hearn earned his early reputation as a student of Creole folklore in New Orleans, and he spent his last years as a teacher and writer in Japan. Both Thomas Bonner, Jr., in "Light in New Orleans: Change in the Writings of Mark Twain, Lafcadio Hearn, William Faulkner, and Walker Percy" (*UMSE* n.s. 10:213–26) and Hephzibah Roskelly in "Cultural Translator: Lafcadio Hearn" (*Literary New Orleans*, pp. 16–28) focus on Hearn's decade in the Crescent City. Whereas Bonner brushes lightly over his Creole sketches, however, Roskelly praises Hearn unreservedly for his pioneering ethnography. Carl Dawson in *Lafcadio Hearn and the Vision of Japan* (Hopkins) contributes an informative study of Hearn's final 14 years, the period of his career for which he is best-known. Melinda Knight also features Hearn, along with Ambrose Bierce and Edgar Saltus, in "Cultural Radicalism in the American Fin de Siècle: Cynicism, Decadence and Dissent" (*Connecticut Review* 14, i:65–75), which connects their resistance to bourgeois literary culture in the 1890s to the larger movements of American modernism.

Three general studies of western American literature pay tribute this year to Owen Wister's role in inventing the modern western formula in *The Virginian*. The most entertaining of these books is Robert Murray Davis's *Playing Cowboys* (Okla.), which traces in its first chapter Wister's careful construction of the bildungsroman. The most scholarly of this trio of books is Blake Allmendinger's richly illustrated *The Cowboy: Representations of Labor in an American Work Culture* (Oxford). Allmendinger analyzes the work patterns of actual cowboys (e.g., cattle branding, livestock castration) as the basis of the "cowboy culture." In this view, Wister's Virginian becomes a "livestock detective" who betrays the "cowboy group" from which he sprang. Perhaps the most controversial of these books, however, is Jane Tompkin's chatty *West of Everything* (Oxford). In stark contrast to Allmendinger, Tompkins discusses only the mythological or imaginary cowboys in popular novels and films, linking them not to a coherent and complex social structure but to a pervasive and overwhelmingly masculine death wish in American culture. The gunfight that climaxes *The Virginian* is, in Tompkins's view, not only "a revolt against the rule of women" but more specifically dramatizes Wister's own rebellion against his genteel mother. Page for page, *West of Everything* contains as many glib assertions as *Sexual Personae*. Of related interest: Edward Watts fits a theory of postcolonial writing to some of Garland's early stories in "Margin or Middle Border?: Hamlin Garland, Henry Lawson and Post-Colonialism" (*ON* 16:149–

63); and Seth Bovey and I exhume Garland's first published essay from the morgue of the *Portland Transcript* (*ANQ* n.s. 5:2–23).

End-of-the-century African American writers, especially Charles Chesnutt, are solidly represented in this year's scholarship. In his fine "Voices at the Nadir: Charles Chesnutt and David Bryant Fulton" (*ALR* 24, iii:22–41), William Gleason compares two novels on the 1898 Wilmington riot, *The Marrow of Tradition* and Fulton's *Hanover*, to underscore the deliberate ambiguities of Chesnutt's text. Richard J. Patton examines the seven Uncle Julius tales not originally collected into *The Conjure Woman* to emphasize the complexities of the character in "Studyin' 'Bout Ole Julius: A Note on Charles W. Chesnutt's Uncle Julius McAdoo" (*ALR* 24, iii:72–79). For the record, too, William L. Andrews compiles and introduces *Collected Stories of Charles W. Chesnutt* (Mentor), a first-rate classroom edition. Lawrence R. Rodger's "Paul Laurence Dunbar's *Sport of the Gods:* The Doubly Conscious World of Plantation Fiction, Migration and Ascent" (*ALR* 24, iii:42–57) provocatively argues that Dunbar's narrative voice in the novel, unlike the speaker of his dialect verse, satirizes the plantation tradition and that his plot of migration to the urban North anticipates the naturalism of Wright, Ellison, and Baldwin. And in "Booker T. Washington as Literary Trickster" (*Southern Folklore* 49:89–107), Frederick L. McElroy makes a convincing case for Washington's revision or reversal, particularly in *Up from Slavery*, of Frederick Douglass's more aggressive rhetorical tropes.

I close this chapter with comments on a few miscellaneous items. Robert L. Gale compiles *The Gay Nineties in America* (Greenwood), a "cultural dictionary" for quick reference. In "Joshua Slocum and the Reality of Solitude" (*ATQ* n.s. 6:59–71), Bert Bender justly restores some of the lost luster to the reputation of the author of *Sailing Alone Around the World*. Finally, I recommend a couple of noteworthy reprinted volumes: the early ethnologist Charles F. Lummis's *Pueblo Indian Folk-Stories* (Nebraska), ed. Robert F. Gish; and *Fairground Fiction: Detective Stories of the World's Columbian Exposition* (Epoch), ed. Donald K. Hartman, containing two late-century pulp novels set at the 1893 Chicago fair, E. M. Van Deventer's *Against Odds* and J. H. Whitson's *Chicago Charlie*.

University of New Mexico

Jo Ann Middleton

The canon continues to explode. New editions of long out of print or previously unpublished works abound, and this year's scholarship is highlighted by a number of noteworthy studies that resurrect recently neglected writers and discover some new ones (mostly women, but a few men). Cather is clearly the major figure, but Wharton, Dreiser, and Stein are holding their own. Several significant books dealing with writers of this period also contributed to another banner year.

i Willa Cather

Clearly the most significant contribution to Cather scholarship this year is *O Pioneers!* (Nebraska), ed. Susan J. Rosowski and Charles W. Mignon with Kathleen Danker, the eagerly awaited first volume in the Willa Cather Scholarly Edition (Susan J. Rosowski and James Woodress, eds.). Intended "to provide to readers—present and future—various kinds of information relevant to Willa Cather's writing, obtained and presented by the highest scholarly standards," this superb first volume meets those standards admirably. *O Pioneers!* includes the critical text that follows Cather's intent in the first edition, a textual commentary tracing the work through its lifetime, a record of all revisions, and illustrations as well as photographs to tie the text to Cather's life and to clarify unfamiliar allusions for present-day readers. David Stouck's fine historical essay locates the novel in its own time and in Cather's career, and he also provides comprehensive explanatory notes. This beautifully produced book is a joy to read and demonstrates the real pleasures to be derived from meticulous attention to detail and the highest standards of scholarship.

   O Pioneers! inspired two very good and quite different essays. Susan

Neal Mayberry convincingly places Cather among 20th-century novelists who offer alternative solutions to the question of female sexuality
and marriage in her excellent essay, "A New Heroine's Marriage: Willa
Cather's *O Pioneers!*" (*ON* 16:37–59). Cather rewrites both the *Liebestod*
and the 18-century " 'heroine's text' of death and descent" by juxtaposing
Marie's adulterous passion and death to Alexandra's story of creation,
which culminates in a new marriage grounded in mutual support,
affection, and friendship. David Laird draws on narrative theory, feminist criticism, and the New Historicism to read *O Pioneers!* as a much
darker novel, asserting that Alexandra finds herself increasingly confined
by social strictures, and he calls the book a "failed pastoral" in his
ambitious essay, "Willa Cather's Women: Gender, Place, and Narrativity
in *O Pioneers!* and *My Ántonia*" (*GPQ* 12:242–53). In *My Ántonia*, Laird
argues, Cather foregrounds the inadequacies and limitations of Jim's
narrative, which allows Ántonia to emerge free from their confines and
"permits the voicing of . . . a kind of *ecriture feminine* the like of which
has no previous analogue in American fiction." In " 'Our' Ántonia: The
Classical Roots of Willa Cather's American Myth" (*CML* 12:111–17),
Mary R. Ryder explains how the classics serve as a structuring principle
to propel the central figure beyond Jim's label of *my* Ántonia until she
becomes *our* Ántonia, "a cultural signifier of all that we value of the
classical western tradition." It's no wonder Ántonia is enshrined as one of
"the principal personages in the changing canon of Western literature"
with the publication of *Ántonia* (Chelsea, 1991), ed. Harold Bloom,
which reprints 26 brief critical extracts as well as nine longer essays and
makes a nice companion to the substantial Rosowski and Murphy
studies (see *ALS 1990*, p. 244).

Several important items make Cather central to a tradition that values
continuity, home, family, and the domestic rituals by which women
create community. Ann Romines's *The Home Plot: Women Writing and
Domestic Ritual* (Mass.) skillfully and compellingly demonstrates that
"linchpins" Harriet Beecher Stowe, Mary Wilkins Freeman, Eudora
Welty, and Cather perpetuate as well as question the ongoing practice of
domestic culture. In fresh and thoughtful readings that point out the
effects of housekeeping on Aunt Georgina, Mrs. Erickson, Clara, Alexandra, Thea, and Ántonia (pp. 120–50), Romines shows that "domestic
ritual is often a battleground, claimed or spurned by competing, collaborating male and female voices." A second chapter (pp. 151–91) concentrates on *Shadows on the Rock,* in which Cather "finally made a full entry

into the life of housekeeping, as practiced by traditional women," and *Sapphira and the Slave Girl,* in which Cather fuses two female plots—the mother's plot of slavery and continuance and the daughter's plot of discovery and liberation, both of which "a woman can—and perhaps *must*—claim." Lynn R. Beideck-Porn's "Celebration of Survival Secured: Food in the Narrative of Willa Cather" (*Images of the Self as Female,* pp. 213–26) traces the thematic treatment of food throughout Cather's canon as one means by which traditional women's roles gain high esteem and as an index of human accomplishment. In *Fiction of the Home Place* (Miss.) Helen Fiddyment Levy investigates fictional strategies devised by Cather, Jewett, Glasgow, Katherine Anne Porter, and Gloria Naylor to reclaim male legend and religion and empower female creativity. Cather's immigrant heroines resemble demigoddesses and replicate heroic males but celebrate "the female maternal source of the home place as the matrix of civilization"; her fiction charts her growing discovery of her own connection as a female artist to the home place (pp. 64–96). Josephine Donovan analyzes Cather's quest for an art connected to its "natural, everyday sources," in "The Pattern of Birds and Beasts: Willa Cather and Women's Art" (*Writing the Woman Artist,* pp. 81–95), noting that she moved gradually from a male-identified view of the artist who imposed his or her ego to an androgynous ideal that abandoned ego and embraced a subject through the "gift of sympathy." In "Willa Cather's Visions and Revisions of Female Lives," her thoughtful contribution to *Images of the Self as Female,* pp. 107–18, Susan J. Rosowski proposes that Cather's legacy was a belief that being female meant having no viable self. Cather confronted the challenge of being a creative woman by "writing a body of fiction that illustrates the 'process, product and progress' of women's artistry.' "

Interest in Cather's late fiction flourishes. Deborah Carlin's *Cather, Canon, and the Politics of Reading* (Mass.), challenges previous canonical assumptions about Cather's five female-centered late fictions. Complementing Merrill Maguire Skaggs's "intellectual history" of Cather's late novels, *After the World Broke in Two* (see *ALS 1990,* pp. 239–40), this study's theoretical approach employs interpretive strategies drawn from narratology, feminism, and deconstruction to focus on issues of narrative structure and gender and to read these works as self-conscious experiments with narrative form that reveal "ambiguous, sometimes contradictory, feminist impulses." Carlin begins with *My Mortal Enemy* as a "test case" for narrative self-referentiality and duplicity, and she offers consistently rewarding and distinctive chapters on each of the novels and "Old Mrs. Harris." Although Carlin asserts that these fictions "undermine their own readability," she offers clearly written and provocative "readings" that will most certainly "elicit and inspire other readings." Unfortunately, Patrick Shaw's *Willa Cather and the Art of Conflict* (Whitston) is a disappointing one-note study which attempts to read all 12 of Cather's novels as expressions of her own "homoerotic tensions," a stance that produces several faulty arguments and tenuous conclusions.

Laura Winters breaks new ground with her superb essay, "*My Mortal Enemy:* Willa Cather's Ballad of Exile" (*WCPMN* 36:31–34). Winters demonstrates that into this complex narrative, which resonates with a compendium of themes found in folk ballads—lost loves, lost havens, mistaken choices, fatal illness, and untimely death—Cather compresses bitter issues of exile that teased her throughout her life; *My Mortal Enemy* concludes with a vision of death in exile that sets the stage for Cather's next two novels, in which her characters must find ways to *live* in exile. The Willa Cather Special Issue of *Legacy* (9, i) contains three fine essays on the later novels, as well as profiles of Dorothy Canfield Fisher by Mark J. Madigan (pp. 49–58) and Louise Pound by Elizabeth A. Turner (pp. 59–64). In her intriguing, well-argued essay, "Reading Marian Forrester" (pp. 35–48), Ann W. Fisher-Wirth draws on Julia Kristeva and Hélène Cixous to probe questions *A Lost Lady* raises about the mother and to speculate on Cather's treatment of Lyra Garber as Marian Forrester. Elaine Sargent Apthorp's "Re-Visioning Creativity: Cather, Chopin, Jewett" (pp. 1–22) seeks to establish the formal complexity and thematic interest of *Lucy Gayheart* by comparing it to Chopin's *The Awakening;* both novels manipulate linguistic and representational conventions to create gaps and force an intersubjective creativity. Also writing on *Lucy Gayheart* is Kevin A. Synott, whose "Painting 'The Tricks That Shadows Play': Impressionism in *Lucy Gayheart*" (*WCPMN* 36:37–39) analyzes Cather's use of a visual mode where color and light supersede linear articulation. The final *Legacy* essay, John N. Swift's "Narration and the Maternal 'Real' in *Sapphira and the Slave Girl*" (pp. 23–34) examines the novel's closing disruptions, which obliterate the boundaries between fiction and autobiography as an expression of Cather's anxious approach to the elusive Lacanian "real."

Sapphira inspired two other noteworthy items. In *Playing in the Dark* Toni Morrison ponders the effect that living in a historically racialized society has had on American writers. Her compelling discussion of

Sapphira and the Slave Girl (pp. 18–28) as a "book that describes and inscribes its narrative's own fugitive flight from itself" explores Cather's struggle to confront the interdependent working of power, race, and sexuality. Elizabeth Jane Harrison's chapter on *Sapphira* (pp. 65–82) in *Female Pastoral: Women Writers Re-Visioning the American South* (Tennessee, 1991) seeks to establish Cather's last novel as an antiplantation romance that offers partial healing for the wounds of slavery through the image of an interracial female community; the novel's final picture of absolution represents Cather's attempt to revise a pastoral genre she inherited as a white writer and suggests a reconciliation with her own morally equivocal past.

Of Cather's novels, *The Professor's House* drew the most attention. David Harrell's impressive, painstakingly researched *From Mesa Verde to The Professor's House* (New Mexico) combines history and literary criticism to elucidate Cather's transformation of historical fact into artistic myth by crafting *The Professor's House* as "a metaphor for the art of composition, for the life of writing from beginning to end." The novel traces the thrill of discovering the Kingdom of Art, which Cather equates with the idealized Cliff City, the tragic costs of allegiance to it, and the anguish of losing it. Harrell's absorbing study makes clear that this book, begun as "a historically inspired narrative to articulate a long-standing personal myth," became for Cather "a bulwark against the sundering of the world." Katherine Joslin proposes that Godfrey St. Peter's rebellion against domesticity revises Edna Pontellier's story in her solid essay, "Finding the Self at Home: Chopin's *The Awakening* and Cather's *The Professor's House*," pp. 166–79 in *Kate Chopin Reconsidered: Beyond the Bayou* (LSU) ed. Lynda S. Boren and Sara deSaussure Davis. Both Edna and Godfrey get what they want by escaping the feminine and masculine versions of domesticity, but both novels suggest that "there is no place beyond the house." Michael Leddy charges, in "*The Professor's House* and the Professor's Houses" (*MFS* 38:444–53), that the "good house/bad house contrast" is a "truism in Cather criticism"; he skillfully explicates details in the novel to demonstrate that the complex and contradictory relationship which St. Peter has to his houses reflects his own complex and contradictory character. In "Cather's *The Professor's House*" (*Expl* 51:31–33) Michael Splinder points out that the ideological tension in the novel can be seen in Veblenian terms; the novel demonstrates how nonpecuniary motives and achievements are first taken over and then absorbed by a system whose basic premise is acquisitive self-interest.

Walter Benn Michaels uses both *The Professor's House* and *A Lost Lady* to illustrate "the rescue of race by culture" in "Race into Culture: A Critical Genealogy of Cultural Identity" (*CritI* 18:655–85). The most powerful literary instance of the process by which identification with the Indian could be seen as an assertion of American identity is *The Professor's House,* but "*A Lost Lady* provides an even clearer picture of how the old regionalist resistance to the American state could begin to be transformed into the defense of what might provisionally be called an American culture."

Two essays in *Desert, Garden, Margin, Range* deal with Cather. In "Frontier Violence in the Garden of America" (pp. 55–69), Reginald Dyke pairs Cather with Wright Morris, exploring narrative strategies each devised to accommodate contradictions between the peaceful garden and the violent frontier—equally powerful myths—within the same story. Linda Pickle addresses the differences in narrative techniques used by fiction writers Cather (*My Ántonia*) and Ole Rølvaag (*Giants in the Earth*) and nonfiction writers Mari Sandoz (*Old Jules*) and John Ise (*Old Sod and Stubble*) to depict the physical and emotional struggles of Plains frontier life in "Foreign-Born Immigrants on the Great Plains Frontier in Fiction and Nonfiction" (pp. 70–89); Cather and Rølvaag are "more successful at evoking the timeless, mythic dimension of their material."

In his persuasive essay "Filters, Portraits, and History's Mixed Bag: *A Lost Lady* and *The Age of Innocence*" (*TCL* 38:476–85), John J. Murphy argues that these novels are important because they communicate "the complexities of history, society, and human relationships," and he places them side by side to find, if not direct influence, significant similarities, particularly between the feminine, but not heroic, Marian Forrester and Ellen Olenska. Elsa Nettels's "Tradition and the Woman Artist: James's *The Tragic Muse* and Cather's *The Song of the Lark*" (*WCPMN* 36:27–31) catalogues the many likenesses that suggest Miriam Rooth might be a model for Thea Kronborg, and a significant difference: there is no central figure of authority and tradition in Thea's story like Miriam's Madame Carre, which "shows how fundamentally Cather's idea of the artist and of her own mission as a novelist had come to differ from James's." In "Whitman and Cather" (*EA* 45:324–32) James Woodress confirms that Whitman *was* an important influence on Cather, "but he had to overcome a lot of competition." With his usual graceful style, Woodress cogently reviews the process by which Cather worked through her "Jamesian period" and came to a real appreciation of Whitman, clearly expressed in both the structure and idea of *O Pioneers!* Robert Thacker's "Alice Munro's Willa Cather" (*CanL* 14:42–57) shows that "Dulse" recapitulates the setting, mood, and "cathartic *denouement*" of "Before Breakfast," and allows Munro to acknowledge Cather as "kindred spirit, influence, foremother."

Essays on Cather's stories increase. Six of the nine essays in the *Nebraska English Journal* Special Issue, "Cather in the Classroom" (37, i [1991]), guest-edited by Susan J. Rosowski, focus on stories. Matthias Schubnell (pp. 41–50), Evelyn I. Funda (pp. 51–62), and Steven Shively (pp. 63–74) discuss "Neighbour Rosicky." Bruce P. Baker writes on "The Enchanted Bluff" (pp. 28–33), John J. Murphy on "The Best Years" (pp. 34–40) and Merrill Maguire Skaggs on the three stages of woman as aspects of the goddess in "Old Mrs. Harris" (pp. 75–84). Essays on *My Ántonia* by Anthea E. Amos-Bankester (pp. 99–109) and Mellanee Kvasnick (pp. 110–17) and on the Cather/Alexander connection by Betty Kort (pp. 10–28) round out this very useful collection. Holly Messitt proposes that Cather invites the reader to join her and Don Hedger in gazing at Eden Bower with a socially determined "panoptic male gaze" in "The Internal Gaze: 'Coming, Aphrodite!' and the Panopticon" (*WCPMN 36:34–37*). "The Unreliable Narrator and Political Reality in 'Two Friends'" (*WCPMN* 36:40–42) is Mark Sherf's explication of the story's central motifs, revealing that this narrator, unlike Cather herself, is unable to mend her universe once it breaks apart. Three articles appeared on that old standby, "Paul's Case." Edward W. Pitcher points out the similarity between Paul's self-destructive acts and Faust's selling his soul to the devil in "Willa Cather's 'Paul's Case' and the Faustian Temperament" (*SSF* 28 [1991]:543–54). In "The Theatricality of Willa Cather's 'Paul Case'" (*SSF* 28 [1991]:553–57) Philip Page argues that the theatrical metaphor provides Cather with the double perspective she needs to portray Paul intimately while withdrawing into the audience who watches him. Michael Salda's somewhat bizarre suggestion that Paul never really leaves the basement seems less so at the end of "What Really Happens in Cather's 'Paul's Case'" (*SSF* 29:113–19).

Two unrelated items are noteworthy. John J. Murphy offers a survey of Cather's attitudes toward religion and her solitary characters' great moments of transcendence in "Cather and the Literature of Christian Mystery" (*R&L* 24, iii:39–56). Advancing *Death Comes for the Archbishop* as "prophetic literature of church in community," Murphy shows how "Neighbour Rosicky" celebrates the sacred in simple life and identifies

"The Best Years" as the story in which Cather "contacts Christian mystery." Applying syntactical and discourse analysis to passages from *My Ántonia* and *Death Comes for the Archbishop,* Janet Giltrow and David Stouck prove the value of linguistics in elucidating Cather's style and the effect of that style on her readers in their remarkably clear and cogent discussion, "Willa Cather and a Grammar for Things 'Not Named'" (*Style* 26:90–113). The *Willa Cather Pioneer Memorial Newsletter* continues to be a dependable source of fine scholarship. In addition to essays already mentioned, this year's volume includes an intriguing Biographical Miscellany (36, ii), Virgil Albertini's annual bibliographical essay (36, iv:47, 53–58), and Susan Rosowski's thoughtful reflection, "Willa Cather and the Intimacy of Art Or: In Defense of Privacy" (36, iv:47–53).

ii Edith Wharton and Ellen Glasgow

Wharton scholarship is substantial, though not equal to last year's flood of books and essays. The first comprehensive collection of its kind, *Edith Wharton: The Contemporary Reviews* (Cambridge), ed. James W. Tuttleton et al., contains a selection of reviews of her work from the 1890s until her death in 1937, checklists of other known reviews, and an introduction that surveys Wharton's career in the context of contemporary critical response. This valuable resource complements Garrison's *Edith Wharton: A Descriptive Bibliography* and Lauer and Murray's *Edith Wharton: An Annotated Secondary Bibliography* (see *ALS 1990,* p. 246).

The 18 first-rate essays collected in *Edith Wharton: New Critical Essays* (Garland), ed. Alfred Bendixxen and Annette Zilversmit, make provocative reading. In addition to previously published studies by Elaine Showalter, Cynthia Griffin Wolff, and Elizabeth Ammons, the book contains Judith L. Sensibar's expanded study of Wharton's revision of the New Representative Man (the emotionally immature bachelor) (pp. 159–80), a translation from the French of E. K. Brown's chapter on Wharton's poetry (pp. 215–30), and a splendid selection of new approaches to Wharton's major novels, neglected novels, poetry, and short stories. The importance of *tableaux vivants* in *The House of Mirth* is the subject of Judith Fryer's illustrated essay (pp. 27–55); Donald Pizer argues that *The Age of Innocence* and Dreiser's *An American Tragedy* represent the artistic maturity and final culmination of American naturalism (pp. 127–42); and Deborah Carlin reads one of Wharton's most neglected novels, *The Fruit of the Tree,* for its Miltonic echoes and Edenic allusions (pp. 57–78). Rebecca Faery relies on feminist theory to illuminate the treatment of both sexual desire and repression in *The Reef* and to demonstrate the degree to which the novel deals with textuality as well as sexuality (pp. 79–96); Judith E. Funston focuses on the mother-daughter relationship to examine issues of female selfhood within a repressive society in "Clocks and Mirrors, Dreams and Destinies: Edith Wharton's *The Old Maid*" (pp. 143–58); and in her "Charity at the Window: Narrative Technique in Edith Wharton's *Summer*" (pp. 115–27) Jean Frantz Blackall exposes the narrative devices Wharton used to render the inner life of her inarticulate protagonist. Carol J. Singley's analysis of the interrelations of sexuality, class, race, and power in "A Bottle of Perrier" (pp. 271–90) concludes that this story should be seen in terms of gender reversals that mask underlying mother-daughter relationships, and Elsa Nettels explores the reasons Wharton chose to rely on male narrators for most of her short fiction in "Gender and First-Person Narration in Edith Wharton's Short Fiction" (pp. 245–60). Abby H. P. Werlock's "Edith Wharton's Subtle Revenge?: Morton Fullerton and the Female Artist in *Hudson River Bracketed* and *The Gods Arrive*" (pp. 181–200) and Catherine Bancroft's "Lost Lands: Metaphors of Sexual Awakening in Edith Wharton's Poetry, 1908–1909" (pp. 231–44) both draw on connections between Wharton's life and art in works from different genres. M. Denise Witzig discovers a revolt in which the silent muse deconstructs and appropriates her own story in "The Muse's Tragedy" (pp. 245–70), and she proposes that the story anticipates Wharton's relationship with Percy Lubbock. Margaret B. McDowell demonstrates that the late ghost stories are essential to an understanding of Wharton's life and thought at the end of her career (pp. 291–314), and Annette Zilversmit concludes this immensely satisfying collection by focusing on Wharton's last completed work, "All Soul's" (pp. 315–29), pointing out that in this story Wharton finally writes compellingly of maternal rejection and female desire, and suggesting that we begin to pay attention to Wharton as "a psychological novelist whose fictional portraits capture fragile, wounded, and doomed women."

In *The Sexual Education of Edith Wharton* (Calif.) Gloria Erlich draws on the theories of D. W. Winnicott, Louise J. Kaplan, Sophie Freud, and Sigmund Freud to probe Wharton's psychic wounds, caused primarily by "flaws in the mother-daughter relationship that derailed her emotional development and caused a massive sexual repression" and what was, at least in essence, an incestuous relationship with her father. Erlich provides a theoretical framework for her ambitious study in which she argues that Wharton actually had three "mothers"—Lucretia Jones, her nanny Hannah Doyle, and an imagined third—then persuasively traces Wharton's struggle to forge a functional gender identity along with a professional identity. *The House of Mirth* extrapolates Wharton's family themes and sexual repression; "The Touchstone" anticipates and *The Reef* elaborates on her affair with Morton Fullerton, whose incestuous inclinations meshed with her own; *Son at the Front* and "The Old Maid" rework themes of sexual inhibition, incest, and complex variations on split parenthood. With the Vance Weston novels, Wharton reinvents herself as a mother whose posterity would be books, and she rewrites her own story in the posthumous *The Buccaneers,* re-creating her lost nanny as a governess who leads a young woman into sexual maturity.

Susan Goodman's charming and informative essay "Edith Wharton's 'Sketch of an Essay on Walt Whitman'" (*WWR* 10:3–9) reviews the important points Wharton "sketched" for an essay she planned on Whitman, then evaluates the extent of Whitman's influence on Wharton's artistic vision. Tamara S. Evans challenges Richard Lawson's thesis that Gottfried Keller was an important influence on Wharton in "Edith Wharton and Poetic Realism: An Impulse: (*GQ* 65:361–68). Evans expertly demonstrates convincing parallels between Theodor Fontane's *Irrungen,* Keller's *Wirrungen,* and Wharton's *Summer,* and comes to the conclusion that, although "the same zeitgeist permeates their works," *none* of the German realists had a significant influence on Wharton's work.

In "The Figure of Edith Wharton in Richard Howard's Poem *The Lesson of the Master*" (*EdWR* 9, ii:11–14) Adeline R. Tintner provides an excellent reading of Howard's 1974 poem, in which a remarkably authentic Wharton discovers the homosexuality of her beloved friend, her imaginary companion, and Henry James himself. On the subject of Wharton's friends, Jackie Vickers traces F. Scott Fitzgerald's compelling perceptions on the nature of women and wealth in *Tender is the Night* through Wharton (whose work he read) to Paul Bourget (whose work he did *not* read) in "Women and Wealth: F. Scott Fitzgerald, Edith Wharton and Paul Bourget" (*JAmS* 26:261–63). Fitzgerald once visited Wharton, but was not invited back. "Punishing Morton Fullerton: Louis Auchincloss's 'The "Fulfillment" of Grace Eliot'" (*TCL* 38:44–53), Tintner's second essay, notes that Auchincloss's second "Wharton" story illuminates the imaginative processes of a gifted writer as he exaggerates and eliminates facts to craft a fictive report.

The House of Mirth took the lion's share of essays this year. First is Elaine N. Orr's intelligent, feminist, and refreshingly different "Contractual Law, Relational Whisper: A Reading of Edith Wharton's *The House of Mirth*" (*MLQ* 52:53–70). Orr explains that, although the image of the cage evokes a *contractual* world in which negotiation means bargain, trade, and profit, the novel also sketches an open space, a " 'dreamed of' or 'whispered' space of *relational* and emphatic problem solving," that offers the possibility of open negotiation as exploration and interrelation with/in the open door. By destroying Bertha's letters, Lily opens the door into another world, admits the possibility of dialogue, and becomes "the text's whisper for community." Ruth Bernard Yeazell asserts that *The House of Mirth* rivals *The Theory of the Leisure Class* both as sociology and as satire in "The Conspicuous Wasting of Lily Bart" (*ELH* 59:713–34); for both Veblen and Wharton, the study of the leisure class is a study of waste. In "The Lying Woman and the Cause of Social Anxiety: Interdependence and the Woman's Body in *The House of Mirth*" (*WS* 21:285–305), Ellen J. Goldner proposes that in Wharton's book cultural anxieties over irresponsible Wall Street trading are displaced into worries over the promiscuous trading of women's sexuality and traces the pattern of lies throughout the novel. Her argument might be more forceful in clearer prose. Lois Tyson considers the consequences of Lily Bart's personal anxiety in "Beyond Morality: Lily Bart, Lawrence Selden and the Aesthetic Commodity in *The House of Mirth*" (*EdWR* 9, ii:3–10). Lily's transcendental project is to escape existential inwardness by becoming an objet d'art, and Lawrence Selden offers her, not an alternative to this goal, but a more effective way of achieving it. In presenting Rosedale as he would have been perceived by her contemporaries Wharton leaves herself open to charges of racism, according to Christian Riegel in "Rosedale and Anti-Semitism in *The House of Mirth*" (*SAF* 20:219–24). Derogatory remarks by other characters and descriptions that rely on racial stereotypes pass on the double standard of seeing things as virtues in gentiles and vices in Jews, but Riegel hesitates to accuse Wharton of fostering anti-Semitism since, in the larger context of the novel, Rosedale represents all the contradictions and social symbolism of the entire group. "When Privilege is No Protection: The Woman Artist in *Quicksand* and *The House of Mirth*," Linda Dittman's contribution to *Writing the Woman Artist* (pp. 133–54), by juxtaposing *The House of Mirth* with

Nella Larsen's *Quicksand,* illustrates the difficulty of withstanding social constructions that deny the woman artist access to her gifts.

Two articles discuss *The Age of Innocence.* Clare Virginia Eby's "Silencing Women in Edith Wharton's *The Age of Innocence*" (*CLQ* 28:93–104) is a skillful and compelling discussion of Wharton's indictment of silences and silencing as Old New York's means of social control. None of the three principal characters escapes the consequences of evasion; even Newland Archer must confront his "inarticulate life-time." In "Concepts and Visions of 'The Other': The Place of 'Woman' in *The Age of Innocence, Melanctha,* and *Nightwood*" (*Women in Search of Literary Space* [Gunter Narr], ed. Gudrun M. Grabher and Maureen Devine, pp. 113–33), Elfriede Pöder investigates significantly different versions of "woman's" future place. Wharton envisions the integration of Ellen Olenska's values into the patriarchal and capitalistic society; Stein denies the possibility of living by the female principle in society, but suggests a place for its enactment in language; Barnes foretells the final destruction of all traces of authentic womanhood. Suggesting that critics sometimes generalize and oversimplify Wharton's "feminism," Julie Olin-Ammentorp in "Wharton's View of Women in *French Ways and Their Meaning* (*EdWR* 9, ii:15–18) makes a very strong case for a rereading of Wharton's war works, which reveal her "conservative (even reactionary), didactic, even preachy" side and clearly demonstrate her "unstated belief in the fundamental inferiority of women."

Several unrelated items deserve attention. In "Deadly Letters, Sexual Politics, and the Dilemma of the Woman Writer: Edith Wharton's 'The House of the Dead Hand'" (*ALR* 24, ii:55–69), Lynette Carpenter focuses on Wharton's early story to illustrate her radical struggle to use language honorably as a woman of letters and to discover her role as a woman writer telling women's stories. Andrew Levy contends that Wharton applied her architectural vision to the short story, transforming Poe's writer as "unmoved mover of his audience's emotions" into "an interior designer mediating among the concerns of her audience," in "Edith Wharton: The Muse's Strategy" (*Genre* 24:155–71). In "Holding Up the Revealing Lamp: The Myth of Psyche in Edith Wharton's *The Reef*" (*CollL* 19:75–90), Wendell Jones, Jr., explores the novel's intricate pattern of allusions to the Greco-Roman myth of Psyche and Cupid. Tony Widdicombe's reading of Wharton's "uncharacteristic" story "The Angel at the Grave" as a problematic memorial to Transcendentalism concludes that Wharton's muted vindication of the movement is accompanied by ironies which leave the reader in an uncomfortable state of ambiguity ("Wharton's 'The Angel at the Grave' and the Glories of Transcendentalism: Deciduous or Evergreen?" [*ATQ* 6:47–57]). The *Edith Wharton Review* continues to publish substantial essays, notices, and occasionally a special issue such as "Edith Wharton in Paris" (9, i), a selection of papers from the 1991 Paris conference.

With interest in Cather and Wharton at white heat, it cannot be long before Glasgow captures a larger share of critical attention. The little Glasgow scholarship that did appear this year is solid, and the publication of *Ellen Glasgow: The Contemporary Reviews* (Cambridge), ed. Dorothy M. Scura, should help raise interest. Collected here are a broad selection of reviews published during Glasgow's lifetime, checklists of other known reviews, and Scura's fine comprehensive introduction. Glasgow's opening speech for the 1931 Southern Writers Conference, "The Southern Author and His Public," can be found in *Friendship and Sympathy: Communities of Southern Women Writers* (Miss.), ed. Rosemary M. Magee, pp. 5–12.

Elizabeth Jane Harrison's clear and persuasive chapter on Glasgow in *Female Pastoral* (pp. 17–42) may be the best in the book. Harrison notes that Glasgow began early in her career to develop an alternate version of the naturalistic novel with the intention of reshaping the southern pastoral, a genre that had hitherto inscribed a racist patriarchal order, and that her depiction of the rural world is connected to her creation of a new kind of pastoral. Glasgow changes the focus of the narrative from the aristocracy to the yeoman farmer and makes the issue of class structure more important than "the love story" as her pastoral vision evolves from "woman as enabler to woman as enabled through her relationship to the land." Helen Fiddyment Levy traces Glasgow's longing for the "woman-centered home despite her initial intellectual inclination toward competitive individualism" in *Fiction of the Home Place* (pp. 97–130). *Virginia* begins a lifelong examination of the intersection of race and economic and gender privilege; *Barren Ground* repudiates the concept of woman's families or equal friendship, valuing instead rationalism, pragmatism, and rugged individualism as the basis of female salvation; *Beyond Defeat,* Glasgow's valedictory, accepts the capacity of individual women to create a loving, intergenerational, supportive community firmly rooted in the land. Finally, arguing that "cultural discourse is gender-specific," E. Lale Demirtürk asserts that Glasgow reconstructs conventional female identity by reversing the patriarchal system, then pairs her with Gilman and Paule Marshall with Alice Walker to compare two versions of the critique of patriarchal values in "In Search of a Redeemed Vision: The American Women's Novel, 1880s–1980s" (*ASInt* 30:78–88).

iii Gertrude Stein and Sherwood Anderson

The ongoing efforts to make Stein's work more accessible (and therefore more central to the canon) get a substantial boost this year from two splendid studies. Elizabeth Fifer tackles Stein's "difficult writing"— *Two, As Fine As Melanctha, Painted Lace, Stanza in Meditation, Alphabets and Birthdays,* three volumes of plays, and *Useful Knowledge*—in *Rescued Readings: A Reconstruction of Gertrude Stein's Difficult Texts* (Wayne State), a clearly written study that concentrates on the interaction between Stein's lesbianism and her art to prove that Stein should not be read "like Eliot or Pound or Joyce." After an excellent review of recent Stein scholarship, Fifer skillfully uses psychoanalytic and reader-response techniques to demonstrate how we can learn to "read" the patterns of complex language and experimental strategies Stein devised to both reveal and conceal the erotic and homosexual content of these texts. In these "obsessively sexual" works, Stein discloses her attitudes of frankness, celebration, fearfulness, and repulsion toward her sexuality and offers the receptive reader a part in making "dangerous meaning."

An equally impressive study is Ellen Berry's *Curved Thought and Textual Wandering: Gertrude Stein's Postmodernism* (Michigan). Berry suggests that it has been difficult to read Stein's work in the past because "our interpretive frameworks have had to 'catch up' with her remarkable innovations," and begins her well-organized and lucid book by defining postmodern categories central to an understanding of Stein's fiction: play with and within the text; decentering; radical indeterminacy; a renunciation of interpretive metanarratives; and an emphasis on the reader's role in constructing multiple textual meanings. Berry draws on these interpretive paradigms and feminist perspectives to read *A Long Gay Book* as Stein's farewell to realism; *A Novel of Thank You* as a text that ruptures the concept of centered structure; *Lucy Church Amiably* as a postmodern performance piece; *Mrs. Reynolds* as a "tactical intervention into the workings of power"; *Blood on the Dining Room* as an example of textual wandering; and *Ida* as a postmodern work containing both the possibilities and limitations of Stein's antimimetic modes. Related to these is

Marianne DeKoven's " 'Why James Joyce Was Accepted and I Was Not':
Modernist Fiction and Gertrude Stein's Narrative" (*SLitI* 25, ii:23–30),
which asserts that, despite certain points of intersection, Stein's work is
"eccentric to the mainstream of modernism" and defines its limits by
transgressing them. DeKoven's second essay, "Breaking the Rigid Form
of the Noun: Stein, Pound, Whitman, and Modernist Poetry" (*American
Modernism,* pp. 225–34) investigates the similarities and differences between Stein and Ezra Pound. Stein, unlike Pound, did not work toward
domination, containment, compression, or "abstract conversion of her
erotic-poetic impulse"; her ambivalence about breaking the rigid form of
the noun emerges in diction of violence and anxiety. Gerard Donnelly
Smith finds differences of another kind between Stein's poetry and
Pound's or Eliot's in "Music of the Spheres" (*Sagetreib* 11, iii:103–23).
Though Stein respects language's musical potential, she also explores
how the sounds of language are instilled with meaning and interpreted
by the listener in texts that mirror the chaotic universe and move toward
"a realistic and meaningless music of the spheres."

Other discussions of the reader/text encounter are James A. Detweiler's "A Piano in the Margin: Gertrude Stein 'Detected' in *Blood on
the Dining-Room Floor*" (*KPR* 7:12–16) and Peter Quartermain's chapter
on Stein (pp. 21–43) in his *Disjunctive Poetics: From Gertrude Stein and
Louis Zukofsky to Susan Howe* (Cambridge). Detweiler does some "readerly 'detecting' " to discover that Stein implicates her readers in subverting narrative authority by assuming the narrator-alias "Everybody,"
contriving a situation in which it is clear that the personality of the
implied author/narrator is an artifice, drawing readers as characters into
a "conversation," then leaving them uncertain of their position relative
to events in the text, to the implied author, and to the historical Stein
herself. Quartermain's timely study of the link between alternative methods of poetic discourse and the alternative cultural backgrounds of many
noncanonical modern writers begins with Stein, who herself learned
English as a second language. In a radical attack on certainty, Stein with-
draws her language from lexical and referential signification, achieves an
"astounding multiplicity of meaning and suggestion," and redefines as
pluralities both the act of reading and the role of the reader.

Asserting that "no writer did more in the business of knowledge destruction than Gertrude Stein," Ronald E. Martin credits Stein with
waging a war against accepting language's characteristics as the pa-
rameters of her thought and with eliminating emotion from the text:

pp. 179–207 in *American Literature and the Destruction of Knowledge: Innovative Writing in the Age of Epistemology* (Duke, 1991). Nancy Gray explains how Stein's remarkable freedom with words ungenders access to language and teaches us to pay attention to things we have always known but did not realize in *Language Unbound: On Experimental Writing by Women* (pp. 38–80). "After the Invention of the Gramophone: Hearing the Woman in Stein's *Autobiography* and Woolf's *Three Guineas*" (pp. 88–96), G. Johnston's ingenious contribution to *Virginia Woolf Miscellanies: Proceedings of the First Annual Conference on Virginia Woolf* (Pace), ed. Mark Hussey and Vara Neverow-Turk, describes the "intertext" between Stein and Woolf in terms of technological culture; both Stein and Woolf present a woman's voice trained in private but heard in public, positing a new relationship between the heard, the observed, and the listener. An interesting experiment is Elizabeth A. Meese's essay in *(Sem) Erotics: Theorizing Lesbian :Writing* (NYU), which places her own "lesbian :writing" alongside Stein's (pp. 63–83).

Alison Rieke devotes a chapter to the language of *Stanzas in Meditation* and *Tender Buttons* (pp. 60–92) in her *The Senses of Nonsense* (Iowa) to demonstrate the hermeticism and play of sense and nonsense that saturates much of Stein's writing. In *Stanzas in Meditation* Stein creates "an autobiography of protective negations which counter and balance the compromises she made in more public writings about herself." Susan M. Schultz, on the other hand, wonders how a writer who professes to believe in the utter separation of the text from the world could write several autobiographies, and she suggests that the self-effacement and obscurity of *Stanzas* "cover up what is actually the opposite impulse" in "Gertrude Stein's Self-Advertisement" (*Raritan* 12, ii:71–87). Calling Stein "the most important early poet and theorist of the prose long poem," Robert Grotjohn examines "Poetry and Grammar" as well as "Patriarchal Poetry" in his "Gertrude Stein and the Long Prose Poem" (*Genre* 24:173–89); Stein's theory and practice of the long prose poem brighten the prospect for an American epic since they lead to a cooperative and democratic poetry dependent on the participation of readers. Marguerite S. Murphy's *A Tradition of Subversion: The Prose Poem in English from Wilde to Ashbery* (Mass.) uses Bakhtin to explore the prose poem as a "dialogical" genre and includes her discussion of *Tender Buttons* to demonstrate the radical subversiveness of the genre (pp. 137–67).

Catherine R. Stimpson's important essay, "Gertrude Stein and the Lesbian Lie," (*American Women's Autobiography*, pp. 152–66) investigates

Stein's complex act of deception, confession, and assertion in handling the lesbian lie—"no lesbians lie here"—in *The Autobiography of Alice B. Toklas* and *Everybody's Autobiography*. Stein's lie is to write as if she were incapable of lying, thereby diverting her readers' attention from the lesbian couple and homosexual realities of her subtext. Gaps between the style's apparent promise of full disclosure and the reality of partial concealment make the autobiographies mimetic, portraying "the homosexual dissimulation of which Colette speaks so cleverly and respectfully." Stimpson concludes this thought-provoking essay by indicating the larger, unresolved problems in feminist theory with regard to lesbian lying and language. Leigh Gilmore agrees that Stein's oblique strategies enable her autobiographical representation of lesbian sexuality in the *Autobiography* in "A Signature of Lesbian Autobiography: 'Gertrice/ Altrude,'" pp. 56–75 in *Autobiography and Questions of Gender* (Cass, 1991), ed. Shirley Neuman. The marginal "Gertrice/Altrude" doodle— comingled names which make visible the invisible—represents her ambivalence about the self as a unified figure, her approach to autobiography, and her acceptance of the "irreducibility of identity, sexuality and self-representation." Georgia Johnson considers the importance of form and context in discovering what a present means within a past in *The Making of Americans* in "Reading Anna Backwards: Gertrude Stein Writing Modernism Out of the Nineteenth Century" (*SLitI* 25, ii:31–38). In "Gertrude Stein and the Deconstruction of Family: *The Making of Americans*," pp. 134–49 in *Women in Search of Literary Space* (Gunter Narr), ed. Gudrun M. Grabher and Maureen Devine, Franziska Gygax argues that, despite its subtitle, "being the history of a family," the book is really about the deconstruction of family/families, the only possible narrative for a woman writer confronted with paternal authority and her own female authorship.

Several unrelated items conclude this section. Marc Robinson seeks to rectify the fact that Stein's plays are largely ignored, even by her admirers ("Gertrude Stein, Forgotten Playwright" [*SAQ* 91:621–43]). In "Out of the Picture: Mrs. Krebs, Mother Stein, and 'Soldier's Home'" (*HN* 12, i:1–11), J. Gerald Kennedy and Kirk Curnutt display the photograph tying Hemingway's story to Stein's "Accents in Alsace" and suggest that the mother-son conflict within his narrative betrays Hemingway's fear of never overcoming his need for Stein's approval. Steven J. Meyer follows Stein's clues in "My Debt to Books" and traces links between *The Autobiography of Alice B. Toklas* and both *Robinson Crusoe* and Boswell's

Life of Samuel Johnson in his clever and competent "Gertrude Stein Shipwrecked in Bohemia: Making Ends Meet in the *Autobiography* and After" (*SWR* 77:12–34). Of note as well are Linda Simon's *The Biography of Alice B. Toklas*, which has been reissued as a Bison Book (Nebraska, 1991) with a new preface, Simon's "Annotated Gertrude Stein" appendix, and 36 pages of photographs; and the first complete translation of Natalie Clifford Barney's 1929 memoir, *Adventures of the Mind* (NYU), with chapters on Stein, Mina Loy, Djuna Barnes, and Anna Wickham, and complete notes by translator John Spalding Gatton.

Until recently Anderson scholarship focused primarily on *Winesburg, Ohio;* this year shows signs of burgeoning interest in his other work. Scholars will certainly welcome the publication of *Certain Things Last: The Selected Short Stories of Sherwood Anderson* (Four Walls), ed. Charles E. Modlin, which includes five previously unpublished stories. Modlin has meticulously edited the 30 stories from Anderson's three post-*Winesburg* story volumes and his manuscripts to present accurate texts; a superb introduction and informative editorial notes make this a valuable contribution to Anderson studies. An appropriate companion volume is Robert Papinchak's *Sherwood Anderson: A Study of the Short Fiction* (Twayne). Papinchak offers a comprehensive survey of Anderson's work and an evenhanded critical appraisal of a good number of the stories, reminding us by his selection that *Winesburg* was, although the "watershed of Anderson's creative efforts," only a small part of his total output. Conforming to the three-part format of the Twayne "Studies in Short Fiction" series, the book contains selections by Anderson on writing, previously published scholarly discussions, and a catalogue of Anderson sites in Clyde, Ohio.

Most of the year's work on Anderson is contained in a special issue of *The Old Northwest* (15, iv), ed. David D. Anderson, which includes a stunning variety of essays. Ray Lewis White introduces Anderson's entertaining 1929 broadcast talk on small-town journalism, "The Newspaper and the Modern Age" (pp. 213–31). "*Winesburg, Ohio:* Serendipities of Form" (pp. 233–43), Philip Gerber's deft analysis, attributes the book's lasting appeal to Anderson's luck in striking on themes and a style predictive of strong American "interests-to-be": the 20th-century conviction that we are all victims, simple prose that reflects colloquial speech, and short episodes that can be read as independent stories. In "Sherwood Anderson's 'Middletown': A Sociology of the Midwestern Stories" (pp. 245–59), William V. Miller applies the classification system used by Helen and Robert Lynd in their sociological study of Muncie, Indiana, to Anderson's portrayal of midwestern rural life. Charles E. Modlin's intriguing contribution, "Sherwood Anderson and Waldo Frank" (pp. 273–80), looks at the "odd-couple friendship" through Anderson's letters and includes a previously unpublished letter regarding *The Dark Mother* that Anderson may or may not have sent. In "Initiation of a Primitive" (pp. 261–71) Welford Dunaway Taylor discusses the significant influence primitivism had on Anderson, specifically identifying the 1913 Chicago Armory Show as an event of real consequence for the maturing writer. Rounding out the issue is "Sherwood Anderson and the River" (pp. 281–93), David D. Anderson's fine discussion of the important part Mark Twain, his language, and his metaphors played in Anderson's life and work.

iv Theodore Dreiser, H. L. Mencken, and Sinclair Lewis

Scholars will applaud the publication of two exciting books: the long-awaited Dreiser Edition text of *Jennie Gerhardt* (Penn.), ed. James L. W. West III, and *Fulfilment and Other Tales of Women and Men* (Black Sparrow), a selection of Dreiser's short fiction collected and edited by T. D. Nostwich. The new *Jennie Gerhardt* restores the text to its complete, unexpurgated form, and will prompt a reexamination of Dreiser's relation to the naturalist and sentimental forms of his day; it also has new work on Dreiser's characterization of Jennie and a reassessment of Dreiser's class and ethnic perspectives. In the first of a series of Dreiser volumes planned by Black Sparrow Press, Nostwich gathers 12 short fiction and semifiction tales drawn from books long out of print, and a previously uncollected, "restored-from-typescript" story. The volume includes splendidly informative notes and will surely inspire a reevaluation of Dreiser's skill as a story writer. In addition to being a good introduction to Dreiser, *Theodore Dreiser Revisited* (TUSAS 614), Philip Gerber's revised and expanded version of his earlier study, contains two new chapters on the evolution of Dreiser scholarship in the past 25 years. Indicative of Dreiser's current prestige, *Dreiser Studies,* always a good source of news, scholarship, and bibliographical information, will now be published under the auspices of the newly established International Dreiser Society.

Dreiser's little-known work is already beginning to interest critics. In "Anne Estelle Rice: Dreiser's 'Ellen Adams Wrynn'" (*Women's Art Journal*

13, ii:3–11), Carol A. Nathanson convincingly demonstrates that Dreiser based his character on the American expatriate painter he met in Paris in 1912. Suggesting that Dreiser forecast methods later used by Eugene O'Neill, Elmer Rice, and Thornton Wilder, Keith Newlin argues in "Expressionism Takes the Stage: Dreiser's 'Laughing Gas'" (*JADT* 4, i:5–22) that Dreiser's first staged play was also "America's first staged expressionistic play" and examines the play's formal innovations and the "new stagecraft" used in the Little Theater Society of Indiana's 1916 production. Douglas C. Stenerson submits that Dreiser got his Buddhism from Sir Edwin Arnold and compares passages from *Hey Rub-a-Dub-Dub, Notes on Life,* and several pieces in *Uncollected Prose* to the nine substantial excerpts from *The Light of Asia* in Dreiser's notebooks to prove it in "Some Impressions of the Buddha: Dreiser and Sir Edwin Arnold's *The Light of Asia*" (*CRevAS* 22 [1991]:387–405).

Of Dreiser's novels, *Sister Carrie* generated the most interest. David E. E. Sloane's Sister Carrie: *Theodore Dreiser's Sociological Tragedy* (Twayne) is a comprehensive, perceptive, informed, and readable study, unified by an emphasis on environmental determinism and enriched by the judicious use of both secondary sources and other turn-of-the-century works. Sloane locates the overpowering reality of the novel in Dreiser's use of city imagery to develop a sociological context for his characters, who are overcome by fatalistic social forces and unobtainable material aspirations. Kevin R. McNamara seeks to correct Bob Ames's bad press and contests both Carrie's status as a spectator and Ames's anachronistic gentility in "The Ames of the Good Society: *Sister Carrie* and Social Engineering" (*Criticism* 34:217–35), in which he casts Ames as a *social* engineer and theorist of self who preaches the careful channeling of desire and capital for individual and social good. In "Dreiser's Debt to Balzac" (*ALR* 24, ii:70–80), Nancy Warner Barrineau surveys evidence in *Ev'ry Month* and in the recently restored text of the Pennsylvania Edition of *Sister Carrie* to demonstrate the extent of Dreiser's significant indebtedness to Balzac.

Irene Gammel provocatively juxtaposes Frederick Phillip Grove's Canadian artist-as-victim to Dreiser's American artist-as-egoist in "Victims of Their Writing: Grove's 'In Search of Myself' and Dreiser's 'The Genius'" (*ArielE* 23, iii:49–70) and throws new light on differences between artistic "failure" in small-town Canada and "egotistical" artistic success in urban America. Dreiser's vision of the artist deliberately moves the arts into the economic arena and raises disturbing questions about the appropriation of art by capitalism. In *Voyage into Creativity: The Modern Künstlerroman* (Peter Lang), Roberta Seret traces Eugene Witla's growth in terms of the American value of tangible achievement, seen most commonly in financial success and sexual prowess, finding that his incessant conflicts and his need to emerge as a superior individual result from a society "that judges its citizens by achievement and not by talent" (pp. 123–42). In his ground-breaking study of religion as a "residual cultural determinant," *American Catholic Arts and Fictions: Culture, Ideology, Aesthetics* (Cambridge), Paul Giles calls Dreiser "the first major American writer to emerge from within Catholic culture," and he argues that despite his conscious dissociation from Catholicism, Dreiser's polarities between conformity and alienation, his metaphors culled from religious liturgy, and his sense of fatality are all linked to his inherited mythology of Catholicism (pp. 134–68).

The major Mencken news is the much-anticipated publication of *My Life as Author and Editor* (Knopf), ed. Jonathan Yardley. The book, two-fifths the length of the original manuscript, retains Mencken's chronological organization and incorporates five of the 34 appendices into the text, retaining three in their proper place at the end. The memoir gets only as far as 1923, and the Mencken in these pages is an unfamiliar, more energetic, more ambitious, and more fun-loving figure, with a gift for portraiture that rivals his best invective and ridicule and wonderfully vivid impressions of Dreiser, Sinclair Lewis, and Anita Loos—and lesser lights as well. It comes as a surprise to discover that Mencken actually *liked* women, and as no real surprise to find evidence of anti-Semitism (and other kinds of bigotry). A work of recollection, not of literary criticism, *My Life as Author and Editor* gives us a valuable first-hand look at Mencken, his time and its people. In "Tarred and Coded: The Papers of H. L. Mencken" (*Wilson Library Bulletin* 67, ii:26–27), Kathleen Hart describes the cataloguing, organization, and treatment of Mencken's papers when they were opened in 1991. Of tangential interest to Mencken scholars (and of primary interest to intellectual historians) is Lawrence J. Oliver's *Brander Matthews, Theodore Roosevelt, and the Politics of American Literature, 1880–1920* (Tennessee), the first full-length study of Matthews's career within the New York literary establishment. Oliver explores Matthews's politics, his literary and cultural "progressivism," his association with Teddy Roosevelt, and his ideological conservatism, which made him a prime target for Mencken, Bourne, and the other "juvenile highbrows."

Essays of note in this year's numbers of *Menckeniana* include Frederick Betz's three-part survey of Mencken's role in the history of the word "patrioteer" (121:1–6, 122:12–15, 123:11–15); "Mencken and the Feds" (123:6–10), Shawn Cunningham's review of the U.S. government file on Mencken; and the transcript of a panel discussion of *In Defense of Women* (121:7–15). Vincent Fitzpatrick's annual bibliography (124:6–15) can also be found here, as well as "The American Mercury" (123:1–6), reproducing his article for *American Literary Magazines: The Twentieth Century* (Greenwood). Finally, Ned D. Heindel and Linda H. Heindel offer a close reading of a Mencken story—and even provide a map—in "H. L. Mencken and 'A Girl from Red Lion, P.A.'" (*PF* 42:136–42).

The newly established Sinclair Lewis Society should do much to rectify the recent dearth of Lewis scholarship; the first number of *The Sinclair Lewis Society Newsletter* sets an agenda: "The first step in revitalizing Lewis studies would seem to be to redefine them in terms other than [Mark] Schorer's." Indeed, the time *has* come for a major reassessment of Lewis's work; the publication of *Sinclair Lewis: Main Street and Babbitt* (Library of America), ed. John Hersey, has elicited laudatory and perceptive reviews. This edition has sound, carefully researched texts, with excellent explanatory notes by the late John Hersey, as well as a 36-page "Chronology" that does not depend solely on Schorer for its facts.

Three fine essays and a brief note make up the remainder of this year's work. Sally E. Parry's intelligent essay, "Gopher Prairie, Zenith, and Grand Republic: Nice Places to Visit, But Would Even Sinclair Lewis Want To Live There?" (*MMisc* 20:15–27) is a clear examination of how Lewis's vision of these apparently pleasant midwestern towns changed; as their hopes and aspirations for these communities are increasingly corrupted by class and ethnic hatred, their citizens reflect more and more dramatically "anger and confusion over the American dream in the 20th century." In "Sinclair Lewis, Paul De Kruif, and the Composition of *Arrowsmith*" (*SNNTS* 24:48–66), James M. Hutchisson applies his considerable investigative skills to extant notes and drafts, de Kruif's autobiography, and two hitherto unpublished letters to confirm that de Kruif's assistance was central to the making of *Arrowsmith* and accounts for Lewis's ability to write a "heroic" novel. Leo P. Ribuffo offers an extended discussion of *It Can't Happen Here* that traces its "odyssey" from Lewis's typewriter through MGM studios to the Federal Theater stage in order to elucidate the cultural, economic, and political realities of the 1930s in *Right Center Left: Essays in American History* (Rutgers), pp. 161–

88. In "Sinclair Lewis, Max Besont, and Henry James" (*HJR* 13:90–91), Martin Bucco identifies Max Besont, author of a "purple eulogy" to Henry James (quoted in full), as Lewis, who was incapable of appreciating James—and proud of it.

v Jack London, John Dos Passos, Upton Sinclair, and Ring Lardner

Recent challenges to the canon have also prompted some reappraisals of the "good old boys" of American letters. A special issue of *American Literary Realism 1870–1910*, "A Symposium on Jack London" (24, ii), contains four substantial essays that propose bold corrections to previous readings of London's work. In "Sea Change in *The Sea Wolf*" (pp. 5–22) Sam S. Baskett argues that the devaluation of the woman has obscured the novel's essential push toward androgyny. Wolf's class-induced nihilism and Humphrey's class-induced sterility can both be alleviated through the ideal of physical, psychological and spiritual balance that Maud Brewster comes to represent. In "The Archetypal Woman as Martyr to Truth: Jack London's 'Samuel'" (pp. 23–32), Earle Labor contends that London's later stories are experimental, containing "passages of lyrical and narrative brilliance," and a rich cluster of archetypal motifs that manifests the dynamic vitality of the Jungian "primordial vision." Labor expertly demonstrates his thesis with a close reading of London's "dialogic story-within-a-story" to explore London's "mythology of the feminine." Although "The Unparalleled Invasion" has been seen as racist, Lawrence I. Berkove in "A Parallax Correction in London's 'The Unparalleled Invasion'" (pp. 33–39) argues that the story, a masterpiece of irony, is more concerned with humanity than fears of "the yellow peril" or notions of white supremacy. The final essay, "Jack London's New Woman in a New World: Saxon Brown Robert's Journey into the Valley of the Moon" (pp. 40–54), is Jeanne Campbell Reesman's feminist analysis of Saxon as a "dialogic character" and *The Valley of the Moon* as an illustration of London's far-reaching redefinition of gender roles for men and women, based on a feminism that is a part of the "hermeneutics of openness to the other." Another intelligent essay is "'A Trade, Like Anything Else': *Martin Eden* and the Literary Marketplace" (*ELWIU* 19:246–59). Christopher Gair explores the ramifications of being a "writer" within the world of magazine fiction, clarifies Martin's status as both producer and marketer of texts, showing that Martin is much closer to the "businessman" than he acknowledges, and describes his suicide as "simultaneously a victory and a failure—a victory over the capitalist marketplace at the cost of his own existence."

Two items deal with biography. William Holtz's "Jack London's First Biographer" (*WAL* 27:37–46) is an account of Rose Wilder Lane's difficulties with Charmain London over the version of London that would emerge from her biography, "Life and Jack London," and the ambiguities that still attend her intentions and actions. "Becky London: The Quiet Survivor Talks About Her Father" (*The Californians* 9:34–39), Lailee van Dillen's intimate portrait of London, is based on two interviews with his younger daughter and offers insights into London's writing habits, his surprising conventionality where his children were concerned, his fascination and respect for words, and his determination that "No child of mine is ever going to be afraid of anything."

Dos Passos continues to engage a few critics. The innovative, interdisciplinary *American Science and Literature* includes Joseph W. Slade's fine essay on "Hart Crane and Dos Passos" (pp. 172–93). Both had misgivings about the consequences of science, but they found ways to integrate technology and new information in expanded literary forms, subjects, and metaphors. Thus, in *U.S.A.* Dos Passos draws on biology to reveal the flow of information as "a public, collective phenomenon," and in *The Bridge* Crane uses physics to narrow theories to images. Ronald E. Martin, however, stresses Dos Passos's deconstructive innovations in language and narrative technique in *Destruction of Knowledge* (pp. 311–52). *Manhattan Transfer* and *U.S.A.* develop the 20th-century sense of "the arbitrary, relativistic and manifold qualities of language"; Dos Passos's "quadripartite system of narration" reveals the political and sociopsychological potentials of the destruction of knowledge.

Janet Galligani Casey's "Nancibel Taylor and the Dos Passos Canon: Reconsidering *Streets of Night*" (*SNNTS* 24:410–22) is an astute examination of the shift in Dos Passos's artistic development and thematic concerns from the exclusively masculine interests of *One Man's Initiation* and *Three Soldiers* to a more integrated vision of women, an important aspect of his most celebrated fiction. *Streets of Night*, despite its obvious weaknesses, is the first of Dos Passos's novels to focus on a female protagonist; Nancibel Taylor, handicapped by her femininity in a world that privileges men, anticipates Ellen Thatcher (*Manhattan Transfer*), Margo Dowling and Mary Fench (*U.S.A.*). In "John Dos Passos and the American Left: Recovering the Dialectic of History" (*Criticism* 34:591–

611) Stanley Corkin places *The 42nd Parallel* within the context of American history and Hegelian Marxism with the help of Georg Lukács and Theodor Ardorno.

After years of relative obscurity, Upton Sinclair is in the spotlight as the candidate who ran on the EPIC (End Poverty in California) platform, provoked the first "media campaign" in American politics, and lost. Based on extensive primary research, Greg Mitchell's important study, *The Campaign of the Century: Upton Sinclair's Race for Governor of California and the Birth of Media Politics* (Random House), a fascinating day-by-day account of "the most astonishing smear campaign ever directed against a candidate," recovers Sinclair's notoriety as a social activist, if not his reputation as a writer. Fourteen pages of photographs and Mitchell's lucid style make this book entertaining as well as illuminating. Sally E. Parry's ambitious and competent "Learning to Fight the Nazis: The Education of Upton Sinclair's Lanny Budd," pp. 47–55 in *Visions of War: World War II in Popular Culture and Literature* (Bowling Green), ed. M. Paul Holsinger and Mary Anne Schofield, traces Lanny's development and growing political awareness through the 11 *World's End* novels to show that these novels, written to explain the dangers of fascism and dictatorship, also document Sinclair's own evolving political consciousness. In *Prophets in Babylon: Five California Novelists in the 1930s* (Peter Lang), Margaret C. Jones concentrates on Steinbeck's *The Grapes of Wrath,* West's *The Day of the Locust,* Huxley's *After Many a Summer Dies the Swan,* and Sinclair's *Co-Op* as parodies that critique the California Dream. *Co-Op,* published two years after Sinclair's run for governor and written to promote the ideals of EPIC, stresses the possibility of harmony between the movement and Christian institutions and beliefs.

Ring Lardner has also made a comeback, with one new essay, a book-length critical study, and *Ring Around the Bases: The Complete Baseball Stories of Ring Lardner* (Scribner's), ed. Matthew J. Bruccoli. This volume includes 33 stories (12 previously uncollected), two articles, a charming foreword by Ring Lardner, Jr., and Bruccoli's introduction, which concedes that these stories represent only a part of Lardner's considerable output, an incomplete and distorted view of his fiction, omitting as they do his examinations of the postwar middle class and the new leisure class. Nevertheless, they make good reading!

One of Douglas Robinson's accomplishments in his important study *Ring Lardner and the Other* (Miss.) is to insist on Lardner's minor status in American letters so persuasively that he risks "majoritization." Another is to enter postfeminist discourse by exploring the contradiction between Lardner's patriarchal masculinity and his rich body of writing permeated with the voices of women and the lower middle class. Brilliantly integrating a wide range of theoretical criticism, Robinson derives his own model from Bateson and Lacan (the double bind, the Other) and demonstrates it with three pairs of essays on "Who Dealt?," Lardner himself, and the reader. Masculinist Robinson also includes Ellen Gardiner's feminist reading of the story to "clear a space for dialogue between men and women." Robinson's essay, "Ring Lardner's Dual Audience and the Capitalist Double Bind" (*AmLH* 4:264–87) applies his theory of the double bind to "Haircut."

vi W. E. B. Du Bois, Nella Larsen, Jean Toomer, and Others

Much of what Du Bois wrote remains unpublished or out of print, but scholars have a new resource in Meyer Weinberg's *W. E. B. Du Bois: A Quotation Sourcebook* (Greenwood). Weinberg has gleaned over 950 entries, grouped into 20 chapters dealing with specific topics, from Du Bois's published and unpublished works, summarized the main sense of each in a brief heading, then constructed a comprehensive index that captures "the distinctive Du Boisian ways of stating matters." Reprints of Du Bois's *Black Reconstruction in America* (Maxwell Macmillan) and Paul G. Partington's edition of *The Rare Periodicals of W. E. B. Du Bois* (Partington) also appeared this year.

Volume 12 of *Critique of Anthropology,* guest-edited by Faye V. Harrison and Donald Nonini, includes Harrison's assessment of Du Bois's formative influence on African American anthropology (pp. 239–60); Ernest Allen, Jr.'s discussion of "double consciousness" and "twoness" in *The Souls of Black Folk* (pp. 261–76); and Nancy Ladd Muller's consideration of Du Bois as a philosopher whose approach to race and racism should be read in the context of the pragmatism which informs his work (pp. 319–38). In addition, Robert Paynter places his own field study of Du Bois's homesite in Great Barrington within the debate of historical archaeology (pp. 277–92); Donald Nonini puts Du Bois's explanation of poor whites' racism in the context of recent historical scholarship (pp. 293–318); and Willie L. Baber argues that Du Bois's works on race and racism provide a major critique of formalism in economic anthropology which, he points out, reveals an institutional ecology of racism (pp. 339–64).

In his thoughtful and evenhanded "Du Bois on the Invention of Race" (*Philosophical Forum* 24:166–83), Tommy L. Lott reinterprets Du Bois's notion of race identity in the context of prevailing African-American social philosophy at the turn of the century, defends the plausibility of Du Bois's sociohistorical view of race history, and explains the consequences for both Du Bois and his critics of blurring the distinctions between race and ethnicity. Michael J. C. Echeruo explores similarities between Edward Blyden's and Du Bois's ideas on the meaning of race which acknowledge "the 'mixed race' created by white intervention in black history" in "Edward W. Blyden, W. E. B. Du Bois, and the 'Color Complex'" (*JMAS* 30:669–84). In "Curing the Blues: W. E. B. Du Bois, Fashionable Diseases, and Degraded Music" (*Black Music Research Journal* 11, ii [1991]:137–55), Tom Lutz says that Du Bois did not like the "blues," first because the blues represented debased, appropriated music and, even more importantly, because both the blues and ragtime were associated with the explicitly virulent and racist "coon" songs of the time. In a more contemporary framework, Alton B. Pollard III discusses the Clarence Thomas-Anita Hill "debacle" in terms of Du Bois's prophecy that race would be the paramount problem of the 20th century in "W. E. B. Du Bois and the Struggle for African America's Soul" (*CCur* 42:370–77).

Dickson D. Bruce, Jr., identifies both European Romanticism and American Transcendentalism as sources for Du Bois's "double-consciousness" and suggests that his use of the term gave his audience a reference point on the tragedy of racism ("W. E. B. Du Bois and the Idea of Double Consciousness" [*AL* 64:299–309]). In "Du Bois, Emerson, and the 'Fate' of Black Folk" (*ALR* 24, iii:8–88), Brian A. Bremen and Keith Byerman link "double-consciousness" specifically to Emerson, demonstrating that nearly all of *The Souls of Black Folk* should be read in dialogue with his 1852 essay "Fate." Byerman's "Race and Romance: *The Quest of the Silver Fleece* as Utopian Narrative" (*ALR* 24, iii:58–71), places the novel in the muckraking tradition. And in a literary hat trick of sorts, Byerman's "The Children Ceased to Hear My Name: Recovering the Self in *The Autobiography of W. E. B. Du Bois* (*Multicultural Autobiography*, pp. 64–93) shows how Du Bois, overriding differences and discontinuities in his life, uses autobiographical narrative to present a "self" that is remarkably consistent, to show that his radicalism places him at the core of American principles, and to assert that he has been central to American history. In " 'Closing Ranks' and 'Seeking Honors': W. E. B. Du Bois in World

War I" (*JAH* 79:96–124), Mark Ellis rereads Du Bois's editorial as an address to the War Department in which he distorted his real beliefs in hopes of getting a commission—and paid a heavy price.

James Weldon Johnson's work is also becoming available again; *Black Manhattan* (Da Capo, 1991), with a new introduction by Sondra Kathryn Wilson, offers a history and a firsthand evaluation of the Harlem Renaissance. *God's Trombones* provoked two very different responses. In "Sharing the Passion: Jacopone de Todi's 'Donna del paradiso' and James Weldon Johnson's 'The Crucifixion' " (*Medieval Perspectives* 7:108–23), V. Louise Katainen discovers striking parallels, including a simplicity of style that evokes a deep affective response from the reader. Robert E. Fleming admits that he finds no direct evidence that Faulkner read Johnson, but he compares the Easter service at Dilsey's church with the sermons in *God's Trombones* to reveal marked similarities of language and structure in "James Weldon Johnson's *God's Trombones* as a Source for Faulkner's Rev'un Shegog" (*CLAJ* 36:24–30). In *The Hammers of Creation: Folk Culture in Modern African-American Fiction* (Georgia), Eric J. Sundquist analyzes Johnson's incorporation of "folk culture," particularly music, into *The Autobiography of an Ex-Coloured Man* (pp. 1–48).

The definitive text of the Harlem Renaissance, Alain Locke's *The New Negro* (Maxwell Macmillan), appears this year with a superb introduction by Arnold Rampersad. Also now available are five of Locke's lectures on cultural diversity from his years as a professor at Howard University, *Race Contacts and Interracial Relations: Lectures on the Theory and Practice of Race* (Howard), ed. Jeffrey C. Stewart. In addition to furnishing a useful introduction, Stewart has carefully edited the transcriptions, meticulously retaining Locke's own text and interpolations whenever possible, filling in gaps judiciously, and supplying substantial explanatory notes. The lone article on Locke is Sandra L. Quinn-Musgrove's "Lost in Blackness: Alain Leroy Locke" (*Ethnic Forum* 12, ii:48–68), in which she reviews evidence for her conviction that Locke "conceived and initiated the means for successful, nonviolent integration of the races in the United States." Tracing Locke's influence through major and minor political philosophers and activists, Quinn-Musgrove argues convincingly and with some indignation that Locke's exclusion from most studies of racial integration arises from the fact that his ideas were far ahead of his time.

Robert B. Jones's brilliant explication of a newly discovered, unpublished story, "Gothic Conventions in Jean Toomer's 'The Eye' " (*SAF*

20:209–17) is the most important essay on Jean Toomer this year. Written during Toomer's Gurdjieff period, the story dramatizes Toomer's monistic vision of reality and conforms to the Gothic "fable of the impossibility of identity" to explore the roles of evil and madness, personal identity and family relationship. "The Eye," which formulates a poetics of terror and dramatizes the idea that good and evil, sanity and insanity, inhere within the self, places Toomer in the Romantic tradition of Hawthorne, Melville, and Poe. R. Baxter Miller takes Toomer's own racially conflicted self as the subject of his "Blacks in His Cellar: The Personal Tragedy of Jean Toomer" (*LHRev* 11, i:36–40), and Frederick L. Rusch identifies Toomer's problems with his racial/ethnic identity and his modernist intellectual friends as the major factors in his avant-garde appropriation of jazz and cubist forms for *Cane* in "Form, Function and Creative Tension in *Cane:* Jean Toomer and the Need for the Avant-Garde" (*MELUS* 17, iv:15–28). Robert Cooperman speculates that, though they probably never met, O'Neill and Toomer "subconsciously borrowed" from each other in "Unacknowledged Familiarity: Jean Toomer and Eugene O'Neill" (*EONR* 16:39–48), and he convincingly focuses on the "Toomerisms" from *Cane* in *All God's Chillun Got Wings* to point out their shared understanding of racial conflict and their "corresponding and complementary visions."

I hope that Kirkland C. Jones's *Renaissance Man from Louisiana: A Biography of Arna Wendell Bontemps* (Greenwood) will fuel some critical analysis of Bontemps's work, missing in this anecdotal portrait which highlights Bontemps's influence as a teacher and cultural archivist. This year, only Eric Sundquist offers some critical perspective in his chapter on Bontemps's examination of history in *Black Thunder* (*The Hammers of Creation,* pp. 92–134).

Tyrone Tillery's *Claude McKay: A Black Poet's Struggle for Identity* (Mass.) is both "a psychological portrait of a complex, deeply conflicted literary figure" and an analysis of "the larger problems of identity, vocation, and politics that confronted black intellectuals" in the 1920s. Well-researched and documented, the book makes use of recently unclassified government documents as well as other archival sources to explore the roots of McKay's radicalism, and traces many of his critical and ambivalent attitudes toward much of African America to his Jamaican origins. Tillery offers some literary analysis (*Home to Harlem* and *Banjo*), but only to support his theses. The comprehensive primary and secondary bibliographies he includes will prove useful for further schol-

arship. McKay's poetry produced two essays this year: Clenora Hudson-
Weems's "Claude McKay: Black Protest in Western Traditional Form"
(*Western Journal of Black Studies* 16, i:1–5) and Barbara J. Griffin's
"Claude McKay: The Evolution of a Conservative" (*CLAJ* 36:157–70).
Hudson-Weems discusses the compatibility of McKay's militant, revolutionary protest themes with his rigidly conventional sonnet form
and reaches contradictory conclusions: his articulation of contempt for
American racism in a form of such rigidity shows that he is in control
of his intense feelings, and/or his sonnets show that, if physical constraints are not enough, "the Black man is reduced to artistic constraints
as well." McKay's "Clyde Manuscript," 54 sonnets written after his
stroke, prompts Griffin to conflicted conclusions as well: the sonnets
describe a process which can be read as just another gesture toward
reconciliation by a 20th-century exile or as an end to the "warring
complexities within himself." In "A Vision of Black Culture in Two
Novels by Claude McKay" (*AmerSS* 23, ii [1991]:78–82), Manfred Wolf
contends that McKay focuses less on the plight of blacks than on "their
manner of living and their way of thinking." *Banjo* and *Home to Harlem*
dare to ask what is so startlingly different about black life and offer
the answer: "blacks live more freely, more immediately, more whole-
heartedly than whites." Hazel V. Carby sees *Home to Harlem* and Carl
Van Vechten's *Nigger Heaven* as "fiction of black urban classes in formation" in "Policing the Black Woman's Body in an Urban Context" (*CritI*
18:738–55), using female characters as the means by which male protagonists achieve or fail to achieve social mobility, and as threats to the
emergence of black masculinity and black male citizenship in the American social order.

In the only article on Jessie Redmon Fauset, Vashti Crutcher Lewis
takes a look at *her* portrayal of female characters, overly class- and color-
conscious mulattas who in passing inform readers of the depth of
personal animosity of whites toward blacks ("Mulatto Hegemony in the
Novels of Jessie Redmon Fauset" [*CLAJ* 35:375–86]) and who must be
measured against the near-caricature stereotypes of white contemporary
writers. Also, Carolyn M. Sylvander's biography, *Jessie Redmon Fauset,
Black American Writer* (Whitston), was reissued.

In his lucid introduction to *An Intimation of Things Distant: The
Collected Fiction of Nella Larsen* (Anchor), editor Charles R. Larson
corrects misconceptions about Nella Larsen's life, summarizes the five
works (short stories and novels) collected here within the context of her

career, and reevaluates her abandonment of her literary career for a return to nursing. Brett Beemyn's "A Bibliography of Works By and About Nella Larsen" (*African American Review* 26:183–88) offers chronological listings of the editions and reviews of Larsen's two novels and periodical publications, alphabetically arranged sections containing criticism of *Passing* and *Quicksand,* and published biographical and bibliographical studies.

Helena Michie focuses on the linked differences within the black community of skin color and sexuality as they are represented in Larsen's *Quicksand* and *Passing,* which work with and against the tradition of the mulatto, the doubly marginal figure, and in Toni Morrison's *Sula,* which breaks free from the tragic mulatta, enters the almost exclusively black community, and translates the problem of skin color into other physical markings (pp. 137–68 in *Sororophobia: Differences Among Women in Literature and Culture* [Oxford]). In "Clare Kendry's 'True' Colors: Race and Class in Nella Larsen's *Passing*" (*Callaloo* 15:1053–65), Jennifer De-Vere Brody convincingly challenges previous readings that see the main creatures as "psychological beings" or "sexual creatures" and demonstrates in a clear and cogent discussion that this "biting critique of Black bourgeois ideologies" is concerned with the "simultaneous representation and construction of race and especially class." Jonathan Little takes critics to task for missing Larsen's irony in "Nella Larsen's *Passing*: Irony and the Critics" (*African American Review* 26:173–83). The ending of *Passing* is consistent with the novel's internal logic and the organic design that explodes the romantic narrative conventions of Larsen's passing-for-white plot. David L. Blackmore offers a close reading of *Passing* to extricate the subversive subtexts in " 'That Unreasonable Restless Feeling': The Homosexual Subtexts of Nella Larsen's *Passing*" (*African American Review* 26:475–84). In "The Quicksands of Self: Nella Larsen and Heinz Kohut," pp. 184–99 in *Telling Facts: History and Narration in Psychoanalysis* (Hopkins), ed. Joseph H. Smith, M.D., et al., Barbara Johnson takes Kohut's model of "narcissistic personality disorder" as a framework for understanding the psychological effects of social conflicts on Helga Crane. She then takes *Quicksand* as a framework for questioning the limits of Kohut's "narcissism" and shows how Larsen tells the story of the neither/nor self from within.

Lastly, John E. Bassett's *Harlem in Review: Critical Reactions to Black American Writers, 1917–1939* (Susquehanna) includes more than 1000 annotated items that chart critical responses to African American writers of the period covered by this chapter in five chronologically arranged chapters; individual titles are followed by a section on general criticism and scholarship. The volume is enhanced by Bassett's interesting introduction.

vii Western Writers

Ole Rølvaag got more attention than usual this year, certainly a reflection of the general interest in American multiculturalism; three noteworthy items appeared in addition to the essays mentioned in the Cather section. In " 'To Lose the Unspeakable': Folklore and Landscape in Ole Rølvaag's *Giants in the Earth*" (*Mapping American Culture*, pp. 89–111), April Schultz places *Giants in the Earth* firmly in the context of immigrant literature, tracing the contrast between persistence and innovation by focusing on the divergence between Per Hansa and his wife Beret. In this important essay, Schultz pays close attention to Rølvaag's use of both pagan and Christian Norwegian folklore to demonstrate the complexities of the novel, uncovering in these allusions Rølvaag's anxiety about the loss of ethnic identity and his message to the Norwegian-American community about "the dangerous hubris of the dominant American narrative of individualism and inevitable expansion." Patrick D. Morrow compares *Giants in the Earth* to Johan Bojar's *The Emmigrants* to illustrate differences between "complex" and "formula" fiction, pp. 109–31 in *The Popular and the Serious in Select Twentieth-Century American Novels* (Mellen). Rølvaag's tragic novel, an amalgamation of Norwegian culture and concerns turned to the frontier experience, anticipates the postmodern novel in its depiction of "seekers after spiritual enlightenment"; Bojar's success story, written to celebrate the centenary of the first Norwegian emigration to the New World, neatly resolves the fundamental American conflict between self-reliant individuality and other-directed human community. Martha Sledge announces that she has discovered a rare diary by Swedish immigrant A. H. Petterson which records his experiences in adjusting to America; she compares it to *Giants in the Earth* and Simon Johnson's *From Fjord to Prairie* to prove that immigrant novels are indeed "chapters of history" in "Truth and Fact: The Rhetoric of Fiction and History in Immigrant Literature" (*SDR* 29, ii [1991]:159–69). Sledge's important, exciting essay also raises provocative questions about defining the lines that distinguish fiction from history.

There was one essay on Owen Wister this year: Gerald Thompson's superb critical review and defense of *The Virginian,* "Owen Wister and His Critics: Realism and Morality in *The Virginian*" (*Annals of Wyoming* 64:2–10). Drawing on Wister's essays, letters, and diary, Thompson argues that critics who attack the realism of the novel miss the point that Wister used a realistic framework to shape a romantic content. More importantly, Thompson demonstrates that critics who oppose the book on moral grounds should look at Beccaria's moral/legal philosophy, which furnishes the "formula" Wister followed in *The Virginian.*

Peter Wild continues in his efforts on behalf of naturalist John C. Van Dyke, editing three of his books for the University of Utah Press: *The Grand Canyon of the Colorado: Recurrent Studies in Impressions and Appearances, The Mountain: Renewed Studies in Impressions and Appearances,* and *The Open Spaces: Incidents of Nights and Days Under the Blue Sky.* Incidentally, Eastern naturalist and writer John Burroughs has been given "new life" with Edward J. Renehan, Jr.'s *John Burroughs: An American Naturalist* (Chelsea). Highly readable, the first biography of the "dean of American nature writers" since 1925 draws on previously unpublished letters, journals, and letters to discuss Burroughs's work, his influence, and his complicated relationships and friendships with figures such as Emerson, Thoreau, Theodore Roosevelt, and Henry Ford.

Mary Austin's nature writing prompted one essay. In "Mary Austin's Disfigurement of the Southwest in *The Land of Little Rain*" (*WAL* 27:37–46), William J. Scheick discusses Austin's first book as her attempt to challenge "the familiar" in both her choice of setting and her search for the transcendent, a drama of frustration in which she fails to appropriate a "metaphysically resistant natural landscape." Karen S. Langlois's "Mary Austin's *A Woman of Genius:* The Text, the Novel, and the Problem of Male Publishers and Critics and Female Authors" (*JACult* 15, ii:79–86) traces the publishing history of Austin's book and reveals the problematic endeavor of publishing feminist fiction in the male bastion of early 20th-century bookselling.

Louis Owens reminds us that Mourning Dove's *Cowega* introduced "the dilemma of the mixedblood, the liminal 'breed' seemingly trapped between Indian and white worlds" (pp. 40–48) in his groundbreaking study, *Other Destinies: Understanding the American Indian Novel* (Okla.). Alanna Kathleen Brown uses manuscript letters to render the intricacies of the Mourning Dove/McWhorter collaboration, evolving dialogue, and growing friendship, and focuses on the difficulties both faced in compiling *Okanogan Sweat House,* the collection of legends that became

Coyote Stories in "The Evolution of Mourning Dove's *Coyote Stories*" (*SAIL* 4, ii–iii:161–80). Amy Ling places Winnifred Eaton in the context of contemporaneous pseudonymic writers to shed new light on her choice of a persona in "Creating One's Self: The Eaton Sisters," pp. 305–18 in *Reading the Literatures of Asian America* (Temple), ed. Shirley Geoklin Lim and Amy Ling. Although both Edith (Sui Sin Far) and Winnifred (Onoto Watanna) chose pseudonyms, Winnifred was the real literary trickster—her *Diary of Delia* is a novel written in Irish-American dialect by a Chinese-Eurasian Canadian published under a Japanese name!

Two general essays pertinent to this section express themes informing much of the year's work—autobiography/biography and sociology. "Utopia and Anti-Utopia in Twentieth-Century Women's Frontier Autobiographies," Lynn Z. Bloom's contribution to *American Women's Autobiography* (pp. 128–51), demonstrates that even the least utopian women's autobiographical constructions were the antithesis of "the hopeless, worn-out drudges" in men's writing about frontier women. Walter Hölbling questions the validity of the "'natural' symbiosis of open space and open mind" in "Open Spaces to Narrow Minds: Soil, Soul, and Intellect in Recent U.S. Writing" (*NDQ* 60, i:147–60) and investigates ambiguities and contradictions inherent in the evolution of the "mythic self-image of the small town as an ideal community."

viii   General Studies and Additional Authors

The most important general work this year is Ronald Weber's solid and valuable study, *The Midwestern Ascendancy in American Writing* (Indiana), focusing on the years between the fading of the New England tradition and the emergence of the southern literary renaissance, when midwestern literature was at the center of American writing. Weber cogently addresses the deeply divided feelings about the region seen in contradictory images of abandonment and celebration, provides insights on the effects of the tremendous social and technological changes during the period, and illuminates the sense of lost promise that permeates much of this work with an elegiac quality. In addition to Cather, Dreiser, Anderson, and Lewis, the book covers a host of others important to this chapter. In her fascinating study, *The Making of Middlebrow Culture* (No. Car.), Joan Shelley Rubin takes on critical "oversimplification of middlebrow culture in the 1920s, 1930s, and 1940s" and gives us perceptive analyses of such cultural phenomena as newspaper book columns, the Book-of-the-Month Club, the "Great Books" movement, the "out-line" vogue, and the proliferation of literary radio programs. In doing so, she also offers assessments of such luminaries as Dorothy Canfield Fisher, Henry S. Canby, and Will Durant. A somewhat different group (Randolph Bourne, Floyd Dell, Max Eastman, H. L. Mencken) is the focus of Steven Biel's study of the new intellectual community that emerged in Greenwich Village and challenged the authority of the university during the 1910s and 1920s, *Independent Intellectuals in the United States, 1910–1945* (NYU).

In *Urban Intersections: Meetings of Life and Literature in United States Cities* (Illinois), Sidney H. Bremer argues that the "economic city" of Dreiser, Sinclair, Dos Passos, and Wright has unfairly dominated our perceptions of urban life, and, in well-argued, absorbing discussions, focuses on images of the "neighborhood city" in women "residential novelists" such as Cather, Wharton, and Chopin, African American authors such as McKay, James Weldon Johnson, and Larsen, and Jewish-American writers such as Anzia Yezierska, Abraham Cahan, and Henry Roth. *White Collar Fictions: Class and Social Representation in American Literature, 1885–1925* (Georgia) is Christopher P. Wilson's splendid exploration of turn-of-the-century literary treatments of and by "the new middle classes." Wilson's fresh readings of O. Henry, Edna Ferber, Robert Grant, Elmer Rice, Sherwood Anderson, and Sinclair Lewis demonstrate how each modified literary forms to engage their audiences, and he uncovers the ways in which these writers helped create a new cultural vocabulary. Laura Hapke's fine study, *Tales of the Working-Girl: Wage-Earning Women in American Literature, 1890–1925* (Twayne), explores the evolution of the working girl from the slum melodramas of the 1890s to the strike fiction of the 1910s to the economic ascension novels of the 1920s, drawing on literary criticism and social history to examine the artistic goals and strategies in the fiction and essays of more than 100 writers, including Crane, Wharton, O. Henry, Dreiser, and Anzia Yezierska.

The Challenge of Feminist Biography: Writing the Lives of Modern American Women (Illinois), ed. Sara Alpern et al., a collection of ten feminist essays on real "New Women," and *Breaking the Ties That Bind* (Okla.), ed. Maureen Honey, a collection of early feminist stories about the New Woman, make an intriguing pair of books that describe one female type. Susan Sipple discusses another, "pre-Depression female hobos and Depression-era transients," and focuses on Meridel Le Sueur's

Women on the Breadlines as fiction which gives them a voice in " 'Witness [to] the Suffering of Women': Poverty and Sexual Transgression in Meridel Le Sueur's *Women on the Breadlines*," pp. 135–53 in *Feminism, Bahktin, and the Dialogic* (SUNY, 1991), ed. Dale M. Bauer and Susan Jaret McKinstry. Roberta Maierhofer sees *Women on the Breadlines* as Le Sueur's creation of an "a-patriarchal space" since, prior to her work, poverty during the depression was presented as a peculiarly male experience in "Meridel Le Sueur: A Female Voice of the Thirties," pp. 150–62 in *Women in Search of Literary Space.*

Mary Loeffelholz challenges traditional male-oriented interpretations of the modern period in *Experimental Lives: Women and Literature 1900– 1945* (Twayne) by highlighting the experiments in literary technique and thematic innovations of women such as Cather, Stein, Austin, and Fauset. Jo-Ann Wallace's "Laura Riding and the Politics of Decanonization" (*AL* 64:111–26) raises questions about the canon, critical reception, and cultural authority as it seeks to account for the critical neglect of "a major woman poet, critic and fiction writer of the 1920s and 1930s." Other efforts to rectify neglect make up the remainder of this section.

In "Dorothy Day and Women's Spiritual Autobiography" Mary G. Mason locates Day's four neglected autobiographical works in the tradition of conversion narrative (*American Women's Autobiography*, pp. 185– 217). Richard Tuerk compares two competing visions of the immigrant experience in autobiographies by Jacob Riis, Louis Adamic, Mary Antin, and M. E. Ravage in "At Home in the Land of Columbus: Americanization in European-American Immigrant Autobiography" (*Multicultural Autobiography*, pp. 114–38). Fictional accounts of the immigrant experience can be found in *How I Found America: Collected Stories of Anzia Yezierska* (Persea, 1991), which contains virtually all of Yezierska's short fiction, including seven previously uncollected stories. Gay Wilentz uses female-centered discourse to examine *Bread Givers* in "Cultural Mediation and the Immigrant's Daughter: Anzia Yezierska's *Bread Givers*" (*MELUS* 17 [1991]:33–41) and demonstrates how the novel's contradictory ending reflects Yezierska's unease with any possibility of mediated existence in the "promised" land. The "pervasive racial and cultural nativism" and "intolerant resentment" of Edna Ferber's *American Beauty* is Stanislas A. Blejwas's topic in "The Inherited and the Disinherited: The Polish Farmer in New England Literature" (*Connecticut Review* 14, ii:49–60). Ferber's novel reflects the prevailing opinions about the "new"

immigrants among the New England intellectual elite, but Blejwas finds
it surprising how easily she "panders" to this nativism.

Linda Tate has compiled "Elizabeth Madox Roberts: A Bibliographical Essay" (*RALS* 18:22–43), which might spur some activity in the
Roberts camp. Ruth Suckow's centenary produced only a new edition of
The Folks (Iowa) and one essay, Mary Jean DeMarr's "An Iowa Woman's
Life: Ruth Suckow's *Cora* (*Midamerica* 18 [1991]:80–96), which considers
the novel, unique in Suckow's inclusion of a lesbian theme, as an exploration of the difficulties for women in a patriarchal society to find both
personal and professional fulfillment. Abigail Ann Martin's *Bess Streeter
Aldrich* (BSWWS 104) saves once-popular, now-neglected, Aldrich from
oblivion; unlike Suckow's Cora and Cather's Alexandra, Aldrich's women
get their strength and fulfillment from "*womanliness.*"

In "Cain, Chandler and the Great California Road Show" (*The
Californians* (9, Nov. [1991]:22–25), David Fine discusses James M.
Cain's centrality to the development of the highway image in Los
Angeles fiction. Richard Fine's *James M. Cain and the American Author's
Authority* (Texas) is a thorough examination of the ideals, goals, and
impact of Cain's proposed central copyright organization, which pro-
voked a controversy splitting East and West Coast writers and sowing
seeds of distrust that later surfaced in the McCarthy era blacklists.

One book this year secures B. Traven's reputation. Heidi Zogbaum's
compelling *B. Traven: A Vision of Mexico* (SR Books) explains how Mexican history shaped the direction and tenor of Traven's writings, shows
how developments in Germany crucially shaped Traven's reading of
Mexican events, and systematically examines and supports the accuracy
of Traven's claim that his novels were "documentaries." Lastly, Edward
N. S. Lorusso is singlehandedly reestablishing Robert McAlmon's reputation by editing and providing substantial introductions for three University of New Mexico Press reprints: *Village* (1990), *Post-Adolescence*
(1991), and *Miss Knight and Others* (1992).

Drew University

14 Fiction: The 1930s to the 1960s

Catherine Calloway

Eudora Welty is popular again this year, as are southern writers in general. In addition to Welty, Vladimir Nabokov, Kay Boyle, and the Beats are represented in book-length studies, and Mary McCarthy, an often overlooked figure, in several books. James Agee, Robert Penn Warren, Saul Bellow, and J. D. Salinger each claim their own essay collections. John Steinbeck and the proletarians continue to remain well-received, while scholarship remains sparse on westerners, iconoclasts, and detectives.

i General

Two works focus on the importance of setting or place. *Prophets in Babylon: Five California Novelists in the 1930s* by Margaret C. Jones (Peter Lang) examines the California Dream—the culmination of the exodus to the West—as it relates to the American Dream in five novels: Arnold B. Armstrong's *Parched Earth,* Aldous Huxley's *After Many a Summer Dies the Swan,* Nathanael West's *The Day of the Locust,* John Steinbeck's *The Grapes of Wrath,* and Upton Sinclair's *Co-op.* Devoting a chapter to each work, Jones examines the historical, sociological, and geographic factors contributing to the American Dream as well as the images and motifs of Hollywood, Edens, and utopias that characterize it. Her study goes beyond earlier studies of utopias in California literature by concentrating on "novels produced during a brief period of crisis, when the socioeconomic disparities and the utopian visions traditionally represented as characteristic of California Society were fictionally depicted as having attained a peculiar intensity and centrality."

Chicago is the subject of James Hurt's *Writing Illinois: The Prairie, Lincoln, and Chicago* (Illinois). Citing a wide range of writers from the late 1800s to the 1990s, Hurt examines the way in which "the prairie landscape, the memory of Lincoln, and the presence of Chicago" have contributed to "the sense of place in Illinois." While Hurt discusses a number of writers representing different periods, he sees as particularly crucial the influence of Abraham Lincoln and the works of Saul Bellow.

Another study, *Jewish-American Fiction, 1917–1987* by Sanford Pinsker (Twayne) focuses on the Jewish-American contribution to American literature. Pointing out the significance of that fiction "as it moved from obscure beginnings to international importance in the decades following World War II," Pinsker's study does not attempt to be comprehensive, but instead selectively examines representative novels by writers such as Henry Roth, Nathanael West, Michael Gold, I. B. Singer, Philip Roth, Norman Mailer, and Cynthia Ozick. He notes the common factors shared among stories of the Jewish journey to American life: the conflict between secular beliefs and Jewish orthodoxy, the American Dream, family conflicts, the search for a Jewish-American identity, and the false attraction of Jewish suburban life. Especially insightful are the lengthy sections on Bernard Malamud and Bellow.

Women's writing has also been a main concern of this year's critical debate. In *Experimental Lives: Women and Literature, 1900–1945* (Twayne), Mary Loeffelholz explores the place of female writers in modernist literature, both English and American. In doing do, Loeffelholz hopes "to convey the degree to which literature participated in the early twentieth century's pitched battles around definitions of masculinity and femininity," to "explore the relationship between challenges to traditional literary forms and challenges to traditional ideas about women's and men's identities," "to suggest something of the sheer variety of women's literary production in these years," and to "ask how our ideas about modernism as a whole might change if we saw Harlem as a modernist center on a par with Paris or London." Americanists will particularly appreciate the sections on Djuna Barnes, Dorothy Parker, Kay Boyle, Katherine Anne Porter, and Zora Neale Hurston.

Another worthy contribution on modern and contemporary American women writers is *Friendship and Sympathy: Communities of Southern Women Writers,* ed. Rosemary M. Magee (Miss.). Magee assembles a wide variety of speeches, essays, reviews, and interviews in which women writers comment on their own and other female writers' work and demonstrate the need for a sense of community, friendship, and tradition among American women writers. Voices within the text include

Ellen Glasgow, Marjorie Kinnan Rawlings, Carson McCullers, Margaret Walker, Porter, Flannery O'Connor, Welty, and Caroline Gordon, as well as such recent writers as Alice Walker, Anne Tyler, Josephine Humphreys, and Bobbie Ann Mason.

ii Proletarians

a. John Steinbeck *East of Eden* continues to be a popular subject for Steinbeck enthusiasts. Ricardo J. Quinones in *The Changes of Cain: Violence and the Lost Brother in Cain and Abel Literature* (Princeton [1991]; pp. 135–52) traces the Cain and Abel motif in *East of Eden,* demonstrating how Steinbeck uses this age-old myth as a "framing device" to portray the emergence of a "national type" in American literature at the end of World War II and to reveal the influence of modernism on the characters' actions. Quinones credits Steinbeck with going beyond the "pattern of guilt and division" to tap "the emotional centers of the Cain-Abel theme."

East of Eden has also been popular with contributors to this year's issues of *Steinbeck Quarterly.* Steven Mulder in "The Reader's Story: *East of Eden* as Postmodernist Metafiction" (*StQ* 25:109–18) sees the novel as a forerunner to postmodernism, a "*pre*-Postmodern" novel in which Steinbeck experiments with a combination of realistic, modern, and postmodern techniques. Mulder concludes that Steinbeck ultimately wrote a metafictional work that actively engages the reader in the process of "*self-creation.*" In "*East of Eden* on Film" (*StQ* 25:28–42) Robert E. Morsberger studies the differences between Steinbeck's novel and movie and television adaptations. He credits Elia Kazan and Paul Osborn's cinematic version with improving on Steinbeck's original by making the Cain figure more cunning and malevolent and by repositioning certain scenes, thus strengthening the story's ending. Morsberger notes that the 1980 television miniseries, despite scriptwriter Richard Shapiro's omission of certain events, particularly those surrounding the Hamilton family, and the condensing of many scenes, follows Steinbeck's outline more accurately than does the film version. Morsberger concludes, though, that both the movie and the television versions are worth viewing. Scholars interested in Steinbeck research will welcome Robert DeMott's helpful "*East of Eden:* A Bibliographical Checklist" (*STQ* 25:14–28), inventorying both primary and secondary sources.

Several essays in *Steinbeck Quarterly* treat other works. Richard S.

Pressman in "Individualists or Collectivists? Steinbeck's *In Dubious Bat-tle* and Hemingway's *To Have and Have Not*" (*StQ* 25:119–33) notes "parallel ambiguities" and concludes that though Steinbeck and Hem-ingway wrote about different locations, their novels remain relevant because they "are simultaneously engagements with the Depression and evasions of it." Christopher S. Busch in "Steinbeck's *The Wayward Bus*: An Affirmation of the Frontier Myth" (*StQ* 25:98–108) examines one of Steinbeck's less well-regarded novels in light of the frontier myth that has permeated much of American literature. Busch views *The Wayward Bus* as an extension of a pattern begun by Steinbeck in his earlier works—that "of contrasting the frontier figure's heroism with the modern person's weakness and degeneration"—and asserts that the novel, which demon-strates how static cultures have become in the United States, is worthy of more critical attention than it has yet received. Mimi R. Gladstein in "*Cannery Row:* A Male World and the Female Reader" (*StQ* 25:87–97) argues that *Cannery Row* does not focus on a gender-neutral society, but instead it portrays a sexist, male-dominated world where, with the exception of Mary Talbot and Dora Flood, the presence of women serves only to facilitate destruction. In fact, many of the women encountered by the male characters are not named or described, thus demonstrating their insignificance and their lack of individuality. As a result, Gladstein suggests, women who read *Cannery Row* from a feminine rather than a masculine point of view will miss much of Steinbeck's humor.

In an effort to call attention to one of Steinbeck's lesser-known achievements, Andrew Welsh in "Lancelot at the Crossroads in Malory and Steinbeck" (*PQ* 70 [1991]:485–502) examines Steinbeck's unfinished version of Sir Thomas Malory's *Noble Tale of Sir Launcelot du Lake*. Particularly significant, states Welsh, is Steinbeck's 17-page expansion of Malory's brief narrative concerning the incident in which four sor-ceresses capture the sleeping Lancelot, hoping to force him into becom-ing the paramour of one of the devious queens. Steinbeck improves on Malory's version by making Lancelot's imprisonment a crucial plot element. Gary D. Schmidt's "Steinbeck's 'Breakfast': A Reconsideration" (*WAL* 26:303–11) focuses on a brief tale from *The Long Valley* later incorporated into chapter 22 of *The Grapes of Wrath*. In the earlier version of the story Steinbeck creates a narrator whose perspective is more evident to the reader. This first narrator does not understand how to enter into the circle of brotherhood that the family which he encoun-ters extends to him. According to Schmidt, the narrator's struggle to express the significance of the experience parallels the difficulty that writers confront in trying to communicate to readers the importance of the experiences they express in writing, for to merely recall the experience is inadequate.

b. Mary McCarthy, James Agee, and Others   Five years after the publication of Carol Gelderman's *Mary McCarthy: A Life* (St. Martin's, 1988), Carol Brightman in *Writing Dangerously: Mary McCarthy and Her World* (Clarkson Potter) offers another extensive yet very readable biography. More than 700 pages long, Brightman's chronicle captures not only the essence of McCarthy, but the settings in which she lived and worked. Like Gelderman before her, Brightman describes McCarthy's sexual rendezvous, her marriages, and her career as a writer.

Brightman differs from Gelderman by detailing McCarthy's involvement in the Vietnam war and, of course, her death, which occurred shortly after publication of Gelderman's text. Brightman's biography is based on personal interviews with McCarthy and numerous family members and friends as well as on letters and journals. A biographical glossary is included.

Coincidentally, Carol Gelderman has also contributed further material about McCarthy's life and work as editor of *Conversations with Mary McCarthy* (Miss., 1991). Gelderman includes 26 chronologically organized, previously published and televised interviews with McCarthy that were conducted by different individuals between 1962 and 1987 and that "give a picture of how multi-faceted a writer Mary McCarthy was— novelist, short story writer, essayist, journalist, memoirist, critic." The volume offers a brief chronology of McCarthy's life and her views on the works of numerous other writers.

The serious McCarthy scholar will welcome the publication of *Mary McCarthy: An Annotated Bibliography*, compiled by Joy Bennett and Gabriella Hochmann (Garland), more than 400 pages of entries on primary and secondary materials. In addition to sections on each of the many genres that McCarthy wrote in some fifty years, the compilers annotate the reviews of McCarthy's 24 books, her biographical sources, and obituaries, and literary criticism and master's theses on McCarthy's work. Bennett and Hochmann's bibliography draws on but surpasses earlier bibliographies on McCarthy, such as Sherli Evans Goldman's *Mary McCarthy: A Bibliography* (1968).

Michael A. Lofaro deserves credit for editing a collection of essays that applauds the sometimes overlooked work of James Agee, *James Agee: Reconsiderations* (Tennessee). Wilma Dykeman's "Introduction: The Agee Legacy" (pp. 1–5) provides an overview of the volume's contents. Biographical and bibliographical information are offered by Kathryn Black Swain in "An Agee Chronology" (pp. 6–11) and "Agee: A Brief Life" (pp. 12–20) and by Mary Moss in "Agee: A Bibliography of Secondary Sources" (pp. 119–43). Framed within these selections are six essays on Agee's *Let Us Now Praise Famous Men* and *A Death in the Family.* In "The Lost World of Agee's *Let Us Now Praise Famous Men*" (pp. 21–31), George Brown Tindall focuses on the environment about which Agee wrote— "the lost world of tenancy and sharecropping—how it came to be and how it has vanished in the years since Agee visited Alabama." David Madden in "The Test of a First-Rate Intelligence: Agee and the Cruel Radiance of What Is" (pp. 32–43) looks at the self-reflexive quality of *Let Us Now Praise Famous Men,* a book of many structures and genres, which has been considered both a success and a failure. Linda Wagner-Martin in "*Let Us Now Praise Famous Men*—and Women: Agee's Absorption in the Sexual" (pp. 44–58) points out the importance of the structure of "Agee's house of fiction [which] becomes a vortex, a single center of focus," and of the women in the novel, particularly Annie Mae (Woods) Gudger, a "romantic heroine," and other female family members. Paul Ashdown's "Prophet from Highland Avenue: Agee's Visionary Journalism" (pp. 59–81) is largely biographical. Ashdown traces Agee's career as a journalist, pointing out his role as a "social prophet," calling *Let Us Now Praise Famous Men* "a stunning example of forthspeaking journalism," and noting the many signs and portents that appear in his works. Eugene T. Carroll in "Mood and Music: Landscape and Artistry in *A Death in the Family*" (pp. 82–103) reminds the reader of the unique position that Agee's novel held in the 1950s, pointing out the significance of musical imagery, small town values, and universal themes. In the last essay in the collection, "Urban and Rural Balance in *A Death in the Family*" (pp. 104–18), Victor A. Kramer reminds the reader of the autobiographical nature of Agee's best writing and of how skillfully he used the technique of remembrance. Significantly, *A Death in the Family* "functions on several levels at once: it is Agee's memorial; it is his examination of self; it is a picture of a particular era when urban and rural were blended; it is an archetypal rendering of what all persons learn, live, and love."

Two other writers from the 1930s receive brief recognition this year. Naomi B. Sokoloff in *Imagining the Child in Modern Jewish Fiction* (Hopkins) devotes one chapter, "Henry Roth—*Call It Sleep*" (pp. 87–106), to a close examination of the significance of language in Roth's novel. According to Sokoloff, the novel is composed of a "many-layered discourse" through which Davey, the protagonist, must travel in order to eventually attain adulthood and recognize "the potential for change." Two essays call attention to a sometimes overlooked writer of the 1930s, Meridel Le Sueur. Roberta Maierhofer in "Meridel Le Sueur: A Female Voice of the Thirties" (*Women in Search of Literary Space*, pp. 150–62) cites Le Sueur's *The Girl* as exemplifying her work in the "socialist-feminist tradition." A more penetrating analysis of her novel can be found in Blanche H. Gelfant's " 'Everybody Steals': Language as Theft in Meridel Le Sueur's *The Girl*," pp. 183–210 in *Tradition and the Talents of Women*, ed. Florence Howe (Illinois, 1991). Gelfant details the change of the unnamed protagonist from a young girl into a grown woman, showing how she acquires a powerful language in the process and noting the many literary genres in which the novel participates—the female bildungsroman, the palimpsest, the fertility myth, and the social protest narrative.

c. Richard Wright, Ralph Ellison, James Baldwin The inclusion of Richard Wright in the Library of America series on important American authors prompts James W. Tuttleton to survey Wright's life and works in "The Problematic Texts of Richard Wright" (*HudR* 45:261–71). While Tuttleton is pleased at long-overdue recognition of Wright, he questions revisions made in the works, arguing that Wright did not approve of some of them and that they should thus be footnoted rather than included in the body of the text. Hilary Holladay's "*Native Son*'s Guilty Man" (*CEA* 54, ii:30–36) focuses on Bigger Thomas's lawyer, Boris Max. Holladay points out the many ironies in the names of Wright's characters before demonstrating the complex personality of Max, who in his weak courtroom argument "fails himself as well as his client." In "*Othello*'s African American Progeny" (*SoAR* 57, iv:39–57) James R. Andreas examines the subject of miscegenation in works by Wright, Ralph Ellison, and Amiri Baraka, noting that Shakespeare's *Othello* is the paradigm for these authors' rewritings of the miscegenation myth in which black men and white women engage in sexual relationships. According to Andreas,

"Wright restages and reinterprets the problematic relationship of Othello and Desdemona; Ellison represents it comically; and Baraka reverses or inverts it."

James Baldwin is the subject of several good essays. In *Forms of Uncertainty: Essays in Historical Criticism* (Virginia) David Levin devotes a chapter solely to Baldwin's works. Chapter 13, "James Baldwin's Autobiographical Essays: The Problem of Negro Identity" (pp. 237–45), considers the role of identity in Baldwin's autobiographical writing, concluding that like earlier writers such as Franklin, Thoreau, Edwards, Bradford, and others, Baldwin is an "original" American author. Pancho Savery in "Baldwin, Bebop, and 'Sonny's Blues'," pp. 165–76 in *Understanding Others: Cultural and Cross-Cultural Studies and the Teaching of Literature,* ed. Joseph Trimmer and Tilly Warnock (NCTE), examines the function of bebop in African American culture, pointing out that Baldwin uses "traditional aspects of Afro-American culture" in "Sonny's Blues" and that the reader needs to take this cultural context into consideration when examining his works. Linda Jo Scott's "James Baldwin and the Moveable Feast" (*MichA* 24:401–8) is one of two essays noting the relevance of Paris to Baldwin's life and writing. Like many American writers before him, Baldwin was fascinated with Paris, went there to learn about his cultural origins, and eventually left, having divorced his puritanical American background, discovered his sexual preference, and recognized his American roots. In "Other(Ed) Americans in Paris: Henry James, James Baldwin, and the Subversion of Identity" (*ESC* 18:335–46), Eric Savoy argues that there is a "connection between James's and Baldwin's problemization of the American 'self,' and Baldwin's consistently deployed trope of the journey, which gradually became a nexus, or a dominant sign, in his analyses of history, the politics of race, and the American refusal to learn the lessons of history."

ii Southerners

a. Robert Penn Warren   Warren scholars will be pleased with *"To Love So Well the World": A Festschrift in Honor of Robert Penn Warren,* ed. Dennis L. Weeks (Peter Lang), a thought-provoking collection of 28 essays offering a wide range of critical approaches to Warren's life and work. Weeks divides the anthology into two sections: "The Legacy," 17 essays by well-known critics and scholars, and "The Beneficiaries," 11 articles by students who have been inspired by their study of Warren's writing. Leading the volume is "Robert Penn Warren: A Selective, Chronological Bibliography," compiled by Donovan Hendricks and William J. Burling (pp. 1–11), that covers Warren's major works, excluding book reviews, individual poems, and foreign translations. Cleanth Brooks in "Homage to R. P. Warren" (pp. 13–17) shares his knowledge of Warren as a coeditor and colleague, providing personal insight into Warren's personality and literary viewpoints. Similarly, Leslie Fiedler in "Robert Penn Warren: A Final Word" (pp. 19–28) meditates on Warren's life and career, noting the influence of Hemingway and tracing the adaptation of *All the King's Men* from novel to play and movie. Several essays compare Warren with other major literary figures. Victor Strandberg in "R.P.W. and T.S.E.: In the Steps of the (Post) Modern Master" (pp. 29–43) compares Warren to T. S. Eliot, noting such similarities in their lives and writing as their faulty marriages, their decisions to live away from their native grounds, their attractions to Renaissance literature, their dislike of art for art's sake, and their anticipation of postmodernist viewpoints. James A. Grimshaw, Jr., in "Shakespeare's *Henriad* and *All the King's Men:* A Study in Parallels" (pp. 45–57) outlines the analogies between the four Shakespeare history plays and Warren's novel, concluding that parallels exist in five main areas: action, language, structure, theme, and characterization. In "Burning Barns in Warren and Faulkner" (pp. 223–28) Jeanette Chaplin compares the issue of race, "the troubled father-son relationship," the similarities between the father figures, and the fact that each author used his story (Warren's "Prime Leaf" and Faulkner's "Barn Burning") as a prototype for a later novel. In "The Medieval Interlace Structure in *All the King's Men*," (pp. 313–25) Lilian Nobles Wooley notes Warren's use of a complex narrative pattern also employed by medieval writers such as Sir Thomas Malory and Chrétien de Troyes and modern writers such as Ezra Pound and Eliot. The adaptation of this earlier form permits Warren to successfully merge Jack Burden's past memories with his present life, to include tales whose relationships are not immediately evident, and to interweave the stories of Cass Mastern, Ellis Burden, Anne Stanton, Willie Stark, and Judge Irwin.

Other articles examine Warren's principal fictional works, especially *All the King's Men,* which continues to be a popular topic. Robert Feldman in "Responsibility in Crisis: Jack Burden's Struggle in *All the King's Men*" (pp. 101–11) argues that the theme of responsibility in the novel is developed more clearly through the character of Jack Burden rather than that of Willie Stark. In "Jack's Unconscious Burden: A Psychoanalytic Interpretation of *All the King's Men*" (pp. 197–209), Martin Lumpkin applies Roy Shafer's psychoanalytic theories to demonstrate how the novel is "a tale of dark, tragically masked, psychic undercurrents below the conscious stories the characters tell themselves." Brian Abel Ragen in " 'We Have Always Gone West': Automobiles, Innocence, and *All the King's Men*" (pp. 189–96) discusses the automobile as a symbol of freedom. Ragen compares Jack Burden to other Americans who went west with no particular goal in mind, except to divorce themselves from their pasts and to try to replace their childhood innocence. Lana K. Payton's " 'Out of the Strong Come Forth Sweetness': Women in *All the King's Men*" (pp. 303–12) takes issue with scholars who feel that Warren does not really develop the female characters in the novel. According to Payton, four central female figures—Anne Stanton, Sadie Burke, Jack Burden's mother, and Lucy Stark—should be treated as major characters because they are courageous, strong, tenacious, and loyal. Lucy Ferris is also concerned with Warren's women in "From Manty to Cassie: The Evolution of Warren's Female Persona" (pp. 259–71). Ferris posits that two of Warren's women characters differ significantly from the typical Warren female. Cassie Spottwood of *Meet Me in the Green Glen* and Amantha Starr of *Band of Angels* are not typical Warren "bitches"; they are physically feminine and not financially independent or sexually aggressive. But they are also dependent on the male presence: Warren presents the "symbiotic nature of bondage" through which these two women must learn self-assurance and the ability to handle freedom.

Fathers are the subject in Thomas A. Hays's "The Two Fathers of Percy Munn: Father-Son Relationships in *Night Rider*" (pp. 273–78) and Randolph Paul Runyon's "Father, Son, and Taciturn Text" (pp. 113–22). Hays suggests that Munn's decision to sacrifice himself instead of killing Tolliver at the end of *Night Rider* enables him to free himself from the two father figures who have complicated his life. Runyon traces "the situation of a son who finds that he has been preceded by his father, and specifically by his father's *text,* and that now he must in his turn speak, act, or interpret that paternal text" through a number of works by Warren, including *Night Rider, Band of Angels,* and *Flood.* In "Warren Mounts His Horse: *Flood's* Author as Southern Gothic/Grotesque Writer" (pp. 279–85), Robert Sterling Long places Warren's *Flood* into the Southern Gothic/Grotesque tradition of Tennessee Williams, Flannery O'Connor, Carson McCullers, and Truman Capote because of its grotesque characters, gruesome imagery, and sexual perversions. Jane Hoogestraat in "*A Place To Come To* and the Problem of History" (pp. 59–73) suggests that the effect of World War II on the characters in *A Place To Come To,* especially Jed, is masqued by Warren, who will not let the characters acknowledge their inability to "come to terms with the scope of the war." Finally, Warren's *World Enough and Time,* receives critical attention from James A. Perkins, who in "The Myth of the Labyrinth in *World Enough and Time*" (pp. 159–69) examines the last 65 pages of the book, determining that "Grand Boz and his island fastness" are there to act "as a physical labyrinth to parallel and expose the mental labyrinth in which Jeremiah Beaumont is trapped."

Two other Warren articles deserve mention. Bryan Dietrich in "Christ or Antichrist: Understanding Eight Words in 'Blackberry Winter' " (*SSF* 29:215–20) provides insight into the much-debated final line of the poem. According to Dietrich, who explores the "religious" reading of the story, Seth's admission that he "did not (necessarily) follow the path of hope, villainy, *or* damnation alone" is an important statement, for "revealed deception is always a seed of hope." Henry Cunningham in "Jack Burden Investigates" (*SoQ* 31, i:35–49) offers a new approach to *All the King's Men* by placing Jack Burden into the tradition of the hard-boiled detective, not only in speech as previous critics have noted, but in action. However, Warren's optimistic ending, where "Jack gains a new understanding of himself and the world," does not fit the archetypal pattern of the detective tale.

b. O'Connor, Welty, and Porter   John Roos in "The Political in Flannery O'Connor: A Reading of 'A View of the Woods' " (*SSF* 29:161–79) examines "the Lockean and Thomistic visions of nature, property, family, and progress" in an often overlooked O'Connor story. Through demonstrating the Lockean view of life and its effect on her characters, O'Connor shows the reader the dangers of self-interest, which may, as Locke advocated, benefit all concerned but overlook "the good of others" in the process. Nancy T. Clasby in " 'The Life You Save May Be Your Own': Flannery O'Connor as a Visionary Artist" (*SSF* 28:509–20) argues that a Jungian reading of "The Life You Save May Be Your Own" is more effective than a Freudian reading because of O'Connor's ironic use of traditional archetypal motifs and myths, particularly that of the waste-land in which the hero forgets the purpose of his quest and neglects to rescue the woman involved. In "The Domestic Dynamics of Flannery O'Connor: *Everything That Rises Must Converge*" (*TCL* 38:66–88), Bryan N. Wyatt traces the domestic theme, O'Connor's focus on home and the family, through the stories in her last book, noting the importance that O'Connor assigns to her female characters in particular.

Eudora Welty's work continues to be well-received. Welty scholars will welcome Barbara Harrell Carson's *Eudora Welty: Two Pictures at Once in Her Frame* (Whitston), a survey of Welty's nonfiction, short stories, and five novels. Examining Welty's vision of life as "holistic rather than dualistic," Carson surveys the background of that vision in Plato, Albert Rothenberg, Michael Polanyi, Albert Einstein, Werner Heisenberg, David Bohn, Carl Jung, Gregory Bateson, and others who might have influenced Welty. Carson points out that in contrast to other believers in holism, who treat this motif marginally and indirectly, Welty includes this holistic viewpoint often, expresses it through a wide variety of literary techniques and genres, and makes it an integral part of her works, yet still manages to avoid repetition and to create "fresh insights into what life is."

James Robert Saunders's " 'A Worn Path': The Eternal Quest of Welty's Phoenix Jackson" (*SLJ* 25, i:62–73), though not especially original, thoroughly inventories Welty's use of characters or situations similar to those in the works of such writers as Faulkner, Margaret Walker, Maya Angelou, Alice Walker, and Toni Morrison. According to Sanders, the character of Phoenix Jackson is significant in several ways: she relates closely to nature, lives and successfully and lovingly accomplishes her errand, and continues her journey. Elaine Orr in " 'Unsettling Every Definition of Otherness': Another Reading of Eudora Welty's 'A Worn Path' " (*SoAR* 57, ii:57–72) takes a fresh approach to Welty's popular story. Instead of considering "A Worn Path" a closed text as many other critics have, Orr argues that the story is an open text that "includes and opens windows to contradiction and paradox." It is the reader, not Phoenix Jackson, who must successfully complete the journey and overcome "the worn path of old readings, tried and untrue assumptions." Two articles focus on Welty's *The Optimist's Daughter*. Sally Wolff in " 'Among Those Missing': Phil Hand's Disappearance from *The Optimist's Daughter* (*SLJ* 25, i:74–88) focuses on Welty's omission of "twenty pages of romantic scenes depicting the meeting, courtship, and marriage of Phil and Laurel" from the final draft of the novel. By analyzing earlier drafts of Welty's writing, now housed in the Mississippi State Archives,

Woolf demonstrates how Phil's physical absence changes the story of Phil and Laurel from one that would reflect a happy courtship and marriage to one of death and mournfulness. Because of his disappearance and absence from the text, Phil's character is "more fully identified," and Laurel is presented as "a woman whose untold love story ended almost before it began."

John Blair in "Nicholas and the Judge: The 'Wrong Book' in Eudora Welty's *The Optimist's Daughter*" (*NMW* 24:25–33) asks why Charles Dickens's *Nicholas Nickleby* was the " 'wrong book' " for Laurel McKelva Hand to read to her father and why Edward Gibbon's *The History of the Decline and Fall of the Roman Empire* might be the right one. Blair suggests that Dickens's novel might be the wrong choice because the Judge is not a true optimist, in spite of his being considered one; instead, Laurel is the real optimist, for it is she who demonstrates the quality of forgiveness and exercises compassion. Jan Nordby Gretlund's "Eudora Welty: Early Acrobatics" (*NMW* 24:35–49) examines one of Welty's earliest stories, "Acrobats in a Park." Its theme—the importance of "family unity and love, the individual seen as being independent of the family and yet as an integral interlocked member of it"—anticipates many of Welty's later works, including the novels *Losing Battles, The Ponder Heart,* and *Delta Wedding.* In spite of a lengthy introduction on "the politics of narrative and the social construction of American law," Eve Kornfeld's "Reconstructing American Law: The Politics of Narrative and Eudora Welty's Empathic Vision" (*JAmS* 26:23–39) presents a clear and cogent argument for Welty's use of "the power of narrative" in *Losing Battles* to reconstruct American law: Judge Moody's perspective is changed after he hears the personal stories of a family in an environment outside the courtroom. That work is also the subject of "The Languages of *Losing Battles*" (*SAF* 21:67–82) by Eben E. Bass, who examines the significance of both spoken and written language in Welty's novel, concluding that even "though the feminine language modes of *Losing Battles* are 'opposites,' they serve a common goal: querying and challenging male-authored decrees." Linda Orr in "The Duplicity of the Southern Story: Reflections on Reynolds Price's *The Surface of Earth* and Eudora Welty's 'The Wide Net' " (*SAQ* 91:111–37) argues that both Price and Welty consider the process of southern storytelling more important than the plot of the story; by having their stories raise questions, they draw readers into the "net," the story, and thus seduce their audiences into wanting more tales. *The Robber Bridegroom* is the subject of Darryl

Hattenhauer's "Absurdism and Dark Humor in Welty's *The Robber Bridegroom*" (*UMSE* 10:167–69). Hattenhauer takes issue with critics who view the novel "as an unsuccessful attempt at light comedy." Instead, he proposes, Welty departs from her previous fictional patterns to write a novel of "absurdist dark comedy" that in some respects parodies earlier works containing dark humor, such as Melville's *Moby-Dick*, Poe's "The Raven," and Twain's *A Connecticut Yankee in King Arthur's Court*. In "*A Curtain of Green:* Eudora Welty's Auspicious Beginning" (*MissQ* 46:91–114), Gina D. Peterman traces Welty's beginnings as a published writer, noting the reactions of early reviewers to her work, especially Katherine Anne Porter's endorsement of her as an important new voice.

Ann Romines includes two chapters on Welty in *The Home Plot: Women, Writing and Domestic Ritual* (Mass.), "Welty's Beginnings: Housekeeping and the Other Way to Live" (pp. 192–246) and "Welty and the Dynamo in the House: 'Why Keep It Up, Old Woman?'" (pp. 247–91). Romines focuses on "lessons in domestic ritual offered by American women's fiction," arguing that such writers as Welty, Willa Cather, Sarah Orne Jewett, Harriet Beecher Stowe, and Mary Wilkins Freeman are an important part of an overlooked canon of American literature, "which both perpetuates and questions the ongoing practice of domestic culture." Using Welty's *Collected Stories, The Golden Apples, Delta Wedding, The Bride of the Innisfallen,* and *Losing Battles* as examples, Romines demonstrates how even women critics have overlooked the domestic language and imagery in Welty's writing and that of other women.

Helen Fiddyment Levy includes chapters on Welty and Porter in *Fiction of the Home Place*. In "The Oldest Root Sometimes Blooms Most: Eudora Welty" (pp. 161–95) and "The Land That is Nowhere: Katherine Anne Porter" (pp. 131–60), Levy argues for the importance of the home place, which "shelters all who seek its protection." Welty and Porter believe "in the female pastoral home with its sustaining creativity and pastoral connections as a model for the loving, just human community . . . and as a model for their own authorial labors."

Merrill Skaggs in "The Louisianas of Katherine Anne Porter's Mind" (*Louisiana Women Writers,* pp. 155–67) examines the Louisiana setting in Porter's fiction as "a place in the mind" as well as a specific geographic locale. Using "Old Mortality" and "Holiday" as examples, Skaggs provides answers to the question Porter asked in her use of Louisiana: "What does it mean to be a southern woman?"

c. Margaret Mitchell and Harriette Arnow   Two Margaret Mitchell items deserve mention. Elzbieta Olesky's "The Keepers of the House: Scarlett O'Hara and Abigail Howland" (*Louisiana Women Writers*, pp. 169–82) compares *Gone With the Wind* and Shirley Ann Grau's *The Keepers of the House* in terms of the years covered by the narrative, patriarchal settings, the early loss of the protagonists' mothers, their marriages to men who are "unscrupulous opportunists," and the later loss of those spouses. According to Olesky, both Mitchell and Grau assert that a "woman's survival depends upon her strength—her will and ability to 'keep' the house" rather than on her aspiration to be a "lady." In "Margaret Mitchell's Feminist Farm Fantasy: *Gone With the Wind*," a chapter in *Female Pastoral* (pp. 43–64), Elizabeth Jane Harrison argues that because of her southern heritage and her gender Scarlett O'Hara is a static character in spite of her strong will, and that Margaret Mitchell could not successfully apply "feminist fantasy" to a "masculist form." In another chapter in this volume, "Harriette Arnow's Exile from the Promised Land: *The Dollmaker*" (pp. 83–99), Harrison views *The Dollmaker* as a kunstlerroman "in which the artist must leave her or his homeland in order to find identity." According to James Devers in "Cain and Abel in Harriette Arnow's *The Dollmaker*: A Comment on War" (*NConL* 22, iii:4–5), Arnow uses a Cain/Abel parallel to show that fratricide pervades any war, even one like World War II that we may feel compelled to fight.

d. Peter Taylor and Thomas Wolfe   Linda Kandel Kuehl in "Peter Taylor's 'The Instruction of a Mistress': The Voice as Executioner" (*SSF* 29:331–39) compares Taylor's narrative voice to that of Robert Browning in "My Last Duchess." The story contains a confessional narrator who forces the reader to become a part of his discourse, "to reassess the nature of the relationship between the older man and the younger woman," and to chillingly conclude that the narrator's lover is dead.

Aside from Suzanne Stutman's "Home Again: Thomas Wolfe and Pennsylvania" (*RALS* 18:44–52), *The Thomas Wolfe Review* is responsible for most of the published work on Wolfe this year. The importance of Wolfe's sometimes overlooked *The Good Child's River* is the subject of

Stephen Douglas Fraser's "The Filters of Fiction: Wolfe, Bernstein, and the Writing of *The Good Child's River*" (16, ii:15–22), Ted Mitchell's "*The Good Child's River:* Some Reflections" (16, i:7–13), and Ted Mitchell and Aldo P. Magi's "Suzanne Stutman Interviewed" (16, i:14–20). David K. Perelman-Hall discusses the influence of Samuel Taylor Coleridge on Wolfe in "The Romantic Tradition: Coleridge and Wolfe" (16, i: 21–30; 16, ii:23–32). The European influence on Wolfe is noted by Klaus Lanzinger in "Jason's Voyage: The International Theme of Thomas Wolfe" (16, ii:34–43).

e. Zora Neale Hurston   Sandra Dolby-Stahl in "Literary Objectives: Hurston's Use of Personal Narrative in *Mules and Men*" (*WF* 51:51–63) argues that too many scholars overlook Hurston's literary talent in *Mules and Men* because they concentrate too heavily on her use of folklore. Dolby-Stahl attempts a reconciliation: it is because Hurston blends more than 25 different types of folklore material into her work that it becomes more than a "standard ethnography" and that "a sense of intimacy between the author and the reader" is formed. As Emily Dalgarno demonstrates in " 'Words Walking Without Masters': Ethnography and the Creative Process in *Their Eyes Were Watching God*" (*AL* 64:519–41), "Hurston's revisions suggest that the play between the narrator and Janie increasingly displays all of the problems of the ethnographer who translates storytelling into a narrative written for a mass readership." In "The Pastoral and the Picaresque in Zora Neale Hurston's 'The Gilded Six-Bits' " (*CLAJ* 35:316–24), Evora W. Jones uses "The Gilded Six-Bits" to show how folklore, the pastoral, and the picaresque operate in Hurston's work. Fred Setterberg in "Zora Neale Hurston in the *Land of 1,000 Dances*" (*GaR* 46:627–43) blends his own personal experiences with music, the blues, and New Orleans with accounts of Hurston's activities as a writer and folklorist. Although Setterberg's article emphasizes biographical information rather than critical analysis, he does argue that Hurston includes in her books "what most of her contemporaries could or would not chronicle: the cohesion, integrity, and stubborn exuberance of rural black culture."

iii   Expatriates and Émigrés

a. Vladimir Nabokov   Several articles focus on Nabokov's *Pale Fire*. James F. English in "Modernist Joke-Work: *Pale Fire* and the Mock

Transcendence of Mockery" (*ConL* 33:74–90) views the novel as a modernist rather than a postmodernist text. The contradictions to the humor in Nabokov's writing emerge from his inverting "the social categories of in-group and out-group," his using the "joke-work" in his own way with characters being both victors and victims of the comic exchanges. John Pier's "Between Text and Paratext: Vladimir Nabokov's *Pale Fire*" (*Style* 26:12–32), although heavily immersed in the jargon of contemporary literary theory, will be useful to those interested in a close study of paratextuality. Pier revises Pekka Tammi's earlier analysis of the narrative levels in *Pale Fire*, concluding that Nabokov's novel reminds the reader "that the literary work depends, finally, on the 'discursivity' of its reader, on the transtextual space that surrounds every text." Philip Sicker in "*Pale Fire* and *Lyrical Ballads:* The Dynamics of Collaboration" (*PLL* 28:305–18) calls attention to the "subordinate position" that Nabokov found himself in after "collaborating" with Edmund Wilson on a project that culminated with only Wilson's part of the work being published. According to Sicker, Nabokov uses *Pale Fire* to comment on Nabokov's own personal experiences with literary collaboration as well as to parallel the character of Kinbote with Samuel Taylor Coleridge, who had a similar problem with William Wordsworth and literary collaboration in their 1798 *Lyrical Ballads*. Scholars looking for critical material on other Nabokov works will welcome Tony Sharpe's *Vladimir Nabokov* (Edward Arnold, 1991), which provides biographical information as well as a survey of Nabokov's autobiography and selected fiction, noting particularly the influence of other writers. Sharpe wisely restricts his study to a close reading of six of Nabokov's 17 novels, his intention being to provide the exposition necessary for a basic understanding of Nabokov's life and work.

b. Djuna Barnes Several recent articles show the disparity of critical opinion on Barnes's work. In " 'That Savage Path': *Nightwood* and *The Divine Comedy* (*Renascence* 44:137–58), Jeanne Campbell Reesman provides a thorough and insightful comparison. She notes, for example, that, like Dante, Barnes includes love as a theme, focuses on the sins of "Incontinence, Violence, and Fraud," uses the structural patterns of descent and ascent, includes inversions, similar characters, and images of doorways, a night wood, and animals, and centers her work on "a static, still figure." Even the ending of *Nightwood* is better understood through its Dantesque connections, which compel the reader to "turn away from the dual vision of the end" and look toward the future. Jane Marcus in "Laughing at Leviticus: *Nightwood* as Woman's Circus Epic," pp. 211–47 in *Tradition and the Talents of Women,* ed. Florence Howe (Illinois, 1991), examining *Nightwood* as a revision of the Old Testament book from a feminist perspective, views the novel as "a brilliant and hilarious feminist critique of Freudian psychoanalysis and a parody of the discourse of diagnosis of female hysteria," as "the reversible world of the circus, the night world of lesbian, homosexual, and transvestite Paris," and as a prediction of the forthcoming Holocaust. The least controversial article on Barnes is "Djuna Barnes Remembers James Joyce" (*JJQ* 30:113–17) by Phillip Herring, who briefly notes the influence of Joyce on Barnes, contending that after Barnes read *Ulysses* she experimented more with style and became more of a modernist.

c. Kay Boyle and Paul Bowles   Kay Boyle is represented this year by one book, Elizabeth S. Bell's *Kay Boyle: A Study of the Short Fiction* (Twayne). Beginning with a chronological study of Boyle's short stories, Bell offers a wide variety of commentary on Boyle's work, examining the stories, then moving to several interviews with Boyle by Bell and other writers, then to reprints of some of Boyle's lectures, essays, and speeches. The third part offers commentary on Boyle's life and work by some of Boyle's friends, supporters, reviewers, and critics, including William Carlos Williams, Katherine Anne Porter, David Daiches, and Vance Bourjaily. A selected bibliography of fiction, of primary and secondary material is included.

The single article on Paul Bowles is Richard F. Patteson's "Paul Bowles/Mohammed Mrabet: Translation, Transformation, and Trans-cultural Discourse" (*JNT* 22:180–90). Patteson discusses Bowles's talent for "project[ing] himself imaginatively into the fabric of an alternative culture," noting that "Bowles's most successful and important collaboration, producing ten books over the past twenty years, has been with Mohammed Mrabet, and their fiction, perhaps inevitably, is a virtual spider web of intertextuality."

iv   **Easterners**

a. Saul Bellow   Saul Bellow was the subject of two books, *Saul Bellow* by Peter Hyland (St. Martin's) and *Saul Bellow: A Mosaic,* ed. L. H. Gold-man et al. (Peter Lang). Calling attention to Bellow's reputation as "the

major post-war American novelist," Hyland traces Bellow's literary career from the 1940s until the 1980s, chronologically examining his novels
and short fiction, documenting the major historical events, social
changes, and personal experiences that influenced his writing, such as
the depression, World War II, postwar society, the urban worlds of
Chicago and New York, and Bellow's trips to Europe, and discussing
major themes and motifs, such as freedom, poor father-son relationships,
responsibility, identity, nature imagery, and moronic infernos. Particularly important is the ambiguity in the works, which, argues Hyland,
marks Bellow's intention to demonstrate to the reader the complexity of
the issues he addresses.

Saul Bellow: A Mosaic grew out of the April 1987 Saul Bellow International Conference at Haifa University in Israel and includes 14 essays in
four sections—"Saul Bellow's Worldview," "Saul Bellow's Style," "New
Directions in the Works of Saul Bellow," and "Saul Bellow on Himself."
The first section examines Bellow's writing in light of his Jewish heritage.
L. H. Goldman in "The Jewish Perspective of Saul Bellow" (pp. 3–19)
surveys a number of Bellow's works, noting that Bellow's Judaism operates on both conscious and unconscious levels. Goldman "relate[s]
Bellow's humanism to his apprehension about Romanticism . . . to his
sensitivity to global injustices, to his early depiction of anti-Semitism,
and to his unremitting assault on Nazi philosophy throughout his
works." Daniel Walden in "Toward Order and Pattern in Urban Society:
Bellow's Journey from the Existentialists to Communicated Experience"
(pp. 27–34) argues that Bellow's protagonists live in dualistic worlds of
order and disorder and must work toward communicating with their
fellow men and acting humanely. In "Engagement and Responsibility in
Saul Bellow's Novels" (pp. 35–47) Ada Aharoni traces "the theme of
engagement and human responsibility" through a number of novels.
Bellow's works center on a moral and ethical dilemma that modern
people face—whether to take care only of themselves or whether to
extend their humanity to other people.

The three essays in the second section analyze Bellow's style. Alan
Lelchuk in "Recent Adventures of Saul Bellow: Reflections on 'What
Kind of Day Did You Have?'" (pp. 59–71) notes Bellow's uniqueness in
abandoning traditional plot lines, constructing memorable characters,
and using "paragraphs [to] work like short stories to reveal whole characters and chunks of history." Marianne M. Friedrich in "Two Women
Protagonists from Bellow's Short Stories: Character Conception and Its

Artistic Realization" (pp. 73–85) focuses on "the close interrelation between the character conception and its narrative form" in two Bellow
short stories featuring women protagonists, "Dora" and "Leaving the
Yellow House." In "Bellow's Endings" (pp. 87–95) Mark Weinstein
examines the endings of ten of Bellow's novels, stressing their uniqueness
as "a kind of genre in themselves" and their "artistic closure." According
to Weinstein, Bellow's endings "suggest that all of Bellow's major novels
are comedies about death."

Gloria L. Cronin's "Searching the Narrative Gap: Authorial Self-Irony
and the Problematic Discussion of Western Misogyny in *Mr. Sammler's
Planet*" (pp. 97–122), the first of four essays on "New Directions,"
provides an insightful examination of Bellow's use of misogyny to characterize Mr. Sammler, who finally craves "total immunity from women."
In "Herzog's Fictions of the Self" (pp. 123–38) Jonathan Wilson examines the role of con artists and tricksters, particularly Moses Herzog
himself. Andrew Gordon in "Acting and Authenticity in the Novels of
Saul Bellow" (pp. 139–58) adds a new dimension to the critical acknowl-
edgment of the acting motif in Bellow's writing by focusing on "Bellow's
ambivalence about acting and theater" and by analyzing the complexity
that results from Bellow's inclusion of an acting and theater motif in so
many of his novels. In "Bellow and Kafka" (pp. 159–72) Harold Fisch
notes the influence of Kafka on Bellow in plot, structure, characterization, theme, use of imagery, archetype, irony, and inversion, with Bellow
parodying some of Kafka's earlier figures. Edward Bloomberg in "Pas-
calian Echoes in *Henderson the Rain King*" (pp. 173–83) sees Bellow as "a
serious Pascal scholar" whose interest in the philosopher-scientist is more
than a passing fancy. Bloomberg views Henderson as an almost perfect
embodiment of a "Pascal likeness," concluding that "Henderson, by
Bellow's design, perfectly illustrates Pascal's dream for all *libertins:* redemption through conversion."

The final two essays, one by Bellow himself, provide insight into
Bellow the man and the writer. In "Literature and Politics: The Bel-
low/Grass Confrontation at the PEN Congress" (pp. 49–57), Daniel
Fuchs describes the attack by Günter Grass on Bellow at the 1986 writers'
congress in New York, a confrontation that centered on "the vexed question of the relationship between truth and power, vision and action."
The anthology appropriately concludes with "Summations" (pp. 185–
99), Bellow's speech at the Haifa conference in 1987, a restatement of his

vision of the artist, who "must turn again to the sources of our permanent strengths to the stronghold of the purest human consciousness."

One other Bellow item merits attention: Eugene Hollahan's "Career
of a Crisis-Watcher: Saul Bellow," pp. 207–37 in his *Crisis-Consciousness
and the Novel* (Delaware). Hollahan demonstrates how the *crisis* trope,
long considered important in literature, is an integral part of Bellow's
writing. Bellow uses it to introduce new themes and motifs, to signal
turning points in the plot and changes in the characters' moods, and "to
connect and judge the mutually exclusive spheres of public life and
private life."

b. Bernard Malamud   Using several of Malamud's stories as examples,
Victoria Aarons in " 'In Defense of the Human': Compassion and Redemption in Malamud's Short Fiction" (*SAF* 20:57–73) argues that in
Malamud's works redemption can be achieved only by people who act
compassionately and who deliberately choose to prove their love for
others. Sharon Deykin Baris in "Intertextuality and Reader Responsibility: Living On in Malamud's 'The Mourners'" (*SAJL* 11:45–61)
draws parallels between Malamud's "The Mourners" and two earlier
American short stories, Melville's "Bartleby the Scrivener" and Crane's
"The Blue Hotel." The theme of responsibility in the stories by Melville
and Crane reminds the reader of the theme of responsibility that emerges
in Malamud's story and forces the reader to respond to the painful issues
behind the story, to "feel personally challenged, acknowledge our world,
and attest to its inhabitants' life stories." John Kimsey in "Dolorous
Strokes, or, Balin at the Bat: Malamud, Malory, and Chrétien," pp. 103–
12 in *The Celebration of the Fantastic: Selected Papers from the Tenth
Anniversary International Conference on the Fantastic in the Arts,* ed.
Donald E. Morse et al. (Greenwood), traces the influence of Thomas
Malory's "Balin, or the Knight with the Two Swords" and Chrétien de
Troyes's *Perceval* on Malamud's *The Natural.* Kimsey points out that
"Malamud treats the Waste Land myth as an allegory of the male quest
for individuation and as an essay on the meaning of heroism."

c. Salinger   *The Catcher in the Rye* continues to attract critical commentary. In "The Personal Narrative and Salinger's *Catcher in the Rye*" (*WF*
51:5–10), Danielle M. Roemer notes that Holden Caulfield plays two
roles, one constructive, one destructive, one in control, one out of

control. Salinger uses Holden to demonstrate to the reader that all people undergo the process of finding their identities. In " 'To Tell You the Truth . . . .' " (*CLAJ* 36:145–56) Susan K. Mitchell offers an explanation as to why there are so many different interpretations of *The Catcher in the Rye*. According to Mitchell, Salinger has created a "writerly text," one that "splits down the middle into positive and negative factions." The "apparent center" of the novel is as phony as its protagonist Holden Caulfield; thus, "the ultimate meaning" of the novel cannot be determined.

New Essays on The Catcher in the Rye, ed. Jack Salzman (Cambridge, 1991), offers six critical articles on Salinger's most popular work. In his introduction to the volume (pp. 1–22), Salzman provides an overview of the history of the novel, noting the many critical responses that it has generated. John Seelye in "Holden in the Museum" (pp. 23–33) notes the influence of Huck Finn and Humphrey Bogart on Salinger's text as well as the influence of *The Catcher in the Rye* on later war novels, particularly those written about Vietnam. In "Holden's Museum Pieces: Narrator and Nominal Audience in *The Catcher in the Rye* (pp. 35–55), Michael Cowan links the "museum routine" in the novel to "the conscious and unconscious strategies that Holden employs in the dual persona of character and narrator" to help him control himself, his listeners, and his world. Christopher Brookeman in "Pencey Preppy: Cultural Codes in *The Catcher in the Rye*" (pp. 57–76) believes that not only most critics overlook an important part of the novel—the "very specific social world" where the American prep school is a main influence—but also that the novel is intertextual—"a finely tuned linguistic and cultural updating of the collegiate tales of F. Scott Fitzgerald." Two final essays, Joyce Rowe's "Holden Caulfield and American Protest" (pp. 77–95) and Peter Shaw's "Love and Death in *The Catcher in the Rye* (pp. 97–114), focus on the character of Holden Caulfield, his prototypes in American literature, and his adolescent crisis.

v Westerners

Native American fiction was represented by one good essay this year. In "Maps of the Mind: John Joseph Mathews and D'Arcy McNickle," pp. 49–89 in *Other Destinies: Understanding the American Indian Novel* (Okla.), Louis Owens offers a detailed analysis of three 1930s novels, Matthews's *Sundown* and McNickle's *The Surrounded* and *Wind from an*

Enemy Sky, showing the ways in which these two writers influenced later writers.

Among the topics discussed in *An Interview With Frederick Manfred* (Midwestern), conducted by Leslie T. Whipp on 5 May 1987, are the family experiences used in Manfred's books, the influence of figures such as Meridel Le Sueur, Ernest Hemingway, William Faulkner, and Karl Marx on his writing, and his belief in writing as process.

Wallace Stegner was only briefly touched on this year. In "Cities of the Living: Disease and the Traveler in the *Collected Stories of Wallace Stegner*" (*SSF* 29:509–15), Anne Ricketson Zahlan examines the medicinal motif in Stegner's short fiction, which ties together the opening and closing stories of his collection and "teaches that acceptance of mortality is necessary to validate the journey of life." Zahlan points out that the Stegner characters who travel abroad become frail and unhealthy rather than recharged and revitalized.

vi Iconoclasts and Detectives

a. Jack Kerouac and Others   The Beats occasioned one book this year, Edward Halsey Foster's *Understanding the Beats* (S. Car.). Foster examines four figures—Kerouac, Ginsberg, Corso, and Burroughs—who "wrote in reaction to the materialistic, conformist America they saw developing in the 1940s." Foster provides biographical information on the writers as well as a solid analysis of their major works and themes. He also demonstrates the ways that the Beats either followed or departed from previous American literary patterns and authors and their influence on later writers.

In "The Artist and the West: Two Portraits by Jack Kerouac and Sam Shepard" (*WAL* 26:293–301), James C. McKelly examines the importance of Dean Moriarty in *On the Road* as an authentic westerner who inspires Sal Paradise, and he discusses the influence of Kerouac, who "offers a vision of a new American frontier," on Sam Shepard in *True West,* the difference between the two writers being that Kerouac's West is a "romanticized projection" and Shepard's is not.

b. Raymond Chandler and Others   Michael F. Logan in "Detective Fiction as Urban Critique: Changing Perspectives of a Genre" (*JACult* 15, iii:89–94) notes the way that urban worlds in detective fiction have been portrayed ambivalently. Citing Raymond Chandler and Dashiell

Hammett as examples, Logan argues "that a misplaced consensus exists within the detective genre: the corrupt and corrupting American city." The corruption of the urban world is also noted by Rick Lott, who in "Signs and Portents: John D. MacDonald's Apocalyptic Vision" (*UMSE* n.s. 10:181–90) traces the growing vision of the apocalypse throughout MacDonald's novels, noting that with the 1971 publication of *A Tan and Sandy Silence* MacDonald relies more heavily on apocalyptic images than he does in earlier Travis McGee novels, to the point where McGee becomes extremely pessimistic, indeed nihilistic. This apocalyptic vision, argues Lott, places MacDonald "in the mainstream of American literature." Robert G. Shoemaker in "Travis McGee: A Fit But Empty Jaundiced Shell" (*Clues* 13:59–65), on the other hand, questions the popularity of the Travis McGee adventure series and the value of Travis McGee as a character, concluding that "McGee is not a character to identify with, but a place-marker, to be filled in by the reader." In fact, Shoemaker argues, readers who compare themselves to MacDonald's protagonist can only appear "the wiser, the more successful, the happier, the braver, and the better." Unlike Lott, who uses numerous examples from McGee novels to support his ideas, Shoemaker discusses McGee in general, rarely offering specific references.

Miriam Fuchs in "Nathanael West's *Miss Lonelyhearts: The Waste Land* Rescripted" (*SSF* 29:43–55) shows how West so parodies, distorts, and inverts rituals, motifs, and characters from Eliot's poem that "the objects from *The Waste Land* are the detritus of *Miss Lonelyhearts.*"

Arkansas State University

15 Fiction: The 1960s to the Present

Jerome Klinkowitz

Throughout the 1970s and 1980s critics strove to establish how contemporary fiction had cast itself free from bondage to the descriptive world. Released from the dictates of representation, writers of novels and short stories would worry less about character and subject. Samuel Beckett's idealistic motive for the work of James Joyce—that it is not about something, but rather is that something itself—was taken literally as a goal achievable by authors from Abish and Barthelme to Vonnegut and Wurlitzer.

The new decade of the 1990s, however, finds many critics turning back to ask just what factors of mimesis remain in the fiction of these same authors. Perhaps the impetus comes from the question asked by story writer Raymond Carver: what do we talk about when we talk about love? For even though subject and character have been discounted at least in the conventional sense, there are still recognizable people in these fictions addressing themselves to matters recognizable from the outside world. Interestingly, love itself figures as an action that helps resolve the issue.

i General Studies

What happens to fiction when interests in character and subject recede was perceived early on by Richard Kostelanetz, whose *On Innovative Art(ist)s: Recollections of an Expanding Field* (McFarland) collects an important 1965 essay, "On the New Arts in America" (pp. 3–16). When fiction "achieves its coherence and makes its points less through se-quences of time," other aspects predominate, such as repeated "images,

My thanks to Julie Huffman for help with the research toward this essay.

attitudes, incidents, comments, rituals, fragmented feelings," and "aspects of character" rather than character itself; here, spatial form comes to the aesthetic fore. This shift accompanies other trends, such as visionary, non-naturalistic styles that "render the invisible visible rather than documenting social and factual experience." The nature of this rendering is explored by Jennie Wang, whose " 'To Wiederfight His Penisolate War': 'The Lover's Discourse' in Postmodern Fiction" (*Crit* 34:63–79) finds that in the works of John Barth, Thomas Pynchon, Kurt Vonnegut, John Hawkes, Robert Coover, and Raymond Federman a "love story" manages to "bridge the gap between the public and the private in a carnivalesque discourse" conducted in much the way Kostelanetz anticipated in the earlier works of these same writers.

William Gaddis and Donald Barthelme join Pynchon, Barth, and Coover as Susan Strehle's subjects in *Fiction in the Quantum Universe* (No. Car.). For Strehle, fiction has not so much abandoned reality as adopted a new definition of it, one borrowed (along with techniques of perception and measurement) from contemporary science. *The Public Burning* and *Gravity's Rainbow* are replete with a "wealth of historically accurate detail"; far from being metafictionists, Coover and Pynchon and the others "comment on a lived reality through the pane of art." For them, interpretation is an interactive process, yielding not reality but a perception of how reality is understood. This latter approach prompts Strehle to borrow a term from the physicist Werner Heisenberg, *actualism,* that she uses to identify a style of fiction neither realistic or metafictive.

Other physical aspects of structuring reality interest Patti White in *Gatsby's Party: The System and the List in Contemporary Narrative* (Purdue). For White, Barth's *The Sot-Weed Factor* dramatizes Ebenezer Cooke's loss of innocence by his involvement with a list (of whores), Pynchon's *Gravity's Rainbow* walks a fine line between real and delusional structures, and Don DeLillo's *White Noise* uses information theory as theme and the nature of sound waves as structure.

Apart from physics, traditional devices such as character and subject are called into new service. In *Narcissus from the Rubble: Competing Models of Character in Contemporary British and American Fiction* (LSU), Julius Rowan Raper takes a conservative view in which character as a stable center avoids the fragmentation of proteanism. He finds Pynchon's *V.* employing characters in terms of intentionality (by means of their focus on objects), Barth's *Chimera* treating phenomenology as a malaise of protean and narcissistic tendencies, and Jerzy Kosinski's *Being There* serving as an existential model of life in which the philosophical *Dasein* is satirized in Freudian terms. My own *Structuring the Void: The Struggle for Subject in Contemporary American Fiction* (Duke) considers what authors write about when the notion of subject has been theoretically disallowed. For Kurt Vonnegut, it is a matter of structuring an unknowable world in terms of the more familiar aspects of his autobiography, an approach Walter Abish fully textualizes in his own fiction; Max Apple turns even the most innocuous of subject matters (such as Disneyland and Post cereals) into rituals, while Gerald Rosen and Rob Swigart construe a carnivalized grammar dealing with comic aspects of California life; ultimately, Stephen Dixon manages a self-contained realism in which all narrative is generated by its own elements, complementing Grace Paley's sociological use of metafiction.

That there was a renewed argument for realism in the 1980s is clear; that this argument turned on paradoxes and led to significant shadings and qualifications in its employment interests the contributors to editor Kristiaan Versluys's *Neo-Realism in Contemporary American Fiction.* Most helpful is Malcolm Bradbury's "Writing Fiction in the 90s" (pp. 13–25), in which the problems of grasping "a terrible contemporary history" are compounded by theoretical issues of the text itself. An inability to see beyond thematics hinders John W. Aldridge's assessment of the minimalists in *Talents and Technicians: Literary Chic and the New Assembly-Line Fiction* (Scribner's), in which fiction by Frederick Barthelme, Ann Beattie, Raymond Carver, and their like is dismissed for not being "about" any significant action. A similar failure to grasp what postmodern fiction is really "about" leads to misreadings of contemporary innovators in Aldridge's *Classics and Contemporaries* (Missouri), to the extent that Donald Barthelme's stories are dismissed as "quite literally verbal immersions in dreck, the evacuated crud and muck of contemporary life," stories that at best "very effectively dramatize the sensations of being suffocated and shat upon and generally soiled and despoiled in soul and mind which accompany our daily experience of contemporary life."

Two authors hoping to provide comprehensive studies fall disappointingly short of the mark. In *American Fiction Since 1940* (Longman) Tony Hilfer skips the 1960s almost entirely, dismissing a decade's innovators as a gloss on Barth's "Literature of Replenishment" essay (itself a rejection of innovative fiction's aesthetic) and describing Kurt Vonnegut as a "black humorist" (a term made obsolete as early as the first wave of serious scholarship about the period in the middle 1970s). Brian McHale's *Constructing Postmodernism* (Routledge) does include coverage of innovators Ronald Sukenick, Steve Katz, Clarence Major, and Raymond Federman, but at the expense of overemphasizing the self-consciously elite avant-gardism of Joseph McElroy and William Gibson. To his book's detriment, McHale writes as a superior-class critic who slums; he makes considerably more references to Pia Zadora, Pee-wee Herman, Pat Sajak, John Ritter, Bryant Gumbel, and Sean Connery than to Kurt Vonnegut, whose fiction engages popular values much more effectively but which stands virtually unread here. A much better understanding of these interests is found in Thomas Reed Whissen's *Classic Cult Fiction* (Greenwood), in which key works by Vonnegut, Richard Fariña, Sylvia Plath, Joseph Heller, Hunter S. Thompson, Ken Kesey, Richard Brautigan, and Stephen King are studied for their role in a counterculture's activity. That much of this counterculture impulse existed a full decade earlier is established by Dan Wakefield's literary memoir, *New York in the 50s* (Houghton Mifflin). From the lyrical sociology influencing the postwar intellectual climate surrounding Columbia University to the alternative values being lived in Greenwich Village, Wakefield recaptures a personal style from which an era's revolt at the American mainstream became the next age's basis for transformation.

ii Women

A new emphasis on what happens to the text written by women (as opposed to what happens to women in these texts) distinguishes the year's scholarship in this field. Introducing *Resurgent: New Writing by Women* (Illinois), editors Lou Robinson and Camille Norton observe that "When women write together, the notion of text as property, author as owner, is questioned, further dismantling traditional ways of reading." The differing nature of experience as it is translated into "reality" interests Nancy Gray in *On Experimental Writing by Women* (Illinois). The universal categories presumed to inform realistic writing are often masculine constructs; these cultural codes must be "broken into and through" so that gender does not function as access or obstacle to language.

Subgenres have been among the recourses for women written out of mainstream forms, but once more the new emphasis is on the unique occasions they provide. *Feminist Fabulation: Space/Postmodern Fiction*

(Iowa) is Marleen S. Barr's account of how such writing has become inclusive rather than exclusive; in addition to Marge Piercy's success with nonpatriarchal storytelling, this "Tralfamadorian method" reveals feminist trends in the works of Barthelme, Vonnegut, and Pynchon. As for romance, a new edition of Janice A. Radway's *Reading the Romance* (No. Car.) reviews its history in the curriculum and reminds us that elite novels do not tell genuinely cultural stories; there is, moreover, an anthropological tendency developing that applies ethnographic interest to reading and not just speaking (important as women's reading becomes an act of declared independence). Important themes in editor Jayne Ann Krementz's *Dangerous Men and Adventurous Women: Romance Writers on the Appeal of the Romance* (Penn.) are Mary Joe Putney's feeling that a potent healing myth distinguishes the romance from women's fiction (a case of fantasy appealing to the nurturing instinct) and Susan Elizabeth Phillips's belief that female empowerment remains rare in both literature and life. Kathy Acker's role as a romance writer is discussed by Diane Elam in *Romancing the Modern* (Routledge). Acker's focus is "interpretive problems raised by gender," and her *Don Quixote* illustrates the difficulty of finding a feminine voice in a male-constructed world. For her, romance is not unreal but rather a reality "invested by desire."

Single-author studies this year are restricted to familiar figures, but with new angles to exploit. For *Sylvia Plath: Confessing the Self* (Peter Lang) Toni Saldívar was given access to Plath's papers, a problem for many previous studies. Saldívar's key is to establish a relationship by means of language, in Plath's case to her dead father; as the letter binds but also separates, the author practices a gnosis in an attempt to write her own scripture. In *Strands of the Cable: The Place of the Past in Jewish American Women's Writing* (Peter Lang), Ellen Serlen Uffen finds Cynthia Ozick questioning her characters' concerns, especially those of past to present in both social and fictive senses. Does the past lie? Can it be defined as their own? To answer these questions, Ozick devises literary borrowings as an intertext, creating levels of invention to mark her characters' search; their effort is praised, for it is better to search and fail than not to look at all. Similar problems with the past interest J. Randal Woodland in " 'New People in the Old Museum of New Orleans': Ellen Gilchrist, Sheila Bosworth, and Nancy Lemann" (*Louisiana Women Writers*, pp. 195–210). Here old stories perpetuate their curse by ensnaring new victims. Protagonists strive against these limits, forcing life narratives into new channels; yet because the old destinies of New

Orleans remain full of life, there is a constant temptation not to struggle for new ones. Fresh attention to the text is given by Qing-yun Wu in "A Chinese Reader's Response to Maxine Hong Kingston's *China Men*" (*MELUS* 17, iii:85–94); the Chinese talk-story prompts Kingston to stress "auricular images" and a "translation of music" that transcends language barriers. A postmodern reconceptualization of space helps Paula E. Geyh better understand a widely studied novel in "Burning Down the House? Domestic Space and Feminine Subjectivity in Marilynne Robinson's *Housekeeping*" (*ConL* 34:103–22): the former objectivity of space fragments and interpenetrates subjectivity; there is "a new *transient* subjectivity which is located in a place outside all patriarchal structures," a situation that demands a rethinking of subjectivity as operative in both feminist and postmodern theory. A corresponding narrative development that replaces an identifiable speaker with a *we* "that becomes the sole constituent of narrating—though not narrated—identity" fascinates Susan Sniader Lanser in *Fictions of Authority: Women Writers and Narrative Voice* (Cornell), especially as used by Amy Tan in *The Joy Luck Club,* where a sequential community voice interlaces segments of personal history.

iii Toni Morrison and Other African Americans

Studies of Toni Morrison and especially of *Beloved* dominate the field. This novel is "in many ways the Ur-text of the African-American experience," according to Henry Louis Gates, Jr., in *Loose Canons: Notes on the Culture Wars* (Oxford). Significant in Gates's view of a "post-Black Aesthetic," *Beloved* "transcends the ultimate horror of the black past—slavery—through myth and the supernatural." Morrison's genius (by which she avoids the "kitsch" that waylays too many other treatments of the subject) is to find "a language by which to thematize the very unspeakability of slavery," a process that involves stepping outside the limits of realism. Thus, *Beloved* is an important part of Gates's larger thesis, that for multiculturalism and diversities to work some means must be constructed to transcend specific limitations in favor of a commonality unrestricted by distracting issues.

    Morrison's fiction also plays a crucial role in Jane Gallop's aesthetic as argued in *Around 1981: Academic Feminist Literary Theory* (Routledge). The tradition of the foremother is a complex one, in which affirmations of the past sometimes threaten the integrity of the future; in similar manner, the empowerment of black women through a voice independent of male domination can "also threaten to silence any difference within," situations that are dramatized in Morrison's work. Morrison's own position is outlined in her *Playing in the Dark* (Harvard) as a protest against white authors' marginalization of black themes and characters; because ignoring matters of race has been accepted as positive, "liberal" behavior, the essence of black literature ceases to be a cultural concern.

No less than seven studies of *Beloved* distinguish two issues of the newly renamed *African American Review* (formerly *Black American Literature Forum*). Chief among them is Bernard W. Bell's "Beloved: A Womanist Neo-Slave Narrative; or Multivocal Remembrances of Things Past" (26:7–15), in which a dialogy of voices transcends the "complex double consciousness" of characters in response to their humanity. This same notion occupies Deborah Ayer Sitter in "The Making of a Man: Dialogic Meaning in *Beloved*" (26:17–29), where the key is Morrison's unsettling of assumptions and heightening of more difficult understandings. Brenda K. Marshall uses "magic realism" to explain the resistance to closure in this novel, an undertaking that becomes "a political act" within the logic of *Teaching the Postmodern: Fiction and Theory* (Routledge). The fantastic deserves consideration as well, says Grace A. Epstein in "Out of Blue Water: Dream Flight and Narrative Construction in the Novels of Toni Morrison" (pp. 141–47), a contribution to editor Nicholas Ruddick's *State of the Fantastic: Studies in the Theory and Practice of Fantastic Literature and Film* (Greenwood). "Dream flight" is a stretching of the reader's conception of reality, incorporating both the empirical and the fantastic as a way of escaping narrative confines and cultural constraints.

Alice Walker's *The Color Purple* continues to draw scholars. For Linda S. Kaufman in *Special Delivery: Epistolary Modes in Modern Fiction* (Chicago), it is a case of struggling with modes of representation in attempting to deal with otherness; multiple forms of enslavement link Celie's and Nettie's stories, making it necessary for one to be constituted as a subject before undertaking the decentering practiced by other novelists such as Doris Lessing. In Patricia Waugh's *Practising Postmodernism, Reading Modernism* (Edward Arnold), "intertextual displacements" are seen as challenges to the notion of history as consisting in the acts of great men; Walker thus expands her narrative to accommodate genuinely alternative discourses. Mapping out "missed readings" does encourage a different style of historical consciousness, James C. Hall agrees in "Toward a Map of Mis(sed) Reading: The Presence of Absence in *The Color Purple*" (*BALF* 26:89–97). Important thematic considerations in Walker's second novel are drawn out by Donna Krolik Hollenberg in "Teaching Alice Walker's *Meridian:* From Self-Defense to Mutual Discovery" (*MELUS* 17, iv:81–95) and Lynn Pifer in "Coming to Voice in Alice Walker's *Meridian:* Speaking Out for the Revolution" (*BALF* 26:77–88).

Gayl Jones, Paule Marshall, Walker, and Morrison have been critical of black male characters, but they are also understanding of the psychic mutilation suffered, according to Richard K. Barksdale in *Praisesong of Survival* (Illinois). Confusions of sex and violence are buried in the chattel status of slavery, he says; as a result, following emancipation black men tended to imitate the behavior of their former white masters. That Amiri Baraka found a different path in cultural nationalism is clarified by William L. Van Deburg, whose *New Day in Babylon: The Black Power Movement and American Culture, 1965–1975* (Chicago) discusses Baraka's belief in race as a felt identity preserved by culture and expressed by art; more than just writing, Baraka has also organized the means for dissemination of his idea that art is a political factor of change. Yet cultural assumptions can still be dismantled by literary means, as Joseph Weixlmann indicates in "African American Deconstruction of the Novel in the Work of Ishmael Reed and Clarence Major" (*MELUS* 17, iv:57–79). Rather than devoting themselves to content, Reed and Major address formal concerns of deconstruction; by challenging notions of what a novel should be, they also unsettle bourgeois beliefs of what African American culture is. That popular culture readily provides some of the tools for this work is established by Carol Siri Johnson in "The Limbs of Osiris: Reed's *Mumbo Jumbo* and Hollywood's *The Mummy*" (*MELUS* 17, iv:105–15).

Intersubjective relations are a special strength in "The Phenomenology of the Allmuseri: Charles Johnson and the Subject of the Narrative of Slavery" (*BALF* 26:373–94) by Ashraf H. A. Rushdy. Fictive language does not so much record an experience as create it, and for Johnson this means that "the art of reading becomes the act of inhabiting the role and place of others, and the art of writing requires an authorial 'act of self-surrender' of such magnitude that the writer finds her or his 'perceptions and experiences' coinciding with ones that preceded her or him." John Edgar Wideman's preface (pp. vii–xi) to a collected edition of his earlier works, *The Homewood Books* (Pittsburgh), indicates his approach to social materials. Shared locales, characters, and events unite these novels, but even more consistent is their investigation of a culture, "of seeing and being seen." Wideman's motive is to "make concrete those invisible planes of existence that bear witness to the fact that black life, for all its material impoverishments, continues to thrive, to generate alternative styles, redemptive strategies, people who hope and cope." Helen Fiddyment Levy finds Gloria Naylor pursuing a similar goal: *Fiction of the Home Place* poses women's community centered on maternal figures as a better model than the conventional heroic ideal, because as society fragments, male-led structures become suspect. When it comes to white writers considering Africa as a subject, the results are often reflexive, says John Cullen Gruesser in *White on Black: Contemporary Literature About Africa* (Illinois), citing Walter Abish's *Alphabetical Africa* as a language game and John Updike's *The Coup* as using the continent as a blank on which to fantasize.

iv Philip Roth, Woody Allen, and Other Jewish Americans

Philip Roth's academic background has always made him an excellent interview subject and intelligent spokesman for his own work; therefore it is no surprise that editor George J. Searles's *Conversations with Philip Roth* (Miss.) is a singularly valuable collection. What stands out from the important pieces collected here is Roth's own humility in the face of the creative process, something that aids his insight into the works of others. That there is much art and substance to Woody Allen's fiction becomes clear in Annette Wernblad's *Brooklyn Is Not Expanding: Woody Allen's Comic Universe* (Fairleigh Dickinson). *Getting Even* employs more complex language than Allen's comic routines, a language meant to be read and not just heard; yet like his early films, this first novel prefers to "mock and retaliate rather than subvert and eradicate." *Side Effects* resembles the middle films in its more fully formed literary sensibility, moving beyond parody and humor to speculate on morality, death, and gender relationships. *Without Feathers* is more topical, yet it deviates successfully from Allen's more familiar schlemiel figure.

Three general studies have special merit. *The Ritual of New Creation: Jewish Tradition and Contemporary Literature* (SUNY) provides Norman Finkelstein a platform for studying how a current of nostalgia lets authors look back to codes in earlier texts; Cynthia Ozick is especially successful with such liturgical codes, writing historically but being ahistorical in matters of religious formulation. In *Follow My Footprints: Changing Images of Women in Jewish American Fiction* (Brandeis), editor Sylvia Barack Fishman describes a tension in tearing away from traditions, with an emphasis on the role of women in these dislocations and displacements. In more recent novels women are getting access to knowledge that "is not for you," Norma Rosen suggests in *Accidents of Influence: Writing as a Woman and a Jew in America* (SUNY); she is also helpful in her commentary on E. L. Doctorow's *World's Fair,* ascribing that novel's lack of intensity to its suffusion in the glow of what is dead, a situation that develops when the future allows no room for carrying Jewish American traditions forward.

v Walker Percy and Other Southerners

Fulfilling the commitments of honor and duty without suffering his ancestors' suicidal depression in doing so was Walker Percy's goal; such is the thesis informing Jay Tolson's *Pilgrim in the Ruins: A Life of Walker Percy* (Simon and Schuster). Tolson is factually strong on family history and interpretively sharp on the role of medical science in shaping the author's beliefs; religiously and philosophically, Dostoevsky is a major influence. Though critics have made much of Percy's Catholicism, Tolson reminds us that previous groundings in science and art tempered this disposition. An argument that Catholic doctrine underlies Percy's novelistic strength is made by Karl-Heinz Westarp in "Message to the Lost Self: Percy's Analysis of the Human Situation" (*Renascence* 44:216–24), a special issue in which editor Joseph Schwartz also presents important essays by L. Jerome Taylor, Jr., Lewis Lawson, Terrye Newkirk, and David Hugh Werning. A fresh view of Percy's first novel is provided by Philip E. Simmons in "Toward the Postmodern Historical Imagination: Mass Culture in Walker Percy's *The Moviegoer* and Nicholson Baker's *The Mezzanine*" (*ConL* 33:601–24). Mass culture enacts cyclical theories of history, a pattern that fits Percy's vision of decline and fall.

In 1963 Walker Percy received a letter from Shelby Foote agreeing that writing is a search for answers but suggesting that those answers were best found in form. *Shelby Foote: Novelist and Historian* (Miss.) has Robert L. Phillips, Jr., citing this letter but arguing that Foote is less of an Emersonian or Whitmanesque romantic than a Jamesian, Proustian researcher of the past. For Foote, form evolves over time as a complex human invention, and it is this action in the past that he finds most fascinating. It is a similar interest in historical uses of social and religious codes that prompts Margaret D. Bauer to consider Alice Walker more as a southern than exclusively African American writer, as argued in "Alice Walker: Another Southern Writer Criticizing Codes Not Put To 'Everyday Use' " (*SSF* 29:142–51). A massive collection of statements on this and similar topics is provided by editor Rosemary M. Magee's *Friendship and Sympathy: Communities of Southern Women Writers* (Miss.), where Walker is represented (but as the only well-known African American writer). For editor Jefferson Humphries's *Southern Literature and Literary Theory* (Georgia), Gina Michelle Collins asks "What Feminism Can Learn from a Southern Tradition" (pp. 75–87), and answers that emotions can be blinded by holding extreme negative views, particularly when modern feminism gets trapped within its own vision in response to patriarchal values.

Although William Styron attracts less work, principally Janet M. Stanford's "The Whisper of Violins in Styron's *Sophie's Choice*" (*SLJ* 25, i:106–17), where the potential for human sensitivity is measured through response to music, George Garrett continues to emerge. His own *My Silk Purse and Yours: The Publishing Scene and American Literary Art* (Missouri) laments how publishers seem more interested in subsidiary rights than in literature itself and that writers have become more broadly concerned with publishing beyond just writing; surveying the scene, Garrett fears that a certain "midlist seriousness" has created reputations (such as Ann Beattie's) rather than forcing them to be earned (as happened with Walker Percy). Garrett's trilogy is of interest to Monroe K. Spears, whose *Countries of the Mind* (Missouri) appreciates how the author plants imagination in fact, staying within limits of the historically probable not just for reality's sake but as a way of interplaying textuality with the imagination. Historical place is given brilliant examination in the contributions to *Literary New Orleans* (LSU), especially by Lewis Lawson in "Pilgrim in the City: Walker Percy" (pp. 51–60), a survey of the city's optimistic and pessimistic aspects as they influenced Percy's emigration from "the French flu, which might also be called the Vieux Carre syndrome" of engendering a sense of place decaying into the bizarre.

vi Leslie Silko, James Welch, and Other Writers of the West and Southwest

A major publishing event is marked with Louis Owens's *Other Destinies: Understanding the American Indian Novel* (Okla.). Owens pays special attention to how Native American writers adapt narrative forms to an otherwise unrecorded subject, praising N. Scott Momaday for being "fully aboriginal" in his handling of otherness, James Welch for taking his readers through "conceptual barriers" to different realities, Leslie Silko for fashioning an identity beyond time, Louise Erdrich and Michael Dorris for weaving meaning from the remnants and relationships of people to the land, and Gerald Vizenor for his Bakhtinian melding of levels. Welch's ability to create necessary grounding stories is detailed by Nora Barry in "'A Myth to Be Alive': James Welch's Fools Crow" (*MELUS* 17, i:3–20), while Catherine Rainwater applies a more sophisticated style of analysis to familiar materials in "The Semiotics of Dwelling in Leslie Marmon Silko's *Ceremony*" (*AJS* 9:219–40), a reminder that reality is a product of semiosis and that American Indian epistemology is a communal function.

Three Chicano/Chicana writers contribute important statements to editors Feroza Jussawalla and Reed Way Dasenbrock's *Interviews with Writers of the Post-Colonial World* (Miss.). Rudolfo Anaya talks about his New Mexico roots, the role of the shaman, and the bilingual rhythms of southwestern Spanish. Rolando Hinojosa makes much of the fact that he writes in two languages, the choice determined by situation. Sandra Cisneros considers the role of Spanish in her written English, something she strives to connect to the spoken word. In sum, these authors make a point that "post-colonial" includes important considerations of language.

When it comes to contemporary writers, Jane Tompkins limits her coverage in *West of Everything* (Oxford) to Louis L'Amour. But his *The Last of the Breed* is important for its cycle of fear and release; his narratives of ordeal invoke the need for seriousness too many readers would deny to the western novel. When reading L'Amour, there is always the sense that something important is at stake. Popular culture is also a factor in Robert Murray Davis's *Playing Cowboys: Low Culture and High Art in the Western* (Okla.), where development is a more important theme than escapism or violent action. In recent times heroes of these works have had to reinvent themselves as thoroughly as any characters in innovative fiction; indeed, the process can be observed in the innovative works of Richard Brautigan and Ishmael Reed, authors too many traditionalist critics do not consider within the subgenre.

vii The Mannerist: John Updike and John Cheever

The importance of John Updike's reworking of Hawthorne's themes and techniques has been apparent in recent scholarship, a trend James A. Schiff brings to fruition with "Updike's *Roger's Version:* Re-Visualizing *The Scarlet Letter*" (*SoAR* 57, iv:59–76), "Updike's *The Scarlet Letter* Trilogy: Recasting an American Myth" (*SAF* 20:17–31), and *Updike's Version: Rewriting* The Scarlet Letter (Missouri). *A Month of Sundays, Roger's Version,* and *S.* are more than just retellings of Dimmesdale's, Chillingsworth's, and Hester's stories. As a trilogy they reveal a new, postmodern Updike, one who explores alternative narrative modes with a Hawthornean depth critics have thought he lacked. In transforming Hawthorne's story, Updike alters an American myth, recasting the American Eden as "the bad conscience of a nation." More predictably, Updike affirms the corporeal, reconciling body and soul. The trilogy in turn exercises the power of language (in a verbalizing sense), enhances visualization, and offers a dissenting view of the self's transformation.

There is also the Rabbit tetralogy, Stacey Olster's subject in "Rabbit Is Redundant: Updike's End of an American Epoch" (*Neo-Realism in Contemporary American Fiction,* pp. 111–29). There is a progressive "menialization" in the Rabbit novels, Olster believes, signaling Updike's belief in a decline evident in life's quality. Indolence and complacency mark this decline, and Harry Angstrom's death is a submission to these facts.

John Neary suggests an interesting pairing in *Something and Nothingness: The Fiction of John Updike and John Fowles* (So. Ill.), based on a common interest in existentialism supported by theology. For Updike, this prompts the familiar influence of Kierkegaard, which in *Rabbit, Run* involves questions of meaning, in *The Centaur* invites symbolic encounters with The Wholly Other, in *Couples* shows that substance (God, marriage, and the form of the social novel) can survive, and in the Hawthorne trilogy reminds readers of the divorce between the divine and the human (a *via negativa* shunning the customary as opposed to a *via affirmativa* building on presence rather than absence). In Updike's hands, a Kierkegaardian faith can exist beyond nothingness, but it is also helpful for deconstructing unwarranted assumptions.

Critical hostility to John Cheever encourages Michael D. Byrne to look for clues in "Split-Level Enigma: John Cheever's *Bullet Park*" (*SAF* 20:85–97). It is in this novel that Cheever "came to the end of the spool" in finding praise for suburbia; at the time it surprised his critics, but in fact it began a trend evident in the novels that followed, where "homeless, deracinated characters" became "nostalgic wanderers searching for a place to exist, an order. Suburbia could no longer provide it."

viii Realists Old and New

The prophetic inclinations of a major writer are given full examination by Robert Merrill in a revised edition of *Norman Mailer* (TUSAS 322). Prophetic desires lead Mailer to impose a narrative pattern on *The Armies of the Night,* part of an attempt to undertake analysis by means of nonfiction. Merrill believes Mailer has become a good critic in the process, less of a Jeremiah and more of a storyteller.

Editor Jay Parini brings attention to the stature of another contemporary in *Gore Vidal: Writer Against the Grain* (Columbia). Most helpful is Catharine R. Stimpson's "My O My O Myra" (pp. 183–98), in which Vidal's view of sexuality becomes the key to *Myra Breckinridge* and *Myron.* With humanity as a bisexual species, such interests are a potential rather than a perversion; aggression is "the motor of eros," a situation that allows sex to be infiltrated with mental images and fantasies.

Interest in Edith Wharton is found by Adeline R. Tintner to be a prevalent concern in "Punishing Morton Fullerton: Louis Auchincloss's 'The "Fulfillment" of Grace Eliot'" (*TCL* 38:44–53). A dialectic with the text far beyond conventional realism concerns Marilyn C. Wesley in "The Transgressive Other of Joyce Carol Oates's Recent Fiction" (*Crit* 33:255–62). And Jacqueline Rose discovers intertextual commentary operative in *The Haunting of Sylvia Plath* (Harvard), a narrative impulse that plays out a troubling underside of domestic and sexual ideals; *The Bell Jar* is easily seen as a "type of pilgrim's progress (peregrination) for girls through the multiple forms and products of twentieth-century cultural life." The literary side of Robert Coles is discussed by Jay Woodruff in *Conversations with Robert Coles* (Miss.), coedited by Woodruff and Sarah Carew Woodruff, who argues that nontechnical language is a strong force in shaping and expressing Coles's vision.

Raymond Carver is not a minimalist, claims Randolph Paul Runyon in *Reading Raymond Carver* (Syracuse). Rather, he is a "self-reflexive metafictional writer" who eschews "extrospective fiction" in favor of introspections akin to John Barth's. The most prominent metafictive quality is the cyclic nature to Carver's stories, many of which employ metastories as part of their plot; as a result, there is an intertextuality of enveloped references which lead his narratives to comment on themselves. Ewing Campbell's *Raymond Carver: A Study of the Short Fiction* (Twayne) sees patterns in Carver's versions and variations; his fringe people practice manners in decay, prompting the articulated chaos of *Cathedral.*

With "Anne Tyler's Emersonian Balance" (pp. 207–30) Sanford E. Marovitz makes an important contribution to editor Alice Hall Petry's *Critical Essays on Anne Tyler* (Hall); his subject is how *Dinner at the Homesick Restaurant* draws on Virginia Lee Burton's 1942 novel, *The Little House,* in which a child's apprehension supplies generational continuity. Paul Jude Beauvais finds a role for narrative in postmodern culture; in "Postmodernism and the Ideology of Form: The Narrative Logic of Joan Didion's *Democracy*" (*JNT* 23, ii:16–30), he shows how politics turns to metafictive technique for parodic intertextuality. A distinctive voice that uses art to instruct, testing ideas by submitting them to the medium in which they work, impresses Per Winther in *The Art of John Gardner: Instruction and Exploration* (SUNY); Gardner's is an "echoic method" that uses collage techniques to incorporate previous texts, allowing him to explore rather than be simply didactic. A well-grounded appreciation supports Douglas Fowler's *Understanding E. L. Doctorow* (So. Car.); especially useful is Fowler's comprehension of why *Big as Life* fails (its science fiction characters are immobilized by size and time, while the author's liberal political sensibility clashes with the intrinsic political implications of the invasion-type narrative). In terms of strength, *The Book of Daniel* is distinguished by its "narrational nerve energy" and *Ragtime* by its ability to generate narratives from images. Similar conclusions are reached by T. V. Reed in "Genealogy/Narrative/Power: Questions of Postmodernity in Doctorow's *The Book of Daniel*" (*AmLH* 4:288–304), who suggests that elements of postmodernism are both represented by its textual field and contained as forces within that field (the elements under discussion are effacement of objectivity and critical distance, refigurations of power, decentering and dispersal of subjectivity, and the collapse of time into space).

There is a special way in which a narrator can double as his own biographer, argues Kim McKay in "Double Discourses in John Irving's

The World According to Garp" (*TCL* 38:457–75), a process that involves languages from both genres and dramatizes conflicts between memory and the imagination. Something of a coterie develops around the works of an important but less studied writer in the special issue of *Review of Contemporary Fiction* (12, ii) devoted to Jerome Charyn. Thankfully, David Seed goes well beyond this appreciative mode in his "Performance, Play, and Open Form in *Going to Jerusalem* and *The Tar Baby*" (12, ii:152–63), a discussion of how Charyn constructs frames within frames and mocks his own attempts to describe.

Writers of realism are inevitably more subject-oriented than others, and in *Testing the Faith: The New Catholic Fiction in America* (Greenwood) Anita Gandolfo shows how the reforms initiated by Vatican II influenced a generation of fictionists. The issues were authority versus the intellectual life, which are prominent concerns in the work of André Dubus and Larry Woiwode (Woiwode making it an eminently personal process). Gregory W. Bredbeck supplies a useful introduction to Emmanuel S. Nelson's *Contemporary Gay American Novelists: A Bio-Bibliographical Guide* (Greenwood) that defines "identity politics" in literary terms (a matter of literature expressing "other" influences and seeking a voice beyond what is heterosexual, homophobic, discriminatory, or repressive).

Then there is nature, a topic that inspires some of Sherman Paul's best work in *For Love of the World: Essays on Nature Writers* (Iowa). Readers of this chapter will value Paul's "Making the Turn: Rereading Barry Lopez" (pp. 67–107), in which Transcendental affinities for light and a "moral exploration" of the original order distinguish an author who makes the necessary adjustment when interior and exterior landscapes fail to correspond.

ix   Experimental Realists

Grace Paley is a politically motivated writer whose themes are irrationally scrambled, says Fred Miller Robinson in *Comic Moments* (Georgia); her stories show time collapsing as actions are stretched beyond their ability to be accommodated in rational forms, which is a pretty good way to describe the actual politics of Paley's tumultuous age. Maxine Chernoff's use of Chicago materials is considered in James Hurt's *Writing Illinois* (Illinois); here, conventional people meet "strange" people, prompting stories that explore the nature of such relationships. High versus low culture works in the same way, as does contrasting such locales as home and hospital.

The grandfather of experimental realism may well be Hubert Selby, Jr., whose innovative forms have never cast themselves free of an especially gritty social awareness. Allan Vorda explores this dimension in "Examining the Disease: An Interview with Hubert Selby, Jr." (*LitR* 35:288–302), in which the disease in question is "lack of love." Influences on Selby range from William Carlos Williams to Gilbert Sorrentino and Michael Stephens; surprisingly, Selby admits that "I adore the work of Joseph Heller." It is no surprise that Kathy Acker makes her readers "imagine different ways for a book to be in the world"; how this corresponds to postmodern thought as propounded by such figures as Deleuze and Guattari is explained by David Brande in "Making Yourself a Body Without Organs: The Cartography of Pain in Kathy Acker's *Don Quixote*" (*Genre* 24 [1991]: 191–209); power relations are located in material signifiers of gender, and Acker reexplores them "as they find their most immediate and fundamental point of application in the imposition of subjectivity." Devotion to principles of realism is a recurrent topic in "An Interview with Paul Auster" (*ConL* 33:1–23) conducted by Larry McCaffery and Sinda Gregory; Auster himself delights in being a detective novelist on the order of Borges, Calvino, Nabokov, and Kafka rather than their more popular cousins.

What has happened to the great "moral fiction" debate conducted more than a decade ago by John Gardner and William H. Gass? Marc Chénetier finds it resolved, in a way, by a new generation in "Metamorphoses of the *Metamorphoses:* Patricia Eakins, Wendy Walker, Don Webb" (*NLH* 23:383–400); here, complicity with the intertext announces writerly and readerly involvement with "the literary debates of the last half-century."

x Innovative Fiction: From Barth to Vonnegut

After suffering at the hands of both advocates and detractors who would use the special nature of his accomplishments for their own partisan purposes, John Barth is finally given excellent analytical treatment in *John Barth and the Anxiety of Continuance* (Penn.), Patricia Tobin's study of how Barth's work not only accommodates but builds positively on "the anxiety of influence" that hampers other authors: "he conducts his self-inventing within the Bloomian schema of oedipal conflict—not inventing himself, like Whitman, once and for all in a miraculous conception aimed at public consumption, but rather *re*inventing himself with each new work of art, as new ephebe to his own precursor, in order that the career might go on." Barth thus transforms Bloom's antithetical revisionism from context to core while at the same time rendering poetic anxiety more conscious; the anxiety of influence becomes the anxiety of continuance in which Barth's "long literary career" becomes "a diachronic progress in creative self-revision that receives its synchronic punctuation with his ten volumes of fiction."

For Thomas Pynchon, critics alternate between thematics and techniques. Judith Chambers's *Thomas Pynchon* (TUSAS 607) finds his attitude perverse yet not despairing. There is a tension between hollowness and affirmation, yet the two are seen as polarities with no way out. Most interesting is Chambers's view of *Vineland,* a work she finds extremely hollow and unredeemed because of its flat language; she speculates that the author here shows how little he can do with our postmodern, kitsch-ridden world. Michael Bérubé takes a more theoretical approach in *Marginal Forces/Cultural Centers: Tolson, Pynchon and the Politics of the Canon* (Cornell). Considering the rubrics of cultural transmission and reception, Bérubé argues for marginality as empowerment, a factor enhanced by the way Pynchon's own academic reception has itself become a narrative as his fiction is institutionalized and recuperated. As for the works themselves, *Gravity's Rainbow* "includes and delimits previous models of literary production" so that postmodernism can be staged as a cultural practice, part of the author's "politics of re-presentation." "Repetition and the Construction of Character in *Gravity's Rainbow*" (*Crit* 33:243–54) by Kathryn Hume presents a scheme by which repetition of key situations and relationships submits characters to "a fixed array of pressures"—these include symbol systems, the void, science and technology, multiple realities, and activities as a game, all of which deemphasize individual character in terms of larger forces, allowing only personal kindness as "a candle lit against the darkness." As always, the most forward-looking work on this author appears in *Pynchon Notes,* which in 1992 regained some distance on its publication schedule by issuing two double issues (numbers 26–27 dated for 1990 and 28–29 for 1991). Most fascinating is Charles Hollander's "Pynchon's Politics: The Presence of Absence" (26–27:5–59), in which every shred of historical and literary evidence is meticulously examined to show Pynchon's political advocacy of the disaffected and disinherited. Several essays in this number are devoted to *Vineland,* as is Johan Callens's "Tubed Out and Movie Shot in Pynchon's *Vineland*" (28–29:115–41), in which television is portrayed as having changed American reality and perception. One of the most important contributions in several years is Marcel Cornis-Pope's "Systematic Transgression and Cultural Rewriting in Pynchon's Fiction" (28–29:77–90), which places Pynchon's work in the context of innovative fiction established by Ronald Sukenick, where fictionalization and deconstruction are less important than tensions between innovation and constraint, randomness and structure, and the "aggregative" and "divisive" impulses of narration.

New insights distinguish Philip Davis's *The Experience of Reading* (Routledge), insights gained from reading Joseph Heller's *Something Happened* with Ben Jonson in mind (by which Slocum's inability to control the world in his own writing is demonstrated by his lack of narrative and syntax suitable for holding intact a jumbled story) and reading Philip Roth's *The Counterlife* in tandem with Lord Byron (as a way of showing what happens when a writer cannot repent of his proclivity when using his own life as material for fiction). Roth's pattern is anticipated by Ken Kesey in *One Flew Over the Cuckoo's Nest* if we agree with Michael André Bernstein, who in *Bitter Carnival: Ressentiment and the Abject Hero* (Princeton) sees generic concerns proper to memoirs controlling the clichés of popular culture; rather than challenging any one tradition, Kesey's approach manages to accept all of them. An excellent review of several decades of Kesey scholarship is provided by editor George J. Searles in *A Casebook on Kesey's* One Flew Over the Cuckoo's Nest (New Mexico), the survey of which reminds one that with this novel Kesey both extended American heroic tradition and radically revised it for a new era.

Welcome attention to some unexamined parts of Kurt Vonnegut's canon is provided by Marc Chénetier in " 'The "Beagle" Sails Again': Darwinism Revisited in Contemporary American Fiction," pp. 140–59 in editors Rob Kroes and S. Ickringill's *Victorianism in the United States: Its Era and Legacy* (Amsterdam: Vrei Universiteit University Press). "The fictional power of Darwinism" is evident in *Galápagos,* not as a scientific element "but as a violently disrupting key placed at the beginning of the mundane and earthly score our life demands we read and interpret every day." But the greater share of this year's attention goes to the late Jerzy Kosinski. In *The Shriek of Silence: A Phenomenology of the Holocaust Novel* (Kentucky), David Patterson sees the boy protagonist of *The Painted*

Bird as one who enfigures silence as a character; in "speaking" the unspeakable, his silence restores the word, a word previously "torn from its meaning, like a tongue torn from a mouth." Naomi B. Sokoloff agrees; her *Imagining the Child in Modern Jewish Fiction* (Hopkins) sees the boy as a focalizer who enables an aesthetic of horror, a narrative device rather than a psychological portrait. The broadest view is taken by Thomas S. Gladsky, whose *Princes, Peasants and Other Polish Selves: Ethnicity in American Literature* (Mass.) credits the author with starting over in order to transcend boundaries. The ethnic center of Kosinski's work is readjusted to the cold war ethic and its new American self. Gladsky offers the first substantial praise for the author's otherwise maligned last novel, *The Hermit of 69th Street,* admiring its rich Polish heritage. "Jerzy Kosinski: Chance Beings" (pp. 31–49), an exceptionally original interview, graces Benedict Giamo and Jeffrey Grunberg's *Beyond Homelessness: Frames of Reference* (Iowa). Trained as a social scientist, Kosinski saw himself continuing as a "societal being," an identity imposed by his wartime childhood. As for homelessness, "we should acknowledge that the homeless cannot be legitimately housed, because we are unable or unwilling to do so," something Kosinski when plotting his fiction has used as a measure of what today's society involves.

A distressing miscomprehension of Donald Barthelme's fiction unsettles the viewpoint of editor Richard F. Patteson's *Critical Essays on Donald Barthelme* (Hall). The problem begins at the start, where unlike other volumes in this generally fine series a somewhat desperately slanted overview takes prefatory prominence. The culprit here is John Barth, who uses the occasion of "Thinking Man's Minimalist: Honoring Barthelme" (pp. 1–4) to misidentify Barthelme's style in order to vent exasperation at what he feels is dismissal of his own work by certain postmodern critics. As Barth himself has admitted in his own *The Friday Book* (see *ALS* 1984, p. 295), "minimalism" is commonly accepted as the designation for a stripped-down realism practiced by Ann Beattie, Raymond Carver, and an entirely different kind of Barthelme—Frederick Barthelme, who like these others made a deliberate about-face from Donald Barthelme's antirealistic innovations more than a decade afterward. Yet because Barth's fiction was perceived as antagonistic to Donald Barthelme's literary experiments, he now tries to change the terms of that writer's success. That Barth's becomes an editorial view is clear from the nature of the volume's reprinted and newly commissioned essays, a collection from which any serious consideration of the author as an innovator is excluded.

Fiction is truly "an embroiled medium" these days, something John M. Unsworth finds to be the case in "William Gass's *The Tunnel:* The Work in Progress as Post-Modern Genre" (*ArQ* 48, i:63–85). Gass is here seen on "the cusp," arguing at times for modernist precepts while having his work betray these ideals of authorial omnipotence. The reviewers' controversy over William Gaddis's *The Recognitions* is reviewed and analyzed by Jack Green in *Fire the Bastards!* (Dalkey Archive), an indictment of compromised standards and sloppy reading. Some of these commercial reviewers might well have admitted that making a commodity of identity was an economic strategy by which the media were forced to work; in *Echo Chambers: Figuring Voice in Modern Narrative* (Iowa) Patrick O'Donnell identifies this as both theme and practice in Gaddis's *JR*, a case of vocal exchanges taking over discourse and reducing all human commerce to the level of instrumentality. Naturalism itself is overthrown, or rather dismantled, in another contemporary work, argues Paul Civello in "Undoing the Naturalistic Novel: Don DeLillo's *Libra*" (*ArQ* 48, iv:33–56). Yet true discourse is still possible if one gives up the desire to speak "for and in place of the other," says Anthony Schirato in "Comic Politics and Politics of the Comic: Walter Abish's *Alphabetical Africa*" (*Crit* 33:133–44), where the key lies in engaging in a true dialogical language.

Steve Katz's eminence as an innovator who draws his strength from language is evident from the essay about himself (pp. 161–80) contributed to editor Joyce Nakamura's *Contemporary Authors Autobiography Series 14* (Gale, 1991) and in the methodology revealed in his collected short stories, *43 Fictions* (Sun and Moon). A New Yorker living in Boulder, Colorado, Katz regrets his adopted home's lack of linguistic diversity, for it is the music of cultures intermixing that has prompted his finest efforts in transforming the observed world into a fictive event. Such events are common in his stories, the breadth of which qualify him as one of the few magical realists writing in the United States.

xi Science Fiction, Fantasy, Crime, and Fantasy

Science fiction combines with postmodernism to produce cyberpunk, according to arguments advanced in a special issue of *Critique* (33, iii).

Brian McHale states in "Elements of a Postics of Cyberpunk" (pp. 149–75) that nothing new must be added to the science fiction side of things, but that a definite shift in dominance among its components has taken place. Since science fiction has always been long on theme and short on form, McHale believes that the subgenre's most recent contribution has been to take "what typically occurs as a motif of narrative structure or a pattern of language in postmodern fiction" and translate these concerns of form "to the level of the projected world"—to "literalize" or "actualize" the metaphors of postmodernism. A more sophisticated approach to this same issue is taken by Lance Olsen in "Cyberpunk and the Crisis of Postmodernity," pp. 142–52 in editors George Slusser and Tom Shippey's *Fiction 2000: Cyberpunk and Future of Narrative* (Georgia). There is a neopragmatic impulse behind such fiction, Olsen suggests, moving beyond antisystematics to maintain politics as its own system; cyberpunk becomes profoundly radical when it operates at the fringes of culture, interrogating the empirical by investing otherness, but like all science fiction it must struggle against neoconservative trends toward realism. Olsen finds these same conditions replicated microcosmically in *William Gibson* (Starmont Reader's Guide 58), especially as this principal cyberpunkist has moved "from experimentation at the level of technique to experimentation at the level of ideas." Gibson's work flatters postmodern criticism by intertextualizing many of its favorite writers and techniques; Thomas Pynchon, whom Gibson considers a "mutant" science fictionist, is an important influence. Yet when cyberspace is considered as "a metaphor for memory," one must ask if there is a difference between human memory and computer memory, which may be the ultimate question on which cyberpunk fiction is based.

"Fantasy and Postmodernism" (pp. 36–50) is one of Brian Attebery's chapters in *Strategies of Fantasy* (Indiana). Whereas modernism has little use for fantasy, postmodernism embraces it as a "replenishing" return to an earlier narrative form (the term is drawn from John Barth's treatment of postmodernism). "Postmodernism is a return to storytelling in the belief that we can be sure of nothing but story," Attebery agrees, reminding critics that fantasy is always metafictional.

Approaches to crime fiction previously unthought of distinguish a cleverly insightful book on William David Spencer, *Mysterium and Mystery: The Clerical Crime Novel* (So. Ill.). To Spencer, the ironic "good news" of Jesus's murder involves unravelling the clues of a murder mystery. "Mysterion" is the holy mystery of rites that unifies devotees with a suffering deity; in the contemporary novel, a cleric takes the place of police when they fail in this function, solving the crime when God's wisdom illuminates the issue. Roots for detection are found in Augustine's *Confessions,* making this an old subgenre indeed.

Much sense is made by Leonard Mustazza in "Fear and Pity: Tragic Horror in King's *Pet Sematary,* pp. 73–82 in editor Tony Magistrale's *The Dark Descent: Essays Defining Stephen King's Horrorscape* (Greenwood). Mustazza sees horror writing as the art of manipulating "phobic pressure points"; evoking the sense of the tragic in life, writers locate flaws as the choice of evil conspiring with forces the hero would oppose. Though there are distractions of pure grossness in such work, readers should attend to how the human mind deals with death, for this is Stephen King's primary goal.

xii The New Journalism, War, and Sport

With two more biographies scheduled for publication in 1993, Paul Perry slips in ahead of the crowd with *Fear and Loathing: The Strange and Terrible Saga of Hunter S. Thompson* (Thunder's Mouth). With a thematic dedication to "the death of the American dream," Thompson pushes writing techniques well beyond normal limits, speaking more as an apocalyptic prophet than as a journalist. And here considerations of Thompson as a fiction writer begin; it cannot be denied that his own revolt against the standards of journalism in the 1960s paralleled the disruptions undertaken by fiction writers such as Ronald Sukenick, Donald Barthelme, and Steve Katz. Perry's own previous work on Ken Kesey makes him comfortable with such affinities, though the intersections detailed here pertain to both writers' involvements with the Hell's Angels motorcycle club and the Merry Pranksters. Therefore, it is important to consider Arthur J. Kaul's "Hunter S. Thompson," pp. 273–79 in *A Sourcebook of American Literary Journalism* (Greenwood), ed. Thomas B. Connery. Apocalyptic religious motifs are a resonant force in Thompson's work, specifically those of "volatile denunciatory literary jeremiads." This style transforms the journalist into a performer.

Fictive responses to the Vietnam war concern no less than three books. In *Vietnam, We've All Been There: Interviews with American Writers* (Praeger/Greenwood), Eric James Schroeder learns from John Sack that *M* began as a foray in black humor (in distinction to the lighter humor evolved from World War II fictions), and from Larry Heinemann how his own literary art tries to measure direct experience. An interesting aside characterizes Michael Herr as having "donated his sanity to journalism" in producing the fictionlike *Dispatches*. The impact of collective defeat interests Owen W. Gilman, Jr., in *Vietnam and the Southern Imagination* (Miss.). Southern writers place Vietnam in the context of their own region, answering the call of history; issues of the Civil War, including race, land, and regional values, occur again in these new works. Larry Heinemann's *Paco's Story* is praised as a radically new departure for American fiction, moving beyond conventions of the war story in order to treat a postapocalyptic world; James Dickey's *Deliverance* is interpreted freshly as "Vietnam fought in the South." An imposed morality burdens Tobey C. Herzog's interpretations in *Vietnam War Stories: Innocence Lost* (Routledge), especially when he argues for a fundamental universality among wars that flies in the face of virtually all understandings of Vietnam as a new and unique experience. Herzog's aim is to bring out all the familiar truisms about losing romantic illusions and finding courage through bonding with other soldiers; he would be unlikely to find a Vietnam veteran who felt the experience was summed up by *The Red Badge of Courage*.

Fiction writers tend to grind their own axes when it comes to drawing on the great American game, says Warren Goldstein in "Inside Baseball" (*Gettysburg Review* 5:410–22), with approaches generally taking either a historical or a cyclical bias. The importance of one key historical event is studied by Richard Gaughran in "Saying It Ain't So: The Black Sox Scandal in Baseball Fiction" (pp. 38–56), one of the many important essays in editor Alvin L. Hall's *Cooperstown Symposium on Baseball and the American Culture: 1990* (Meckler); in most cases, novelists see the occasion as one that violated ideals, but in W. P. Kinsella's *Shoeless Joe* idealism returns to reverse the damage.

University of Northern Iowa

16   Themes, Topics, Criticism

Michael Fischer

Literary theory has not been faring very well in the popular press. Dinesh D'Souza, George Will, Roger Kimball, and others have charged contemporary theorists with everything from bad writing and hatred of literature to reverse racism and an intolerant insistence on political correctness. Most of the books under review here belie this simplistic picture. From many contemporary theorists we get anxious questions rather than ironclad answers, questions often focused on the political efficacy of the enterprise, interrogating what has been accomplished and wondering what more can be done.

i Literary Theory

Loose Canons: Notes on the Culture Wars (Oxford) by Henry Louis Gates, Jr., is a case in point. A collection of essays (most of them previously published) on canon formation and African American studies, *Loose Canons* evinces Gates's considerable skepticism. "It's heady stuff," Gates says of the politically charged rhetoric rumbling through much contemporary theoretical writing: "Critics can feel like the Sorcerer's Apprentice, unleashing elemental forces beyond their control. But we know, on some level, that it's mostly make-believe, that the brilliant Althusserian unmasking of the ideological apparatus of film editing you published in *October* won't even change the way Jon Peters or Mike Ovitz treats his secretary, let alone bring down the house of patriarchy." Despite his reservations about the political pretensions of recent theory, Gates defends its value for advancing previously excluded texts. *Loose Canons* is a readable, often humorous plea for diversity in the texts we teach and the approaches we take.

Gerald Graff's *Beyond the Culture Wars: How Teaching the Conflicts*

Can Revitalize American Education (Norton) similarly concedes the shortcomings of theory while trumpeting its larger value. Instead of lamenting the disappearance of consensus, Graff celebrates disagreement as evidence that new voices are getting the chance to be heard. But he argues that in our teaching we have done a poor job explaining our differences to our students and involving them in our debates. Theorists have settled for preaching to the already converted, thus participating in the avoidance of conflict that characterizes American higher education. Graff's solution: expose students to the controversies that divide us; overcome the much-lamented loss of community not by resurrecting some exclusionary unanimity but by grounding community in democratic debate. I sometimes feel that Graff fails to appreciate why some professors feel threatened by the conflicts he urges them to take part in. Nevertheless, *Beyond the Culture Wars* is an indispensable book for anyone interested in the issues that unsettle contemporary literary study. These issues include determining when something is political, revitalizing our teaching of canonical texts, and dealing with the hostility of students to book culture.

Redrawing the Boundaries: The Transformation of English and American Literary Studies (MLA), a collection of essays edited by Stephen Greenblatt and Giles Gunn, is another constructive response to the changes overtaking the academy. Virtually every field in literary study gets addressed—from medieval studies and Renaissance/early modern studies to gender criticism and composition studies, not to mention several subdivisions of contemporary literary theory (Marxist criticism, feminist criticism, psychoanalytic criticism, deconstruction, New Historicism, cultural criticism, and postcolonial criticism). The best chapters—Marjorie Perloff on modernist studies and Philip Fisher on American literary and cultural studies since the Civil War, to cite two of many examples— sketch the recent history of a field, noting where scholarship and teaching are headed, and why. Some chapters fall short of the high standards set by the book as a whole: Deborah Esch's treatment of deconstruction, for instance, struck me as uncritical and predictable, and Anne Middleton's turgid discussion of medieval studies fails to shed much light on an interesting problem—"the generation-long self-marginalization of the field." But, all in all, *Redrawing the Boundaries* is a very useful reading of the shifting terrain. The second edition of *Introduction to Scholarship in Modern Languages and Literatures* (MLA), ed. Joseph Gibaldi, has also appeared, with helpful essays and ample bibliographies on a variety of topics, from linguistics, rhetoric, and composition to textual scholarship, literary theory, and feminist and gender studies. Contributors include Jonathan Culler, Gerald Graff, Naomi Schor, Giles Gunn, and Henry Louis Gates, Jr.

Still another fine collection of essays, *The Politics of Liberal Education* (Duke), ed. Darryl J. Gless and Barbara Herrnstein Smith, ably defends current trends in the study of literature against conservative attacks. This volume originated as a conference on "Liberal Arts Education in the Late Twentieth Century: Emerging Conditions, Responsive Practices," held in 1988 at Duke University and the University of North Carolina at Chapel Hill. Some of the essays (for example, Henry A. Giroux's "Liberal Arts Education and the Struggle for Public Life: Dreaming about Democracy," pp. 119–44) are too content with simply bashing the William Bennetts of this world. In "Two Cheers for the Cultural Left" (pp. 233–40) Richard Rorty accordingly likens the original conference to a rally for the cultural left and goes on to explain his own more ambivalent attitude toward contemporary theory and the people—E. D. Hirsch, in particular—it attacks. Other important essays in the book include Mary Louise Pratt on the Western culture debate at Stanford (pp. 13–31); Gerald Graff on teaching the conflicts (pp. 57–73); Henry Louis Gates, Jr., on the African American literary tradition (pp. 95–117); and Eve Kosofsky Sedgwick on antihomophobic pedagogy (pp. 145–62).

The political repercussions of theory also occupy *Pedagogy Is Politics: Literary Theory and Critical Teaching* (Illinois), ed. Maria-Regina Kecht. Many of the contributors express disappointment in theory for reinforcing what Kecht calls "dogmatism and orthodoxy, authority and hierarchy, privilege and exclusiveness": "What has flourished is the arrogance of self-righteous academics eager to impress and silence those who have not acquired proficiency in theoretical newspeak." Nevertheless, despite these reservations about theory, the contributors share Kecht's hope that it can still serve "as an effective instrument of critique and emancipation." The essays become a little repetitive in their talk of empowerment, counterhegemonic critical awareness, and the subversion of official truths and hierarchies. The best contributions, however, defend the liberationist potential of theory while acknowledging the institutional obstacles in its way. See especially Kathleen McCormick's "Always Already Theorists: Literary Theory and Theorizing in the Undergraduate Curriculum" (pp. 111–31); Richard Ohmann's "Teaching Historically" (pp. 173–89); Reed Way Dasenbrock's "English Department Geography:

Interpreting the *MLA Bibliography*" (pp. 193–214); and Peter J. Rabino-witz's "Against Close Reading" (pp. 230–43).

Paul A. Bové's *Mastering Discourse: The Politics of Intellectual Culture* (Duke) features 11 essays (all but one of them previously published) on such topics as "Variations on Authority: Some Deconstructive Transformations of the New Criticism" and "Paul de Man: Critic Against Consensus." Bové is guardedly optimistic about the readiness of literary critics to relate literature to other kinds of cultural discourse. In his view, such a move, while not sufficient, is nevertheless a step in the right direction—a step toward making the study of literature a means of fostering critical consciousness. Not content to take the activist claims of theory at face value, Bové rigorously specifies the preconditions for a genuinely oppositional literary criticism: "Postmodern critical intelligence can complete the legitimation of its oppositional ideology only if it becomes part of the public sphere by placing itself within the context of other oppositional forces and theorizes the counterhegemonic in light of their local struggles." I do not see how Bové's often tangled and abstract writing places criticism in the public sphere, but he is right to emphasize that postmodern criticism cannot be oppositional if it remains sequestered in the academy. Bové is also a contributor to *Critical Conditions: Regarding the Historical Moment* (Minnesota), ed. Michael Hays, a collection of essays probing the theoretical and institutional underpinnings of recent theory. The volume includes Bové discussing Sacvan Bercovitch in "Notes Toward a Politics of 'American' Criticism" (pp. 1–19); Donald Pease dealing with Stephen Greenblatt in "Theory, Criticism, Dissent: Toward a Sociology of Literary Knowledge" (pp. 20–38); and Daniel T. O'Hara taking on Stanley Fish in "Critical Change and the Collective Archive" (pp. 39–55).

Whereas *Critical Conditions* zeroes in on the current historical moment of criticism, three other books deal more generally with the involvement of criticism in history. *Studies in Historical Change* (Virginia), ed. Ralph Cohen, has essays concentrating on change and continuity in history. Two are especially pertinent to theory: Murray Krieger's "Literary Invention, Critical Fashion, and the Impulse to Theoretical Change: 'Or Whether Revolution Be the Same'" (pp. 179–206) and Deborah E. McDowell's "Recycling: Race, Gender and the Practice of Theory" (pp. 246–63). In *Is Literary History Possible?* (Hopkins) David Perkins argues skeptically against the cognitive claims of literary history while conceding its indispensable role in our experience of literature. In a curiously disengaged tone, Perkins takes up several crucial questions, among them narrative form in literary history and the legitimacy of periodization. While I remain unconvinced by Perkins's skepticism, I am impressed by his lucid discussion of complex questions.

The editor of an important anthology of English romantic writing, Perkins notes that "fundamental premises of literary history as a discipline come to us from the romantic period." The example of English romanticism helps him formulate the problems surrounding periodization. Another eminent romanticist, Jerome J. McGann, recapitulates in *The Textual Condition* (Princeton) his influential defense of historical criticism. The first several essays in this book establish the relevance of textual editing to literary theory, arguing that "we must attend to textual materials which are not regularly studied by those interested in 'poetry': to typefaces, bindings, book prices, page format, and all those textual phenomena usually regarded as (at best) peripheral to 'poetry' or 'the text as such.'" McGann concludes his study of textuality with a reading of Ezra Pound's *Cantos* along "the double helix of [its] reception history and its production history." Although *The Textual Condition* goes over familiar McGann themes, it provides an accessible introduction to his recent work.

Three fine books, all of them building on American intellectual history, aid the current revival of pragmatism in American theory: Giles Gunn's *Thinking Across the American Grain: Ideology, Intellect, and the New Pragmatism* (Chicago); Richard Shusterman's *Pragmatist Aesthetics: Living Beauty, Rethinking Art* (Blackwell); and Richard Poirier's *Poetry and Pragmatism* (Harvard, 1991). Gunn carefully discusses some major exponents of American pragmatism—William James, Henry James, Sr., John Dewey, and Richard Rorty—and then applies their pragmatism to several current issues in American studies, among them the appeal of interdisciplinarity and the effects of academic pluralism. Shusterman, a philosopher, uses Dewey as a springboard for rethinking the organic unity of literary works and the cognitive claims of interpretation. Shusterman's Deweyan pragmatism leads him to attack invidious distinctions between high culture and popular art. He defends popular art in a lively chapter on "The Fine Art of Rap," rap being for Shusterman "a postmodern popular art which challenges some of our most deeply entrenched aesthetic conventions, conventions which are common not only to modernism as an artistic style and ideology but to the philosophical doctrine of modernity and its sharp differentiation of cultural spheres."

Poirier's *Poetry and Pragmatism* begins to sketch a family portrait of American pragmatism, with Emerson at its center circled by various other figures—from Emerson's contemporaries Henry David Thoreau and Emily Dickinson through John Dewey, Robert Frost, Gertrude Stein, Kenneth Burke, R. P. Blackmur, Stanley Cavell, and other writers. Poirier does an excellent job describing the experience of reading Emerson. He follows the flow of Emerson's writing, an unrelenting movement of undoing and redoing, which Poirier encourages us to hear and track in time rather than sum up once and for all. *Poetry and Pragmatism* stands in sharp contrast to the automatic writing and hasty reading that mar much academic criticism. Although Poirier shies away from specifying the value of reading Emerson, he puts Emerson at cross-purposes with neoconservatives and their theoretical antagonists. He will not, for example, call reading literature "subversive" because the term is "too grandiose": "the Glendowers of literary theory are forever using it, as if at its mention 'the frame and huge foundation of the earth / Shaked like a coward'." Poirier's reticence here makes *Poetry and Pragmatism* hard to classify and maybe even to use, like the writing of Blackmur, Burke, and the other critics he admires, all of them still "highly suspect in the academy." Poirier brilliantly practices a kind of criticism that he thinks "might show literary and cultural studies how it is possible to move ahead of their current tedium, rancor, confusion, and professionalist overdetermination." But "might" is a key word here: more needs to be done to clarify the social benefits of "reading in slow motion."

Geoffrey Harpham's *Getting It Right: Language, Literature, Ethics* (Chicago) is broadly concerned with the ethics and politics of criticism. Instead of proposing what criticism ought to do, Harpham is interested in what facilitates an ethical imperative—any ethical imperative. He wants to flesh out the prerequisites of ethical discourse—the preconditions to be satisfied in making an ethical appeal rather than a threat, for example, or a practical recommendation. Delimiting "ethics itself" takes Harpham through a wide range of texts, from recent literary theory and philosophical writing on ethics to Joseph Conrad's *The Secret Agent*. The result is an impressive, consistently intelligent study.

So is J. Hillis Miller's *Illustration* (Harvard), particularly part one ("The Work of Cultural Criticism in the Age of Digital Reproduction"), a clear, insightful introduction to the problems and goals of cultural studies. Miller declares his "wholehearted allegiance" to a cultural studies that "would preserve and productively transform cultural difference in the new technological conditions while at the same time working for a more just social order everywhere." He argues that cultural critics must be more, not less, involved with theory if they are to circumvent the various "aporias" faced by cultural studies today (for instance, how to enhance diversity without falling back into nationalistic strife or ethnic essentialism). By "theory," Miller in part means deconstruction or rhetorical reading, and I agree with his tacit claim that deconstruction can help keep cultural studies open and honest. Even so, I have a harder time seeing that deconstruction is what cultural studies needs to keep its interpretations in line: "Without some grounding in procedures of verification, for which rhetorical reading offers the best precedents, the cultural critic might be free to say anything she or he likes about the film, the piece of advertising, or whatever." Many would contend that deconstruction needs the procedures of verification that Miller calls on deconstruction to enforce.

Even more emphatically than Miller, Betty Jean Craige in *Laying the Ladder Down: The Emergence of Cultural Holism* (Mass.) endorses many of the changes remaking literary study and American culture: for example, affirmative action in hiring and admissions, opening the canon to previously excluded works, and seeing nature as an ecosystem to be worked with rather than dominated. According to Craige, these changes herald an inclusivist social order characterized by, among other things, "a respect for differences, an appreciation of diversity, a preference for cooperation over competition." Craige sometimes oversimplifies things, as when she predicts that the battle between neoconservatives and their multiculturalist adversaries will be decided "not by the momentary persuasiveness of either side's arguments but rather by the racial and cultural composition of the population"—as if ethnicity or racial heritage guaranteed a progressive point of view. But Craige does a good job analyzing the conservative backlash against recent theory, as well as criticizing some of the measures multiculturalists have advocated (for example, hate speech codes).

Interest in diversifying the canon continues to spawn theoretical studies of ethnocentrism, neocolonialism, and marginalized literatures. Going against the grain of much recent theory, Zhang Longxi's *The Tao and the Logos: Literary Hermeneutics, East and West* (Duke) claims that the East and West share exegetical traditions, which he wants to place in dialogue. Longxi explains that "the goal of this East-West comparative study is unabashedly the finding of the sameness [in literary hermeneutics] despite profound cultural differences, while so many contemporary or postmodern Western theories are predicated on the assumption of cultural, ethnic, gender, or some other difference." *Interviews with Writers of the Post-Colonial World* (Miss.), ed. Feroza Jussawalla and Reed Way Dasenbrock, features insightful interviews with such writers as Chinua Achebe, Raja Rao, and Sandra Cisneros, and a useful introduction on postcolonial, international writing in English. *Decolonizing Tradition: New Views of Twentieth-Century "British" Literary Canons* (Illinois), ed. Karen R. Lawrence, also deals with the canonization and marginalization of a diversity of writing in English. This useful volume includes theoretical essays on the politics of genre (among them, Lillian S. Robinson's "Canon Fathers and Myth Universe") as well as essays examining specific test cases of canonization: *Lady Chatterley's Lover, The Waves,* Scottish and Irish women's writing, Nadine Gordimer's *A Sport of Nature,* and J. M. Coetzee's *Foe* are some examples. *Rewriting the Dream: Reflections on the Changing American Literary Canon* (Rodopi), ed. W. M. Verhoeven, also includes theoretical essays on race, class, gender, and the American literary canon, along with case studies of Henry James, Pound, T. S. Eliot, Thomas Pynchon, and others.

Pynchon is one of the writers taken up by the best book on canonization to appear this year, Michael Bérubé's *Marginal Forces/Cultural Centers: Tolson, Pynchon, and the Politics of the Canon* (Cornell). As Bérubé notes, Melvin Tolson and Pynchon make up an odd couple. Tolson was an African American modernist who sought but failed to win academic acclaim for his work; Pynchon is an Anglo-American postmodernist who spurns the considerable academic attention that his novels have garnered. Juxtaposing the two cases allows Bérubé to study "how canonization works, or fails to work, for writers in the age of institutional criticism." Bérubé's opening theoretical chapter on institutional authorizations should be mandatory reading for anyone interested in investigating how academic literary study affects the legitimation or neglect of certain writers.

Arnold Krupat's *Ethnocriticism: Ethnography, History, Literature* (Calif.) does not so much analyze canonization as thoughtfully advocate "ethnocriticism," a multiculturalist kind of criticism "which engages otherness and difference in such a way as to provoke an interrogation of and a challenge to what we ordinarily take as familiar and our own." Ethnocriticism is concerned with borders and interrelationships rather than reductive, Manichean dualisms (for example, between center/margin, majority/minority, us/them, and so on). Krupat relates this ideal to anthropological studies of cultural difference by Franz Boas and James Clifford; he then tries to implement ethnocriticism by reading Native American literature.

Also concentrating on Native American materials, Hertha Dawn Wong's *Sending My Heart Back Across the Years: Tradition and Innovation in Native American Autobiography* (Oxford) uses contemporary autobiography theory as well as literary and anthropological approaches to track the development of Native American autobiography from precontact oral and pictographic personal narratives through late 19th- and 20th-century life histories and contemporary autobiographies. Difficult larger questions frame Wong's study: for instance, how does "a Native American express a genuine sense of self when that self is mediated by the language of a member of the dominant culture?" Louis Owens's *Other Destinies: Understanding the American Indian Novel* (Okla.) is another impressive study of Native American literature, in this instance the novel writing of American Indians from the late 19th-century work of Mourning Dove through the contemporary postmodernist writing of Gerald Vizenor. In his excellent introduction Owens problematizes the notion of Indian identity—as both a historical construct and a worldview—and shows that an oral heritage complicates how American Indian writers represent their identity in novel form. His comments are enriched by his readings of literary theory—postmodern theory as well as theories of difference—and his ability to contextualize American Indian literature within the American canon and the emergent writings of postcolonial cultures.

The shifting contours of identity—and the advantages and drawbacks of identity politics—are key concerns of Kwame Anthony Appiah's *In My Father's House: Africa in the Philosophy of Culture* (Oxford). Appiah's first two chapters—on Alexander Crummell and W. E. B. Du Bois and the development of Pan-Africanist discourse—will be especially interesting to American literary critics. After arguing forcefully against fixed biological notions of race and tribe, Appiah goes on to explore how Pan-African solidarity can be supported by intellectuals like himself, "whose understanding makes [them] skeptical that nationalism and racial solidarity can do the good that they can do without the attendent evils of racism." Toni Morrison also probes literary and cultural constructions of whiteness and blackness in *Playing in the Dark*. Citing several American writers, Morrison wonders whether the major characteristics of our national literature—for instance, "individualism, masculinity, social engagement versus historical isolation"—"are not in fact responses to a dark, abiding, signing Africanist presence."

In dealing with the canon and other issues, literary theorists tap a broad range of other disciplines, including philosophy, psychology, history, and anthropology. *A Ricoeur Reader: Reflection and Imagination* (Toronto), ed. Mario J. Valdés, offers a good introduction to the work of Paul Ricoeur, one of the most important philosophical critics of literature. Essays by Ricoeur on a variety of topics—from individual theorists (including Habermas, Hirsch, Geertz, and Frye) to more general problems in hermeneutics—make up the volume. Ricoeur's major study of identity, *Oneself as Another* (Chicago), trans. Kathleen Blamey, is now available in translation, as is Maurice Blanchot's *The Step Not Beyond* (SUNY), trans. Lycette Nelson. Three other philosophically oriented books are *Rules and Conventions: Literature, Philosophy, Social Theory* (Hopkins), ed. Mette Hjort, a strong collection of essays on the role of convention in interpretation; *Interpretation and Overinterpretation* (Cambridge), ed. Stefan Collini, a fascinating set of essays on Eco's work that includes contributions by Rorty, Culler, and Eco himself; and Leonard Lawlor's *Imagination and Chance: The Difference Between the Thought of Ricoeur and Derrida* (SUNY).

As Lawlor's interest in Derrida suggests, critics and philosophers remain committed to assessing and explicating his writing. Timothy Clark's *Derrida, Heidegger, Blanchot: Sources of Derrida's Notion and Practice of Literature* (Cambridge) distinguishes Derrida's philosophical work from the literary criticism that claims allegiance to him. Clark is especially interested in tracking Derrida's indebtedness to Heidegger and Blanchot. Examining the dialogue between Derrida and Levinas, Simon Critchley's *The Ethics of Deconstruction: Derrida and Levinas* (Blackwell) argues that Derridean deconstruction poses an ethical demand, if we define "ethical" in Levinas's terms. Ernst Behler's *Confrontations: Derrida, Heidegger, Nietzsche* (Stanford, 1991), trans. Steven Taubeneck, uses Derrida's writings on Nietzsche to shed light on Derrida's critique of philosophy, especially in relation to Heidegger's thought.

The appearance of these calm, rather conventional studies of Derrida and his connections to other thinkers does not mean that deconstruction now transcends polemical advocacy or assault. David H. Hirsch's *The Deconstruction of Literature: Criticism after Auschwitz* (Brown, 1991) mounts a blistering attack on de Man, Heidegger, Jauss, and other writers important to contemporary literary theory. Much like Christopher Norris in *Uncritical Theory,* discussed below, Hirsch measures the politics of these writers by their response to a painfully real historical event: in this case, the Holocaust. According to Hirsch, Heidegger's rapprochement with Nazism and de Man's collaborationist wartime writings indicate the more general totalitarianism of deconstruction. Some of Hirsch's comments strike me as cheap shots, as when he suspects "that those same scholars who were shocked to learn about de Man's past would be equally surprised to learn about the existence of German death camps." And I think he goes too far in rejecting contemporary theory, virtually equating it with Nazism. Nevertheless, *The Deconstruction of Literature* deserves to be read—and answered—by anyone concerned about the politics of contemporary criticism. In Hirsch's view, "the inability of European postmodernist literary theorists and their followers in this country to face the implications of the recent cultural past of Nazism and of a genocide committed on, and in full view of, the European continent, has rendered contemporary criticism incapable of dealing with the human dimension in literature." Instead of brushing off this charge as so much reactionary nonsense, contemporary theorists need to prove it wrong.

Although also taking up the Holocaust and de Man's wartime writings, Andrew J. McKenna's *Violence and Difference: Girard, Derrida, and Deconstruction* (Illinois) is a more temperate book than *The Deconstruction of Literature.* McKenna sees political shortcomings in Derrida's work: as he says very well, "Derrida repeatedly warns against oversimplifying but the symmetrical danger of overcomplexifying is not considered. It is no good having clean hands if the process renders them incapable of grasping anything." But instead of discarding deconstruction, he supplements it with Girard's notions of mimetic violence and the victim. McKenna thus tries to sharpen the political impact of deconstruction, which is otherwise blunted by "deconstruction's reticence, its irresolution or resolute nonpositionality." Although I am not persuaded that Girard is the missing link between deconstruction and political consequentiality, I like how McKenna wants to improve on deconstruction rather than scrap it. The troubling issue confronted by Hirsch and to a lesser extent McKenna—the possible complicity between totalitarianism and modernist/postmodernist thought—is carefully discussed in *Fascism, Aesthetics, and Culture* (New England), ed. Richard J. Golsan, a collection of essays dealing with modernist writers (Wyndham

Lewis and Ezra Pound) as well as philosophers and theorists (see especially Steven Ungar's "Scandal and Aftereffect: Martin Heidegger in France" [pp. 212–28] and Reed Way Dasenbrock's "Paul de Man: The Modernist as Fascist" [pp. 229–42]).

As indicated by the spate of recent work on Derrida, the death of deconstruction is much exaggerated despite lingering, possibly intensifying, doubts about its politics. Interest also persists in Roland Barthes, although, as Andrew Brown mentions in *Roland Barthes: The Figures of Writing* (Clarendon), "a general unease about the status and usefulness of his works" has slowed the work being done on him. Brown's study combats this neglect by attending to the stylistic moves of Barthes's writing. Brown is particularly good on how Barthes contests political dualisms (proletariat versus bourgeoisie, communism versus capitalism, and so on) but still "attempts to stay political while creating a slightly different and less binary model of how political evaluation might be carried out." Michael Moriarty's *Roland Barthes* (Stanford, 1991) is a comprehensive introduction to Barthes's writings.

Another measure of the continuing importance of Derrida and Barthes is the fact that genre theorists, especially narratologists, still feel obligated to come to terms with their work. In *Narrativity: Theory and Practice* (Clarendon) Philip J. M. Sturgess develops "a logic of narrativity" in opposition to deconstruction (and Marxism). Sturgess fleshes out his theory with readings of diverse novelists, including Conrad, Joyce, and Maria Edgeworth. Anthony Paul Kerby in *Narrative and the Self* (Indiana) looks at narrative from a philosophical viewpoint, emphasizing the crucial role of narrative in human experience. Taking as examples epistolary novels, diaries, oral tales, and other kinds of stories, Bernard Duyfhuizen's *Narratives of Transmission* (Fairleigh Dickinson) explores the preconditions necessary for the transmission of narratives. In *Stories, Theories, and Things* (Cambridge, 1991) the novelist and critic Christine Brooke-Rose reflects on the relationship between creative writing and modern theoretical thinking. Susan Derwin's *The Ambivalence of Form: Lukács, Freud, and the Novel* (Hopkins) employs Freud to extend Lukács's analysis of the novel and to show its continuing relevance to literary interpretation and theories of realism. *Jane Eyre* and *The Second Coming* are among Derwin's examples.

Although Freud remains an important influence on literary theory, he is now almost always discussed in relation to Lacan. Volney P. Gay's *Freud on Sublimation: Reconsiderations* (SUNY), in developing a new theory of sublimation, argues against Lacan's reduction of the ego to a linguistic entity. In *Looking Awry: An Introduction to Jacques Lacan through Popular Culture* (MIT), Slavoj Žižek approaches Lacan by way of Alfred Hitchcock's *Vertigo,* Stephen King's *Pet Sematary,* and other instances of popular culture. Jean-Luc Nancy and Philippe Lacoue-Labarthe's legendary reading of Lacan's essay "The Agency of the Letter in the Unconscious or Reason Since Freud" is finally available in English translation as *The Title of the Letter: A Reading of Lacan* (SUNY), trans. François Raffoul and David Pettigrew. Not for beginners, *The Title of the Letter* was hailed by Lacan himself as a "model of good reading" when it appeared in 1973. James M. Mellard's *Using Lacan, Reading Fiction* (Illinois, 1991) explicates Lacan's thought, then applies it to *The Scarlet Letter,* "The Beast in the Jungle," and *To the Lighthouse.*

Three books make good use of Derrida, Barthes, Lacan, and other recent French theorists. Michele Barrett's *The Politics of Truth: From Marx to Foucault* (Stanford, 1991) subjects the Marxist definition of ideology to a post-structuralist critique indebted to Foucault and other theorists. Starting with the writings of the *Tel Quel* group of the mid-1960s and early 1970s, John Mowitt in *Text: The Genealogy of an Anti-disciplinary Object* (Duke) unfolds how the development of textuality poses a crisis for disciplinary reason. Steven Connor's *Theory and Cultural Value* (Blackwell) is a wide-ranging analysis of the theories of cultural value provided by psychoanalysis, neopragmatism, feminism, and postmodernism (among other theories). Derrida, Barthes, Jameson, Lyotard, Geertz, and Bourdieu are some of the writers discussed.

Several worthwhile books can only be cited here. Edward Jayne's *Negative Poetics* (Iowa) explores the importance of misrepresentation and distortion to literature, while Mario J. Valdés's *World-Making: The Literary Truth-Claim and the Interpretation of Texts* (Toronto) studies how literary works make and readers enact truth claims. Timothy J. Reiss's *The Meaning of Literature* (Cornell) follows the development of the modern concept of literature from the mid-16th through the 19th centuries. *Visionary Poetics: Essays on Northrop Frye's Criticism* (Peter Lang), ed. Robert D. Denham and Thomas Willard, presents essays on Frye and the contexts of his criticism, in particular the *Anatomy of Criticism. Culture and Cognition: The Boundaries of Literary and Scientific Inquiry* (Cornell) by Ronald Schleifer, Robert Con Davis, and Nancy Mergler examines scientific and humanistic discourse by studying points of intersection among semiotics, cognitive science, and psychoanalysis.

Joseph F. Graham's *Onomatopoetics: Theory of Language and Literature* (Cambridge) takes a linguistic approach to key issues in literary theory. John O'Neill's *Critical Conventions: Interpretation in the Literary Arts and Sciences* (Okla.) analyzes how various forms of knowledge achieve the status of disciplinary knowledge.

ii Gender Studies

I put bell hooks's *Black Looks: Race and Representation* (South End) here even though hooks is primarily concerned with the colonizing images of blackness perpetrated by American culture. Nevertheless, hooks studies these images with a keen eye for their construction of gender. In one chapter she comments on black gender relations in light of the Clarence Thomas-Anita Hill hearings in the U.S. Senate for the Supreme Court nominee; in another she speculates on reconstructing black masculinity. *Black Looks* does not seem to me to be on the same high level as some of hooks's earlier work, but I like her frank approach to several features of American popular culture, including films such as *Heart Condition*, television shows like "In Living Color," and performers such as Tina Turner and Madonna. In an acerbic chapter entitled "Madonna: Plantation Mistress or Soul Sister?" hooks charges Madonna (in the film *Truth or Dare: In Bed with Madonna*) with appropriating "black experience for her own opportunistic ends even as she attempts to mask her acts of racist aggression as affirmation."

   (En)Gendering Knowledge: Feminists in Academe (Tennessee, 1991), ed. Joan E. Hartman and Ellen Messer-Davidow, brings together several important essays assessing the impact of feminist theory on fields ranging from sociology, classics, and biology to literature, philosophy, anthropology, and art history. I am not convinced by Joyce A. Joyce's claim (in "Black Woman Scholar, Critic, and Teacher: The Inextricable Relationship Among Race, Sex, and Class," pp. 159–78) that "adopting poststructuralist ideology requires Black critics both to renounce the history of African-American literature and criticism and to estrange themselves from the *political* implications of their *black* skin." But the best essays in the volume are less reductive, as the writers try to measure the gains as well as the losses brought about by the recent academic success of feminist theory. Of special note: Bonnie Zimmerman's "Seeing, Reading, Knowing: The Lesbian Appropriation of Literature"

(pp. 85–99); Sandra Harding's, "Who Knows?: Identities and Feminist Epistemology" (pp. 100–120); and Naomi Scheman's "Who Wants to Know? The Epistemological Value of Values" (pp. 179–200). Zimmerman speaks for the volume's contributors when she says "the only perspective that has no place in feminist inquiry is one born of prejudice and maintained in anger or fear."

The place of feminist criticism in the university is also a major preoccupation of Jane Gallop's *Around 1981: Academic Feminist Literary Theory* (Routledge). The title refers to the year Gallop was tenured, but she is right to link this personal milestone with a new development in feminist criticism: "Around the same time, American feminist literary criticism entered the heart of a contradiction. It became secure and prospered in the academy while feminism as a social movement was encountering major setbacks in a climate of new conservatism." Gallop properly objects to feminist critics more or less disingenuously deriding one another's work as "academic." By examining key anthologies of feminist criticism from 1981 through 1987, Gallop wants not to wring her hands over the academization of feminist criticism but to understand it—"to understand why we are located here [in the university], how we got here, what we sacrificed to get here, what we gained: all as preliminaries to the question of how we do the most good, as feminists, as social and cultural critics, speaking from this location." I do not think Gallop makes much headway with these questions, but—for her—at least they are questions. She challenges academic feminist critics to acknowledge the fact that they are professors, with all the opportunities and limitations that this professional status implies.

Both *(En)gendering Knowledge* and *Around 1981* urge us to assess the impact of feminist criticism on the university, the workplace of most feminist scholars. *Explorations in Feminist Ethics: Theory and Practice* (Indiana), ed. Eve Browning Cole and Susan Coultrap-McQuin, similarly includes several important essays on the difference that feminism may make to everyday ethical decisions, the organization of the workplace, and even global prospects for peace. Feminism in this book represents a distinctive ethical stance, which many of the contributors are at pains to define. "Distinctive" does not mean separatist or cleanly cut off from traditional moral thought. Elizabeth Ann Bartlett finds support for feminist ethics in Albert Camus's existentialism, and Julie K. Ward locates a kind of feminist care ethic among the women members of the ancient Pythagorean schools. Other essays move from theory to practice, plumbing the possible significance of a feminist ethic to the workplace and other institutional settings. I say "possible" because in these contexts the potential of feminist ethics seems clearer to me than its accomplishments.

Zimmerman's affirmation of "the lesbian appropriation of literature" in *(En)gendering Knowledge* finds reinforcement in two other valuable collections of essays. *Inside/Out* (Routledge, 1991), ed. Diana Fuss, brings together some of the most important critics working in gay and lesbian studies, among them Judith Butler ("Imitation and Gender Insubordination," pp. 13–31), D. A. Miller ("Anal *Rope*," pp. 119–41), and Fuss herself (who wrote the book's introduction, pp. 1–10). Although some of the contributors lapse too comfortably into theoryspeak, the volume deals in a sophisticated way with film, opera, fiction, pornography, and the discourse and political activity surrounding AIDS. A special issue of *Discourse* (15, i[Fall 1992]), guest-edited by Cheryl Kader and Thomas Piontek, also features interesting essays on topics from lesbian murder mysteries and pornography to cultural criticism in the age of AIDS.

Jonathan Dollimore's *Sexual Dissidence: Augustine to Wilde, Freud to Foucault* (Oxford, 1991) makes a major contribution to gay and lesbian studies. Dollimore deals with many important issues: the claims of theory and history; essentialist versus antiessentialist accounts of the self; the vicious logic of homophobia; and the difficulty that the majority has in defining homosexuality even as it reacts violently against it: "the more homosexuality emerges as culturally central, the less sure become the majority as to what, exactly, it is: a sensibility, an abnormality, a sexual act, a clandestine subculture, an overt subculture, the enemy within, the enemy without?" Oscar Wilde and André Gide are pivotal figures in Dollimore's treatment of homosexuality, but the range of texts he examines here is daunting—from *Othello* through Freud and Foucault. A more concentrated, less encyclopedic approach, however, might have given his argument more force.

Richard D. Mohr's *Gay Ideas: Outing and Other Controversies* (Beacon) is less successful. Mohr is interested in addressing how gays ought to represent themselves in the wider world as well as intervene in one another's lives. He focuses on politics (the outing controversy, ACT UP), culture (opera, the AIDS quilt, photography, and the visual arts), and identity (various models for the social construction of homosexuality). Although Mohr has a keen sense of the questions facing gay and lesbian critics, his specific recommendations—for example, "the time has come for gay intellectuals to stop being afraid of nature"—sound simplistic.

Kari Weil's *Androgyny and the Denial of Difference* (Virginia) is a thorough study of attitudes toward androgyny in European literature and recent feminist literary criticism. Like many feminist critics leery of essentializing gender differences, Weil asks: "Is there a stable line dividing the sexes, or is the division between male and female always rhetorically constituted on a shifting ground of criteria?" Weil examines androgyny as a response to the unstable, socially constructed boundaries of gender difference.

Like Weil, anyone commenting on feminist theory today must come to terms with French feminist theory. Julia Kristeva's writings are the focus of the essays gathered in *Body/Text in Julia Kristeva: Religion, Women, and Psychoanalysis* (SUNY), ed. David Crownfield. *Revaluing French Feminism: Critical Essays on Difference, Agency, and Culture* (Indiana), ed. Nancy Fraser and Sandra Lee Bartky, collects essays dealing with the many issues raised by recent French feminist writing. Homogeneous, static definitions of "woman" are a major concern. Many of the contributors criticize these definitions, while worrying about what feminist politics will put in their place. These writers join Fraser in seeking "to navigate safely between the twin shoals of essentialism and nominalism, between reifying women's social identities under stereotypes of femininity, on the one hand, and dissolving them into sheer nullity and oblivion, on the other." The problem becomes, in Fraser's view, how to "accept the critique of essentialism without becoming postfeminists."

Although French feminism has been a major concern of American feminists for several years now, other kinds of feminism are finally getting the attention they deserve. In *Talking Back: Toward a Latin American Feminist Literary Criticism* (Cornell), Debra A. Castillo provides an excellent introduction to Latin American feminisms. After sketching an overview of Latin American feminist strategies and problems, Castillo looks at several literary examples. Most of the works she studies come from Latin America, but one of her chapters focuses on Denise Chavez, Maxine Hong Kingston, and what Castillo calls the bicultural text. Castillo's theoretical concluding chapter brings out the larger implications of her readings for feminist theory. She challenges many of the truisms of recent feminist criticism, including its presumably authenticating appeal to experience: "For whereas the basic fact of experience can both authorize and empower a speaker/writer, I have too often seen experience deployed as a tactic to close off discussion, to control the audience, and to foment guilt." Fresh insights like these make *Talking Back* a lucid, original contribution to feminist theory.

British feminism gets represented in *Feminist Criticism: Theory and Practice* (Toronto, 1991), ed. Susan Sellers, a collection of essays by 13 British feminist critics on diverse literary works (among them Mary Shelley's *The Last Man* and Henry Miller's *Tropic of Cancer*). British imperialism—often the target of British feminism—enters into *De/Colonizing the Subject,* which studies how various women, in voicing their experience of domination, recast traditional Western autobiographical forms. The editors' jargon-ridden introduction fortunately does not set the tone for the essays that follow, which include writing on autobiography from an impressive variety of vantage points. Janice Gould's "The Problem of Being 'Indian': One Mixed-Blood's Dilemma" (pp. 81–90), Gita Rajan's "Subversive-Subaltern Identity: Indira Gandhi as the Speaking Subject" (pp. 196–224), and Kateryna Olijnyk Longley's "Autobiographical Storytelling by Australian Aboriginal Women" (pp. 370–86) indicate the coverage.

A similar breadth characterizes *Third World Women and the Politics of Feminism* (Indiana, 1991), ed. Chandra Talpade Mohanty et al. This important, if sometimes repetitive, volume examines the often strained relationship between feminism and Third World women, with the latter being defined to include women of color in the United States as well as women from other countries (Trinidad and Tobago, Brazil, Iran, and Jamaica are some of the countries discussed). In the eyes of many of the contributors, the collision between Third World concerns and feminism brings out the racism, classism, and homophobia that limits middle-class white feminism. The variety of women's situations proves that "there is no logical and necessary connection between being 'female' and becoming 'feminist'," as Mohanty puts it in her helpful introduction. Even more strongly, Mohanty rightly wants to challenge "the notion 'I am, therefore I resist!' "—"the idea that simply being a woman, or being poor or black or Latino, is sufficient ground to assume a politicized oppositional identity."

Like Mohanty, many feminist theorists want feminist theory to be responsive to differences among women: hence, the interest in anthologies and essay collections attuned to the debates within feminism. One example is *Destabilizing Theory: Contemporary Feminist Debates* (Stanford), ed. Michele Barrett and Anne Phillips, which features essays advancing the dialogue between feminism and post-structuralist theory. Contributions include "The Politics of Translation" (Gayatri Chakravorty Spivak, pp. 177–200), "Sexual Practice and Changing Lesbian Identities" (Biddy Martin, pp. 93–119), and " 'Women's Interests' and the Post-Structuralist State" (Rosemary Pringle and Sophie Watson, pp. 53–73). The best essay in the volume, Anne Phillips's "Universal Pretensions in Political Thought" (pp. 10–30), appreciates feminist suspicion of universal rights but cautions against abandoning "the aspiration towards universality": "In the reworking of contemporary political theory and ideals, feminism cannot afford to situate itself *for* difference and *against* universality, for the impulse that takes us beyond our immediate and specific difference is a vital necessity in any radical transformation."

Modern Feminisms: Political, Literary, Cultural (Columbia), ed. Maggie Humm, is an anthology that also tries to do justice to the differences among feminist theories. Among the topics covered are socialist/Marxist feminism; Asian, black, and women of color lesbianisms/feminisms; and liberal feminism. Contributors include writers from Kate Millett and Susan Brownmiller to Gloria Anzaldúa and Mitsuye Yamada. Unfortunately, the volume only reprints snippets of essays and books. We get breadth but not much depth. *Feminisms: An Anthology of Literary Theory and Criticism* (Rutgers, 1991), ed. Robyn R. Warhol and Diane Price Herndl, does a much better job, as it reprints important essays in their entirety: among them, Myra Jehlen's "Archimedes and the Paradox of Feminist Criticism" (pp. 75–96); Annette Kolodny's "Dancing Through the Minefield: Some Observations on the Theory, Practice, and Politics of a Feminist Literary Criticism" (pp. 97–116); and Nellie McKay's "Reflections on Black Women Writers: Revising the Literary Canon" (pp. 212–26). No textbook can cover such a rapidly changing, multifaceted field; even so, *Feminisms* succeeds in providing a useful sample of the diversity that characterizes feminist theorizing today.

In a similar spirit Betsy Erkkila's *The Wicked Sisters* attends to the struggles and conflicts not only among women writers but among feminists. Erkkila sees herself correcting the emphasis of earlier feminist critics on "mutuality, nurturance, and familial bonding among literary sisters and/or mothers and daughters as the essential form of women's literary history": "The almost exclusive focus on sexual difference—the difference of woman from man—as the primary historical and cultural divide, along with the corresponding emphasis on women's culture, women's writing, and women's language, virtually erased the multiple

and various race, class, ethnic, cultural, and other locations of women
within a particular social field." This is by now a familiar complaint—the
charge that in mainstream academic feminism "'woman' was equated
with white middle-class women, and 'woman's sexuality' was equated
with heterosexuality and motherhood"—but Erkkila breathes new life
into the accusation by focusing on some interesting specific examples,
primarily the lives and works of Emily Dickinson, Marianne Moore,
Elizabeth Bishop, Adrienne Rich, and Gwendolyn Brooks. Along similar
lines, Helena Michie's *Sororophobia: Differences Among Women in Literature and Culture* (Oxford) looks at how differences among women have
been textually represented in a variety of contexts, from Victorian mainstream fiction to African American mulatto novels, as well as late 20th-
century lesbian communities and contemporary country music. Michie
is also interested in feminist invocations of sisterhood, a concept she
criticizes for being overly reliant on a family model and for homogeniz-
ing women. *Sororophobia* expands differences among women to include
personal differences—envy, jealousy, competition—as part of women's
relations to each other.

Fiction is the subject of Susan Sniader Lanser's *Fictions of Authority:
Women Writers and Narrative Voice* (Cornell), which takes up an especially important problem in feminist narrative theory: how noncanonical texts acquire authority while questioning the prevailing cultural
construction of authority. Lanser makes the good point that "every
writer who publishes a novel wants it to be authoritative for her readers,
even if authoritatively antiauthoritarian, within the sphere and for the
receiving community that the work carves out." Citing numerous novels
by women, Lanser differentiates among several ways of fashioning narrative voice. Also concerned with writing by women, Laurie A. Finke's
Feminist Theory, Women's Writing (Cornell) has several objectives, one of
them being to broaden the scope of feminist inquiry to include writing
before 1800 (one chapter deals with the courtly lyric, another with
medieval mysticism). Finke's opening and concluding chapters carefully
pose (without resolving) several crucial problems for feminist theory,
including the problem of claiming truth for feminism while recognizing
the contingency of all such cognitive claims.

Narrative also is the focus of a lucid collection of essays, *Gender,
Language and Myth: Essays on Popular Narrative* (Toronto), ed. Glen-
wood Irons. Contributors who concentrate on the role of gender in
popular narratives include Tania Modleski on the Harlequin romance,

Jane Tompkins on the western, Irons on new women detectives, Carol J. Glover on slasher films, and Robin Wood on Stephen King. Mary Gerhart's *Genre Choices, Gender Questions* (Okla.) probes the complex relationship between gender and the selection (or transformation) of genre. This well-informed, thorough book deals with classical and modern approaches to genre theory; gender and genre in the biblical hermeneutical tradition; and specific cases that test the limits of literary genres, such as extending genre to nonliterary texts and making sense of the "new novel." Finally, the bearing of gender on genre choice surfaces in Diane P. Freedman's *An Alchemy of Genres: Cross-Genre Writing by American Feminist Poet-Critics* (Virginia). The poet-critics who interest Freedman include Adrienne Rich, Gloria Anzaldúa, Cherrie Moraga, and Marge Piercy. Their hybrid blendings of autobiography, criticism, and poetry are meant to challenge more argumentative, impersonal forms of academic critical writing.

Jane Miller's *Seductions: Studies in Reading and Culture* (Harvard, 1991) is an unusual book, even though it takes up many of the questions occupying feminist critics. Refreshingly personal and sharply written, *Seductions* chronicles the author's own susceptibility and resistance to male theorizing. Topics discussed include the exclusion of women from Raymond Williams's work on the working class and the marginalization of women in Edward Said and Frantz Fanon's writings on colonialism. Miller punctuates her argument with clear observations and honest self-questioning.

I can only mention *Politics, Gender, and the Arts: Women, the Arts, and Society* (Susquehanna), ed. Ronald Dotterer and Susan R. Bowers, a selection of papers from the 1988 Susquehanna University National Conference on Women, the Arts, and Society. *Constructing and Reconstructing Gender: Links Among Communication, Language, and Gender* (SUNY), ed. Linda A. M. Perry et al., offers essays by feminist communications scholars on defining, learning, and reconstructing gender in a variety of cultural settings: for example, in the workplace (J. K. Alberts, "Teasing and Sexual Harassment: Double-Bind Communication in the Workplace," pp. 185–96) and across cultures (Margaret Riley, "Gender in Communication: Within and Across Cultures," pp. 219–28). Literary critics put off by the empirical data, charts, and graphs that accompany communications scholarship will feel more at home with Nancy Gray's *Language Unbound: On Experimental Writing by Women* (Illinois), a study of Gertrude Stein, Virginia Woolf, Dorothy Richardson, and others.

iii Modernism and Postmodernism

In turning to modernism and postmodernism, I am not leaving feminism behind. Much recent work in this area investigates feminist responses to modernist and postmodernist writing. Margery Wolf's *A
Thrice-Told Tale: Feminism, Postmodernism, and Ethnographic Responsibility* (Stanford) contests the postmodernist critique of anthropology—
the critique set in motion by *Writing Culture,* the 1986 collection of
articles edited by James Clifford and George Marcus. Although Wolf has
learned from postmodernist critics to distrust the objectivity and innocence of ethnography, she defends the value of research into other
cultures. As a self-described feminist anthropologist, she cautions that
"feminists who have only recently gained some academic security might
think carefully about whether intense reflexivity in their research and
writing will be evaluated as being in the new postmodernist mode or as
simply tentative and self-doubting."

Marleen S. Barr is also leery of postmodernism in *Feminist Fabulation:
Space/Postmodern Fiction* (Iowa), but by "postmodernism" she means the
canon of postmodernist literary works—a canon that by and large ex-
cludes writing by women. Barr aims at adding to this canon contemporary fiction by women, especially feminist science fiction, supernatural
fiction, and utopian fiction. Getting into the canon and acquiring
academic respectability seem unequivocally positive goals for her. She
apparently does not share the concern of other feminist critics about the
costs of institutional success.

Whereas Barr wants to expand postmodernism to include writing by
women, Somer Brodribb in *Nothing Mat(t)ers: A Feminist Critique of
Postmodernism* (Spinifex) urges us to reject postmodernist theory as
irredeemably misogynist. While I think feminists should cautiously
approach Foucault, Derrida, and the other theorists that enrage Brodribb, her wholesale dismissal of these theorists is too one-sided. She is
especially unfair to feminist critics (Nancy Fraser, Elizabeth Meese, and
others) who find something of value in postmodernism as well as something to criticize. For Brodribb, any interest in postmodernism implicates the critic in the "Father Knows Best" attitude that postmodernism
allegedly fosters.

"Postmodernism" has taken on many, not always compatible meanings in literary studies and other fields. Like Barr in *Feminist Fabulation,*
the contributors to *Fiction 2000: Cyberpunk and the Future of Narrative*

(Georgia), ed. George Slusser and Tom Shippey, use "postmodernism" to describe recent fiction. The essays in this volume relate cyberpunk not only to postmodernist literature but to traditional science fiction. Even if cyberpunk best expresses our "postmnemotechnic" "infosphere," I am not convinced that "fiction at this threshold is taking leave of two thousand years of mimetic tradition." Mixing critical theory and literary practice, *Contesting the Subject: Essays in the Postmodern Theory and Practice of Biography and Biographical Criticism* (Purdue), ed. William H. Epstein, examines how postmodernist critiques of the autonomous subject can enrich the writing of biography. A distinguished cast of contributors includes Stanley Fish (on biography and intention), Michael McKeon (on novelistic anticipations of literary biography), and Shannon O'Brien (on feminist theory and literary biography).

In philosophy, the category "postmodernism" embraces several antifoundationalist, postmetaphysical thinkers who have become familiar to literary critics, among them Derrida, Rorty, Heidegger, Lyotard, and sometimes Ludwig Wittgenstein. *Merleau-Ponty, Hermeneutics, and Postmodernism* (SUNY), ed. Thomas W. Busch and Shaun Gallagher, is a sophisticated collection of essays on Maurice Merleau-Ponty's work, with several of the contributors comparing him to Derrida and other postmodernist philosophers. Stephen H. Watson's *Extensions: Essays on Interpretation, Rationality, and the Closure of Modernism* (SUNY) analyzes the fate of rationality in Continental philosophy from Kant through Derrida. And in *The High Road Around Modernism* (SUNY) Robert Cummings Neville draws on Charles Sanders Peirce, Alfred North Whitehead, and other philosophers in constructing an alternative to postmodernism, which Neville much too hastily dismisses as a "clever trick": "the ambiance of critique fostered by postmodernism alienates people from culture universally; the message undergraduates take from 'critical theory' is that they do not need to read books, and that rock music wholly supplants any music written before the Beatles."

Social thinkers such as Max Weber and philosophers from Descartes through Rorty figure prominently in Anthony J. Cascardi's *The Subject of Modernity* (Cambridge). Cascardi intelligently discusses numerous features of modernity: the disenchantment of the world, the autonomy of art, secularization, and the subject's relation to the state. His conclusion reinterprets Kant's critique of aesthetic judgment "in an attempt to draw out the postmodern possibilities for positioning subjects with respect to heterogeneous discursive spheres."

Many commentators take an ethical or political approach to modernism and postmodernism. Albert Borgmann's *Crossing the Postmodern Divide* (Chicago) is a clear, thoughtful book. Like many observers, Borgmann feels that while modernism has "lost its theoretical confidence and credibility," postmodernism can offer "no more than the weakest of constructive proposals." We consequently feel stuck between two worlds, one dying and the other unable to remedy the problems we face, the chief problem being that "we live in self-imposed exile from communal conversation and action." "The public square is naked. American politics has lost its soul." Borgmann aims at recovering public life by working through rather than rejecting the postmodernist critique of the truths once thought to be self-evident. While Borgmann's solutions may feel too good to be true, his reflections are both wide-ranging and specific. In this book philosophical thinking retains its connection with everyday life—with layoffs at IBM, for example, and baseball games in Missoula, Montana.

In *The Ennobling of Democracy: The Challenge of the Postmodern Age* (Hopkins), Thomas L. Pangle also thinks American society stands at a historical turning point. He worries about our public life in the face of the threat postmodernism apparently poses to such democratic values as natural human rights. Pangle's chief examples of postmodernism are Heidegger, Lyotard, and Rorty. While acknowledging the insights of their work, Pangle objects to "the civic irresponsibility, the spiritual deadliness, and the philosophic dogmatism of this increasingly dominant trend of thinking." Building on classic Socratic rationalism, Pangle tries to rehabilitate the claims of universal reason. He conducts his argument, however, at a high level of abstraction; his solution is consequently less clear than his neoconservative revulsion from what he sees as "the deepening malaise of American life."

Gianni Vattimo, in *The Transparent Society* (Hopkins), trans. David Webb, is more optimistic about contemporary America (if still cautious). He thinks we live in a postmodern society where the mass media play a decisive role in making life more complex and chaotic. Nevertheless, "it is in precisely this relative 'chaos' that our hopes for emancipation lie." Voicing a question on the minds of many who write about contemporary American culture, Vattimo asks, "Should we counterpose to this world the nostalgia for a solid, unitary, stable and 'authoritative' reality?" His answer is no. With a univocal standard of rationality under attack, ethnic, sexual, religious, and aesthetic minorities are finally getting the chance to speak up for themselves: "They are no longer repressed and cowed into silence by the idea of a single true form of humanity that must be realized irrespective of particularity and individual finitude, transience and contingency."

In one of the best recent books on our current prospects, Charles Taylor in *The Ethics of Authenticity* (Harvard, 1991) argues against the ennervating nostalgia and uncritical optimism that tempt commentators on modernism and postmodernism. Taylor addresses three "malaises of modernity"—that many observers experience as loss or decline—as evidence that modern life has fallen from some better past. These malaises are individualism (which can seem to license self-centered narcissism); the disenchantment of the world and the consequent primacy of instrumental reason; and alienation from public life. In lucid, engaging prose, Taylor writes about "how to steer these developments towards their greatest promise and avoid the slide into debased forms."

Three other books ponder the social as well as intellectual ramifications of postmodernist thought. Thomas McCarthy's *Ideals and Illusions: On Reconstruction and Deconstruction in Contemporary Critical Theory* (MIT, 1991) investigates the limitations of Foucault's genealogy, Rorty's pragmatism, and Derrida's deconstructionism. McCarthy thinks that Habermas's reconstruction of communicative reason offers a way of overcoming the limitations of postmodernism while conserving its strengths. Richard J. Bernstein's *The New Constellation: The Ethical-Political Horizons of Modernity/Postmodernity* (MIT, 1991) brings together his essays on the postmodernism-modernism debate staged by Rorty, Habermas, and other contemporary philosophers. *Between Totalitarianism and Postmodernity* (MIT), ed. Peter Beilharz, Gillian Robinson, and John Rundell, examines the fate of democracy in light of several late-20th-century developments, including the fall of communism, upheavals within Western democracies, and the rise of postmodernist skepticism.

Three books pinpoint the social impact of postmodernism by highlighting its implications for education. William B. Stanley's *Curriculum for Utopia: Social Reconstructionism and Critical Pedagogy in the Postmodern Era* (SUNY) aims at developing a critical pedagogy indebted to the social reconstructionist movement of the 1920s and 1930s and to such postmodernist theorists as Derrida. Similarly, *Postmodernism, Feminism, and Cultural Politics: Redrawing Educational Boundaries* (SUNY), ed. Henry A. Giroux, features essays by several critics interested in bringing postmodernism, modernism, and feminism into a constructive dialogue that will benefit them all. This dialogue will generate "a political and theoretical discourse which can move beyond a postmodern aesthetic and a feminist separatism in order to develop a project in which a politics of difference can emerge within a shared discourse of democratic public life." While I applaud this volume's intentions, the essays become hortatory and redundant. The goals of the contributors—for example, Giroux's dictum that "all schools should have teachers and students participate in anti-racist curricula that in some way link up with projects in the wider society"—are clearer than the means of achieving them. Finally, David W. Orr's *Ecological Literacy: Education and the Transition to a Postmodern World* (SUNY) is a clear attempt to show that a postmodern education must be "life-centered," or responsive to the ecological crisis that grips the globe. Orr includes two chapters advocating ecological literacy as a rejoinder to Allan Bloom's Great Books model of education.

Several books see modernism and postmodernism as multidimensional movements, with cultural, political, and intellectual repercussions. *Beyond Recognition: Representation, Power, and Culture* (Calif.), ed. Scott Bryson et al., posthumously reprints Craig Owens's essays on postmodernism in the visual arts, dance, and literary theory. Paul Mann's *The Theory-Death of the Avant-Garde* (Indiana, 1991) is a thought-provoking meditation on the many difficult questions avant-garde movements have occasioned: for example, can avant-garde artistic and literary movements align themselves with political modes of opposition? has the much-reported death of the avant-garde left anything vital behind? Joseph Natoli's *Mots D'Order: Disorder in Literary Worlds* (SUNY) is an often cryptic attempt to show how literature transforms our ways of seeing through its internal play of order and disorder. In *Social Theory and Psychoanalysis in Transition: Self and Society from Freud to Kristeva* (Blackwell), Anthony Elliott challenges what he sees as the premature dismissal of subjectivity by Lacan and other postmodernist theorists. And in *Deliberate Criticism: Toward a Postmodern Humanism* (Georgia) Stephen R. Yarbrough takes up the seemingly quixotic task of "seeking and articulating *within the discourse of postmodernism* a still center of common experience from which to order the world."

Virtually everyone who writes on postmodernism sooner or later gets around to discussing Jean-François Lyotard and Jean Baudrillard, who, along with Fredric Jameson, dominate consideration of this topic. Two more of Lyotard's works are now available in translation: *The Postmodern*

Explained: Correspondence, 1982–1985 (Minnesota), trans. Don Barry et al., with an afterword by Wlad Godzich; and *The Inhuman: Reflections on Time* (Stanford, 1991), trans. Geoffrey Bennington and Rachel Bowlby. Recent French postmodernists are criticized from a socialist-materialist vantage point in Stuart Sim's *Beyond Aesthetics: Confrontations with Poststructuralism and Postmodernism* (Toronto). Brian Massumi's *A User's Guide to 'Capitalism and Schizophrenia': Deviations from Deleuze and Guattari* (MIT) provides a more sympathetic commentary on two other important French thinkers. Pierre Bourdieu and Loïc J. D. Wacquant's *An Invitation to Reflexive Sociology* (Chicago) focuses on Bourdieu's presentation of his work at the University of Chicago and at the École des hautes études en sciences sociales.

Baudrillard and Lyotard, along with Stanley Fish and Rorty, are the targets of the liveliest book to appear on postmodernism this year, Christopher Norris's *Uncritical Theory: Postmodernism, Intellectuals and the Gulf War* (Mass.). This repetitive, impassioned polemic was set off by an article written by Baudrillard a few days before the outbreak of the Gulf War. Baudrillard predicted that a Gulf War would never take place, that it would be lost in the "hyperreal" media coverage blanketing it. Norris wants not only to vindicate the independent, terrible reality of the war but to argue against what he describes as a complacent postmodern-ist, neopragmatist skepticism that dispenses with politically necessary distinctions between truth and disinformation, fact and fiction. His contempt for postmodernism runs so deep that he has a hard time accounting for its appeal (faddishness, dogmatism, ignorance of contem-porary philosophy, and an end-of-ideology quietism presumably explain the susceptibility of literary intellectuals to postmodernist doubt). Norris strains to exempt Derrida and even de Man from the nihilism that disturbs him; they join Habermas, Noam Chomsky, Terry Eagleton, Said, and other writers in reinforcing the appeal to truth that for Norris underlies political critique. Much of *Uncritical Theory* seems to me hastily written and unconvincing. But Norris rightly holds theorists accountable for their ideas; he takes seriously the impact of theory (however indirect) on our political discourse. He calls on theorists not to stay out of politics but to acknowledge that they are already involved— and to make sure that their discourse is responsible.

The University of New Mexico

i   Italian Contributions: Algerina Neri

Ethnic literature—Native American, Italian-American, Jewish, and His-
panic—seems to attract an increasing number of Italian scholars. This
year's output has not just equaled but surpassed that of last year; still, the
trend has changed. While in 1991 a number of books were collections of
essays from conferences, this year Italian Americanists have preferred to
devote their work to specific authors or periods and to careful translations of contemporary authors and poetry. Americans in Italy and Italians or Italian culture in the United States are never-ending sources of
interest. Even so, the centenary of Melville's death and the 20th anniversary of Pound's take center stage.

a. General Work, Criticism   Brief, penetrating strokes portray Henry
James and Robert Louis Stevenson's unusual friendship and Flannery
O'Connor's secluded, suffering life in the writer and critic Pietro Citati's
Ritratti di donne (Milan: Rizzoli). In his afterword Citati explores how
important are unaccountable details to portray a literary figure and how
much more difficult the literary critic's task compared to a portrait
painter's, and he adds that as the critic's work is a secondhand activity, it
must be entertaining or risk the reader's boredom. This is doubly true, I
think, if one reviews other critics' criticism. However, Italians do not
seem easily bored by criticism. Three of Harold Bloom's works have been
translated into Italian: *Rovinare le sacre verità* (Garzanti), *Il libro di J.*
(Milan: Leonardo), and *I vasi infranti* (Modena: Mucchi), this last with a
useful introduction by Giovanna Franci. Bloom's mentor/antagonist
Northrop Frye has always been much admired by Italian scholars. A
conference on Frye held in Rome in 1987—the proceedings of which

constitute *Ritratto di Northrop Frye* (see *ALS 1989*, p. 424)—the honorary degree awarded him by the University of Bologna, and the Mondello prize (1990) have now been followed by a selection of critical essays, *Reflections on the Canadian Literary Imagination* (Bulzoni), with an introduction by Branko Gorjup and an afterword by Agostino Lombardo. Caterina Ricciardi publishes *Northrop Frye o delle finzioni supreme* (Rome: Empiria) in which, besides two contributions already published (see *ALS 1987*, p. 468, and *ALS 1989*, p. 424), Ricciardi explores Frye's work in relation to T. S. Eliot's and Bloom's.

A more disquieting and provocative work is Alessandro Portelli's *Il testo e la voce: oralità, letteratura e democrazia in America* (Rome: manifestolibri). The book, the author affirms, is offered as "an interpretation of the national American identity through literature and an interpretation of literature through the written and oral foundation of the language." The first part (the voice under the text) shows how unacknowledged orality moves and displaces the certainties of institutions and writing; the second (the voice in the text) studies the impact of orality in literature as far as form of composition, mimesis, and symbolism are concerned; the third part (the text on the voice) traces the way in which word technologies have tried to rebuild language. Portelli's long, meditative, and deep involvement with the subject, the actuality of the issues discussed, and the suggestive proposal to maintain a more dialectic and dynamic approach between the two forms of linguistic communication make this book a stimulating contribution, indeed a conversation in which the reader feels like an active participant. Paola Castellucci traces the effort of expressing silence, expectation, and void in literary production in her *Letteratura dell'Assenza* (Bulzoni). Castellucci tries both to define this interpretative mode and to reconstruct the ongoing process of expressive research in her perceptive analysis of short stories by Edith Wharton, Henry James, William Faulkner, Raymond Carver, and Carmelo Samonà, resulting in stimulating new insights into narrative technique.

Translating has always been both the nightmare and the dream of Italian scholars, either because they have to review doubtful contemporary commercial translations or because they themselves confront the uneasy task of putting Wallace Stevens's and Ezra Pound's poetry into another language. Conferences and discussions attract scholars interested in the activity. Translation is necessary, Agostino Lombardo argues in "Sul tradurre," pp. 35–44 in Rosario Portale, ed., *La traduzione poetica nel segno di Giacomo Leopardi* (Pisa: Giardini), the proceedings of a conference held in Macerata in 1988. Lombardo states that translation is central to the literary life of a country, and the work of the translator must be faithful to the original text and to the translator's language and tradition. While the poet's language is atemporal, the translation remains of its own time. After discussing why and how Pound used translation in "Ezra Pound as Translator of Leopardi" (pp. 79–88), Gabrielle Barfoot points out that Pound's translations of Leopardi were an act of homage to the Italian poet. In "Quelle 'bizzarre imitazioni' di Robert Lowell" (pp. 115–30) Alfredo Rizzardi argues that Lowell's products were neither translations nor imitations but studies, notes, sketches "a la maniere de," even musical variations. In "Traduzioni e recensioni: l'esempio di *Spanking the Maid*," pp. 463–70 in Sergio Perosa et al., eds., *Venezia e le lingue e letterature straniere* (Bulzoni, 1991), Giovanna Covi also discusses the difficult art of translation and objects to the attitude of Italian critics who tend to consider the original texts in their reviews rather than the quality of translation. Taking as an example *Spanking the Maid,* she speaks about the feasibility of translation, drawing on Walter Benjamin's assumption concerning the saying of the unknowable to conclude that translation can be nothing but a continuously evolving attempt.

b. Colonial Literature   None of Sacvan Bercovitch's works had been translated into Italian until his longtime friend Agostino Lombardo convinced him to prepare a volume collecting 11 previously published but newly revised essays, carefully translated by Giovanni Nori in *America Puritana* (Rome: Editori Riuniti). The volume includes material on the colonial period as well as on 19th-century Puritan thought and imagination. The New England Puritans' view of the Indians is discussed, as are those of Maryland Catholics and Virginia Anglicans, in Clara Bartocci's *Gli Inglesi e l'Indiano: Racconto di una invenzione (1580–1660)* (Alessandria: Edizioni dell'Orso). Bartocci's historical and literary criticism, the fruit of long and careful study, traces the image of the Indians through a limited number of texts to conclude that neither the Puritans, Anglicans, nor Catholics ever discovered the native identity, but only invented it in order to celebrate and promote the colonial enterprise. The formation of an American identity is the subject of Itala Vivan's perceptive contribution, "The Other As It Enters the European Text: Birth and Rebirth of the American Gaze" (*Culture* 6:21–38). Vivan shows how "the American gaze was born in the perennial movement to and from Europe, from settlement to wilderness and viceversa, from reality to imagination and once again to reality . . . a process of growth in which the subject can never go back to the same point, nor find what he left or dreamed of." The vicissitudes of a Puritan minister's life among the Indians have fascinated Paola Loreto, who translates and introduces John Williams's *Ritorno a Sion: un pastore puritano tra i Pellerossa 1704–1706* (Bergamo: Lubrina).

Angela Vistarchi has published the work done during a seminar with her students on the American ballad in *Note di un seminario* (Sassari: Centro Stampa Università). After Vistarchi's general introduction to the American ballad and its development, Ferdinando Ledda examines the ballad and the frontier, Susanna Sanna speaks about the adaptation of the ballad to northern and southern ideologies during the Civil War, and Gabriella Ortu about the music in western movies. A well-informed survey of American studies in Italy has been published by Michele Bottalico in "A Place for All: Old and New Myths in the Italian Appreciation of American Literature," pp. 148–60 in Huck Gutman, ed., *As Others Read Us: International Perspectives on American Literature* (Mass.). Bottalico traces the Italian interest in American literature from Cesare Pavese's pioneering work to recent trends; he deplores the translation policies of Italian publishers, although he acknowledges that translation is the only way to make American literature available to a large audience. The American "myth," however, Bottalico concludes, still pervades Italian culture: "myth is, after all, a guide toward and a stimulus for the search for new and unexpected interpretations."

c. 19th-Century Literature   The year has produced new translations with competent introductions, book-length studies, and articles on Poe, Hawthorne, Melville, Twain, James, and Stephen Crane. Poe's letters have been translated by a team of six dauntless female students at the University of Turin after two years of discussion and work under the professional guidance of Barbara Lanati, who has written a stimulating introduction to *Vita attraverso le lettere 1826–1849* (Turin: Einaudi). Poe's personal history, derived from the letters, is his hypothetical life, Lanati argues; this fragmented and contradictory autobiography is at the same time a coherent romance of the self, whose ultimate aspiration and impossible dream was to be his own editor. Poe's complete short stories have been collected in *Tutti i racconti* (Milan: Mursia), with a useful introduction by Ornella De Zordo closely examining the different kinds of Poe stories and his notion of the function of art to build a harmonic and rigorous utopia to oppose to the chaos of life. If there were a gastro-philosophical literary genre, "Bon-Bon," one of Poe's short stories, discussed by Roberto Cagliero's entertaining "His Essays and His Omelettes: Poe a tavola," pp. 398–403 in Maria Grazia Profeti, ed., *Codici del Gusto* (Milan: Franco Angeli), would be a good entry. Through the ironic treatment of gastronomic choices, Poe shows his fastidiousness toward European models and their American emulators in favor of a new national literature. Cagliero also explores the influence of Poe on Joris-Karl Huysmans in "Edgar Allan Poe e la decadenza del pensiero," pp. 9–20 in Elio Mosele, ed., *Joris-Karl Huysmans e l'immaginario decadente* (Fasano: Schena). Huysmans reads Poe through Baudelaire's misreading so that Poe's Huysmans is just a fiction, the result of a fruitful mistake. Paola Zaccaria interprets and questions figures of repetition and stylistic, semantic, and thematic redundancy in Poe's and Samuel Beckett's short fiction in her stimulating *Forme della Ripetizione: Le ipertrofie di Edgar Allan Poe: I deficit di Samuel Beckett* (Turin: Tirrenia). Repetition, Zaccaria argues, points to something unsolved and unutterable which has to be deconstructed through linguistics, psychoanalysis, philosophy, and aesthetics. Starting from these premises, Zaccaria's work, after taking into account the other aspect of repetition—changing and becoming—asserts that Poe's amplification practice and narrative methods make his texts more modern than Beckett's and anticipate authors such as Kafka, Borges, and Henry Berhard.

In his afterword to a new translation of Thoreau's "Civil Disobedience" and "A Plea for Captain John Brown," *Dissobedienza Civile* (Milan: SE Studio Editoriale), Franco Meli explores Thoreau's attitude toward the establishment and possible ways to oppose unacceptable realities like slavery. While John Brown used firearms, Thoreau used words; and in his Transcendentalist idea that individual conscience is supreme, his sense of justice justifies the right to a violent opposition, if necessary. Not the ambiguous representation of reality, but the representation of the ambiguous reality of the world is the starting point of Marina Gradoli's perceptive essay on "L'ambigua presentazione dei personaggi in *The Scarlet Letter*," pp. 175–90 in *Sei tipi di ambiguità III* (Naples: E.S.I., 1991). The continuous shift of positive and negative representations of character and situation, the everchanging point of view enriches the world of the novel and builds up that ambiguity, which suspends our power of judgment. Last year Paola Russo's scholarly book,

Il Bosco delle Ninfe, discussed classical mythology and its connection with historical and Puritan themes. This year another sound contribution comes in Alide Cagidemetrio's *Fictions of the Past.* Hawthorne's *Legends of the Custom-House* and his unfinished romances and Melville's *Israel Potter* are examined "as experiments in writing the past 'anew.'" Although in different ways both writers represent the past as a modern compromise, their works suggest "parallel projects which deny the nationally acclaimed absence of the past . . . and make the American past a past of universal value."

During the Columbus celebration in 1992 the theater of Genoa presented "Ulisse e la balena bianca" (Ulysses and the white whale), written and directed by Vittorio Gassman. Coincidental with the play appeared the volume *Rotte di lettura attorno a "Moby-Dick"* (Genoa: Marietti), gathering various contributions by Italian and American critics. Enrico Groppali discusses the possibility of reading *Moby-Dick* as a theatrical romance; Earl Rovit talks about Melville and the discovery of America; Guido Fink competently discusses the fortunes of *Moby-Dick* as a movie and a theater piece, while Guido Almansi analyzes the use that Gassman makes of *Moby-Dick* in his new production; Edward Rosenberry gives a stimulating political reading of Ahab as a dangerous chief of state; Massimo Bacigalupo provides a poetical introduction in "Al mare, sulle tracce di Eliot e Melville," as well as a useful dictionary and bibliography of the book. Bacigalupo also offers a lively and subtle introduction to his scholarly translation of *Bartleby e altri racconti americani* (Milan: Mondadori). "Tartarus of Maids," one of the short stories included in this selection, is the theme of Gordon Poole's "A Medieval Source of Melville's 'Tartarus of Maids'" (*Annali-Anglistica* 34, i [1991]: 73–80). Poole shows that the most likely literary influence on Melville's writing is Ywain and Gawain, the 14th-century free rendering of Chrétien de Troyes's *Le Chevalier au Leon,* rather than the poem itself. Ruggero Bianchi has edited and introduced the seventh and what should be the last volume of Melville's complete narrative works, although the fourth (*Moby-Dick*) has not come out yet. This year's book is dedicated to *Billy Budd, marinaio: Racconti e frammenti: Diari* (Milan: Mursia). Bianchi's ample introduction, "Ed è subito sera," examines Melville's writing process and structural mode as shown in the short stories and the fragments, then goes on to evaluate the two thoroughly different travel journals. While "Visit to London and the Continent" presents a busy, feverish world, "Visit to Europe and the Levant," is encumbered by the shadow of the immemorable past. "Billy Budd" is read as Melville's last attempt to portray the image of a possible happiness. In *"Billy Budd, sailor:* una storia di omosessualità" (*Nuovi Argomenti* 41:127–30), Francesco Dragosey reduces the narrative to a homosexual story disguised as a sea tale.

Humor in the old Southwest and the life and work of Mark Twain's predecessor Johnson Jones Hooper is examined by Mario L. Togni in "Flush Times/Hard Times in Alabama: Aspetti della vita e dell'opera di Johnson Jones Hooper, umorista dell'Old Southwest (1815–62)" (*Annali di Ca' Foscari* 31:329–55). Twain has always been considered an entertaining author for children, like Swift or Cooper, by the Italian public; bitter remarks and sour meditations about human nature, art, and writing, the themes proposed by several translations published this year, certainly are going to change that image. Besides *L'uomo che corruppe Hadleyburg* (Rome: e/o) and *Appunti sparsi su una gita di piacere* (Florence: Passigli), Giovanni Baldi has offered a good translation with a skillful introduction of *Le avventure di Huckleberry Finn* (Milan: Garzanti), with a foreword by Enzo Giachino. Salvatore Marano proposes *A Double-Barrelled Detective Story, Storia di Doppi e Doppiette* (Rome: Biblioteca del Vascello) in a nice little edition with a lively afterword in which Marano searches for doubles and duplicates. If Marano has been seduced by Twain's ironic treatment of Arthur Conan Doyle and the detective genre, Guido Carboni has been fascinated by Twain's ironic and yet pessimistic attitude toward the debates on evolutionary theories that divided the United States in this period; he translates *Some Learned Fables, Favole Dotte* (Venice: Marsilio), which appears in an attractive bilingual booklet. Carboni has also prepared a lengthy introduction to Mark Twain's life and work in a series meant for the larger public, but it is indispensable to the scholar when it is so able and comprehensive a study as *Invito alla lettura di Mark Twain* (Milan: Mursia). After a thorough presentation of Samuel Clemens's life and times, Carboni discusses the works in depth and adds a critical bibliography.

Henry James has enchanted mostly women scholars this year. Donatella Izzo, an expert on James's world, has collected and translated five short stories about the condition of women in *Rose-Agathe e le altre* (Macerata: liberilibri). Choosing the early 1878 "Rose-Agathe" and moving through the 1909 "Mora Montravers," Izzo skillfully and subtly analyzes James's evolving treatment of women from objects to subjects in Victorian society. Alessandra Contenti also has translated "Rose-

Agathe," although she has presented it as *Dietro la vetrina* (Milan: Tranchida Editori). Contenti's presentation is more attentive to James's re-creation of the Paris of the 1870s and to the comic misunderstanding between the two friends. Another "French" short story, *Gabrielle de Bergerac* (Florence: Passigli), has been presented in a fine edition by Agostino Lombardo, who finds the story enchanting and already presenting the favorite themes of the later James. Lombardo points out how George Sand's name comes immediately to mind while one reads the story. James's admiration of Sand's fluid style and warmth is well-known, as Bianca Tarozzi suggests in her well-balanced book, *Un magnanimo arrendersi alla vita: George Sand vista da Henry James* (Venice: Arsenale). Tarozzi divides the book into James's position toward Sand as a woman and writer, and James's critical appreciation of Sand's works from his 1868 reviews onward. James seemed to have mixed feelings toward this French writer. Although he often criticized Sand's works because they are vague in outline, he was fascinated by her enchanting capability to reproduce the music of places and atmospheres. James's connection with Victorianism is well-known; it is more interesting to explore his escape into modernism and the avant-garde, which is the topic of Sergio Perosa's able essay, "The Case of Henry James: From Victorianism to the Avant-Garde" (*Victorianism in the United States,* pp. 61–75). Perosa shows how James disrupts Victorianism from the inside, combining experimental and revolutionary literary techniques with a sound apprehension of visible reality, in this way bypassing the Decadent Imagination.

Giorgio Mariani has published an original and highly illuminating book on Stephen Crane, *Spectacular Narratives: Representations of Class and War in Stephen Crane and the American 1890s* (Peter Lang). Influenced by Fredric Jameson's thesis on the dialectical relationship that connects mass culture to high culture, Mariani reads *Maggie* and *Red Badge* against the popular genres parodied by Crane, and he explores how Crane differs from the culture industry. At the same time, Mariani shows that Crane's texts embody yet contain the social anxieties of his time, so what appears to be a critique of certain social realities falls prey to ideologies neither more subversive nor more enlightening than those in popular culture that Crane castigates.

d. Americans in Italy/Italy and Italians in America   The image Americans have of Italy has always been a fruitful topic for Italian scholars, and this year the crop seems to be particularly bountiful. This special interest emerges from books, articles, and conferences, organized mostly by the Centro Interuniversitario di Studio sul Viaggio in Italia (C.I.R.V.I.), whose active director, Emanuele Kanceff, publishes a magazine, a special collection of travel books, and conference papers. Joel Barlow's frequent travels to Europe, his composite personality as writer, lawyer, editor, ambassador, and defender of liberty and independence, and his relation to the French Revolution emerges from the agile presentation of Bianca Tarozzi's "Joel Barlow e la Rivoluzione francese," pp. 371–88 in Anna R. Poli et al., eds., *Voyage et Révolution, I: Viaggio, Scrittura, Rivoluzione* (Turin: C.I.R.V.I.). In the same volume Marilla Battilana publishes "An American in Revolutionary Paris: Gouverneur Morris" (see *ALS 1990*, pp. 440–41). Battilana also presents both English and American travelers to Piedmont and Milan in two publications whose texts are harmoniously embellished with old reproductions of engravings, paintings, miniatures, and frescoes of the period: Franco Paloscia, ed., *Il Piemonte dei grandi viaggiatori* (Casale Monferrato: Edizioni Abete, 1991) and Franco Paloscia, ed., *Milano dei grandi viaggiatori* (Casale Monferrato: Edizioni Abete).

Being the first great American writer to visit Italy and use it in his own work, Washington Irving established a whole mode of looking at "picturesque" Italy, a country inhabited by fierce but sometimes likable banditti. This attitude, common in English culture at the time because of Ann Radcliffe's tales, was influential in shaping the 19th-century American image of Italy. Irving and that image are the subjects of Rosella Mamoli Zorzi's "Genova, porta d'incanti e di perigli: i 'banditti' di Washington Irving," pp. 189–202 in Emanuele Kanceff, ed., *Viaggiatori Stranieri in Liguria* (Turin: C.I.R.V.I.). Irving was also the first American writer to visit Sicily (1805), as Gaetano Prampolini points out in his "Washington Irving in Sicilia," pp. 317–34 in Emanuele Kanceff and Roberta Rampone, eds., *Viaggio nel Sud I: Viaggiatori stranieri in Sicilia* (Turin: C.I.R.V.I.). Prampolini skillfully juxtaposes Irving's diary, where he wears the mask of the typical travel writer of his time, and his travel notes to show how much more revealing are the notes. James Fenimore Cooper's diary description of the picturesque Bay of Naples when he reached it in 1829 is the starting point of my "Natura, società, arte nella Campania di James Fenimore Cooper," pp. 531–39 in Emanuele Kanceff and Roberta Rampone, eds., *Viaggio nel Sud II: Verso la Calabria* (Turin: C.I.R.V.I.). More than by the "lazzaroni" and the innumerable Roman remains he never tired of praising, Cooper was seduced by the landscape.

A comparison of that description to the later, more dreamy entry in Cooper's 1838 *Gleanings in Europe: Italy,* and then to the sublimity of the same scene in *The Wing-and-Wing* (1842), where nature is contrasted to the futility of human actions, shows the development of Cooper's ideas and ideals.

Henry P. Leland's *Americans in Rome* is a satirical attack on his countrymen that preceded Twain's famous book, argues Leonardo Buonomo in his "Henry P. Leland's *Americans in Rome* (1863): The Popular Face of the Eternal City According to the American Artist/Ethnographer" (*Annali di Ca' Foscari* 31:7–14). Leland was attentive to the Italian common people, who he thought were the real representatives of that Italian culture and life that he saw rapidly disappearing. A well-documented study of Titian and American artists and writers is discussed by Rosella Mamoli Zorzi in "Titian and XIX Century American Writers" (*Annali di Ca' Foscari* 30 [1991]:173–201). Mamoli Zorzi traces the first copies of Titian that could be seen in the United States, then presents American artists copying Titian, and goes on to discuss the mixed feelings Nathaniel and Sophia Hawthorne had toward Titian's Venuses. The essay concludes with an analysis of the views of Wharton, Pound, and Lowell, among others.

The relation between figurative arts and literature is a controversial issue that Andrea Mariani presents in his concise but sound contribution, "Arte e letteratura: The Pattern Which Connects," pp. 293–98 in Vita Fortunati et al., eds., *Bologna: La cultura italiana e le letterature straniere moderne* (Ravenna: Longo). In his work Mariani follows Gregory Bateson's theory, supporting the idea of the existence of "the pattern which connects," not only through various forms of life and different ways of perceiving beauty, but through various interpretations and expressions of beauty in different forms of art. This also is the starting point of Mariani's fine book, *Il sorriso del fauno: La scultura classica in Hawthorne, Melville e James* (Chieti: Solfanelli). His aim is not so much to explain why writers used classical sculptures in their works, as to identify the consequences of this use. Although the focus is on Hawthorne, Melville, and James, Mariani also reflects thoughtfully on the effect that classical sculpture had on 19th-century American intellectuals generally. F. Marion Crawford, an honorary citizen of Rome, has received deserved and much-awaited attention in Alessandra Contenti's *Esercizi di nostalgia: La Roma sparita di F. Marion Crawford* (Rome: Archivio Guido Izzi). Besides evaluating Crawford as a writer, Contenti carefully and pleasantly reconstructs that Roman world, so dear to the writer who lovingly described every stone of his adopted country, before Italian unification. A 19th-century transatlantic crossing took several weeks of sometimes bad weather or dangerous storms. The Italian actress Adelaide Ristori did not seem to be scared, however, having traveled to the United States four times between 1866 and 1885. In her lively and pleasant presentation, "Ristori on the American Scene" (*Voices in Italian Americana* 3:29–40), Cristina Giorcelli traces Ristori's career, pointing out the features that made her successful and unforgettable to the American public.

The American writer Bernard Malamud's involvement with Italy is completely different. He grew up in Brooklyn and married an Italian-American. Although he visited Italy three times, he left no travelogue or diary, so to discover his impressions, one must read his fiction. *Pictures of Fidelman* and *Dubin's Lives* show what Malamud looked for, color and human warmth, as Marilla Battilana underlines in her lively presentation "L'Italia di Bernard Malamud," pp. 143–59 in *Viaggio nel Sud II*. James Laughlin's reason for visiting Italy was to see Pound in Rapallo and to take advantage of the lesson of the Master, as Rita Severi explains in her essay, "In un altro paese: James Laughlin a Rapallo," pp. 229–40 in *Viaggiatori Stranieri in Liguria*. In addition, Massimo Bacigalupo presents Laughlin in Rapallo and translates some of the poems that Pound sent him, together with some autobiographical pages about his sojourn and his first love in Rapallo (*Poesia* 52:66–73).

e. 20th-Century Prose   In 1990 AISNA published *The City as Text*, a collection of conference proceedings (see *ALS 1990*, p. 438). This year some stimulating papers on the same subject, which were read at another conference in Turin in 1991, have been published as *La città delle donne: l'immaginario urbano nelle letterature di lingua inglese* (Turin: Tirrenia), ed. Marina Bianchi. Besides dealing with Great Britain and other English-speaking countries, the book offers a section about five American women writers. Edith Wharton's use of New York and its mansions as outward signs of their inhabitants' wealth or taste emerges from the three novels that Gianfranca Balestra examines, *The House of Mirth, The Custom of the Country,* and *The Age of Innocence,* in "La città geroglifica di Edith Wharton" (pp. 87–100). The relation between female characters and the city is ambiguous; Wharton does not propose positive models, but only criticizes the devastating social construction of femininity.

Gertrude Stein's and Anaïs Nin's views of Paris are juxtaposed by Barbara Lanati in "Chiaroscuri di una città: Gertrude Stein and Anaïs Nin" (pp. 101–22). Lanati subtly follows the two women's different perceptions of the city—Stein's reduction of her Paris neighborhood to the essentials, Nin's hunger to experience every bit of Parisian life, even houseboat living along the Seine. In "All of Detroit Is Melodrama: Joyce Carol Oates' *Them*" (pp. 123–40), Winifred Farrant Bevilacqua effectively shows how Detroit becomes a maze beyond escape; although the characters try to flee, none is truly able to imagine where to go or what future to create. Following the distinction that Ursula Le Guin made between yang and yin utopia, Daniela Guardamagna suggests the existence of brilliant, rigid, geometric cities as opposed to obscure, harmonic, passive, organic entities in "Geometria e groviglio nelle città di Ursula K. Le Guin" (pp. 141–49).

Giovanna Covi examines the views of New York of several women writers. In "La violenza di New York: mito per Tama Janowitz, denuncia per Kathy Acker," pp. 77–96 in Marina Bianchi, ed., *Sguardi di scrittrici sulle società contemporanee* (Milan: Franco Angeli), Covi stresses Janowitz's illusionary aseptic reportage technique in describing New York and acknowledges Acker's exposition of the cruel and dehumanizing reality of pornography and sexual relations in a postcapitalist society. In "The Islands in New York: Jamaica Kincaid's *Lucy*" (*Culture* 6:37–52), Covi suggests that Kincaid's work makes an important contribution to the current debate among feminist theorists on the related concepts of women and gender. In another interesting contribution, " 'This Sphynx of Countries': il Messico di Katherine Anne Porter" (*LAmer* 41–42 [1990, but published 1992]:31–59), Gabriella Ferruggia, after analyzing the position of American intellectuals toward Mexico in the 1920s, speaks about Porter's three sojourns there. Ferruggia goes on to object to the current interpretation of Porter's "Maria Concepción" (1922) as offering a positive view of Mexico.

An analysis of Stein's techniques as a way to throw light on the whole phenomenon of modernism is Salvatore Marano's aim in *La Rosa senza perché: Gertrude Stein e la scrittura* (Catania: Marino Editore, 1991). Such a task is not easy to achieve, although Marano's concise study is a perceptive introduction to the subject. According to Roberto Serrai, H. P. Lovecraft has never received sufficient recognition in Italy, critics preferring to underline his themes and content rather than his writing techniques. Serrai divides Lovecraft's output into three narrative streams rather than treating it in chronological order in "Howard Phillips Love-craft: da cinquant'anni un 'nome nuovo' (*Il Ponte* 48, xii:91–100). Igina Tattoni has published a full-length scholarly study of Thomas Wolfe, *The Unfound Door: Innovative Trends in Thomas Wolfe's Fiction* (Bulzoni). Born from the need for a better understanding of the experimental trends in Wolfe's fiction and a wish to reevaluate his work, the book shows how some critical attacks on Wolfe's writing techniques can be transformed into evidence of the "mighty innovative effort and unique performance of his writing."

Last year Agostino Lombardo lovingly edited a major contribution to Faulkner studies, *The Artist and His Masks*. This year Faulkner scholar-ship has not been so well-served. However, Mario Materassi, in *Storie di New Orleans* (Milan: Anabasi) translates five early stories where Faulk-ner through the experience of describing the city decides, at Sher-wood Anderson's suggestion, to write about his own piece of territory. Two contributions by Italian scholars have been included in Walde-mar Zacharasiewicz's *Faulkner, His Contemporaries, and His Posterity* (Francke). In "Two Southern Gentlemen and Their Unsavory Upstarts: Verga's Mazzarò and Faulkner's Flem Slopes" (pp. 102–9), Materassi shows how similar the two main characters are, although there is no record that Faulkner ever read Lawrence's translation of Verga. In "Faulkner and a Contemporary Feminist Novel: From Faulkner's *The Bear* to Aritha Van Herk's *The Tent Peg*" (pp. 309–16), Rosella Mamoli Zorzi shows how much this Canadian feminist novel ironically owes to Faulkner's narrative techniques.

The effort and patience of Italian scholars is often required to rescue some good American writing from oblivion. After receiving the Interna-tional Award Chianti Ruffino Antico Fattore in Florence, Peter Taylor, for example, has been well-translated by Gaetano Prampolini, who has collected five of his best and most representative short stories in *L'Antica Foresta* (Rome: e/o). In his attentive afterword Prampolini makes the Italian reader aware of Taylor's complexity and a skill that places him on the level of James and Faulkner. Michele Bottalico has made a fine translation and introduction to Ron Arias's *La strada per Tamazunchale* (Bari: Palomar), which Bottalico finds an interesting example of the cultural stratification that has occurred in a large area of the American Southwest. Other contemporary writers receive modest attention. Don DeLillo is interviewed by Maria Nadotti in "I benefici dell'invisibilità: incontro con Don DeLillo" (*Linea d'Ombra* 77:63–69). Daniela Daniele translates and introduces William Gass's "Esilio" (*Linea d'Ombra* 76:83–93). Marisa Bulgheroni reviews the latest translations of Tom Wolfe's *A caccia della bestia da un miliardo di piedi* (Milan: Leonardo), Norman Mailer's *Il fantasma di Harlot* (Milan: Bompiani), John Updike's *Riposa Coniglio* (Milan: Rizzoli), and Maxine Hong Kingston's *La donna guerriera: Memorie di una gioventù tra i fantasmi* (Rome: e/o) in "Un miliardo di Specchi" (*Indice* 4 [1993]:8), where she critically evaluates contemporary American fiction. In "Esempi di smisuratezza americana" (*Indice* 2:11–12) Guido Carboni reviews recent translations of the work of two cult writers, Robert Pirsig's *Lila* and Thomas Pynchon's *V.*, trying to assess the real "value" of these books. Maria Vittoria D'Amico's close reading of Pynchon's early short stories collected in *Slow Learners* has been published in *Le Matrici dell'Apprendista: I racconti di Thomas Pynchon* (Bari: Adriatica). Through the study of Pynchon's themes in these early works, D'Amico shows how the author adheres to a sort of anarchic faith—that is, an American way to be both democratic and true to authentic literary tradition. Sandro Veronesi's enthusiastic review of Pynchon's *Vineland* in "Thomas Pynchon: *Vineland*" (*Nuovi Argomenti* 40:112–15) shows the high regard he has achieved in Italy.

f. Ethnic Literature   The cultural historian Mario Maffi has composed a fascinating story of the multicultural patchwork of New York's mythical Lower East Side, using literature, cultural anthropology, music, geography, history, urbanism, and gastronomy. *Nel mosaico della città: Differenze etniche e nuove culture in un quartiere di New York* (Milan: Feltrinelli), born out of a 12-year continuously evolving relationship between Maffi and this ever-changing part of New York, is the fruit of long study, research, and direct involvement with a sociocultural microcosm full of creative energy, a laboratory of Americanization and ethnicity. Valuable photographic and iconographic documentation enriches Maffi's passionate work. Although the admitted strategy in Furio Colombo's *La città profonda* (Milan: Feltrinelli) is that of a Baedeker guidebook, the interesting feature of Colombo's volume is his repressed yet obvious love for New York.

Not New York, Paris, or Tokyo but the red earth is the center of the world for the Creek poet Joy Harjo, as she affirms in the opening poem of her collection *Segreti dal centro del mondo* (Urbino: Quattroventi). This slim, well-prepared volume combines Harjio's poetry, Stephen Strom's pictures of Navajo country, and Laura Coltelli's fine translation and her afterword, which dwells on the secrets that govern the Indian world and the dialogue that both poet and photographer have with the earth. Coltelli and Gaetano Prampolini also edit Indianamericana, a series of Native American, mainly contemporary narrative works carefully translated with useful afterwords and published by La Salamandra in Milan. D'Arcy McNickle's *L'accerchiamento* has been translated by Giancarlo Baccelli with a cogent afterword by Marina Gradoli, who shows how McNickle (Cree and Scottish-Irish) was one of the first writers to explore the complex fate of the half-bloods who try to reconcile two cultures. In *Parolefrecce,* a collection of short stories in four parts translated by Lucia Ponzini, Gerald Vizenor (Chippewa and French) is in the same privileged but trying position. Maria Vittoria D'Amico perceptively traces Vizenor's word-arrows that move in four directions to illustrate the shifting condition of the Chippewa from being masters of their own land to their present condition; she stresses Vizenor's realistic, acute, postmodern, cultured use of language. A minute and passionate tracing of Kiowa cultural roots is the basis of *I Nomi* by N. Scott Momaday, the best-known and first American Indian writer to be translated into Italian. Laura Coltelli has provided the translation of Momaday's second autobiography, where childhood recollections in a culturally and linguistically assimilated American family coexist and clash with Kiowa traditions and Indian imagination, as Coltelli points out in her competent afterword. Coltelli also edits *Native American Literatures 2* (Pisa: Servizio Editoriale Universitario). Following the procedure established in the first issue, this number gathers an original unpublished poem by Paula Gunn Allen, exchanges of ideas and perspectives between American and European scholars (Helen Jaskoski on narrative art in a Hopi tale, Louis Owens on cultural survival in John Joseph Mathews's *Sundown,* Bernadette Rigal-Cellard on the prologue of *House Made of Dawn,* Elaine A. Jahner on literary analysis in the wake of the "Ten Cent Treaty"), and interviews focusing on Momaday's *The Ancient Child* by Prampolini and on Vizenor's *Heirs of Columbus* by Coltelli. In "I viaggi di Aby Warburg tra gli Indiani Pueblos," pp. 215–29 in Elemire Zolla and Marina Maymone Siniscalchi, eds., *Il Bosco Sacro: Percorsi iniziatici nell'immaginario artistico e letterario* (Foggia: Bastogi), Fedora Giordano shows the importance of German art historian Warburg's 1895 travels among the Pueblo Indians for his successive elaboration of the iconographic method.

After her collection of 20 Chicano poets, *Sotto il Quinto Sole* (see *ALS*

1990, p. 449), Franca Bacchiega continues to present and translate Chicano writers. Alberto Alvaro Rios's bitter and disquieting story *The Child* has been translated and introduced in "Varcando la frontiera" (*Città di Vita* 47:261–74). Some of the problematic poems of Bernice Zamora have been presented in "Bernice Zamora: una donna fra le resurrezioni," pp. 140–58 in *Si Scrive* (Cremona: Amministrazione Provinciale). The difficult experience of being born in Mexico and living in Texas and of writing in two languages makes Angela de Hoyos's poems particularly sensitive to interracial differences, as Anna Santoliquido notes in "Poesia dall'estremo Ovest: Angela de Hoyos," pp. 36–46 in Santoliquido's *Stelle Zingare* (Bari: Editrice La Vasilia).

This year there has been only one African American contribution; however, it is an outstanding one. Marisa Bulgheroni and Chiara Spallino have lovingly given to the press Zora Neale Hurston's *Tre quarti di dollaro dorati* (Venice: Marsilio), a bilingual collection of three short stories—"Sweat," "The Gilded Six-Bits," "Story in Harlem Slang." Spallino has translated Hurston's language, full of African American idioms and slang, besides giving a biographical sketch of the writer; in her foreword, "Zora Neale Hurston: tre volte nera," Bulgheroni examines Hurston's achievement through a close reading of these stories.

Studies about Italian-American writing, on the other hand, have unexpectedly received more attention than usual. Besides a useful critical bibliography by Cosma Siani (*L'Indice* 5:19–27), Paolo Valesio discusses the position of Italian-American writers in "Lo scrittore fra i due mondi: osservazioni sulla scrittura italiana negli Stati Uniti," pp. 105–20 in the second volume of Vita Fortunati et al., eds., *Bologna: La cultura italiana e letterature straniere moderne* (Ravenna: Longo). In the first volume of the same publication Raffaele Cocchi traces the career and life of a Bolognese woman who migrated to the United States in 1902 and wrote in order to survive, in "Rosa Zagnoni Marinoni: From the Bolognese Hills to the Ozarks" (pp. 313–21). In "A Progress Report on the Orality of Sardinian Migration to America" (*Victorianism in the United States*, pp. 198–205), Lina Unali explains the different steps that Franco Mulas and she are undertaking to record the Sardinian migrants' experience in the United States. The return of a second-generation Italian to Sicily just after World War II is Jerre Mangione's subject in *Riunione in Sicilia* (Palermo: Sellerio), competently and carefully translated by Maria Anita Stefanelli.

Memories of their origins and a desire to become indistinguishable are the poles between which Jewish-American writers' feelings shift when they leave the oppression of Europe and meet the American dream of liberty. In *Memoria e desiderio* (Turin: UTET) Giodano De Biasio traces the great Jewish migration at the beginning of the 20th century, and through a clear analysis of autobiographies, stories, and novels he focuses on the crucial moment that gives birth to Jewish-American literature. In the second part of the book De Biasio offers interesting readings of Henry Roth, Bellow, Malamud, and Philip Roth. In his short but sound contribution, "La presenza ebraica nella letteratura americana" (*Il Ponte* 48:150–62), Mario Materassi questions what Jewish-American literature is, and he suggests that it be called literature of American Jews. After an analysis of the various generations of Jews and their literary output, Materassi affirms that American pragmatism is now dissolving the basic conditions of the Diaspora that had kept it alive for thousands of years. While translating *Il Messia di Stoccolma* (see *ALS 1991*, p. 443), Materassi interviewed Cynthia Ozick on how she became a writer, who were her masters, and what prompted her to write the book; he records her responses in "Imagination Unbound: An Interview with Cynthia Ozick" (*Salmagundi* 94–95:85–111). In "Parlami di Mauschwits" (*Indice* 3 [1993]:4) Guido Fink declares that Art Spiegelman's *Maus* (Milan: Rizzoli) is a great American Jewish book, the like of which has not been seen for some time. Gabriella Morisco chooses to review critical works and articles on Malamud published in the United States from 1970 to 1988 in "Bernard Malamud e la critica anglo-americana negli anni Ottanta" (*Il Lettore di Provincia* 82 [Dec. 1991]:99–104).

g. 20th-Century Poetry and Drama   Twenty years after his death, Ezra Pound is still the object of special interest in his adopted country. This year, besides a huge exhibition held at the Museum of Modern Art of Bolzano which opened in 1991, a large number of books have been devoted to him. The works gathered at Bolzano were by artists associated with him from the beginning of the century to the 1950s as well as by more recent artists influenced by him, and the collection testifies to the respect in which he was held. A rich catalogue, *Beauty is Difficult: Homage to Ezra Pound* (Milan: Scheiwiller, 1991), was provided by Vanni Scheiwiller and Rossana Bossaglia. Pound's friendships, discoveries, and disillusions within the Parisian expatriate community in the early 1920s were recorded in his correspondence for the New York *Dial*, now translated and carefully annotated by Marina Premoli in *Lettere da Parigi 1920–1923* (Milan: Archinto). During his stay in Paris, Pound made several trips to Italy, mainly to Romagna to study Sigismondo Malatesta, the principal character of the first *Cantos,* composed in Paris. Pound's love for Romagna and "the stones of Rimini" is celebrated in a collection of poetry, *Il cielo del Tempio: Un libro di pietra per il Malatestiano e per Ezra Pound* (Ravenna: Essegi, 1991) by Luca Cesari and others, with reproductions of paintings on slate by Massimo Pulini. The artists cherish Pound for his inexhaustible textual dexterity, for his unrelinquished will to oppose the status quo, and for the stimulation he offers. The writer and artist Tonino Guerra certainly shares these attitudes; his *L'albero dell'acqua* (*dedicato soprattutto a Ezra Pound*) (Milan: Scheiwiller), ed. Luca Cesari, gathers a series of fresh evocations of Pound based on visits to the Malatesta sites and an extraordinary imitation of the Canto dell'Usura in the dialect of the Romagna. These books, together with the 1991 output, have been expertly reviewed by Massimo Bacigalupo in "Pound in terra santa" (*Indice* 11:13). Bacigalupo has also introduced a small book, Ezra Pound's *Prologo di Natale* (Milan: Scheiwiller), trans. Elio Fiore. In his perceptive foreword, Bacigalupo dwells on the various themes of the work, which can be read as a "prologue" to Pound's output, "immense in its ramifications but simple and unified in its fundamental trends." The literary magazine *Leggere* publishes an interesting interview with Pound that the filmmaker Pier Paolo Pasolini made for Italian television in 1970 in "Due vite violente" (*Leggere* 43:14–23).

The publication of Andrea Mariani's "Da *Divine Commedie* e altre poesie" (see *ALS 1991,* p. 445) prompted Bacigalupo to discuss some of James Merrill's poems (*Poesia* 56:67–69). In a later issue (58:36–41) Ermanno Krumm and Bacigalupo present Wallace Stevens's *The Auroras of Autumn,* translated by Nadia Fusini as *Aurore d'Autunno* (Milan: Garzanti). Fusini and Bacigalupo seem to be playing Ping-Pong. In 1986 Bacigalupo offered *Il Mondo come meditazione: Ultime Poesie 1950–1955* (see *ALS 1986,* p. 464); the following year Fusini published *Note verso la funzione suprema* (see *ALS 1987,* p. 474); then Bacigalupo edited *L'angelo necessario* (see *ALS 1988,* p. 525); now Fusini presents this competent bilingual translation of a difficult collection of poetry to the Italian public, which as a result has different volumes at its disposal as a means of entering into Stevens's world. Although Fusini insists in her helpful and cogent introduction that Stevens's verses are prosaic, the poetry is still a challenge to most readers. A more approachable collection, James Dickey's *Elmetti* (Florence: Passigli), is offered by Franca Bacchiega, who

presents this bilingual translation with her usual finesse. In her perceptive introduction, Bacchiega, a poet herself, points out Dickey's originality and subtle celebration of life.

In "Una parte per il tutto: 'The Corn Harvest' di William Carlos
Williams," pp. 271–81 in Vita Fortunati, ed., *Bologna: La cultura e le
letterature straniere moderne, II* (Ravenna: Longo), Cristina Giorcelli
argues that nature is the depository of the world's energies both for
Brueghel and for Williams; seasons, the details of the painting, the part
that is the emblem of the whole, must flow back to nature. In "Il
paesaggio nella poesia di Elizabeth Bishop," pp. 209–311 in the same
volume, Gabriella Morisco dwells on the authentic relation that many
American painters and writers, Bishop among them, have with the
environment. Paola Zaccaria devotes a paper to Gyn-ecology, the science
which describes the process of women's self-knowledge. In "Dal testo
misogino al testo gin-ecologico," pp. 497–516 in Andrea Milano, ed.,
Misoginia: La donna vista e malvista nella cultura occidentale (Rome:
Edizioni Dehoniane), Zaccaria affirms that Gyn-ecology is the world of
women who live, love, and build their own selves and their world,
discussing Robin Morgan's "The Network of the Imaginary Mother" as
an example. The same poem from Morgan's *Lady of the Beasts* is analyzed
in depth as the journey that a woman's conscience makes to discover the
divine within her in "Ragnatele e tele: Figure della nascita di un io
femminile in 'The Network of the Imaginary Mother' di Robin Morgan"
(*Il Lettore di Provincia* 84:61–74). In "The Metamorphoses of Hermes:
On Italo Calvino's *Six Memos*—Towards a Reading of American Poetry"
(*Strathclyde Modern Language Studies* 9 [1991]:54–56), Maria Anita Stefanelli applies Calvino's *Six Memos* to poetry reading. Hermes (mobility,
change, communication), hidden in Calvino's text where he controls the
author's writing as well as the reader's activity, is also an overwhelming
presence in American poets whom Calvino admired, such as Eliot, Frost,
and Stevens. The magic power of Hermes is to enable infinity to be
contained in the finite mind during the process of reading.

Very sound are the only two contributions this year devoted to
American drama. In "O'Neill e la problematicità del canone" (*Quaderni
di Lingue e Letterature* [Verona] 17:27–33), Roberto Cagliero asks why
Anna Christie was not published with O'Neill's consent in *Nine Plays*
(1932). Cagliero explains this exclusion from the canon as the writer's
temporary hesitancy about the possibility of writing tragedy. In " 'London, Texas': gli elementi pinteriani nel teatro di Sam Shepard" (*Il

Confronto Letterario 15:211–25), Marco Francioni studies the influence of Pinter's *The Homecoming* on Shepard's *Buried Child* and *True West*. Although Francioni finds several similarities between the two writers, he also notes that Shepard appears to have a more constructive attitude toward the external world—a world that can be dangerous but also the object of desire. The continuous shift from the internal world (the room) to the external one (the wilderness) is a metaphor of the self, continuously moving from one identity to another. As in Kerouac's *On the Road,* Shepard's true goal is movement itself.

University of Pisa

ii Japanese Contributions: Hiroko Sato

One pleasure of reviewing achievements in the study of American literature is to encounter stimulating articles by young scholars. To find great scholars still active after retirement, though, gives me just as much pleasure. This happy experience occurred with Kenzaburo Ohashi's *Koten Amerika Bungaku o Kataru* [Talking about classic American literature] (Nanundo). Therefore, I begin my review with homage to his book, although the usual chronological pattern of this chapter will be interrupted.

Ohashi clearly chose his title with D. H. Lawrence's book in mind. This volume consists of six chapters, each treating a great literary figure of the 19th century: Poe, Hawthorne, Melville, Whitman, Henry James, and Mark Twain. Ohashi's stance is similar to that of Lawrence; the American literature of the past is far more attractive than that of today because it represents "new feelings," such as the idea of freedom, the escape from any kind of bondage, and the idea of the radical self, which form the basis of what is distinctive about the United States. Ohashi rereads the works of 19th-century masters in terms of the present disrupted situation of American writing. He is strongly aware of how recent literary criticism has treated classic works, and he regards this treatment as a kind of dissection that sometimes robs them of their charm. So he tries to restore the original works, all the while appreciating the contributions *some* new literary theories have made to interpretation. However, Ohashi's principal purpose seems to be to show readers the energy and beauty of the works of these masters by recounting how he himself has read them. He believes that in doing so America's strength can be conveyed.

Another book that should be mentioned is *Kawa no Amerika Bungaku* [The river in American literature] (Nanundo), ed. Keiko Beppu and Taijiro Iwayama. This collection of essays by 15 scholars in the Kansai area begins in Washington Irving's Sleepy Hollow, then follows the river through Poe, Melville, Whitman, Hart Crane, Twain, Hemingway, and Faulkner, and into Toni Morrison's Ohio River and Joyce Carol Oates's fictional Eden River. Most of the essays regard rivers as a symbol of the Edenic ideals prevalent in American literature. Among these essays, Keiko Beppu's extensive introduction to the book, Nobunao Matsu-yama's discussion of Poe's rivers as passageways to the Garden, and Atsuko Furomoto's analysis of Toni Morrison's concept of the river as memory seem to be the most stimulating.

Before reviewing this year's other achievements, I note that the articles examined will be restricted to those in the major Japanese periodicals— *Eigo Seinen, Studies in English Literature, Chu-Shikoku Studies in American Literature,* and the *American Review.* Unless otherwise indicated, all books were published in Tokyo.

a. 19th-Century Prose Two outstanding studies of the period's intellectual history have been published, one a book, the other a series of eight articles in *EigoS:* Toshio Yagi's *Amerikan Goshikku no Suimyaku* [The lineage of American gothic] (Kenkyu-sha) and Masayuki Sakamoto's "Poe, Hawthorne, Emerson—An Attempt at Intellectual History" (*EigoS* 138:20–21, 79–81, 134–35, 184–86, 233–35, 294–95, 354–55, 409–11). Through an examination of such works as William Bradford's *Of Plymouth Plantation,* documents concerning the Salem witch trials, and Jonathan Edwards's writings, as well as those of Charles Brockden Brown, Poe, Hawthorne, and Melville, Yagi tries to clarify the characteristics of American Gothic and compare them with that tradition in England. Yagi points out that the vector of English Gothic is to the outside, while that of the United States moves inward. Consequently, Yagi contends, Puritan documents of the colonial period can be read as a kind of Gothic romance. Sakamoto tries to find the common threads among the three literary men in his title through a close textual examination of Poe's "Ligeia," Hawthorne's "Rappaccini's Daughter," and Emerson's *Journal.* Their shared ideas about beauty, nature, death, and eternity are made clearer through juxtaposition with the period's general tendencies.

Indeed, Hawthorne seems to have attracted many younger scholars this year in which six articles appeared in major periodicals. Yoko Tsujimoto's "The Gender Conflict: A Study of *The Scarlet Letter*" (*SALit* 29:19–33) is a feminist reading of the novel. Tsujimoto investigates the half-veiled gender bias that Hawthorne fictionalizes and points out that, while Hawthorne worships maternity, he secretly protects male authority by keeping for himself men's privilege of manipulating words to their own advantage. Yuichi Takeda regards Hester's discourse "in the forest" as an aberration, just like her original deed of adultery; in "The Allegory of Silence: Speech Act in *The Scarlet Letter*" (*SELit* 69:63–76), Takeda takes it to be a subversive speech act that disordered the Puritan norm. Ryoichi Okada's "A Drama about Pearl: A Study of *The Scarlet Letter*" (*EigoS* 138:106–10) attempts to place Pearl in the center of the novel, using an identification of Julian Hawthorne with Pearl as the key. How Hawthorne treated Transcendentalism is examined in Masahiko Narita's "New England's Buried Life: The Transcendental Spirit in Hawthorne's *The House of the Seven Gables*" (26:185–200). Narita says that because Transcendentalism is a product of New England, Hawthorne's native soil, the philosophy seemed to him to be a revitalization of New England's buried life. Satomi Saito's "Narrative Structure of *The Blithedale Romance*" (*SALit* 29:35–51) deals with the questions of the narrator and with textual interpretation, Saito insisting that interpretation consists of a double dialectic between the reader and the text. Computer graphics come into the reading of literary text in Kazuko Uda's "Reading 'Wakefield' by Fractal" (*EigoS* 137:514–16, 569–72), an interesting attempt to read the story using the concept of fractional dimension. Although the idea seems new and fascinating, the result is not wholly convincing. It is appropriate to be interested in Hawthorne, but I suspect the desire to try out new critical theories mostly for their own sake lies behind this sudden enthusiasm.

Yoshitaka Niizeki tries to clarify the function of the "Symphony" chapter in *Moby-Dick* in "The Reader's Composition of 'The Symphony'—Function of Chapter 132 in *Moby-Dick*" (*SALit* 29:53–70). Employing Roland Barthes's ideas of "proiaretic code" and "symbolic field," Niizeki asserts that the reader will be able to compose "The Symphony" through his understanding of the binary opposition between the sequential and the intertextual. Along with Barthes, René Girard is one of the most influential theorists among young Japanese scholars. Keiko Nishiyama analyzes two stories by Poe using Girard's concept of a triangular relationship among the subject, the object, and the mediator in "The Double and Death in Poe's 'William Wilson' and 'The Man of the Crowd' " (*SALit* 29:1–17).

Hirotsugu Inoue's *Henry Thoreau Kenkyu* [A study of Henry Thoreau] (Kirihara-shoten) is an ambitious attempt to "capture" Thoreau, whose elusiveness has long tormented scholars. Inoue discusses Thoreau's views on the earth, rivers, oceans, history, and labor. He also refers to Thoreau's attitude toward Christianity, his prose style, and his relationships with the Concord literary world. This effort to describe Thoreau as a living presence is not fully successful, but nonetheless impressive. Makoto Nagahara's *Mark Twain o Yomu* [Reading Mark Twain] (Kyoto: Yamaguchi-shoten) is a fruit of Nagahara's 40 years' study of Twain's novels. The writer's deep interest in Twain and his careful reading of the texts in their social context are admirable.

b. 19th-Century Poetry   Two books on Emily Dickinson were published almost simultaneously: Masayuki Sakamoto's *Kotoba to Eien— Emily Dickinson no Sekai Sozo* [Words and eternity: The creation of Emily Dickinson's world] (Kenkyu-sha) and Takao Furukawa's *Dickinson no Shiho no Kenkyu* [A study of Dickinson's poetics] (Kenkyu-sha). Sakamoto's book takes the form of a biography of the poet and tries to show how she came to create her own sanctuary in the world of her imagination. Sakamoto places Dickinson in the social context of the New England of her time and asserts that the idea of "true womanhood," which was prevalent in the society in which Dickinson lived, must have had a strong, though negative, impact on her. Furukawa's study, based on his doctoral dissertation, takes a different approach. His interest in Dickinson centers on the structure of her artistic rather than her social world. Furukawa terms Dickinson's world as "layered," a structure in which love, poetry, God, and death are simultaneously connected. This framework induces various readings of her poetry. Midori Asahina's "Emily Dickinson and 'Letter to a Young Contributor' " (*EigoS* 137:598– 602) examines the influence of Thomas Wentworth Higginson's 1863 essay in the *Atlantic Monthly* on the poet. Asahina tries to find the reason why Dickinson, after having read the article, called herself Higginson's "scholar" and why she tried to find her identity in that submissive status. Kuniko Yoshizaki's *Whitman—Jidai to tomoni Ikiru* [Whitman: Living in his time] (Kaibun-sha) attempts to read *Leaves of Grass* in a feminist mode. Through the analysis of "One's Self I Sing" and the Preface to the first edition, Yoshizaki asserts that Whitman was the first American "feminist" poet, one who tired to liberate women both physically and mentally.

c. 20th-Century Prose   In his *1920 Nendai Amerika Bungaku—Hyoryu no Kiseki* [American Literature in the 1920s: Traces of drifting] (Kenkyusha), Shuji Muto summarizes the spirit of the time as "drifting" and indicates how such writers as Fitzgerald, Cather, O'Neill, Hemingway, Dos Passos, and Hart Crane reacted to that tendency. The relationship between literature and the American economic system is specifically treated in two articles, Kiyohiko Murayama's "Recovering Dreiser's Criticism of Capitalism" (*American Review* 26:165–83) and Nobuo Kamioka's "*The Great Gatsby* and Three Economic Systems" (*EigoS* 138:210–14). Through an analysis of *Sister Carrie* and *The Bulwark,* especially, Murayama attempts to reestablish Dreiser's criticism of capitalism as a highly important part of his writings, although that criticism caused a lifelong contradiction within the author. It has been pointed out that Gatsby's dream features two contradictory elements—materialism and spirituality. Kamioka considers this dilemma by discussing three economic systems in America—those of the West, the South, and the East—and points out how the overlapping of these systems can be regarded as the cause of Gatsby's confusion and destruction.

Problems of neighborhood and ethnicity are the central theme of David R. Mayer's *Door Stoops and Windowsills: Perspectives on the American Neighborhood Novel* (Kyoto: Yamaguchi-shoten), a sequel to Mayer's *The American Neighborhood Novel* (reviewed in *ALS 1986*). This time the locales considered extend from Chicago to New York, from Oakland and Seattle to Pittsburgh, while the racial groups include Italians, Japanese, and African Americans as well as Irish and Jews. Mayer uses the concept of "neighborhood" tactfully to capture the elusive elements of ethnic literature. This is a solid scholarly work, based on sociological and historical perspectives. Jewish myth and history are taken up in Reiko Sugisawa's "From History to Narrative: A Study of Bernard Malamud's *The Fixer* and *God's Grace*" (*SALit* 29:71–89). Applying Mircea Eliade's discussion of cosmos and history to these novels, Sugisawa traces Malamud's transition from belief in history to a return to the narrative world so as to save humanity from the terror of history.

Attention also should be paid to three studies of women writers. In

"Paintings as Sources in *The Golden Apples*" (*SELit* 69:77–90), Naoko F. Thornton notes that Eudora Welty has often characterized her own perception and creative process as visually oriented. Thornton points out that *The Golden Apples* is a remarkable example of how nonverbal art can contribute to literature in the hands of a perceptive writer. Hajime Noguchi's *Flannery O'Connor Kenkyu* [A study of Flannery O'Connor] (Bunkashobo) is a study of O'Connor's literature through biography and thematic analysis. Noguchi reveals some new biographical facts about O'Connor's Iowa days—products of his own research in Iowa City—and then goes on to deal with O'Connor's use of "the double" and her interest in music. Although the individual chapters seem unrelated, this volume will be helpful to students. Maki Tonegawa's "Toni Morrison's Exploration of the Relational Self in *Sula* and *Beloved*" (*SALit* 29:91–106), written in English, is an interesting study of the 1993 Nobel Prize winner's novels. Focusing on the mother/daughter relationships in these two novels, Tonegawa tries to read *Sula* as an embryonic form of *Beloved*.

The psychoanalytical method is employed in Hitomi Nakatani's "Reading Reading—Vladimir Nabokov's *Pale Fire* (1962)" (*SELit* English no.:61–74). Nakatani says that the act of reading *Pale Fire* can be called "reading reading"; it is like reading Freud's model of the human psyche. Through this manner of reading, Nakatani indicates that an unexpected bridge between Freud and Jung is suggested. Psychological issues in Steve Erickson's novels are also featured in Yoshiaki Koshikawa's "'Power' in Literature—Reading Steve Erickson" (*EigoS* 138:326–30). Citing mainly *Rubicon Beach* and *Days Between Stations,* Koshikawa observes the relation between stuttering and suppression by "power." Many in the Japanese reading public encounter Clyde Edgerton's name for the first time in Hajime Sasaki's essay, "Clyde Edgerton: The Recitor of North Carolina" (*EigoS* 138:118–20).

d. 20th-Century Poetry and Drama   The year produced only a few studies in this field. Seikichi Hara's introductory article on Gary Snyder, "The Poet Who Came from Turtle Island—Gary Snyder" (*EigoS* 137:567–68), was the only item on modern poetry. Atsushi Katayama's "The Poetic Feeling of O'Neill as a Playwright" (*EigoS* 138:60–62) examines O'Neill's poems and letters of the 1910s and traces the connection between the romantic feelings expressed there and in his later plays. Konomi Ara takes up Charles Johnson's *Middle Passage* in "'Republic' Bound for the *Middle Passage*" (*American Review* 26:109–24). Ara follows the changes in the treatment of black history by African American writers and points out that Johnson makes use of black experiences in American society not for protest but for growth and affirmation.

e. American Studies   More and more literary scholars are employing interdisciplinary approaches, using literary works as their text. In Koji Ohi's "Harriet Monroe and the Chicago Exposition" (*EigoS* 138:8–10), for instance, the architectural design of the buildings at the Exposition, Monroe's long poem *The Columbian Ode*, and Frederick Jackson Turner's pessimistic essay on the disappearance of the American frontier are juxtaposed to illustrate the course the United States took after the event. Shoko Ito's "The Disappearance and the Presence of the American Eagle" (*EigoS* 138:54–58) is an interesting study of the bird as the symbol of American spirituality. Referring to works by Emerson, Thoreau, Hawthorne, and Melville, Ito closely follows the secularization of the symbol through the industrialization of the country. Hiroko Sato's lengthy study of American women and the widening of their consciousness from colonial times to the end of the 19th century, "The Lineage of the American Girl," which began to appear in *EigoS* in April 1991, is concluded in the December 1992 issue. With the popularity of New Historicism and a cultural materialistic approach in criticism, interdisciplinary studies of American literature are likely to become even more popular.

Tokyo Woman's Christian University

iii Scandinavian Contributions: Jan Nordby Gretlund, Elisabeth Herion-Sarafidis, and Hans Skei

Scandinavian work in American literature this year ranges widely, but most of the scholarship is still devoted to 20th-century literature, with an obvious emphasis on fiction. This predominance is also manifest in the year's two impressive surveys of contemporary developments in American literature. There also are book-length studies on John Gardner's achievement, Robert Coover's short fiction, and Flannery O'Connor's novels. Gardner's name comes up again in connection with his debate with William Gass. Hemingway's reputation and influence in Norway and Sweden are the subjects of two essays, and as usual William Faulkner has received due attention. There are essays on Walker Percy's Catholicism, Carson McCullers's prose style, Truman Capote's light-footed novel, *Breakfast at Tiffany's,* and on one of Eudora Welty's first stories. Of the African American writers, only Alice Walker and Paule Marshall have been written about this year. There is an essay on Saul Bellow's American Jewish theme, and one on Thomas Pynchon's shortest novel, *The Crying of Lot 49.* Of recently popular writers, the most attention has been paid to Paul Auster. Auster is mentioned almost as often as Hawthorne, who seems to serve as a permanent reference point. And James Fenimore Cooper, who has always been a Scandinavian favorite, is discussed primarily for his view of man's place in the virgin wilderness. Other Scandinavian concerns in 19th-century American letters are diaries and journals by southern women, travel narratives by women, and also literary work by Scandinavian immigrants. Except for translations of Emily Dickinson's poetry, no publication this year deals with the poetry of that century, but essays on modern American poetry do appear. The growing European interest in the poetry of Wallace Stevens and Randall Jarrell is reflected in two studies. In Denmark there is also a growing interest in the development and impact of contemporary American critical theory, marked by several essays, primarily on deconstructionist critics Harold Bloom and Geoffrey Hartman.

a. 19th-Century Prose   In "Authority in Fenimore Cooper's *The Path-finder*" (*AmerSS* 24:97–109) Domhnall Mitchell gives a close reading of some aspects of this novel, emphasizing its interest in social status within an American democratic framework. The hypothesis is that "the concern with antithetical orders of authority arises as much from cultural consid-erations as literary ones." Mitchell uses Balzac's reaction to the novel as a starting point for a discussion of the portrayal of the French and British characters, before engaging in a closer scrutiny of the heroes and the villains. Disagreeing with Balzac, Mitchell finds that it is not Sanglier but Lieutenant Muir who is the principal antagonist, the most important rivalry being that between Muir and the Pathfinder. Included in the article is a detailed and interesting discussion of the use of nature in the novel, and the way in which Eden is suggested there as a kind of Paradise Regained. Cooper's text is finally described as "an act of homage to the first errand into the wilderness of the New World as well as a tacit legitimization of the material side of America's future pioneering power."

Clara Juncker's "Southern Diamonds: The Diaries of Ella Gertrude Clanton Thomas, Floride Clemson, Margaret Sloan, and Magnolia Le Guin" (*MissQ* 45:201–11) is an essay-review of recently published diaries and journals by southern women. Their entries span the years 1848 to 1913 and offer a contemporary view of "historic events," ranging from the Civil War to a baby's first tooth. It is the South's isolation from the literary establishment that made it a fertile area for self-narratives not written for publication, Juncker asserts. She sees the four "women-authored journals" as occupying "a particularly provocative position within the destabilization of metaphysical notions of self-presence." And she argues that despite the simplicity and immediacy of the diaries, the authors practiced literary techniques characteristic of fiction, which today "invite de-coding and deconstruction."

Anka Ryall's "Domesticating Geographical Exploration: Fredrika Bremer's American Travel Narrative" (*AmerSS* 24:24–36) presents the Swedish author's well-known book *Hemmen i den nya världen* [Homes of the New World] in a new context. As the title indicates, Ryall investigates this travel narrative form in relation to the genre, which here is "domesticated," and relates the use of the form, in turn, to Bremer's experience as a writer of popular novels and to her role as a woman. Drawing on her knowledge of travel accounts, especially by women writers of the 19th century, Ryall invokes modern feminist criticism, which enables her to consider the ways in which Bremer is guided by the narrative model—with its obvious ideal of heroic individualism—and the ways in which she is not. Since Bremer's travels in the New World simply take her from home to home, the experience of the new and exciting becomes less heroic. That adventurous experience and domestic ideals do not go too well together, Ryall demonstrates convincingly.

In "Literary Milieus in a Swedish-American Community," pp. 110–31 in *Swedish Life in American Cities,* ed. Dag Blanck and Harald Runblom (Uppsala: Centre for Multiethnic Research), Lars Wendelius focuses on the middle-sized industrial town of Rockford, Illinois, where between 40 and 45 percent of the population in the first decades of the 20th century were Swedes. His discussion brings out the ways in which the cultural life of these Swedish-Americans can be seen to reflect their need not only to show the existence of a glorious past, but their constructive contribution to American society. Both Wendelius's essay and Anna Williams's *Skribent i Svensk-Amerika: Jakob Bonggren, Journalist och Poet* [Writer in Swedish-America: Jakob Bonggren, journalist and poet] (Almqvist and Wiksell, 1991) are part of a larger ongoing research project, "The Swedish-American Literature," in the Department of Comparative Literature at Uppsala University. During the last decades of the 19th century and the beginning of the 20th, Swedish immigrants created their own culture in the United States, including an ethnic literature with a large number of newspapers and journals. Interested in the literary activity of the Swedish-American immigrant group, the study gives an in-depth portrait of one of the more influential figures of this community with the intention of examining "the consequences of Jakob Bonggren's cultural removal and transposition to a new literary field." Using Pierre Bourdieu's terminology, and focused mainly on the period from 1880 through the 1930s, the period when Jakob Bonggren (1854–1940) was professionally active in the literary life of his transposed ethnic group, Williams places him in a larger context and sees him as a representative for the Swedish-American literary elite, an ethnic leader. A poet and a journalist, Bonggren was for more than half a century employed as editor and editor-in-chief at the Chicago-based *Svenska Amerikanaren* [*Swedish-American*], Swedish-America's largest newspaper. As the period of his professional years coincides roughly with the cultural flowering of Swedish-America, his example may serve as an aid in illustrating the function of Swedish-American literature in creating an ethnic identity.

b. 20th-Century Literary History and General Studies   Paul Levine's "Sammenbrud og gennembrud: Litteratur efter Anden Verdenskrig" [Breakdown and breakthrough: Literature after World War II] (*Amerikansk kultur efter 1945* [Copenhagen: Spektrum, pp. 9–78]) is a useful survey of American literature. Levine structures his essay according to themes and trends, but he makes it complicated by also structuring according to ethnicity, regions, and decades. In short, the survey, as it often happens, piles up subjects, names, and titles, while it goes off in several directions at once. The best parts of the essay deal with Jewish American fiction, which is seen as the most important contribution to American literature during this period; indeed, all other American fiction of the time is evaluated against the achievement of Bellow, Roth, and Doctorow. It is obvious that Levine is not up-to-date on developments in some areas; this is true of the section on southern literature, where Clyde Edgerton, Kaye Gibbons, Josephine Humphreys, and their entire generation are not mentioned. There are a number of obvious factual errors (Welty's *Losing Battles* is *not* about the burden of history, and Flannery O'Connor never wrote about somebody called "the Outsider"). But Levine is good at showing how the divisions between literary genres are disappearing with the ascendancy of new writers (Oates, Morrison, Tan, DeLillo), new techniques (new realism, metafiction, minimalism), and new topics (Vietnam, feminism, apocalypticism). And he is successful in bringing out the importance of the 1960s for this development, even though he has very little space to devote to the poets of the Beat Generation. In general, the treatment of the development of American poetry is unconvincing and lacks enthusiasm; poetry after Berryman, Jarrell, and Lowell is rejected mainly for its "intellectual elitism." On the other hand, the development of American drama is given careful attention and much space, and the essay is very informative on directors (Sellars and Papp), dramatists (Hwang and Wilson), and eclectic trends based on the deconstruction of the tradition.

In "American Literature in Sweden: A Threat to the Indigenous Culture?" pp. 106–15 in *Networks of Americanization* ed. Rolf Lundén and Erik Åsard (Almqvist and Wiksell), Rolf Lundén addresses a question that has been the subject of an ongoing and heated debate in Swedish cultural circles: the matter of the strong influence that American business values and sales methods have exerted on Swedish publishing. In recent years the Anglo-Saxon dominance in translated fiction in Sweden has been solid, to say the least, comprising some 80 percent of all fiction in translation; only 25 percent of the books on the market are of Swedish origin. The influx of American fiction, making up the bulk of the English-speaking contribution—both popular and serious—is considerable, having grown steadily during the last two decades. Of the books translated, the majority are novels, there being scant interest in story collections, experimental writing, and postmodern texts. The question in the title of this essay is answered neither in the affirmative nor the negative. The "threat" to Swedish high culture, in Lundén's view, comes mainly from the field of popular culture in general, regardless of national origin.

In his *Ind i det amerikanske: En bog om amerikansk kultur* [Into the American essence] (Borgen), Bo Green Jensen surveys recent literary developments by collecting 99 of his essays from the last decade. The collection includes essays on American regions, movies, pop music, media, and popular culture, but the best parts are on 17 classic American writers from Edgar Allan Poe to Carson McCullers and on 19 writers, mainly white males, who are still publishing. Some of the 1992 essays are on Robert Bly and the whole man, Norman Mailer and *Harlot's Ghost* with special praise for *Ancient Evenings*, Jay McInerney's realism and minimalism, and Ethan Canin as realist in *Blue River*. But the essay on Hawthorne called "Den kritiske hvirvel" [The critical whirl] deserves to be singled out for the author's awareness of Hawthorne's consciousness of the ambiguity of all things and of "the fluid values in the critical whirl between past and future," which can "never be reduced to a simple dogmatic program." The final part of the book is a collection of interviews with Amy Tan, Kathy Acker, and John Irving, and there is a particularly interesting conversation with Paul Auster from September 1991.

c. 20th-Century Prose   Part of a special issue of *Passage* (Aarhus) on American literature, Frits Andersen's "Månen aborteret og genfødt" [The moon miscarried and reborn] (*Passage* 11/12:95–112) is a very personal reading of Paul Auster's *Moon Palace*. The novel is seen as a fantastic, most unreasonable, and most literary experience; and yet it is also set in a realistic landscape. For the reader there is always an element of interpretative doubt, the same doubt that often motivates the main character, because events presented as facts in one respect are in another respect understood as fiction. The life and the fiction in the novel are related by the reader to his own life and his fiction of himself, as Auster inspires us to create a world, not by dreaming but by editing and rewriting. Auster raises the question of how you can hope to understand your own biographical identity, when every other story, true or not, presents itself as apparent versions of your life story. Andersen points out that Hawthorne and Auster offer the same formal analyses of social, historical, and linguistic conditions for the creation of the self, so that the self is always masked, even to itself. The two writers are, it is argued, equally fascinated with material objects, and they share a negation of allegory. For Auster, the negated and yet still obvious "difference" between allegory and realism is not an obstacle, but a resource from which he can write and live. Auster's own essay "The Art of Hunger" (1970) has appeared in Danish (*Kritik* 101:55–64) in a translation by Peter Kirkegaard, who adds a note on the young Auster's fascination with Knut Hamsun's novel *Sult* [Hunger].

In her "*The Bellarosa Connection* and the Hazards of Forgetfulness" (*AmerSS* 24:65–82), Kathleen Jeanette Weatherford sees Bellow's short novel as an innovation in technique, "exploratory into the genre of semihistorical fiction," and an experiment with narrative perspective. In the tradition of Conrad and Fitzgerald, the focus in Bellow's novel is more on the narrator's response to a "bizarre figure" than on the figure himself, and it is finally the narrator's attempt at self-discovery that holds the reader's attention. In terms of themes, Weatherford sees the continuity with Bellow's previous works in its focus on Jews and their loss of self among the distractions of modern America. But *The Bellarosa Connection* is, it is argued, primarily an important addition to literature portraying different American responses to the Holocaust; in questioning his own role as a Jew and an American, Bellow "finds himself inevitably drawn back to the darkest of all subjects."

The single most important Norwegian contribution to American literary scholarship this year is Per Winther's *The Art of John Gardner: Instruction and Exploration* (SUNY). This slightly revised version of the author's 1985 doctoral dissertation at the University of Oslo is a carefully written, well-argued, and well-researched study of a writer whose untimely death in 1982 put a stop to a career that simply begs to be explored and explained. Gardner's ideas and art deserve attention if only because his name will always be associated with moral fiction and with moral art, or with the ethics of fiction. His blunt and clumsy attacks on the writers of fantasy and metafiction in *On Moral Fiction* are often taken at face value; Winther wants to set a few things right in his book in this respect, and he demonstrates very successfully that Gardner *has* a theoretical platform and that coherent thinking and systematic convictions can be found behind *On Moral Fiction*. Winther places great emphasis on Gardner's ideas, since he has to explain why Gardner chose to work with one set of them rather than with another. But his interest centers on Gardner's voice, in his manner of developing themes, his way of dramatizing ideas. This basic understanding becomes a guideline for the structural arrangement of Winther's study. He does not follow the author's career chronologically, nor does he feel obliged to treat all works at length. He is bold enough to study Gardner's artistic accomplishment on the basis of the individual works he finds to be the writer's best— *Grendel, The King's Indian, The Sunlight Dialogues, Jason and Medea*. Obviously, he has to devote considerable space to a discussion of *On Moral Fiction*, and Winther's book is, all in all, a structured and controlled attempt to show how Gardner's ideas are translated into fiction, how life follows fiction, how fiction instructs and teaches, and, finally, how all-important fiction is (or should be) in the lives of human beings in the second half of the twentieth century.

It being impossible to present all aspects of Winther's study, a quotation will reveal its organization: "My study is organized in keeping with a clearly definable line of reasoning which I have found to influence the conception of Gardner's works, a line of reasoning which explains why his books come to us in the shape and form that they do. . . . In Gardner's opinion art affords man the best instrument there is for probing the depths of human understanding." After the opening chapter, "Life Follows Fiction," a theoretical basis is established for an examination of Gardner's ideas, which are dramatized through close readings of selected works. Two chapters develop and demonstrate the "collage" technique, and another deals with the kind of "experimental fiction" that Winther terms "dialectical." Showing an authoritative command of Gardner's work—ideas, themes, techniques, beliefs—Winther's discussion of *On Moral Fiction* clears up many misunderstandings, although one does not have to share his views. Thorough as is Winther's treatment of the dialectics of Gardner's works, of the collage technique, and his metaphorical language, one misses a theoretical discussion broader than the novelist's rather simple and pragmatic theories. The study would have gained considerably if it had included a study of intertextuality and metafiction, or a combination of these.

Per Winther has also contributed the essay "Hemingway in Norway since 1964" to the special European issue of *The Hemingway Review* (12, iii:20–27). The year 1964 is chosen because Sigmund Skard had published a review article covering the topic to that date, *The Literary Reputation of Hemingway in Europe* (1965). Winther finds overwhelming evidence of continued wide interest in Hemingway, although a low rate of library circulation of his books seems to contradict this point. The republication of several Hemingway novels (and a selection of short stories) by Norway's largest book club has been a tremendous success. *A Farewell to Arms* sold 60,000 copies in 1989; book-of-the-month sales of *The Garden of Eden* reached 45,000 copies; and a collection of 47 stories in 1985 sold 22,000 copies. Winther also surveys the reception of these books by newspaper reviewers, taking the fact of wide reviewing as an indication of Hemingway's popularity. Scholarly attention has been scarce, however, and Winther lists the few articles that have appeared.

Finally, Hemingway's *influence* on Norwegian writers has declined, and it is indeed hard to find any direct link to contemporary Norwegian writing. The Swedish contribution to this issue of *The Hemingway Review* (12, iii:51–62), Rolf Lundén's "Hemingway in Sweden Since 1965," presents a picture that in many respects mirrors the Norwegian situation. Hemingway's reputation in Sweden has been marked by ups and downs, Lundén writes; the first 20 years since 1965 showed a noticeable decline in public interest and a distinct decline in critical estimate. Since the mid-1980s a "renaissance" of sorts can be observed, in part occasioned by the widespread interest in the translations of Anthony Burgess's and Kenneth Lynn's biographies, and at present few writers attract such wide popular interest. Hemingway also can be said to have been something of a writer's writer: in the 1930s and 1940s one could actually talk of a Hemingway school in Sweden, and Lundén offers a number of examples of later writers who acknowledge stylistic debts to him. Also in Sweden, however, the academic community has remained uninterested in Hemingway's work: Lundén points out that not a single book-length study or dissertation has been devoted to Hemingway's fiction since 1965. Of his novels, *A Farewell to Arms* and *The Old Man and the Sea* seem to be the most highly appreciated, having been re-printed eight times each. Hemingway's short stories, however, have always been neglected in Sweden, both before and after 1965, probably the result of a general lack of interest in this form.

Dale Carter's "Alt hænger sammen: Oedipa Mass' Moebius trip in *The Crying of Lot 49*" [Everything coheres] (*Passage* 11/12:123–32) is as diffi-cult to read as the Pynchon novel that is his subject. Carter argues that at the end of the novel Oedipa has just moved from one trap to the other, or possibly from one corner of a trap to the other. Oedipa plays the role of detective, and the way she collects and systematizes evidence is "typically American." Carter argues that "the driving force behind the paranoid American mind is that the nation was created on the borderline between experience and faith, knowledge and imagination, fact and assumption, the founded and the unfounded." Pierce Inverarity's will and everything else is finally ambiguous. Carter concludes that the only approach to Pynchon's novel is to try to unmask or experience its apparently innu-merable conspiracies or counterconspiracies. But, he wonders, if we presuppose that everything does cohere in a final analysis, how can we ever hope to realize just how or what coheres when Pynchon has proved all the tracking methods to be so utterly compromised?

Thomas E. Kennedy's *Robert Coover: A Study of the Short Fiction* (Twayne), a contribution to a popular series, restricts itself to Coover's short fiction, as the nature of the series demands. In view of Coover's achievement as a novelist, this severely limits the value of this study, which as a result cannot consider the natural dialogue between the short and the long fiction. But within the restrictions imposed, Kennedy does an excellent job. He studies three collections of stories, devoting the most space to *Pricksongs & Descants,* which he considers Coover's most powerful stories. Kennedy sees Coover as "a great innovative writer," who plays with realistic technique and strips away established conventional ploys. He also sees him as "a brilliant metafictional strategist" and praises his "astounding originality" in creating comic nightmares that stimulate "dark visions" *and* "belly laughs." Kennedy complains that too few have enough imagination to really appreciate Coover's short fiction, an unfortunate situation because the material is a good "antidote for the mental poison of our times."

Karen Blixen's (Isak Dinesen) 1960 essay on Truman Capote has finally appeared in English in a volume in the same series on short fiction, Helen S. Garson's *Truman Capote: A Study of the Short Fiction* (Twayne) (pp. 122–24). Blixen saw *Breakfast at Tiffany's* as a product of a magic flute that for once had lured Capote from his habitual gloom. She saw that with Capote it would be either/or, and she asked prophetically whether the transformation would last? She seems to have suspected that the old darkness and gravity would defeat Capote's new magic airiness.

In his "Adverbials, Direct Objects and the Style of Carson McCullers" (*POET* 18:121–34), John M. Dienhart argues that McCullers enhanced her style by placing her adverbials in surprising positions. Dienhart enumerates seven predicator-adverbial-object constructions, of which the last, a construction involving an object group without modification, is the most marked (he "lighted *for him* his cigarette"). Dienhart argues that such constructions are both poetic and freakish, the "syntactic abnormalities" and their lyrical cadences helping to reinforce McCullers's themes, such as estrangement and difference. McCullers's characters are often as out of place as the locative adverbials in her sentences, and she is seen as a writer who pushes at the boundaries even in her style. Dienhart does not consider that many of his examples are everyday southern speech and that McCullers shares her adverbial positioning with other southern writers.

Drawing on the many statements made by William Faulkner about how *The Sound and the Fury* was his favorite among his own books, Hans H. Skei's Norwegian introduction to a new edition of this novel (in a booklet accompanying the new edition, published by Den norske Bokklubben in its Library of the Century series) places this complex novel in Faulkner's career, provides readers with guidelines for reading it, and tries to persuade them to read beyond the tricky passages in the Benjy section. If they do this, *The Sound and the Fury* will take them beyond time and place in the way that only great art is able to do. Skei's paper at the 1990 Faulkner and Yoknapatawpha Conference is now included in *Faulkner and the Short Story.* The essay, "Beyond Genre? Existential Experience in Faulkner's Short Fiction" (pp. 62–77), discusses whether genre concepts are of any importance in a study of Faulkner's short fiction and goes on to investigate the possible interdependence of short form and existential experience. Skei refers to the short story theorist Charles May and to Heide Ziegler's German doctoral dissertation on this theme, and he tries to isolate key moments in a few Faulkner stories, that is, epiphanic moments of clarity and possible insight. A close reading of the central scenes in the long (and generally underrated) "A Mountain Victory" demonstrates Skei's point of view, and the article ends with a note concerning the *ethics* of Faulkner's short fiction. Skei is also the editor of a selection of Faulkner's short stories in Norwegian, *William Faulkner: Noveller* (Ekstrabokklubben). Altogether 28 stories, more than half of them in Norwegian for the first time, are collected in the volume, which is a selection from Faulkner's original *Collected Stories.* Skei's introduction outlines Faulkner's life and career, and it gives a fairly detailed survey of his accomplishment in short fiction.

Erik Nielsen's *Flannery O'Connors Romaner* [Novels] (Odense) is the first Danish study to focus exclusively on O'Connor's relatively longer works. The first chapter, on *Wise Blood,* focuses primarily on Hazel Motes, "the despondent atheist," and his conversions from an inherited fundamentalism to a belief in his own soullessness, then to a virulent nihilism, and finally to an all-conquering new faith in God. Nielsen sees O'Connor's first novel as depicting a worldly struggle against the persistent intrusion of the divine, whereas in *The Violent Bear It Away,* O'Connor's second novel, the aesthetic-nihilistic views struggle for access to the Christian universe. The analysis of this novel, the most rewarding part of Nielsen's book, is preceded by short considerations of the nature of O'Connor's concept of sacredness and of her art seen in the light of her Thomism. Surprisingly, Nielsen does not see the two novels, except in their conclusions, as religious novels; rather, they are contributions to an idea-debating genre, initiation stories that express a philosophy of religion. He does argue that the novels are finally similar: the two main characters go through similar metamorphoses toward salvation, and the novels are akin in narrative structure, comic and ironic tone, point of view, style, concreteness, values, and themes. The discussion of her technique is substantiated by a groundbreaking chapter on O'Connor's poetics, which includes a provocative comparison of O'Connor's ideas of Christian alienation and Bertolt Brecht's theory of *Verfremdung*. Nielsen also offers a chapter on O'Connor's secular world, in which the church, the (social) sciences, the South, and her readers are seen as major influences. Nielsen concludes that O'Connor's art dwarfs her artistic intentions. The artist is, he claims, fully integrated in her art and can be identified with her work.

Karl-Heinz Westarp's "Message to the Lost Self: Percy's Analysis of the Human Situation" (*Renascence* 44:216–24) surveys the religious views that Walker Percy had adopted before he started writing fiction. Percy saw himself as an artist, but, it is argued, he acted like an Old Testament Prophet and was really an apostle *malgré lui*. The proof of this claim is Percy's willingness to see our symbolic capacity and its immaterial nature as mysterious and finally scientifically inexplicable in origin. Percy's Catholic faith was a way of seeing everything, and he accepted Aquinas's understanding of faith as a special kind of knowledge. His art, Westarp maintains, does not make sense without an idea of the origin of Percy's vision. The reader must make the connection between Percy's preoccupation with language, as something uniquely human, and his religious conviction that God's Word was made flesh to save us.

In his "Eudora Welty: Early Acrobatics" (*NMW* 24:35–49) Jan Nordby Gretlund shows that Welty in her early story "Acrobats in a Park" was inspired by Picasso's painting "La famille des saltimbanques" and possibly influenced by Rainer Maria Rilke's *Duino Elegies*. But it is made clear that the identification of writer with town was already unmistakable in the mid-1930s, as Welty demonstrated her sense of place in choosing a local park in Jackson as the setting for her story. And the difficulty of balancing on "a family wall of love," which is the theme of the story, has remained a topic of central interest in Welty's fiction.

Clara Juncker's "Black Magic: Woman(ist) as Artist in Alice Walker's *The Temple of My Familiar*" (*AmerSS* 24:37–49), argues that through her "decentered existence" Walker's artist is associated with magic and even madness. By placing female creativity in the realm of magic, Walker has managed to place her artist "outside of phallogocentric discourse" and written her into the African American trickster tradition. The power of Walker's black women artists has its origin, Juncker claims, in her ability to represent in her art the incompatible dividing forces of her life. The masculine impulse toward "unity and wholeness of textual voice" cannot be the ideal of the black woman artist, who "must assume her own division." The essay's terminology is mandarin Cixousian.

Seeking to provide what has elsewhere been called a "diaspora perspective," Brita Lindberg-Seyersted in her essay "New World Black Heritage in Paule Marshall's *The Chosen Place, the Timeless People* and *Praisesong for the Widow*" (*SN* 64:183–94) points to the continued importance of African, Afro-Caribbean and African American lore in Marshall's texts, and she outlines the ways in which African cultural values are privileged in these narratives. Appearing as history, myth and legend, this heritage is manifestly visible in plot and characterization as well as in descriptions of places and people: "the black heritage in fact determines the entire character of [Marshall's] novels; it is the very core of both text and meaning." The two books discussed bear witness to Marshall's decision to assume the role as her people's storyteller: these texts, Lindberg-Seyersted argues, reverberate with the author's belief that to keep the heritage alive, the old stories and myths must be told, dramatized, and sung again and again.

d. 20th-Century Poetry   Jan Rosiek's "Intethedens Metier og Salighedens Figurationer" [The occupation of nothingness and the figurations of blessedness] (*Passage* 11/12:79–93) is a call for a reevaluation of Wallace Stevens's long poems from the final 20 years of his career. The essay is a history of the reception of Stevens's poetry at home and abroad. Rosiek argues that American criticism has not been alone in its slow recognition of the true strength of the poems; inadequate translations have compounded the problem abroad. If Stevens is now attracting even more attention than Pound and Eliot, it is mainly because of new renderings of his long poems. Rosiek illustrates his claim by showing Stevens's musicality in "Le Monocle de Mon Oncle" and the poet's exceptional ability to create imaginative fables, as in "The Auroras of Autumn." In his enthusiasm for Stevens's poetry, Rosiek also tries to focus on the poems on poetry, the poet's "Nietzschean yes to life," and Stevens as the poet of death, an ambitious set of topics for just one essay. The essay precedes seven poems by Stevens translated into Danish by Poul Borum. Stevens's poetry is also important for Deborah Ford in her "The Snow Not the Sentence: Image and Meaning in Contemporary American Poetry" (*P.E.O.* 60:1–15). Ford sees Stevens's "the mind in the act" as the metaphor for contemporary poetry, and her essay deals with the relation of image and meaning, posing the question: how and when does the image become a metaphor? It is argued that Gary Snyder's rejection of metaphor leads to "separation and distance from things," for example, in his poem "The Bath." W. D. Snodgrass's "April Inventory" is seen as a poem that takes the relation of image and meaning "a step further" toward a developing and organic relationship. Randall Jarrell's poems "A Camp in the Prussian Forest" and "The Woman at the Washington Zoo" are singled out for praise, because Jarrell masterfully works the principle of metaphor. It is the Stevens-like "disinterested passion," Ford claims, which enables Jarrell to embrace metaphor and to give the "things of the world" his accurate attention.

e. Theory and Criticism   In her "Minimalisme—en introduktion" (*Passage* 11/12:113–22) Karin Knudsen argues that in any attempt at defining minimalism it is essential to keep in mind the impossibility of distinguishing clearly between minimalism and postmodernism, as minimalism can be understood only in a postmodernist context. After a report on the discussion between William Gass and John Gardner on literary mimesis, communication, fiction as independent object, moral fiction, and reader relations, Knudsen concludes that most of the disagreement about minimalism is about its name and not so much about the characteristics of the genre—which is not what the Gass-Gardner discussion implies. It is obvious, Knudsen writes, that minimalism does not participate in the general love of playful stylistic experiments that characterizes postmodernism. But it is also obvious that the new genre is not a return to mere realism; a century of questioning language and its meaning makes a return to innocent mimesis impossible.

In Inge Birgitte Siegumfeldt's essay on "Bloom, Derrida, and the Kabbalah: The Invocation of Ancestral Voices" (*P.E.O.* 62:1–12), Western culture is seen as a contest between Hellenism and Judaism, with Hellenism so far presiding and Judaism an undercurrent. But Siegumfeldt argues that the present deconstruction of philosophy and literature indicates a reversal of the roles. The de-Hellenizing is furthered by the ruptures and displacements that accompany restorations and revisions central to kabbalistic achievement. Harold Bloom is seen as a deconstructionist critic who acknowledges the influence of Jewish kabbalistic speculation, which also is seen as influencing Derridean grammatology.

The work of another deconstructionist critic is the subject of Claus

Schatz-Jakobsen's "Post-modern American Literary Criticism and the
Law of Genre: The Case of Geoffrey Hartman" (*P.E.O.* 66:1–16), an
essay that attempts to place Hartman's post-1970 "performative rather
than constative variety of creative criticism" in the history of criticism of
the last 20 years. The focus is on Hartman's attack on the distinction
between primary and secondary literature and the resulting leveling, or
transcending, of established genre distinctions between literature and
"related kinds of discourse." The essay outlines the discussion between
Hartman and Jürgen Habermas over the former's conflation of philosophical literary criticism with literature.

Lars Ole Sauerberg's "First and Further Readings: On a Neglected
Aspect of the Phenomenology of the Literary Text" (*OL* 47:1–10) points
out that ignoring the dynamics of the first reading in relation to further
readings deprives a text of something vital for its mode of existence.
Sauerberg argues that any interpretation that considers the text as exist-
ing in its "arrived state," or as its accumulated readings only, reduces its
potential for meaning. With a reading of Shirley Jackson's "The Lottery"
as an example, he suggests that the difference between a first reading and
subsequent readings is not simply quantitative but qualitative. What
Cleanth Brooks and other New Critics often overlook is the knowledge
gradually acquired *during* the first reading, for example, the experience
of first recognizing the source of an allusion (without the aid of a note).
Sauerberg concludes that a sound consideration of the phenomenology
of a literary text demands an awareness and examination of the differences between its first actualization and further readings.

One textbook should be briefly mentioned: Fredrik Chr. Brøgger's
*Culture Language Text: Culture Studies Within the Study of English as a
Foreign Language* (Scandinavian). Although not a work of literary schol-
arship, it emphasizes the linguistic basis for all sorts of cultural studies, so
that literature must be by necessity an integral part of the broad approach
to the teaching of English as a foreign language that Brøgger advocates.
In one chapter, "Culture Studies as a Literary-Oriented Discipline,"
Brøgger analyzes three "cultural texts" in literary terms.

Odense, Uppsala, Oslo Universities

18   General Reference Works

David J. Nordloh

The advance of "electronic information delivery" deeper and deeper into the reference room—dragging a clutter of computer terminals with it—has so far not significantly changed the look on the shelves. The same kinds of printed reference resources continue to appear, in about the same quantity. The chief areas of attention this year are ethnic literature and regional studies, with drama and theater close behind; women's literature gets somewhat less attention than in the past five years; and the rapidly enlarging field of book and publishing history generates its own support structure. I detect in much of this work a general improvement in quality, for which the computer can claim at least a part, making greater comprehensiveness and accuracy possible. Using a new technology to enhance our knowledge of the products and methods of an essential old one makes sense.

Despite its pedestrian title the most productive of the reference items published this year is John E. Bassett's *Harlem in Review: Critical Reactions to Black American Writers, 1917–1939* (Susquehanna). The volume is intended to "provide a representative sense of critical responses to writers of the Harlem Renaissance" by means of an inventory of contemporary commentary on their publications appearing in historical and biographical works, black journals and newspapers, and the "standard" journals and magazines of the period. The material is divided into four chronologically organized chapters. Works by black authors are recorded in their order of publication, each entry followed by a listing of relevant items, also organized chronologically. Four chapters cover 1919–37 thoroughly; a fifth concentrates on major titles published between 1940 and 1944 and not already covered by other checklists, among them Langston Hughes's *The Big Sea* and Melvin B. Tolson's *Rendezvous with America*. The primary items are briefly annotated, and the book reviews assigned a favorability grade. With Bassett's help we are able to better establish a fuller and more authentic historical valuation of the Harlem past.

From place to theme. Two overview bibliographies, one dealing only peripherally with literature, take war as their subject. Frank J. Wetta and Stephen J. Curley's *Celluloid Wars: A Guide to Film and the American Experience of War* (Greenwood), whose central feature is a selected filmography divided by specific wars, also includes a lightly annotated "War Film Bibliography" of the 100 most important books and articles dealing with the war film as a genre (the list was originally published in *Film & Television* 18, ii [1990]:72–79). Not wars but the most written-about American war is the subject of Philip K. Jason's *The Vietnam War in Literature: An Annotated Bibliography of Criticism* (Salem Press). The book lists selected secondary items by type of material. The most significant sections are the first, "Special Collections," and the last, "Authors and Works"; sections on general and genre criticism among others lie between. The annotation is well-focused, effectively combining description and evaluation. In its thoroughness the Jason list is a good starting point for study of the Vietnam experience, although a somewhat repetitious one, since its organization requires that such major treatments as Philip D. Beidler's *American Literature and the Experience of Vietnam* (1982) appear in so many categories and in conjunction with so many authors.

There is a certain quirkiness, only partly appropriate to the topic, in Don L. F. Nilsen's treatment of the material in *Humor in American Literature: A Selected Annotated Bibliography* (Garland), another title in the omnium-gatherum Garland Reference Library of the Humanities. Nilsen concentrates on items published after 1970, arguing that most literary criticism of humorous works has appeared only in the last two decades and that "much pre-1970 criticism was simply not available" to him. Possibly his dim view of the longer past is influenced by his not seeing much of it. He offers 1,293 entries in all, more than 1,000 of them in four chapters covering "Humor of Individual Authors." These chapters are divided chronologically, although it is not made entirely clear that the division is dictated by the dates of publication of relevant works, not by authors' dates of birth; thus, Charlotte Perkins Gilman is placed in chapter 4, "Twentieth-Century American Literary Humor," because *Herland,* her humorous (?) take on utopia, appeared in 1915. The balance of the entries are then too finely chopped into another 12 chapters—one of those with nine subsections!—on such topics as humor in children's literature and black/gallows humor. The annotation is mostly summary and paraphrase, with little distinction between major and minor issues. The quirkiness extends even to the index, a single list combining authors, critics, topics (Algonquin Wits, Anecdotes, Animals), and even characters (Babbitt, Huck Finn). Still, used carefully, this is an acceptable enough entry into the uniquely American perspective on the world.

Three other bibliographies suggest the difficulty of handling topical issues successfully. Michael Kowalewski covers travel writing as a genre in "Travel Writing Since 1900: A Selective Chronology and Bibliography," pp. 287–356 in his *Temperamental Journeys: Essays on the Modern Literature of Travel* (Georgia). Kowalewski allows a few volumes of poetry into his listing of primary works, but he concentrates mostly on nonfiction prose, dividing it into anthologies, special issues of journals, and then nationalities, with each group organized chronologically by date of publication. He also presents a modest secondary bibliography of criticism dealing with the genre. Neither list is annotated. Unfortunately, Kowalewski does not supply an author index, and one has to roam a bit to locate Henry James or Vladimir Nabokov. Science is the subject in Robert J. Scholnick's "Bibliography: American Literature and Science Through 1989," pp. 251–72 in Scholnick's *American Literature and Science,* a collection of commissioned essays. Entries are grouped alphabetically by author under topic headings including "History and Theory of Literature and Science," "History of Science in America," and century sections on "Literature and Science in America." In its modesty this is a solid selection and a good launch point. Leo F. O'Connor sees the world in his own way in *The Protestant Sensibility in the American Novel: An Annotated Bibliography,* another item in the Garland group. O'Connor divides his materials into categories like "The New England Novel: Liberal/Orthodox Controversy" and "Social Gospel: Reform and Utopian Fiction," but he then brings the division process into doubt by also repeating the title of the book as a category—and lumping 150 of the total of 701 entries into it. The novels are annotated in such a way as to demonstrate their relevance, in O'Connor's view, to the heading under which he has placed them. Since his categories are not exclusive, however, and since there is no author index, the volume is very inadequate for reference use: finding a specific author or a work by that author requires page-by-page searching—I still have not found anything by Harold Frederic, although I did come across Kurt Vonnegut's *Sirens of Titans* [*sic*].

The chief contributions to general author bibliography this year consist of additions to continuing projects. James Nagel and Gwen L. Nagel, with the assistance of Judith S. Baughman, have edited *Bibliography of American Fiction 1866–1918* (Facts on File), the second part of a three-part series completing itself in reverse order. What I said in praise last year about coverage and editorial plan on the appearance of the last/first part, covering 1919–1988 (see *ALS 1991*, p. 474), holds here. The longer-lived Dictionary of Literary Biography series, now well beyond 100 volumes, appears to be slowing a bit, with indications that it may be close to exhausting the list of eligible authors, genres, and periods. But there remains some unfinished business, as two new volumes attest. R. S. Gwynn has edited *American Poets Since World War II. Third Series* (DLB 120), treating 66 writers in the now well-established DLB verbal-pictorial format. Rita Dove, Diane Ackerman, Alicia Ostriker, and Dana Gioia are in the list. Gwynn's introduction tries to untangle the intended editorial distinction among the three series on postwar poets: the first (DLB 5 [1980]) was intended to cover poets born between 1904 and 1950, the second to cover those born from 1920 until 1960; then when the second (DLB 105 [1991]) began to bulk too large, it was further divided, with one volume meant to cover writers born before 7 December 1941 and another for those born after; but that division fell apart in number three when additional writers not fitting the deadline were identified—and so this volume actually covers the late 1920s to the mid-1950s, and the division of the *American Poets Since World War II* set relinquishes all claim to logic. Once more we must turn to the comprehensive series index that concludes each new addition to the DLB series; the trick for the occasional user is knowing which is the latest DLB volume, and so which is the current index. The other DLB volume is also a continuation of a segment. *Chicano Writers. Second Series* (DLB 122), ed. Francisco A. Lomeli and Carl R. Shirley, adds 64 author entries and an essay—"A Forerunner of Chicano Literature: Miguel de Quintana (1671–1748)," by Clark Colahan—to the 54 entries and appendices on Chicago history, language, and culture supplied in the first series (DLB 82 [1989] by the same editors. In this instance the editors proffer no organizational logic for the placement of writers in one volume or the other: men and women, 19th and 20th centuries, and novelists, dramatists, and poets are fairly evenly distributed between them.

Two new bibliographies on ethnic literature also appeared. Despite the length of the title, David R. Peck's *American Ethnic Literatures:*

Native American, African American, Chicano-Latino, and Asian American Writers and Their Backgrounds: An Annotated Bibliography (Salem Press) is not accurately named, treating the literatures more fully than the writers. After introductory chapters on general reference bibliographies and related works, on the social and historical record, on the teaching of ethnic literature, and on general studies, Peck gets down to the groups. These latter chapters feature a brief narrative history of each group, a selected list of primary works, and finally a list of secondary works on that literature—but not on individual authors. The annotation of the secondary material is specific, mostly descriptive rather than valuative, in efficient prose. A briefer and narrower compilation is provided by Héctor Calderón et al., "A Selected and Annotated Bibliography of Contemporary Chicano Literary Criticism," pp. 260–73 in their *Criticism in the Borderlands: Studies in Chicano Literature, Culture, and Ideology* (Duke, 1991). The list, supplementing the 15 new essays on the subject gathered into the volume, is intended "to offer to the widest interested audience a basic knowledge of the field." It includes more than 100 books and articles, supported by brief factual annotation, and in its brief compass reflects matters of both theory and practice, culture and context.

Only opening the book will resolve the ambiguity of the title of *Twentieth-Century Western Writers* (St. James, 1991), the second edition of which has been prepared by Geoff Sadler. We are talking here not about Europe and the United States as the West but about works of fiction "set in or relating to the American frontier experience of the last century" or "that embody that experience in a modern setting." The blanket is wide enough, then, to include James Fenimore Cooper and Catharine Maria Sedgwick as well as Larry McMurtry and Tillie Olsen. Author entries appear in alphabetical order, each including a biography, an index of titles both western and otherwise, and a signed critical essay. The essays are tightly focused and unfussy, and the volume deserves a title doing it more justice.

Two other specialized author and topic bibliographies deserve brief mention. Dorothy H. Brown supplies a comprehensive "Bibliography of Louisiana Women Writers" to enhance the essays in *Louisiana Women Writers* (pp. 214–34). Marcela Breton's "An Annotated Bibliography of Selected Jazz Short Stories" (*AAR* 26:299–306) is mostly plot summaries of her choice of 50 items "whose jazz element plays a primary role." And persons with regional interests should note the availability of several continuing annual bibliographies appearing in journals focused on regional matters: "A Checklist of Scholarship on Southern Literature" in *Mississippi Quarterly,* which I mentioned in last year's essay (*ALS 1991,* p. 480); the "Annual Bibliography of Midwestern Literature" in *Midamerica;* the "Annual Bibliography of Studies in Western American Literature" in *Western American Literature;* and "North Carolina Bibliography" in *North Carolina Historical Review.*

As I noted at the outset, drama gets a major portion of reference attention this year. Floyd Eugene Eddleman has added "Supplement III to the Second Edition" to his *American Drama Criticism* (Shoe String), thus making his inventory of discussions of dramatists and their plays current through 1990. Through the combined exhaustiveness of the lists and separate indices for critics, play titles, and playwrights, even books and journals cited, *American Drama Criticism* is a valuable, time-saving resource. Less useful—both because it is directed primarily to students and because it indulges in vague valuative annotation like "excellent study" or "representative and helpful"—is R. Baird Shuman's *American Drama, 1918–1960: An Annotated Bibliography* (Salem Press). After opening sections on general reference works and resources and on "Little Theater, Theater Groups, and Regional Theater," Shuman identifies both general studies and commentary on specific plays by 22 playwrights. Two other drama bibliographies, nicely exclusive of each other in chronological coverage, deal specifically with women. Gwenn Davis and Beverly A. Joyce expand their planned series of pre-20th century surveys of female authorship—already represented by *Personal Writings by Women to 1900* (1989) and *Poetry by Women to 1900* (1991; see *ALS 1991,* p. 477)—with *Drama by Women to 1900: A Bibliography of American and British Writers* (Toronto). In a single alphabetical list they report each woman author's name, her husband's name, birth and death dates, pseudonyms, major works (first editions only), and the chief sources and locations of copies. Appendices group authors chronologically by 50-year periods and by subjects. The downside here is absence of nationality information; the upside is 2,800 authors. Frances Diodato Bzowski's compilation *American Women Playwrights, 1900–1930: A Checklist* (Greenwood) picks up where Davis and Joyce leave off chronologically and pays as much attention to works as to authors. Bzowski concentrates on identifying dramatists, their work (very briefly described), and proof that a work exists by reference to either a published version or a library holding of some form of it. Since Bzowski is concerned primarily with establishing the existence of works, not locations of copies, she provides no census; and since she did the bulk of her work at the John Hay Library at Brown, the greatest number of plays in her list are recorded as being there. If in doubt whether an author is a woman, she takes the prudent course and adds the name, and she has apparently made no attempt at verifying either gender or nationality. But even given these limitations, this bare record is a substantial beginning, offering some 10,000 items. Less comprehensive in their coverage but still useful on specific dimensions of American stage history are Paul Metzger's "American Musical Theater: A Guide to Information Sources" (*BB* 49:251–61), briefly annotating 120 items organized by categories of information (catalogs, biography, libraries and collections, discography, and so on); and Charles S. Watson's "Early Southern Dramatists: An Introduction and a Checklist of Their Plays" (*MissQ* 43 [1989–90]:45–58), which manages to identify 35 plays and record locations of print or manuscript copies.

The continuing expansion of what was once called the history of the book into the territory of the newspaper, the magazine, and even the mimeograph newsletter elicits relevant reference material. Most notable of recent contributions on the subject is Loss Pequeño Glazier's *Small Press: An Annotated Guide* (Greenwood), "a selective enumeration of sources about the small press phenomenon, its constituent small presses and little magazines, and its cultural and commercial significance." The focal period is literary publishing from 1960, identified as the beginning of "The Mimeo Revolution," through 1992, and Glazier leaves no doubt in the selection or organization of the volume that its emphasis is on "phenomenon": the volume identifies no single-author bibliographies, lists no essays on individual presses or even regional publishing. The 174 entries, each thoroughly if dryly described, are divided into "Current Information," "Core Sources" (subdivided into "Culture" and "Commerce"), and "Supplementary Sources." The austerity of perspective is alleviated somewhat by brief discussions of "Bibliographic Precedents" (i.e., previous work on the subject) and "Coterminous Sources" (i.e., other current directories and guides). Actual publications and not the general phenomenon are the subject of *American Literary Magazines: The Twentieth Century* (Greenwood), ed. Edward E. Chielens, the completion of a project that already includes Chielens's volume on the 18th and 19th centuries (1986) and is part of a Greenwood series that also published Barbara Nourie's *American Mass-Market Magazines* (1990). The principal feature of Chielens's new book is its "Profiles of American Literary Magazines, 1900–Present," historical and valuative signed essays, extensively footnoted and accompanied by lists of information sources, on the 76 most prominent journals of the period, from *Accent* and *The American Mercury* to LeRoi Jones and Hettie Cohen's *Yugen*. But there is more: appendices listing minor literary magazines in the order of their inception, a parallel chronology of social and literary events, 1900–1991, and best of all "The Archives: An Analysis of Little Magazine Collections in the United States and Canada," capsule descriptions of 28 depositories crucial to the subject. *American Literary Magazines* is altogether a thoughtfully designed and executed resource, and an up-to-date complement to Frank Luther Mott's one-man epic.

I will briefly mention new editions of several standards. The second edition of David Cutler's *Literary Washington: A Complete Guide to the Literary Life in the Nation's Capital* (Madison Books) shamelessly mixes "the popular and the highbrow, the traditional and the contemporary, the classic and the not-so-classic." Where else could Henry Adams and Art Buchwald be found in such comfortable proximity? *DLB Yearbook: 1991,* ed. James W. Hipp (Gale), includes the usual *Yearbook* essays on the latest Nobel Prize in Literature, overview essays on genres (those by George Garrett on the short story and literary reviewing are especially good), installment seven on literary research archives (this time it is the University of Virginia Libraries), obituaries, and lists of awards and honors. Cambridge has issued a "revised edition" (whose difference from the "updated" paperback edition of 1991 I have difficulty detecting) of *The Cambridge Guide to Literature in English,* ed. Ian Ousby. Responding to the reviving interest in publishing history, Columbia has republished William Charvat's *The Profession of Authorship in America, 1800–1870.*

Though not specifically national in their perspectives, the essays contributed to *The Book Encompassed: Studies in Twentieth-Century Bibliography* (Cambridge), ed. Peter Davison, supply worthwhile survey discussions on topics relevant to the history of real books. Especially fruitful are G. Thomas Tanselle's "Issues in Bibliographical Studies Since 1942" (pp. 24–36), David McKitterick's "Book Catalogues: Their Varieties and Uses" (pp. 161–75), Robin Alston's "Bibliography in the Computer Age" (pp. 276–89), and D. F. McKenzie's "The History of the Book" (pp. 290–301).

I note the demise after volume 15 of *Literary Research: A Journal of Scholarly Method and Technique,* which occasionally ventured into territories American.

Indiana University

Author Index

Subject Index